LEGAL FOUNDATIONS OF TRIBUNALS IN NINETEENTH-CENTURY ENGLAND

Nineteenth-century governments faced considerable challenges from the rapid, novel and profound changes in social and economic conditions resulting from the industrial revolution. In the context of an increasingly sophisticated and complex government, from the 1830s the specialist and largely lay statutory tribunal was conceived and adopted as the principal method of both implementing the new regulatory legislation and resolving disputes, between the state and the subject, or between subject and subject. The tribunal's legal nature and procedures, and its place in the machinery of justice, were debated and refined throughout the Victorian period. In examining this process, this book explains the interaction between legal constraints, social and economic demand and political expediency which gave rise to this form of dispute-resolution. It reveals the imagination and creativity of legislators who drew on diverse legal institutions and values to create the new tribunals, and shows how the modern difficulties of legal classification and analysis were largely the result of the institution's nineteenth-century development.

CHANTAL STEBBINGS is Professor of Law and Legal History at the University of Exeter. Her research is in the commercial legal history of the nineteenth century, with special reference to the law of taxation, trusts and commercial property. She has written extensively in this field, including *The Private Trustee in Victorian England* (Cambridge University Press, 2002).

CAMBRIDGE STUDIES
IN ENGLISH LEGAL HISTORY

Edited by
J. H. BAKER
Fellow of St Catharine's College, Cambridge

Recent series of titles include

The Rise and Fall of the English Ecclesiastical Courts,
1500–1860
R. B. OUTHWAITE

Law Courts and Lawyers in the City of London,
1300–1550
PENNY TUCKER

Legal Foundations of Tribunals in Nineteenth-Century England
CHANTAL STEBBINGS

Pettyfoggers and Vipers of the Commonwealth
The 'Lower Branch' of the Legal Profession in Early
Modern England
C. W. BROOKS

Roman Canon Law in Reformation England
R. H. HELMHOLZ

Sir Henry Maine
A Study in Victorian Jurisprudence
R. C. J. COCKS

Sir William Scott, Lord Stowell Judge of the High Court of
Admiralty, 1798–1828
HENRY J. BOURGUIGNON

The Early History of the Law of Bills and Notes
A Study of the Origins of Anglo-American Commercial Law
JAMES STEVEN ROGERS

The Law of Treason in England in the Later Middle Ages
J. G. BELLAMY

William Sheppard, Cromwell's Law Reformer
NANCY L. MATTHEWS

LEGAL FOUNDATIONS OF TRIBUNALS IN NINETEENTH-CENTURY ENGLAND

CHANTAL STEBBINGS

CAMBRIDGE UNIVERSITY PRESS
Cambridge, New York, Melbourne, Madrid, Cape Town,
Singapore, São Paulo, Delhi, Mexico City

Cambridge University Press
The Edinburgh Building, Cambridge CB2 8RU, UK

Published in the United States of America by Cambridge University Press, New York

www.cambridge.org
Information on this title: www.cambridge.org/9780521869072

© Chantal Stebbings 2006

This publication is in copyright. Subject to statutory exception
and to the provisions of relevant collective licensing agreements,
no reproduction of any part may take place without the written
permission of Cambridge University Press.

First published 2006

A catalogue record for this publication is available from the British Library

ISBN 978-0-521-86907-2 Hardback
ISBN 978-0-521-10751-8 Paperback

Cambridge University Press has no responsibility for the persistence or
accuracy of URLs for external or third-party internet websites referred to in
this publication, and does not guarantee that any content on such websites is,
or will remain, accurate or appropriate. Information regarding prices, travel
timetables, and other factual information given in this work is correct at
the time of first printing but Cambridge University Press does not guarantee
the accuracy of such information thereafter.

FOR MY DAUGHTER, JENNIE

CONTENTS

Acknowledgements	*page*	*viii*
Table of statutes		*ix*
Table of cases		*xxii*
List of abbreviations		*xxviii*

1	Challenges to the legal process	1
2	The ideological and theoretical context	73
3	Composition and personnel	110
4	Jurisdiction and functional powers	147
5	Procedure and practice	184
6	Judicial supervision	229
7	Principles, place and perception	273
Index		335

vii

ACKNOWLEDGEMENTS

This project was made possible by the generous funding of the British Academy, whose support, both financial and otherwise, I gratefully acknowledge. I would like to thank Dr Ken Emond of the British Academy for his patient efficiency, Mr Roger Brien of the Devon and Exeter Institution for providing the perfect working environment, and a great many friends and colleagues in many universities in legal history and in tax law who have patiently discussed aspects of this work with me. Their interest and advice have been invaluable. Any remaining errors are, of course, my own. My special thanks to my husband Howard who, while far from his own field of cell biology, has read every draft of every chapter with unfailing patience, care, humour and wise counsel.

TABLE OF STATUTES

Poor Relief Act 1601, 43 Eliz. c. 2	11
Act of Settlement 1662, 13 & 14 Car. II c. 12	11
Conventicle Act 1670, 22 Car. II c. 1	270
s. 6	270
s. 13	270
Land Tax Act 1688, 1 Will. & M. c. 20	35, 114–115
s. 7	115, 148, 149
s. 8	149, 150
s. 9	35, 40
s. 10	138, 142
s. 17	150
s. 18	262
s. 26	149
Land Tax Act 1692, 4 Will. & M. c. 1	115
s. 7	148
s. 8	140, 149
s. 9	149
s. 10	135
s. 11	142
s. 12	138, 142
s. 20	150, 203
s. 22	162
s. 51	115
Houses and Windows Duties Act 1747, 20 Geo II. c. 3	
s. 6	115, 141, 149
s. 7	149, 190
s. 8	149
s. 9	141, 149, 190
s. 10	149

Table of Statutes

s. 12	157, 202, 215
s. 13	236
Houses and Windows Duties Amendment Act 1747, 20 Geo. II c. 42	
s. 2	141
Houses and Windows Duties Amendment Act 1748, 21 Geo. II c. 10	
s. 3	116
s. 8	157
s. 10	236, 240
s. 23	141
Servants Duties Act 1777, 17 Geo. III. c. 39	
s. 7	115
ss. 9, 14	141
s. 18	113
Inhabited House Duty Act 1778, 18 Geo. III c. 26	
s. 10	115
ss. 12, 18	141
s. 20	190
s. 40	215
ss. 41–42	240
Inhabited House Duty Act 1779, 19 Geo. III c. 59	
s. 14	113
Servants Duties Act 1785, 25 Geo. III c. 43	
s. 18	113
Horses and Carriages Duties and Taxes Management Act 1785, 25 Geo. III c. 47	
s. 11	115
ss. 19, 25	141
ss. 30, 31	215
ss. 33, 34	240
Horses and Carriages Act 1789, 29 Geo. III c. 49	
s. 12	113
Land Tax Act 1797, 38 Geo. III c. 5	148, 150, 214, 236
ss. 2, 6	148
s. 8	149, 203, 204, 205, 236
s. 13	142
s. 14	138, 142
s. 15	138
s. 17	150, 236

Table of Statutes

s. 18	151
s. 19	140
s. 22	149
s. 23	150, 236, 262
s. 28	151, 236
s. 54	236
s. 84	214
Taxes Management Act 1798, 38 Geo. III c. 16	189, 237
Triple Assessment Act 1798,	
38 Geo. III c. 16 113, 142–3, 150, 152, 157, 198, 222, 262	
s. 4	151
s. 5	113
s. 43	284
s. 44	141
s. 45	115, 150
s. 48	150
s. 54	236
s. 55	204
s. 56	139
s. 60	113
s. 61	262
s. 63	198, 201, 205
s. 64	157
s. 65	222
s. 67	204
s. 78	138, 143
s. 79	143
Houses and Windows Duties Amendment Act 1799, 39 Geo. III c. 13	
s. 27	116
Income and Property Taxes Act 1799, 39 Geo. III c. 13	26, 113, 123, 237
ss. 11–15	115
s. 16	153, 251
s. 22	113
ss. 23, 24	115, 124
ss. 25, 26	116
ss. 34, 35	113
s. 36	152
ss. 38, 39	189

xii *Table of Statutes*

ss. 51, 52	190
s. 57	190
s. 63	190
s. 64	153, 157, 215
s. 98	124, 209
ss. 105, 106	113
s. 111	124
s. 114	124

Income and Property Taxes Act 1799, 39 Geo. III
c. 22

s. 22	209

Inclosure Clauses Consolidation Act 1801, 41 Geo. III

c. 109	163, 170, 192, 216, 262, 271
s. 1	112
s. 2	262
s. 3	170, 203, 216, 244, 271
s. 4	163
s. 6	163, 205
s. 7	171
s. 8	163, 170, 244
s. 33	216
s. 34	217
s. 35	163, 274

Health and Morals of Apprentices Act 1802, 42
Geo. III c. 73 · 23, 83

Land Tax Redemption Consolidation Act 1802, 42

Geo. III c. 116	152
s. 197	137, 152, 198, 215

Income and Property Taxes Act 1803, 43 Geo. III

c. 122	26, 154, 155, 215
s. 3	115
s. 12	116
s. 17	117
s. 28	141
s. 31	154
s. 43	190
s. 47	190
s. 64	154
s. 75	154
s. 84	154

ss. 105–109	189
ss. 110–124	154
s. 136	190
s. 143	189
s. 144	154, 204, 205
s. 145	203, 204
s. 146	204
s. 148	220
ss. 151–153	215
s. 184	190
s. 187	190
ss. 198–199	154
Schedule A	154, 190
Schedule B	154, 190
Schedule C	154
Schedule D	154, 189, 190, 203, 204, 205
Schedule E	154, 190
Taxes Management Act 1803, 43 Geo. III c. 99	155, 156, 222
s. 9	138, 141
s. 26	156, 157, 222
s. 29	237
Income and Property Taxes Act 1806, 46 Geo. III c. 65	
ss. 126–35	155
Uniformity of Process Act 1832, 2 & 3 Will. IV c. 39	188, 320
Real Property Limitation Act 1833, 3 & 4 Will. IV c. 27	188, 320
Factories Act 1833, 3 & 4 Will. IV c. 103	65
s. 17	29
ss. 32, 33	29
s. 38	29
s. 45	30
Poor Law Amendment Act 1834, 4 & 5 Will. IV c. 76	23, 30, 77, 83, 86, 90, 113, 158–9, 258
s. 1	111
s. 2	214, 218
s. 7	139
s. 11	113
s. 17	159
s. 43	58
ss. 105, 106	258

xiv   *Table of Statutes*

Common Fields Inclosure Act 1836, 6 & 7
    Will. IV c. 115   92, 120, 163, 244, 271
    s. 1   203
    s. 7   197, 203
    s. 8   203
    s. 9   142
    s. 15   170, 171, 244
    s. 17   245
    s. 19   171
    s. 44   245
    s. 53   170, 245, 271
Ecclesiastical Commissioners Act 1836, 6 & 7 Will. IV
    c. 77   36
Parochial Assessments Act 1836, 6 & 7 Will. IV c. 96   58, 171
    s. 1   26, 171
    s. 6   249
    s. 7   249, 271
Tithe Commutation Act 1836, 6 & 7 Will.
    IV c. 71   24, 32, 67–8, 96, 131, 133, 159, 160, 191, 266
    s. 1   122, 160
    s. 4   139
    s. 7   141, 142
    s. 9   112
    s. 10   216, 219
    s. 17   161
    s. 24   164, 293
    s. 27   161
    s. 32   191
    s. 33   161, 191
    ss. 34–35   191
    ss. 36–43   161, 191
    s. 44   161, 191, 197
    s. 45   165, 237, 265
    s. 46   165, 242, 243
    s. 51   166, 197, 203, 204, 205
    s. 52   161, 166
    s. 53   161, 162, 191
    s. 54   162
    s. 61   167, 203, 204, 205
    s. 63   162, 167

ss. 73 ff.	221
s. 95	258, 271
Tithe Commutation Amendment Act 1837, 7	
Will. IV & 1 Vict. c. 69	168, 169, 258–9
s. 2	168, 216
s. 3	243, 258
Chartered Companies Act 1837, 7 Will. IV & 1 Vict.	
c. 73	293
Conveyance of the Mails by Railways Act 1838, 1 & 2	
Vict. c. 98	
s. 16	60
Railway and Canal Traffic Act 1840, 3 & 4 Vict. c. 97	
ss. 10, 18–19	60
Regulation of Railways Act 1840, 3 & 4 Vict. c. 97	33, 174
s. 18	175
s. 19	175
Tithe Commutation Amendment Act 1840, 3 & 4 Vict. c. 15	
s. 24	219
Copyhold Act 1841,	
4 & 5 Vict. c. 35	24, 32, 96–7, 159, 160, 162, 219, 293
s. 4	116, 139
ss. 5, 6	116
ss. 13, 14, 15	191
s. 21	169
s. 22	293
s. 23	162, 193
s. 24	191
s. 25	192
s. 27	192
s. 29	169, 293
s. 31	162, 192
s. 32	162, 192, 193
s. 33	193
s. 36	163
s. 39	169, 216, 237, 293
s. 40	159, 243
s. 43	171, 219
s. 56	163
s. 96	271

xvi *Table of Statutes*

Income and Property Taxes Act 1842, 5 & 6 Vict. c. 35	198
ss. 4–6	116
s. 14	117
s. 16	117
s. 19	113
s. 23	216
ss. 118–119	155
s. 120	155, 220
ss. 121–126	155
s. 130	155, 198
s. 131	155, 241
Schedule F	113, 209
Regulation of Railways Act 1842, 5 & 6 Vict. c. 55	
s. 11	60, 175, 176
Joint Stock Companies Act 1844, 7 & 8 Vict. c. 110	293
Companies Clauses Consolidation Act 1845, 8 & 9 Vict. c. 16	
ss. 144, 147, 159	59
Gaming Act 1845, 8 & 9 Vict. c. 109	243
s. 19	243
Schedule 2	243
Inclosure Act 1845, 8 & 9 Vict. c. 118	24, 32, 86, 131–2, 159, 160, 163, 170, 259, 283
s. 1	87, 160
ss. 6, 7	142
s. 8	112
s. 9	216, 217, 219
s. 25	163, 192
s. 26	164, 192
s. 27	164, 192
s. 33	164, 193
s. 35	132, 170
s. 38	112
s. 39	170, 204, 245, 259
s. 42	246
s. 44	246, 259
s. 48	170, 204, 205
s. 49	171

s. 54	237
s. 55	170, 197, 201, 204, 205
s. 56	245
s. 57	237
s. 60	245
ss. 63, 64	245
s. 104	170
s. 128	139
s. 166	271
Land Clauses Consolidation Act 1845, 8 & 9 Vict. c 18	61
Railway Clauses Consolidation Act 1845,	
8 & 9 Vict. c. 20	92, 180, 278
s. 12	60, 92
ss. 36, 60, 69	59
s. 126	278
s. 129	278
s. 133	278
s. 134	278
Commissioners of Railways Act 1846, 9 & 10	
Vict. c. 105	34, 174
Public Money Drainage Act 1846, 9 & 10 Vict. c. 101	92
Recovery of Small Debts Act 1846, 9 & 10	
Vict. c. 95	46, 188, 320
Poor Relief Act 1848, 11 & 12 Vict. c. 110	
s. 4	159
Public Health Act 1848, 11 & 12 Vict. c. 63	23, 62, 90
s. 4	30
ss. 5–8	31
s. 86	23
s. 120	66
ss. 123–8	62
ss. 129, 135, 136	59
Summary Jurisdiction Act 1848, 11 & 12 Vict. c. 43	260
Poor Relief Act Continuance Act 1851, 14 & 15	
Vict. c. 105	
s. 12	65, 159
Chancery Reform Act 1852, 15 & 16 Vict. c. 80	275
Common Law Procedure Act 1852, 15 & 16	
Vict. c. 76	188, 320

xviii   *Table of Statutes*

Enfranchisement of Copyholds Act 1852, 15 & 16
    Vict. c. 51
    s. 1   97
    s. 5   219
    s. 7   97
    s. 8   244
Common Law Procedure Act 1854, 17 & 18
    Vict. c. 125   188, 320
    s. 241   301
Merchant Shipping Act 1854, 17 & 18 Vict. c. 104   37, 68, 301
    ss. 241–242   301
Railway and Canal Traffic Regulation Act 1854,
    17 & 18 Vict. c. 31   45, 53–6, 57, 68, 177, 180, 182,
                                  194, 262, 275, 290
    s. 2   25, 177, 180
    s. 3   56, 126, 177, 195
    s. 4   195
Queen's Remembrancer's Act 1859, 22 & 23 Vict. c. 21
    s. 10   241
Railway Companies Arbitration Act 1859, 22 & 23
    Vict. c. 59   60
Merchant Shipping Amendment Act 1862, 25 & 26 Vict. c. 63
    s. 23   301
Union Assessment Committee Act 1862, 25 & 26
    Vict. c. 103   26, 121, 171–4, 206, 249, 306
    s. 2   172
    s. 14   171, 194
    s. 17   172, 194, 204
    s. 18   173, 194, 205, 206
    s. 19   173, 194, 205, 249, 305, 306
    s. 20   194
    s. 21   194
    s. 32   249
    s. 33   249
Railway Clauses Consolidation Act 1863, 26 & 27
    Vict. c. 92   180
Union Assessment Committee Amendment
    Act 1864, 27 & 28 Vict. c. 39
    s. 1   173
Regulation of Railways Act 1868, 31 & 32 Vict. c. 119   180

Table of Statutes

Bankruptcy Act 1869, 32 & 33 Vict. c. 71	47
Valuation of Property (Metropolis) Act 1869, 32 & 33 Vict. c. 67	206, 249
s. 11	206
s. 18	249
s. 19	249
s. 20	249
s. 23	249
s. 32	250
s. 40	250
s. 63	198, 201
Elementary Education Act 1870, 33 & 34 Vict. c. 75	69
ss. 9, 33	69
Railway and Canal Traffic Act 1873, 36 & 37 Vict. c. 48	25, 34, 68, 127, 181, 206, 223, 262
s. 5	262
s. 6	180
s. 7	296
s. 8	181
s. 10	180
s. 11	181
s. 12	180
s. 14	180
s. 15	181
s. 19	60, 181
s. 21	141
s. 22	142
s. 23	127
s. 24	141
s. 25	180, 217–18, 299
s. 26	180, 246, 247
s. 27	195, 200
s. 28	227
s. 29	180, 195
Ord. 2	206
Ord. 13	206
Ord. 14	195
Ord. 17	196
Ord. 18	206
Ords. 23, 25	205

xx — *Table of Statutes*

Ord. 28	196
Ord. 29	196
Ord. 30	218
Ord. 31	218
Ord. 33	218
Ord. 35	196
Ord. 42	246, 247
Ord. 43	246
Ord. 54	195, 278

Supreme Court of Judicature Act 1873, 36 & 37
Vict. c. 66   65, 126, 135, 188, 202, 234, 247, 293, 294, 309, 320

s. 19	234
s. 56	126

Building Societies Act 1874, 37 & 38 Vict. c. 42

s. 34	62

Customs and Inland Revenue Act 1874, 37 Vict. c. 16   241

Public Health Act 1875, 38 & 39 Vict. c. 55   66

ss. 179–81, 268–9   59, 66

Supreme Court of Judicature Act 1875, 38 & 39
Vict. c. 77   65, 202, 247, 294, 309

Prison Act 1877, 40 & 41 Vict. c. 21

ss. 9, 13–14   69

Summary Jurisdiction Act 1879, 42 & 43 Vict. c. 49   303

Taxes Management Act 1880, 43 & 44 Vict. c. 19   138

s. 41	138
s. 57(6)–(8)	155
s. 57(9)	222

Bankruptcy Act 1883, 46 & 47 Vict. c. 52,   58, 76

ss. 66–70   58, 76

Corrupt and Illegal Practices Prevention Act 1883, 46 & 47
Vict. c. 51   223

s. 38   223

Local Government Act 1888, 51 & 52 Vict. c. 41   303

Railway and Canal Traffic Act 1888, 51 & 52
Vict. c. 25   34, 135, 136, 182, 200, 225, 248, 268, 287

s. 2	181, 251
s. 3	136
s. 4	136
s. 5	137, 200

s. 5(2)	201
s. 8	181
s. 9	181
s. 10	182
s. 12	182
s. 17	248
s. 17(6)	268
s. 20	195
ss. 50, 51	223, 225
Arbitration Act 1889, 52 & 53 Vict. c. 49	239
Official Secrets Act 1889, 52 & 53 Vict. c. 52	114
Copyhold Act 1894, 57 & 58 Vict. c. 46	
s. 53	244
Workmen's Compensation Act 1897, 60 & 61 Vict. c. 37	62
Schedule 2	47, 62
s. 23	62
Finance Act 1898, 61 & 62 Vict. c. 10	
s. 16	223
Education Act 1902, 2 Edw. VII c. 42	258
National Insurance Act 1911, 1 & 2 Geo. V c. 55	9, 328
Electricity (Supply) Act 1919, 9 & 10 Geo. V c. 100	258
Tribunals and Inquiries Act 1958, 6 & 7 Eliz. II c. 66	2

TABLE OF CASES

AG *v.* BBC [1980] 3 All ER 161   306, 310
Allen *v.* Sharpe (1848) 2 Ex 352   240
Andrew Knowles & Sons Ltd *v.* McAdam (1877)
    1 TC 161   223

Barker *v.* the Tithe Commissioners (1841) 9 M & W 129   265
Barrett *v.* the Great Northern Railway Company and the
    Midland Railway Company (1857) 1 CB NS 423   57, 178–9
Baxendale *v.* the Great Western Railway Company
    (1858) 5 CB NS 309; (1862) 12 CB NS 758   178, 179
Board of Education *v.* Rice [1911] AC 179   258, 263
Dr Bonham's Case (1610) 8 Co Rep 113b   260
Boulter *v.* Kent Justices [1897] AC 556   256, 303
Broughton and Plas Power Coal Co. Ltd *v.* Kirkpatrick
    (1884) 2 TC 69   201
Brown *v.* Trant (1701) 2 Vern 426   106
Bruce *v.* Wait (1840) 1 Man & G 1   251

Cardiffe Bridge Case (1700) 1 Salk 146   254
Caterham Railway Company *v.* the London, Brighton, and
    South Coast Railway Company and South Eastern
    Railway Company (1857) 1 CB NS 410   57, 178
Chabot *v.* Lord Morpeth (1844) 15 QB 446   257, 265, 267
Church *v.* Inclosure Commissioners (1862)
    11 CB NS 664   123, 164, 192, 227, 266
Churchwardens and Overseers of West Ham *v.* Fourth City
    Mutual Building Society [1892] 1 QB 654   172
City of London *v.* Wood (1702) 12 Mod 669   260
Collier *v.* Hicks (1831) 2 B & Ad 663   207, 221, 275, 305

xxii

Table of Cases

Colonial Bank of Australasia Ltd *v.* Willan
(1874) LR 5 PC 417 — 271
Commins *v.* Massam (1643) March NR 196 — 253
Commissioners of Sewers for Yorkshire Case (1724) 1
Str 609 — 269
Cooper *v.* Wandsworth Board of Works
(1863) 14 CB NS 180 — 264

Darlaston Local Board *v.* London and North Western
Railway Company [1894] 2 QB 45 — 182
Daubney *v.* Cooper (1829) 10 B & C 237 — 207
Dawkins *v.* Lord Rokeby (1873) 8 LR QB 255 — 302
Dimes *v.* Grand Junction Canal (1852) 3 HLC 759 — 260
Dyson *v.* Wood (1824) 3 B & C 449 — 251

Earl of Stamford and Warrington *v.* Dunbar (1844) 12 M
& W 414 — 167, 243, 268
Edwards *v.* Bowen (1826) 5 B & C 206 — 255
Evans *v.* Rees (1839) 10 A & E 151 — 167
Ex parte Evans (1846) 9 QB 279 — 275, 305
Ex parte Phillips (1835) 2 A & E 586 — 255

Foxham Tithing Case (1705) 2 Salk 607 — 261

Gateshead Union Assessment Committee *v.* Redheugh
Colliery Ltd [1925] AC 309 — 121, 213
Girdlestone *v.* Stanley (1839) 3 Y & C Ex 421 — 134, 165–6,
216, 227
Goffin *v.* Donnelly (1881) 6 QBD 307 — 302
Goslings and Sharpe *v.* Blake (1889) 2 TC 450 — 223
Great Charte *v.* Kennington (1742) 2 Str 1173 — 261
Dr Grenville *v.* College of Physicians (1700)
12 Mod 386 — 269
Griesley's Case (1588) 8 Co Rep 38a — 298
Groenvelt *v.* Burwell (1697) 1 Ld Raym 454; 3 Salk 265
(1696); Carth 421 (1697); Holt KB 184, 395, 536 (1697,
1700); 1 Ld Raym 213 (1697); 3 Ld Raym 278 (1697);
1 Salk 144, 200, 263, 396 (1698, 1700);
Carth 491 (1699); 12 Mod 386 (1700);
1 Comyns 76 (1700) — 251–2, 254, 298

xxiv   *Table of Cases*

Hall *v.* Norwood (1663) 1 Sid 165   265
Harris *v.* the Cockermouth and Workington Railway
    Company (1858) 3 CB NS 693   179
Hopkins *v.* Smethwick Local Board of Health (1890) 24
    QBD 712   264

Jaques *v.* Caesar (1670) 2 Wms Saund 100   251
Jones *v.* the Eastern Counties Railway Company (1858) 3
    CB NS 718   262

Lee *v.* Birrell (1813) 3 Camp 337   113
Leeds Permanent Benefit Building Society *v.* Mallandaine
    (1897) 3 TC 577   201
Liverpool Corn Trade Association Ltd *v.* London and
    North Western Railway Company [1891] 1 QB 120   19
Luard *v.* Butcher (1846) 15 LJ NS CP 187   243

Manchester, Sheffield & Lincolnshire Railway *v.*
    Brown (1883) LR 8 App Cas 703   44
Mayor and Aldermen of City of London *v.*
    Cox (1867) LR 2 HL 239   250, 253, 311
Miller *v.* Seare (1777) 2 Black W 1141   255

National Telephone Company *v.* HM Postmaster General
    [1913] AC 546   299
Nicolson *v.* the Great Western Railway Company (1858) 5
    CB NS 366   179

Oxlade *v.* the North Eastern Railway Company (1857) 1 CB
    NS 454   179

Palmer *v.* the London and Brighton Railway Company
    (1871) 40 LJ CP 133   179–80
Pelsall Coal and Iron Co. Ltd *v.* London and North
    Western Railway Company (1889) 23 QBD 536   180
Pickering *v.* Noyes (1823) 1 B & C 262   219

R. *v.* Aberdare Canal Company (1850) 14 QB 854   257
R. *v.* Assessment Committee of St Mary Abbotts,
    Kensington [1891] 1 QB 378   173, 187, 228, 255, 275, 298,
                                             300, 304–6

Table of Cases

R. *v.* Barker (1762) 3 Burr 1265	268
R. *v.* Berkley and Bragge (1754) 1 Keny 80	270
R. *v.* Bloomsbury Income Tax Commissioners [1915] 3 KB 768	38
R. *v.* Board of Education [1910] 2 KB 165	257, 258, 268
R. *v.* Bolingbroke [1893] 2 QB 347	261
R. *v.* Bowman [1898] 1 QB 663	256
R. *v.* Cambridge University, ex parte Bentley (1723) 1 Str 557	230
R. *v.* Chancellor of St Edmundsbury and Ipswich Diocese [1948] 1 KB 195	254
R. *v.* Chantrell (1875) LR 10 QB 587	271
R. *v.* Cheltenham Commissioners (1841) 1 QB 467	261
R. *v.* Coles (1845) 8 QB 75	252
R. *v.* the Commissioners for the General Purposes cf the Income Tax for Kensington [1914] 3 KB 429	266
R. *v.* Commissioners for Special Purposes of the Income Tax (1888) 21 QBD 313	268
R. *v.* Commissioners of Income Tax for the City of London (1904) 91 LT 94	269
R. *v.* Commissioners of the Land Tax for St Martin in the Fields, Westminster (1786) 1 TR 146	268
R. *v.* Edward Pryse Lloyd (1783) Cald 309	255
R. *v.* Electricity Commissioners [1924] 1 KB 171	256, 258, 264, 267
R. *v.* Glamorganshire Inhabitants (1700) 1 Ld Raym 580	48
R. *v.* Inhabitants in Glamorganshire (1701) 1 Ld Raym 580	254
R. *v.* Inhabitants of Uttoxeter (1732) 2 Str 932	269
R. *v.* Johnson [1905] 2 KB 59	256
R. *v.* Justices of County of London and London County Council [1893] 2 QB 476	231
R. *v.* Justices of London [1897] 1 QBD 433	173, 206
R. *v.* Justices of Shrewsbury (1733) 2 Str 975	269
R. *v.* Kensington Income Tax Commissioners [1913] 3 KB 870	267
R. *v.* King (1788) 2 TR 234	269
R. *v.* Legislative Committee of the Church Assembly [1928] 1 KB 411	256
R. *v.* Light Railway Commissioners [1915] 3 KB 536	267
R. *v.* Local Government Board (1882) 10 QBD 309	257

xxvi   *Table of Cases*

R. *v.* London County Council [1892] 1 QB 190,   256
R. *v.* Mansel Jones (1889) 23 QBD 29   187, 223
R. *v.* Moreley (1760) 2 Burr 1040   270
R. *v.* Nat Bell Liquors Ltd [1922] 2 AC 128   270
R. *v.* North Worcestershire Assessment
    Committee [1929] 2 KB 397   256
R. *v.* Northumberland Compensation Appeal Tribunal
    [1951] 1 KB 711; [1952] 1 KB 338   260
R. *v.* Poor Law Commissioners (1837) 6 A & E 1   258
R. *v.* Rand (1866) LR 1 QB 230   261
R. *v.* Sharman [1898] 1 QB 578   256
R. *v.* Shoreditch Assessment Committee
    [1910] 2 KB 859   311
R. *v.* Sunderland Justices [1901] 2 KB 357   256
R. *v.* Tomlinson (1866) LR 1 CCR 49   301
R. *v.* the Vestry of St Pancras (1890) 24 QBD 371   268
R. *v.* Woodhouse [1906] 2 KB 501   256
Ransome *v.* the Eastern Counties Railway Company (1857)
    1 CB NS 437   179
Re the Appledore Tithe Commutation (1845)
    8 QB 139   162, 167, 217, 266
Re Clifford and O'Sullivan [1921] 2 AC 570   267
Re Constables of Hipperholme (1847) 5 Dowl & L 79   255
Re Crosby Tithes (1849) 13 QB 761   165, 266
Re Dent Tithe Commutation (1845)
    8 QB 43   168–9, 217, 258–9, 310
Re Glatton Land Tax (1840) 6 M & W 689   150
Re Lediard (1751) Sayer 6   255
Re Macqueen and the Nottingham Caledonian Society
    (1861) 9 CB NS 793   221
Re Nathan (1884) 12 QBD 461   268–9
Re Schmidt's Trade-Mark (1887) 35 Ch D 162   305
Re Tithes of Crosby-upon-Eden (1849) 13 QB 761   253
Re Ystradgunlais Tithe Commutation (1844) 8 QB 32   168, 266
Redheugh Colliery Ltd *v.* Gateshead Assessment
    Committee [1924] 1 KB 369   174
Reid's Brewery Co. Ltd *v.* Male (1891) 3 TC 279   223
Royal Aquarium and Summer and Winter Garden Society
    Ltd *v.* Parkinson [1892] 1 QB 431   256, 303, 306, 307

Table of Cases

San Paulo (Brazilian) Railway Co. Ltd *v.*
   Carter (1895) 3 TC 344 — 223
Scott *v.* Bye (1824) 2 Bing 344 — 251–2
Seaman *v.* Netherclift (1876) 2 CPD 53 — 302
Sharp *v.* Wakefield [1891] AC 173 — 256, 303
Shell Company of Australia Ltd *v.* Federal
   Commissioner of Taxation [1931] AC 275 — 306
Society of Medical Officers of Health *v.*
   Hope [1960] AC 551 — 306
Special Commissioners *v.* Pemsel (1891) 3 TC 53 — 144

Tillam *v.* Copp (1847) 5 CB 211 — 277

Watney & Co. *v.* Musgrave (1880) 1 TC 272 — 222
Williams *v.* Steward (1817) 3 Mer 472 — 106, 152
Winsford Local Board *v.* Cheshire Lines Committee (1890)
   24 QBD 456 — 182
Wood *v.* Woad (1874) LR 9 Ex 190 — 263
Worthington *v.* Jeffries (1875) 10 LR CP 379 — 253

ABBREVIATIONS

LAW REPORTS

Source: Donald Raistrick, *Index to Legal Citations and Abbreviations*, 2nd edition (London: Bowker-Saur, 1993). The relevant volume of the *English Reports* (ER) is also indicated.

A & E   *Adolphus and Ellis' Reports* (110–13 ER) 1834–40

AC   *Law Reports Appeal Cases* 1891–

All ER   *All England Law Reports* 1936–

B & Ad   *Barnewall and Adolphus' King's Bench Reports* (109–10 ER) 1830–4

B & C   *Barnewall and Cresswell's King's Bench Reports* (107–9 ER) 1822–30

Bing   *Bingham's Common Pleas Reports* (130–1 ER) 1822–34

Black W   *Sir William Blackstone's King's Bench Reports* (96 ER) 1746–80

Burr   *Burrow's King's Bench Reports* (97–8 ER) 1757–71

Cald   *Caldecott's Magistrates and Settlement Cases*, 1776–85

Camp   *Campbell's Nisi Prius Reports* (170–1 ER) 1808–16

Carth   *Carthew's King's Bench Reports* (90 ER) 1686–1701

CB   *Common Bench Reports* (135–9 ER) 1845–56

Abbreviations

CB NS	*Common Bench Reports, New Series* (140–4 ER) 1856–65
Ch D	*Law Reports, Chancery Division* 1876–90
Co Rep	*Coke's King's Bench Reports* (76–7 ER) 1572–1616
Comyns	*Comyns' King's Bench Reports* (92 ER) 1695–1741
CPD	*Law Reports, Common Pleas Division* 1875–80
Dowl & L	*Dowling and Lowndes' Bail Court Reports* (67–82 Revised Reports) 1843–9
Ex	*Exchequer Reports* (154–6 ER) 1847–56
HLC	*House of Lords Cases* (9–11 ER) 1847–66
Holt KB	*Holt's King's Bench Reports* (90 ER) 1688–1711
KB	*Law Reports, King's Bench* 1901–52
Keny	*Kenyon's Notes of King's Bench Cases* (96 ER) 1753–9
Ld Raym	*Lord Raymond's King's Bench Reports* (91–2 ER) 1694–1732
LJ NS CP	*Law Journal Reports, New Series, Common Pleas* 1832–1949
LR App Cas	*Law Reports, Appeal Cases*, 1875–90
LR CCR	*Law Reports, Crown Cases Reserved* 1865–75
LR CP	*Law Reports, Common Pleas* 1865–75
LR Ex	*Law Reports, Exchequer* 1865–75
LR HL	*Law Reports, English and Irish Appeals* 1866–75
LR PC	*Law Reports, Privy Council* 1865–75
LR QB	*Law Reports, Queen's Bench* 1865–75, 1891–
LT	*Law Times Reports* 1859–1947
M & W	*Meeson and Welsby's Exchequer Reports* (150–3 ER) 1836–47

xxx   *Abbreviations*

Man & G   *Manning and Granger's Common Pleas
                 Reports* (133–5 ER) 1840–4

March NR   *March's New Cases, King's Bench* (82 ER)
                 1639–42

Mer   *Merivale's Chancery Reports* (35–6 ER)
                 1815–17

Mod   *Modern Reports* (86–8 ER) 1669–1755

QB   *Queen's Bench Reports* (113–18 ER) 1841–52

QBD   *Law Reports Queen's Bench Division* 1875–90

Salk   *Salkeld's King's Bench Reports* (91 ER)
                 1689–1712

Sayer   *Sayer's King's Bench Reports* (96 ER) 1751–6

Sid   *Siderfin's King's Bench Reports* (82 ER) 1657–70

Str   *Strange's King's Bench Reports* (93 ER) 1716–49

TC   *Reports of Tax Cases* 1875–

TR   *Durnford and East's Term Reports*
                 (99–101 ER) 1785–1800

Vern   *Vernon's Chancery Reports* (23 ER)
                 1680–1719

Wms Saund   *Williams' Notes to Saunders' Reports* (85 ER)
                 1666–73

Y & C Ex   *Younge and Collyer's Exchequer Reports*
                 (160 ER) 1834–42

OTHER ABBREVIATIONS

DRO   Devon Record Office

HCPP   House of Commons Parliamentary Papers

Parl. Deb.   Parliamentary Debates

TNA:PRO   The National Archives: Public Record Office

Report/Minutes, Copyholds Enfranchisement, 1837–8
     'Report from, and Minutes of Evidence before, the Select
     Committee on Copyholds Enfranchisement', *HCPP*
     (1837–8) (707) xxiii 189

Abbreviations xxxi

Report/Minutes, Commons' Inclosure, 1844
'Report from, and Minutes of Evidence before, the Select Committee on Commons' Inclosure', *HCPP* (1844) (583) v 1

Minutes, Railways, 1844
'Minutes of Evidence before the Select Committee on Railways', *HCPP* (1844) (318) xi 17

Report/Minutes, Copyholds Bill, 1851
'Report from, and Minutes of Evidence before, the Select Committee on the Enfranchisement of Copyholds Bill', *HCPP* (1851) (550) xiii 1

Minutes, Income and Property Tax, 1852
'Minutes of Evidence taken before the Select Committee on the Income and Property Tax', *HCPP* (1852) (354) ix 1

Report/Minutes, Railway Amalgamation, 1872
'Report from, and Minutes of Evidence before, the Joint Select Committee of the House of Lords and the House of Commons on Railway Companies Amalgamation', *HCPP* (1872) (364) xiii 1

Minutes, Railways, 1881
'Minutes of Evidence before the Select Committee on Railways', *HCPP* (1881) (374) xiii 1

Minutes, Railways (Rates and Fares), 1882
'Minutes of Evidence before the Select Committee on Railways (Rates and Fares)', *HCPP* (1882) (317) xiii 89

Minutes, Income Tax, 1919
'Minutes of Evidence taken before the Royal Commission on the Income Tax', *HCPP* (1919) (288) xxiii (Parts 1 and 2)

1

CHALLENGES TO THE LEGAL PROCESS

Statutory tribunals today surpass the courts of law in terms of numbers of disputes heard and resolved. They are recognised as adjudicative bodies of central importance to the efficient operation of the regular courts themselves and the administration of justice in general. It has been shown that an individual citizen's personal contact with a formal adjudication process is far more likely to be in the context of an administrative tribunal than of a court of law. Tribunals operate in a wide range of aspects of everyday life,[1] hearing and determining appeals by individuals aggrieved by an administrative decision taken by an organ of the state. Their principal feature is that they do so in an effective, accessible, expeditious and inexpensive way.[2] They are today of a known constitution, applying clear rules to the dispute before them and arriving at a determination. Within this broad characterisation, however, there exist a very large number of tribunals,[3] varying considerably in their functions, jurisdictions, procedures and personnel. A tribunal's objective might be to adjudicate, investigate, regulate, advise or award, or perform a combination of two or more of these functions.[4]

---

[1] Modern tribunals deal with 'the whole range of political and social life, including social security benefits, health, education, tax, agriculture, criminal injuries compensation, immigration and asylum, rents, and parking': Sir Andrew Leggatt, *Tribunals for Users: One System, One Service: Report of the Review of Tribunals* (London: HMSO, 2001), para. 1.16.

[2] These were described by the permanent secretary to the Lord Chancellor as 'the outstanding attributes of the administrative tribunal' in 'Minutes of Evidence before the Committee on Administrative Tribunals and Enquiries' (London: HMSO, 1956), Cmnd 218, p. 190, para. 4.

[3] The diversity and lack of coherence render even the enumeration of tribunals difficult. Depending on the definition adopted, numbers today range from 200 to the 70 considered by the Leggatt Review.

[4] H. W. Arthurs, 'Rethinking Administrative Law: A Slightly Dicey Business' (1979) 17 *Osgoode Hall Law Journal* 1 at 38.

2   Legal Foundations of Tribunals in 19th-Century England

Though modern tribunals retain some degree of executive provenance, they are often almost entirely adjudicatory in function. They establish facts and apply legal rules, albeit within a very specific jurisdiction, but are bodies existing outside the formal structures of the courts of law. Their place is, accordingly, ambiguous. Furthermore, while many individual tribunals are working well enough in practice,[5] as standards of administrative justice have risen a close scrutiny of individual tribunals' structures, jurisdiction and procedures has revealed weaknesses and anachronisms, which undermine their effectiveness as dispute-resolution organs.[6] This diversity and uncertainty of place renders any concept of a system of tribunals fallacious, makes definition or classification impossible[7] and principle unreachable. Though the situation has been improved immensely by the parameters necessarily drawn by the Council on Tribunals for its supervisory purposes, modern tribunals as an institution lack any unifying underlying principles other than of the most general kind. The work of the council, indeed the need for its creation in 1958,[8] reflects the lack of uniformity and consistency in constitution, process and personnel across the range of past and present tribunals. The diversity of form and process among modern tribunals undermines modern government's aim to arrive at a coherent structure for the delivery of administrative justice. The enduring concern and difficulty with the theoretical place of tribunals and with the practical work of reforming them to achieve some consistency in their nature and operation is reflected in the number of governmental reviews and inquiries into tribunals from the late 1990s.[9]

---

[5] Even the oldest extant tribunal, the General Commissioners of Income Tax, created by William Pitt in 1799 when he first introduced the income tax.

[6] See C. Stebbings, 'Historical Factors in Contemporary Tribunal Structure, Process and Reform', in Martin Partington (ed.), *The Leggatt Review of Tribunals: Academic Seminar Papers*, Bristol Centre for the Study of Administrative Justice Working Papers Series 3 (Bristol: University of Bristol, 2001), Chapter 8.

[7] See J. A. Farmer, *Tribunals and Government* (London: Weidenfeld & Nicolson, 1974), pp. 184–5; Arthurs, 'Rethinking Administrative Law', 3; R. E. Wraith and P. G. Hutchesson, *Administrative Tribunals* (London: George Allen and Unwin, 1973), pp. 14–15, 43–4.

[8] Tribunals and Inquiries Act 1958, 6 & 7 Eliz. II c. 66.

[9] JUSTICE, *Review of Administrative Law in the United Kingdom* (London: JUSTICE–All Souls Review, 1981); Lord Woolf, *Access to Justice: Final Report on the Civil Justice System in England and Wales* (London: HMSO, 1996); Tax

Challenges to the Legal Process

The reasons for the diversity, lack of coherence, uncertainty of status and inherent individual weaknesses which have rendered both theoretical analysis and practical reform so problematic lie to a considerable extent in the historico-legal context of the statutory administrative tribunal as an institution in the nineteenth century. Its formative period began in broad terms at the height of the industrial revolution in the 1830s. The novelty of the social and economic demands they were created to meet, the complexity and diversity of governmental patterns and administrative practices and the legal context of the response rendered the classification of the new statutory tribunals difficult and ultimately unsatisfactory. The diversity of tribunals was as much a feature of the nineteenth century as of the present day, and the problems of definition existed then as now. The term 'tribunal', not being a term of art, referred to any dispute-resolution body or process, from the regular courts of law, through domestic bodies regulating clubs, societies and professions, to ministers making decisions in the course of their administrative duties. The nature of dispute-resolution powers, their prominence in the work of the body in question, the extent to which they were appellate or first-instance powers and to which they were discrete adjudicatory powers both in practice and in the intention of the legislature, all varied according to the tribunal. Furthermore the structure, powers and the guiding procedural principles of all tribunals were settled when the tribunals were first created. And yet within a period of fifty years political, social and legal demands had combined to construct the legal foundations of a new institution, albeit one broadly conceived: the statutory administrative tribunal, composed of predominantly lay adjudicators, hearing and determining appeals arising from administrative action in specialised fields of human activity. The formative period of statutory tribunals can be regarded as culminating with the creation of the Railway Commission of the 1870s, arguably the prototype of the modern tribunal.[10]

The aim of this study is to elucidate the legal foundations of modern statutory tribunals which perform an extra-judicial

---

Law Review Committee, *Interim Report on the Tax Appeals System* (London: Institute for Fiscal Studies, 1996); Leggatt, *Tribunals for Users.*
[10] Wraith and Hutchesson, *Administrative Tribunals*, p. 27.

4   *Legal Foundations of Tribunals in 19th-Century England*

adjudicatory function and have become, in effect, a first tier of civil dispute-resolution and an independent replacement for the regular courts.[11] The study examines the evolution of the modern concept of the tribunal and the legal rules and doctrines which developed to sustain it within the context of the legal system itself and of legal theory. It explores the reasons for its emergence, the legal foundations of its constitution, processes and jurisdiction, and how it attained its place in the modern legal system. It is concerned with the coherence of the legal doctrines and their legal effect, explaining how the concept of the modern statutory tribunal and its procedures developed and how they were created by certain legal values and ideas.

The reason for undertaking a doctrinal legal study of this nature is to promote a more profound understanding of the tribunal as a legal institution, both for its own sake, and to permit the effective reform and adaptation of the law and the institution to modern conditions and changing values. In providing an analysis of legal evidence it also provides a resource for scholars in other disciplines pursuing alternative discourses, since any student of the nineteenth century, whatever his perspective, requires technical rigour and a degree of accessible legal contextualisation, and it thereby aims to illuminate the familiar history of government growth in the nineteenth century. The doctrinal approach is a traditional one, and one of the assumptions on which it is based is the orthodox view that law is formal and impartial with a discrete existence and a purpose and momentum of its own.[12] The doctrinal approach values the legalistic discourse as providing a disciplined legal analysis of a branch of modern law of considerable contemporary importance that has hitherto been somewhat neglected, partly because of its inherent intractability and partly because of the dominance of other perspectives. Indeed, the role of legal doctrine in the machinery of central government intervention has been largely untouched. Its study reflects the essential importance of the law in the historical continuum and ensures that legal issues are addressed as issues of importance and that they do

---

[11] Arthurs, 'Rethinking Administrative Law', 38.

[12] This centralist perspective of law has been challenged, notably by Professor Arthurs: H. W. Arthurs, *'Without the Law': Administrative Justice and Legal Pluralism in Nineteenth-Century England* (Toronto and Buffalo: University of Toronto Press, 1985), pp. 2–4.

Challenges to the Legal Process

not become too diffuse. It asserts that the law was not purely reactive, but that it was influential in its own right. Furthermore, as one of the three traditional professions, and with a training even wider than its practice, the values, processes and perspectives of the law formed the intellect and values of many of the leading protagonists in the evolution of the statutory tribunals – ministers, politicians, the leaders in trade and industry, and intellectuals.

The doctrinal approach can be viewed as somewhat exclusive, self-referential and technically legalistic, and as such of value to and accessible only to lawyers. Though it makes the law itself the focus of study, it does not argue that law is necessarily the principal factor, or even of equal weight, in determining an historical trajectory, and so does not deny or diminish the further dimensions that exist alongside the purely legal one. It acknowledges and values the political, social and ideological influences that affected the choice and nature of the statutory tribunals' legal foundations, and as such is based on a broader intellectual infrastructure and seeks to sustain the permeability of intellectual boundaries. It will be seen that the genesis of the modern statutory tribunal as a genre was as political as it was legal in that it was rooted in the development of an increasingly centralised, interventionist and regulatory state, and that accordingly the political dimension to the law, and its interaction and interrelation with the legal dimension, is of undoubted importance in the formation of the law itself. The legal and political discourses are closely linked, with a strong relationship both historical and intellectual.[13] Since both entail the study of the same institutions and relationships on the basis of much common source material, to adopt a doctrinal study of the law of such institutions and relationships is essentially a difference in emphasis. In the case of the tribunal as a legal institution, social conditions made regulation imperative, political ideology dominated the highly controversial issue of the desirable degree of state intervention, while political policy initiated the legislation and dictated the subsequent pattern of law-making. The conception of law as the product of the political process is therefore particularly apposite in the context of the statutory tribunal. Within the political process, however, the values, traditions,

---

[13] See generally Martin Loughlin, *Sword and Scales: An Examination of the Relationship between Law and Politics* (Oxford: Hart Publishing, 2000).

6   *Legal Foundations of Tribunals in 19th-Century England*

practices and existing institutions of the law were potent forces that contributed to the creation of the statutory tribunal as a new concept and the determination of its nature, structure and processes. In enacting the new regulatory legislation the state had clear political objectives, objectives that could not be fulfilled in practice through the traditional system of legal institutions, and were ultimately resolved by the development of new ones, the statutory tribunals, which form the subject of this study.

The tribunal that today constitutes such an important part of the civil justice system is the appellate tribunal, hearing and determining appeals against decisions made by a public authority. It is the elucidation of the legal foundations of this type of tribunal that forms the subject of this study. In theory each new tribunal, being created for a highly specific and self-contained purpose, is a new creation standing isolated from its contemporary and historical context and looking no further than its own parent Act. However, in terms of its essential nature and characteristics it belongs to a genre, and it is the legal foundations of that genre which can directly be traced to a relatively small group of implementing bodies created in the nineteenth century, and indeed to general legal values and traditions before then. The nineteenth century had relatively few tribunals in the sense of recognisable adjudicatory bodies in the public sphere, and yet it is those tribunals that form the lineal ancestors of the tribunals of today, despite a wide diversity of subject-matter, in the sense that it is through the former that the salient characteristics of the latter were formed and refined. The legal foundations of the modern statutory tribunal can therefore be discerned most clearly through the features and practices of those organs of the nineteenth century which enjoyed discrete, express and unambiguous dispute-resolution powers, the extremes of the judicial function allowing for clearer study. Those bodies determined appeals by individuals against administrative decisions, albeit with significant or even dominant administrative purposes, with oral hearings, proceeding according to some rules of guidance or process that were available to the public, following quasi-judicial processes and possessing a measure of independence from the executive. Even within this paradigm there was variation, notably in the balance of administrative and judicial functions, the nature of the powers as inquisitorial or adversarial and the character of the process. Some, for example,

Challenges to the Legal Process

were inquisitorial bodies with a subsidiary though important dispute-resolution function.[14] Some bodies held hearings in private and some in public, some published their decisions and some did not, some members were paid and some were not, some decisions could be appealed against to the regular courts and some not. While these diverse emphases undoubtedly reinforced the unique nature of each tribunal, they did not entirely obscure the fundamental underlying principle of their creation. Four groups have been identified through which the study will be conducted, each possessing prominent and formal adjudicatory functions though exhibiting a different emphasis: the fiscal tribunals are selected as the oldest; the tithe, copyhold and inclosure tribunals as the most inquisitorial; the Assessment Committees as the most administrative; and the Railway Commissioners as ultimately the most judicial.[15]

In order initially to discern those nineteenth-century tribunals with clear dispute-resolution functions, and subsequently to explain a major factor in the evolution of the statutory tribunal from governmental body to legal institution, a distinction has been drawn between judicial and administrative functions. That such a distinction can be drawn at all is a controversial assumption that has been the subject of considerable scholarly debate.[16] The distinction is problematic since it has inherent theoretical weaknesses on close analysis. Yet addressing as it does one aspect of the boundary between the judicial and the executive, it is central to the development of the legal foundations of the modern statutory tribunal. However, for the purposes of such a study, and in that context, the distinction need be made only in the broadest and most practical terms. Only for specific purposes such as the application of judicial review and the claiming of privileges enjoyed by the regular courts did the distinction have to be drawn with any degree of real precision, and the problems in so doing

---

[14] These, notably the land rights tribunals, would now be perceived as statutory inquiries.

[15] Other tribunals perform a wide variety of non-adjudicative and essentially administrative functions. The study excludes public officials deciding questions according to internal rules.

[16] See H. W. R. Wade, ' "Quasi-Judicial" and its Background' (1949) 10 *Cambridge Law Journal* 216–40 and the authorities there cited; Carol Harlow and Richard Rawlings, *Law and Administration*, 2nd edition (London: Butterworths, 1997), pp. 31–3.

8   Legal Foundations of Tribunals in 19th-Century England

were considerable.[17] The point of importance in tracing the legal evolution of the modern predominantly adjudicatory tribunal is to be able to identify the dispute-resolution or 'judicial' function of each tribunal within its overall duties. A tribunal's purpose was to implement, as an organ of the executive, the statutory regime consigned to it, work which in the nineteenth century comprised an admixture of legislative, administrative, ministerial and judicial functions.[18] The definition adopted for the purpose of this study is that the tribunals were exercising their judicial functions where they were resolving disputes arising from their implementation of the legislation, on their merits and objectively by the establishment of facts and the application to those facts of legal rules. In practice when the tribunals exercised their statutory powers to 'hear and determine' disputes, they did so in a manner discrete from the overall administrative process. When they met to hear appeals and objections, they did so on the basis of a specific statutory provision to that effect, and with sufficient formality of procedure, to indicate to the adjudicators themselves and the parties appearing before them that they were engaged in an activity of a character distinct from the general administrative and ministerial process, though within the context of that process. Procedural distinctiveness accordingly compensated to some extent for theoretical obscurity.

The necessary focus on the adjudicatory tribunals also inevitably relegates to the background those tribunals that were predominantly regulatory and administrative, notably the implementing organs relating to the poor law and the legislation for factories, public health, prisons and education. Political and social studies of the nineteenth century often concentrate on such bodies, because in social and political terms that legislation constituted the most important of the nineteenth century. First, it was principally through them that the social evils of the nineteenth century were relentlessly exposed and pressure for their amelioration sustained. Secondly, they epitomised the nature of the growth of the administrative state. In this respect the focus on adjudicatory tribunals has the effect of masking two important features of the period. It does

---

[17] See below, pp. 297–309.

[18] For an analysis of the terminology see S. de Smith, *Judicial Review of Administrative Action*, 4th edition (London: Stevens & Sons, 1980), pp. 68–89.

Challenges to the Legal Process

not fully reveal the scope and degree of central government activity in English life in the nineteenth century, particularly in the field of social welfare. It also obscures the full extent of the tensions between centralism and localism that permeated this political revolution and suggests that central control of local administration was less than it actually was. When hearing and determining disputes in the course of fulfilling their overall regulatory functions, the adjudicatory tribunals were acting judicially and independently in the sense that they were administering their own particular statutory regime of law, with further recourse, if any, to the regular courts of law and not to any higher executive body. Those bodies engaged principally in regulation and inspection, however, did so through local authorities under the control of central government in Whitehall. This shift in administrative power was the real political revolution inherent in the early growth of the administrative state, and one that is most clearly seen in the regulatory tribunals rather than the adjudicatory tribunals. The independence of action of tribunals exercising their judicial functions can, therefore, be misleading in that it undermines the reality of the relationship between the tribunals and the central government, a reality that is revealed by political scholarship. It must be remembered, however, that it is a question of degree, and that nearly all tribunals possessed both administrative and judicial powers.

While the regulatory bodies are important as the prime examples of the efforts of Victorian governments to address major social and economic problems created by the industrialisation of Britain, their formal dispute-resolution function was relatively minor and they contributed little to the modern conception of an extra-judicial dispute-resolution legal institution. When the era of the modern tribunal began with the passing of the Liberal social welfare legislation in the early twentieth century, notably the National Insurance Act 1911, legislators looked to the adjudicatory tribunals of the nineteenth for the essential features and processes of their new implementing bodies. Paradoxically, therefore, while today the social welfare tribunals are particularly prominent in extra-judicial dispute-resolution, they owe their nature, structures and procedures more to the adjudicatory tribunals of the nineteenth century, notably those concerned with taxes, railways and land rights, than to their predecessors in the social welfare field. The conclusions drawn from this study will

10   *Legal Foundations of Tribunals in 19th-Century England*

therefore necessarily be based on an examination of those tribunals that were predominantly adjudicatory in the sense that their judicial functions were clearer and more distinct than in the other early tribunals. The conclusions, however, relate to the function rather than the individual tribunal, to the presence of a judicial function within an administrative context, and so are valid for all statutory tribunals whatever the balance of administrative and judicial functions within the particular work of each and whatever the subject-matter.

Victoria's reign opened in 1837 at the height of a new challenge to the existing legal process to meet the demands of a new and dynamic industrial economy that was transforming the country. The immense expansion in commerce and industry which had gathered pace throughout the eighteenth century was, by the beginning of the nineteenth century, not only gaining momentum itself, but was also bringing other phenomena in its wake. The trebling of the population in less than a century, the migration from the countryside to the towns and changing working practices all engendered directly or indirectly a need for some kind of reforming social provision or regulation in almost every aspect of national life. The breadth of these areas of concern, dictated by prevailing ideologies, was astonishingly wide. Crowded towns, slum dwellings, disease and epidemic, dangerous working conditions in mines and factories, lack of education provision for children and the ever-present and increasing problem of pauperism were all obvious consequences, to varying degrees, of the industrialisation of Britain. Less obvious were deficiencies in the system of land tenure and taxation that rendered the country less able to support its growing population. Then there came issues emerging from advances in technology, such as new forms of transport, new public utilities and new inventions, or from the increased pace of commercial enterprise, such as bankruptcy. And underpinning these were issues of the public revenue, raised for the finance of foreign conflict but levied from the property and profits of the transformed British economy.

Inherent in the industrial revolution was a technological revolution that created one of the earliest and most severe social evils. The new machinery introduced into the textile industry required the construction of factories where the scale of operations was considerably increased from the cottage production of the

Challenges to the Legal Process

eighteenth century. The powerful and unguarded machinery, the exploitation of the labour force in terms of working hours and the appalling working conditions could not be tolerated, especially when it was clear that young children were subject to them as much as, if not more so than, their adult colleagues. The situation was exacerbated as the introduction of steam power allowed the scale of manufacturing to increase further and factories moved to urban areas to tap a plentiful supply of labour. The Royal Commission of 1833 exposed the full evils of the emerging and, in practice, unregulated factory system.[19]

If the exploitation of minors in the factories was the earliest welfare problem of the industrial revolution, pauperism was the principal problem in the 1830s. The Elizabethan poor law,[20] even if it had ever worked, was overwhelmed by the poverty spawned by the industrial revolution, and pauperism was growing unchecked and unrelieved. Poverty itself was not a new evil born of industrialisation, but it was undoubtedly exacerbated by it as the traditional support of cottage employment declined.[21] The existing law was administered by the justices of the peace through the appointment of local overseers, who levied a poor rate to fund its administration. It aimed to relieve the sick and the old and to either set to work or punish the able-bodied poor, but it was inherently divisive, widely abused, undermining of economic stability, corrupted and corrupting.[22] As a result it was inadequate, hugely and increasingly expensive to operate and did little to relieve the utter misery of poverty. Furthermore, it fuelled discontent among the rural population, already unstable as a result of bad harvests, low wages and the high price of wheat, which often found violent expression. It was a system that was widely accepted as failing in both fundamental principle and operation. Not only did the poor

---

[19] 'First Report of the Central Board of Commissioners for Inquiring into the Employment of Children in Factories', *HCPP* (1833) (450) xx 1 at 36.

[20] Poor Relief Act 1601, 43 Eliz. c. 2; Act of Settlement 1662, 13 & 14 Car. II c. 12.

[21] See generally S. G. and E. O. A. Checkland (eds.), *The Poor Law Report of 1834* (London: Pelican Books, 1974), Introduction.

[22] See generally W. Blake Odgers, 'Changes in Domestic Legislation', in Council of Legal Education (eds.), *A Century of Law Reform* (London: Macmillan & Co. Ltd, 1901), pp. 131–41; Derek Fraser, *The Evolution of the British Welfare State* (London: Macmillan, 1973), pp. 28–50; David Roberts, *Victorian Origins of the British Welfare State*, reprint of Yale University Press edition 1960 (Hamden, CT: Archon Books, 1969), pp. 38–9.

12   Legal Foundations of Tribunals in 19th-Century England

law fail to address the practical problem of pauperism, with outdoor relief being granted to the undeserving, and the conditions of indoor relief in the workhouses scandalising Victorian society, its machinery of operation, based on the maintenance of paupers by their own parishes, led to complex and highly technical litigation in the courts of Quarter Sessions and King's Bench between parishes as to which parish was responsible for a pauper. The evils and abuses of the administration of the poor law were considerable and were revealed in 1834 following a comprehensive investigation.[23]

The intense and rapid industrialisation of Britain gave rise to severe problems of public health, hitherto virtually unknown. It was the huge rise in population and its migration to the towns that caused these problems.[24] The rise in population resulted in cramped and unsuitable accommodation, the emergence of slums and an almost total lack of amenities. Water for drinking and drainage and sewerage was in short supply, and sanitary arrangements virtually non-existent. This in turn gave rise to epidemics of cholera and typhus and endemic diseases such as tuberculosis. The combination of overcrowding and poverty gave rise to further problems of immorality, vice and crime. These conditions, and the link between a dirty, cramped and polluted environment and disease, were exposed and established by Edwin Chadwick's analysis of 1842.[25]

The need to feed a growing population not only acted as a stimulus to the development of new methods of agriculture, but also focused public attention on those aspects of land tenure that prohibited its full exploitation. Tithes, the ancient though still extant payments of a tenth of the produce of land to support the incumbent of a parish,[26] were hugely unpopular and caused particular difficulties. They were in some instances in 1836 still paid in kind, in crop or livestock, to the rector of the parish or to the tithe owner where the tithes had come into lay hands,[27] an

---

[23] See generally Checkland (eds.), *Poor Law Report*, pp. 398–414.

[24] Fraser, *British Welfare State*, pp. 51–5; William C. Lubenow, *The Politics of Government Growth* (Newton Abbot: David and Charles, 1971), pp. 69–106.

[25] Poor Law Commissioners, *Report on an Inquiry into the Sanitary Condition of the Labouring Population of Great Britain* (London: HMSO, 1842).

[26] See generally Percy W. Millard, *Law Relating to Tithes* (London: Butterworths, 1938), pp. 1–4.

[27] A lay tithe owner was known as an impropriator.

Challenges to the Legal Process 13

exercise of expense and immense practical difficulty.[28] Furthermore the law that had grown up around this form of taxation was complex and the issue highly contentious. It caused significant dissent and acrimonious dispute between tithe owner and tithe payer, the former demanding and needing the tax, the latter reluctant to pay it. Not unusually it poisoned the relationship between the clergyman and his parishioners,[29] and bullying and intimidation on both sides were common. When the clergy took their tithes in kind, and for many it was a vital element in their income, it was observed in Parliament in 1836, 'they were looked upon as the fleecers rather than as the protectors of their flocks'.[30] Furthermore, such dissension, like most property disputes, all too frequently resulted in tedious and costly litigation in the regular courts of Chancery and Exchequer and the ecclesiastical courts. By the 1830s tithes were regarded as an expensive and anachronistic irritant, and, more importantly, a hindrance to the improvement in agriculture promoted as desirable in the later years of the eighteenth century, a reform which became increasingly urgent as the population grew and as the proportion thereof engaged in agriculture decreased.[31] The widespread demand for tithe reform was ultimately supported even by the church,[32] and the issue was regarded as one of national importance, not only in its own right as an issue concerning private property rights but also because of its context of the place and status of the established church.[33] They were, nevertheless, valuable private rights of property[34] whose financial importance is shown by the considerable efforts of tithe owners to claim that the new crops, such as

---

[28] Eric J. Evans, *The Contentious Tithe* (London: Routledge and Kegan Paul, 1976), pp. 21, 23.

[29] See for example *Parl. Deb.*, vol. XXXIII, ser. 3, col. 892, 12 May 1836 (HC).

[30] *Ibid.*, vol. XXXIV, ser. 3, col. 977, 27 June 1836 (HC).

[31] Adam Smith, *An Inquiry into the Nature and Causes of the Wealth of Nations*, 4th edition, 2 vols. (Edinburgh: Oliphant and Others, 1814), vol. II, pp. 92–3. For other reasons, see Eric J. Evans, *Tithes and the Tithe Commutation Act 1836*, Standing Conference for Local History, 3rd revised edition (London: Bedford Square Press, 1997), pp. 5–8; Evans, *Contentious Tithe*, p. 16.

[32] The church saw a choice between its status as the established church and state interference with its property; it chose the latter.

[33] The Marquess of Lansdowne regarded it as 'only inferior in importance to that great measure...the amendment of the Poor-laws', *Parl. Deb.*, vol. XXXIV, ser. 3, col. 1291, 7 July 1836 (HL).

[34] Though some Radicals such as William Cobbett did not regard tithes as private property at all, but rather as public property which could be 'disposed of as the

14   Legal Foundations of Tribunals in 19th-Century England

turnips and potatoes, were subject to tithe, and to reclaim the right to tithes which had not been claimed for many years[35] or which were subject to an unrealistic private agreement to commute, when the land in question was improved and brought into better production.[36] They were classified as incorporeal hereditaments, descended as real property at Common Law, and lay owners could deal with them as they could with any other species of private realty.

In the same period the evils of copyhold tenure were similarly recognised. Copyhold was an ancient and common form of tenure that was widely applicable when Victoria came to the throne. It was governed by a mixture of manorial custom and Common Law that was as complex and technical as the law applying to tithes.[37] Customs varied from manor to manor and in many instances were uncertain, since such titles were evidenced by the records of the lord's court and those were often recorded negligently, or were not recorded at all but were fixed by oral tradition. Copyhold land was frequently mixed with freehold land, and it was often difficult to distinguish them, particularly where they were held by the same owner and boundaries had been forgotten. Its nature rendered conveyancing difficult, uncertain and expensive, and frequently led to litigation. It was described as creating 'a number of endless disputes, heartburnings, and bickerings'.[38] Its characteristics limited the extent to which the land could be exploited for its mineral wealth or its timber, the minerals belonging to the lord, and the tenant being entitled only to so much timber as he needed for fuel and repairs. Accordingly the agreement of both lord and tenant was a prerequisite to such exploitation, so mines remained unworked and timber unplanted. A common saying was that 'the oak scorns to grow except on free land', and apparently in

---

Parliament shall please'. See William Cobbett, *Rural Rides*, Everyman's Library, 2 vols. (New York: J. M. Dent, 1912), vol. II, p. 106.

[35] The normal limitation periods did not apply to tithes.

[36] Some of the tithe settlements made during the inclosure movement of the late eighteenth and early nineteenth centuries had allowed tithe owners as much as one-quarter of the arable land itself in compensation for the loss of tithe: Evans, *Tithes*, p. 5 n. 18.

[37] See Sir William Holdsworth, *A History of English Law*, 17 vols. (London: Methuen & Co. Ltd, 1925), vol. VII, pp. 296–312.

[38] *Parl. Deb.*, vol. CXXI, ser. 3, col. 1111, 25 May 1852 (HL) *per* Duke of Cleveland.

Challenges to the Legal Process

Sussex one could tell copyhold land from freehold simply by comparing tree growth on either side of the boundary.[39]

The greatest evil of copyhold tenure, as perceived in the nineteenth century, was its prevention of any improvement of the land and its consequent damage to the public interest.[40] On descent and alienation, a fine was to be paid to the lord. Not only was this in itself a real practical grievance, by the 1830s this fine was generally two years' improvement of the land, and as such it was a clear disincentive to the tenant to improve his land, amounting to nothing less than a tax on the capital the tenant laid out in improvement. Tenants were unwilling to expend significant amounts of capital on improving their land in terms of cultivation, building and drainage. It was believed that copyhold land was very much worse cultivated than freehold land in England. Not only did this mean that neither the lord nor the tenant benefited, but it was damaging to the public interest.[41] Of the other fines and dues which a copyhold tenant was liable to pay to the lord the most pernicious was the heriot. This varied according to custom, but the principle was that when a copyholder died, the lord could seize the best chattel of which a tenant died possessed, and though it was a right that was rarely enforced by the nineteenth century, it was still viewed with some anxiety. Indeed, it seems that Sir Robert Peel had been anxious, as a tenant of a manor to which heriot attached, that his painting *Chapeau de Paille* might be seized, and to ensure it was not, he bought the manor itself.[42] Though in effect it resembled freehold, its intricate, anachronistic and inherently contradictory nature was no longer appropriate to contemporary conditions and it had become a nuisance. It was injurious to the lord, the tenant and the public interest and was described, in 1838, as 'a blot on the juridical system of the country'.[43] As with tithes, therefore, there were forceful reasons of public policy for its abolition. Copyhold

---

[39] 'Third Report of the Real Property Commissioners', *HCPP* (1831–2) (484) xxiii 321 at 335.

[40] See generally Anon., 'The Enfranchisement of Copyholds' (1853) 18 *Law Magazine* N.S. 117.

[41] 'Third Report of the Real Property Commissioners', *HCPP* (1831–2) (484) xxiii 321 at 335. See too Arthur Underhill, 'Changes in the Law of Real Property', in Council of Legal Education (eds.), *Century of Law Reform*, pp. 310–14.

[42] *Parl. Deb.*, vol. CXXI, ser. 3, cols. 1100–1, 25 May 1852 (HL).

[43] *Report, Copyholds Enfranchisement, 1837–8* at p. 191.

16   *Legal Foundations of Tribunals in 19th-Century England*

tenure, however, had some value to both lord and tenant. The lord was entitled to his receipts from fines on death and alienation, and could demand heriot even if it was not willingly granted. The copyholder enjoyed the benefits of a clear and registered title.

A similar mischief existed in relation to the inclosure of common land. Several million acres of common and waste land were under-productive or unproductive, with landowners prevented from introducing new crops or new methods of agriculture, and the government wanted it brought into cultivation to feed the growing population. Social reformers were acutely aware of the prevalence of crime arising from common rights, the low morals of people who subsisted on the common land and its generally brutalising effect. Commoners were regarded by many contemporaries as being, as a class, dishonest, not industrious and prone to committing petty crimes.[44] Sheep stealing was relatively easy on common land, and the killing of sheep in order to take the grazing was not unusual. The benefits of tithe, copyhold and inclosure reform were accordingly perceived as immense. Between them they would increase agricultural production, bring about improvements in standards of behaviour and morality, reduce litigation, simplify the law and, in the case of inclosure, bring immediate and widespread employment in fencing, ditching and draining. The remedy proposed by the legislature was to bring about, with varying degrees of compulsion and interference, the end of tithes, copyhold tenure and common land.

The main problem with the land rights was not so much the principle of their existence but the process of their removal. In principle, commuting tithes, enfranchising copyholds and inclosing common land had long been possible, but the machinery provided was cumbrous and expensive. In the case of inclosure in particular, the available machinery was a discouragement, being prohibitively expensive,[45] often unreasonably long and sometimes

---

[44] See evidence of Robert Graham, solicitor, in *Minutes, Commons' Inclosure, 1844* qq. 4212 ff.

[45] One inclosure of 1,500 acres of waste in Denbighshire in 1842 took two years and cost in all some £1,700. The cost was made up of commissioners' fees, the fees of their clerk, legal fees, making the maps and constructing roads and drains. It was met by selling a portion of the land: *Ibid.*, qq. 1922–44, and see too qq. 2700, 6258, 6277, 6278. See 'The New Tribunals for Railway and Other Private Bills' (1846–7) 5 *Law Review and Quarterly Journal of British and Foreign Jurisprudence* 53.

Challenges to the Legal Process

incompetently executed. Each inclosure required a private Act of Parliament. Apart from the parliamentary fees involved, the process required the employment of lawyers and agents, and travel and lodging in the capital for the parties and witnesses, expenses which increased as the process was prolonged, as well as all the costs of surveyors, solicitors and the manual labour to carry out the inclosure itself. With copyhold enfranchisement too, it was felt that the process was a real hindrance to those parties who wished to enfranchise.[46] It was acknowledged that the private bill procedure undermined the property rights of poorer parties. One land agent believed the private Acts were often 'carried without reference to the comforts, convenience, or presumed rights of small parties'.[47] Such parties were generally worried about cost, and this deterred them from pursuing any appeal to establish their rights.

The industrial growth of nineteenth-century Britain was fuelled by innovation on an unprecedented scale, most notably in the development of new methods of transport. In arguably one of the most formative developments of the modern age, the Victorians created a railway network unrivalled anywhere in the world. The scale of the enterprise and the speed of its growth were remarkable. Railway building reached its peak in 1846, with a record number of railway bills, and by 1854 there were 232 incorporated railway companies, 12,688 projected miles of railway, ninety-five million passengers carried in a year, 80,000 workers employed in the enterprise and a total authorised capital of £356 million.[48]

The scale and the speed of railway development brought with it considerable problems of network organisation, competition and public safety which had to be addressed. Ralph Littler QC described the issue of railways as 'almost the greatest domestic question of the country. Next to religion and education', he said, 'I regard the question of the management of railways as the most important internal question of the country.'[49] Many problems

---

[46] *Report, Copyholds Enfranchisement, 1837–8.*
[47] *Minutes, Commons' Inclosure, 1844* qq. 3388, 3390 *per* Thomas Woolley, land agent and Assistant Tithe Commissioner.
[48] *Parl. Deb.*, vol. CXXXII, ser. 3, col. 585, 6 April 1854 (HC) *per* Edward Cardwell.
[49] *Minutes, Railways (Rates and Fares), 1882* q. 3672.

18   *Legal Foundations of Tribunals in 19th-Century England*

were unexpected, largely as a result of a failure to appreciate the true nature of railway communication. In the earliest days, Parliament regarded railways as comparable to canals, and sought to prevent the railway companies from obtaining exclusive control over the carriage of passengers and goods over their lines, for that tended to monopoly. It was thought that the companies would merely collect the tolls, and allow others to compete between themselves for business on the lines. But this ideological insistence on free competition over individual lines and the prohibition of monopoly was soon recognised to be impossible in terms of public safety.[50] Furthermore, the uncontrolled railway companies were, under the extensive powers granted in their parent Acts, interrupting roads and taking private land for the temporary storage of equipment or works, with slight consideration for the interests and convenience of the public or the landowners. There was also little effective control over the building of bridges and other public works, for it was largely in the hands of the justices of the peace or the superior courts, who were not qualified or appropriate bodies to judge matters such as the dimension and inclination of new or altered bridges. There was evidence too that some railway companies were not fulfilling the duties placed on them by their Acts, and there was some uncertainty as to how these obligations were to be enforced.[51] The only central control was, as with inclosures, the private bill committee system, where each individual railway bill was scrutinised, but the machinery did not ensure the protection of the public. It was too individualistic, lacking in specialist expertise, dominated by the local interests of landowners or the capitalist interest of the railway companies,[52] and lacking any representation of the interests of the public.[53] It was enormously expensive, again because of the need to summon

---

[50] For the early history of railway legislation see 'Third Report from the Select Committee on Railway Communication', *HCPP* (1840) (299) xiii 167.

[51] See Henry Parris, *Government and the Railways in Nineteenth Century Britain* (London: Routledge and Kegan Paul, 1965), Chapter 1.

[52] 'Minutes of Evidence before the Select Committee of the House of Lords (on Railways)', *HCPP* (1846) (489) xiii 217 qq. 1419–20 *per* Captain J. M. Laws, railway director and manager.

[53] See 'Fifth Report from the Select Committee on Railways', *HCPP* (1844) (318) xi 17 at pp. 21–6.

Challenges to the Legal Process

witnesses and lodge them in London often for many weeks[54] and the employment of counsel.[55]

The principal problem with railway companies in 1854 was the common lack of co-operation between railway companies to ensure that facilities for continuous travel were provided for the public. It seems that timetables were deliberately arranged so as to deny through facilities and small railway lines connecting main lines were not thought worth the expense of construction. A passenger would arrive at one place by means of one company's railway and find he could continue his journey only on that of another, if at all, after a delay of some hours. So the general public suffered through deliberate non-co-operation by the various railway companies. Such disputes between railways had been going on for years, causing real inconvenience to users of the railways. The lack of provision of proper facilities for forwarding traffic was identified as 'one of the principal evils of railway management'.[56] Furthermore, the railway companies were not treating all traders and passengers fairly, affording facilities to some and not to others through unequal charges. Some railway companies were giving preferential rates to certain firms of carriers, and thereby driving others out of business and as Wills J observed in 1891, 'nothing has been alleged against railway companies which has been more bitterly resented by the trading community than the differential treatment of two different districts by railway companies serving both localities'.[57] By the last quarter of the nineteenth century the main problem was the intensification of monopoly through company amalgamation and all the problems arising when the restraining influence of competition was absent. In 1872 a Joint Select Committee inquired into the issue,[58] but it had been a problem from the early 1850s with individual railway companies seeking to amalgamate, and

---

[54] 'Minutes of Evidence before the Select Committee of the House of Lords (on Railways)', *HCPP* (1846) (489) xiii 217 qq. 5–8, 70–81, *per* George Webster, parliamentary agent; q. 941 *per* Charles Saunders, secretary to the Great Western Railway Company.

[55] See generally 'Railway Tribunals' (1846) 3 *Law Review and Quarterly Journal of British and Foreign Jurisprudence* 415.

[56] *Report, Railway Amalgamation, 1872* p. 13.

[57] *Liverpool Corn Trade Association Ltd* v. *London and North Western Railway Company* [1891] 1 QB 120 at 129.

[58] *Report, Railway Amalgamation, 1872.*

20 Legal Foundations of Tribunals in 19th-Century England

those few and immensely powerful bodies creating a virtual monopoly, leading to high rates and inadequate services and facilities, and with no provision for the protection or interests of the public or of smaller companies. The public interest demanded some kind of central control over amalgamated railways to ensure the system provided the fair, safe and free transit of passengers and goods. The challenge was to find some method of control sufficiently robust to ensure the immensely powerful amalgamated companies served the public and not themselves.

The growth in Britain's wealth, the financial exigencies of the war with France at the beginning of the nineteenth century and the domestic demands of poor relief and improved public amenities attracted the attention of the taxing authorities. The novelty of the problems lay not in the principle but in the scale. The established taxes were the land tax and the assessed taxes on certain luxury goods, but both were limited in the extent to which they were suited or could be made to suit the increasing demand for public revenue. The land tax had long become unrealistic through being based on out-of-date valuations and was of little fiscal significance. The assessed taxes were numerous and rendered complex and relatively unproductive by the many exemptions they allowed. Customs and excise duties bore the burden of supplying the public revenue, but were inherently unpopular with the powerful free trade movement. Income tax had been in suspension since 1816 and so was not an available source of revenue, and its reintroduction was not necessarily straightforward. In 1837 the compulsory taxation of income was still a novelty, for not only could a proportion of the working population remember its introduction less than forty years before, a significant number had no experience of it at all. William Pitt had faced acute problems in introducing income tax in 1799, and any reintroduction after such a long period would almost amount to the institution of a new tax, with all the political and practical problems associated with it. Ideological objections to direct income taxation as inquisitorial, though weaker, were still widely held. Fiscal problems were, however, acute at the beginning of the Victorian age and action was necessary.

When Sir Robert Peel's Tories took over the reins of government in 1841, they were faced with an empty Treasury. The deficit was largely due to the debt resulting from the French Wars

Challenges to the Legal Process

earlier in the century which was still taking over half of the total gross central government expenditure. Navy and army costs were high, while central government expenditure on domestic issues was slight. A series of bad harvests and depressed wages had increased the demand for relief from the established indirect taxes, and the earlier remission of a number of taxes to promote Whig free trade had absorbed what surplus there was. In the years leading up to Peel's second ministry widespread repeals had resulted in the deficit of some £5 million which Peel's administration had to address. The problem facing the government was not only to secure new sources of public revenue, but equally to ensure its steady and consistent flow to central and local government to enable them to sustain the rapid and widespread reforms and to meet the increased expenditure of a developing bureaucratic state. That was a question of process rather than principle. In income tax a particular problem faced was that the machinery of assessment did not ensure that the great wealth of the industrial revolution, namely commercial income, was fully subject to the tax. The taxation of this income had been undermined by the reluctance of the commercial community to be assessed by local men who were often their competitors in trade for fear of commercial espionage or simply a desire for the preservation of secrecy in personal financial affairs.[59] Local taxation posed a different challenge. Any social reforms would almost certainly be financed by local rather than central taxation.[60] By the middle of the nineteenth century there was all too often a difference between the real value and the rateable value of property in many parishes, and the need for a new system of rating, to ensure the uniform and correct valuation of property rateable to parochial assessments, with uniformity both of rating within individual parishes and between parishes, was a pressing need. Furthermore, if the overseers returned an incorrect valuation, through incompetence, carelessness or self-interest, the only remedy was for the ratepayers to appeal to the Quarter Sessions, but that was an expensive and tedious process, and accordingly the evil was often left to

---

[59] *Parl. Deb.*, vol. LXII, ser. 3, col. 657, 18 April 1842 (HC). See too C. Stebbings, 'The Budget of 1798: Legislative Provision for Secrecy in Income Taxation' (1998) *British Tax Review* 651.

[60] For the history of rating, see generally Holdsworth, *History of English Law*, vol. X, pp. 168–70, 276–99; *Ibid.*, vol. XIV, pp. 214–20.

22 Legal Foundations of Tribunals in 19th-Century England

stand. Taxation, both central and local, was, therefore, a continuous preoccupation of central and local government, and one which, in the context of a significantly increased national wealth and expenditure, was of growing consequence. In some instances, such as rating, its machinery was beginning to be incapable of ensuring the efficient raising and collection of revenue. Another problem with taxation was a political one, namely the demand for the implementation of a free trade policy and the need to fund it from other sources of revenue.

Such were the major domestic challenges that faced British society at the beginning of the reign of Queen Victoria.[61] Since their magnitude, in terms of both severity and breadth, were such that the state had to intervene to an unprecedented extent, they also constituted a major challenge to government and to current ideologies. The degree of initiative, authority and control necessary to implement the reforms uniformly and effectively could come only from central government. Past experience, particularly in the field of poor relief, had shown that a strong and expert central agency was necessary to implement the reforms necessary to address challenges of such magnitude, otherwise they would be ignored or undermined and accordingly patchy in their implementation. A central agency would also distance the reforms from local vested interests and would, as indeed happened, build up an expertise and good practice that it could then, in theory, disseminate. It was believed that a strong and centralised body would act as a deterrent to wrongdoing by those subject to the legislation. The government met these domestic challenges by reforming legislation in the wake of intensive investigation. Proposed legislation arose from the considerable and detailed work of various Select Committees and Royal Commissions, followed by the formulation of legislative proposals into bills which were subject to close examination and extensive debate in Parliament, the newspapers and in the various specialist and generalist journals which abounded in Victorian England. The outcome was a programme of centralising legislative reform of almost unparalleled importance, spanning the whole of the nineteenth century and creating the English administrative state.

---

[61] They were the principal, but not the sole, evils of an industrialised society. For other problems faced in early Victorian England, see Roberts, *Victorian Origins*, pp. 85–7.

Challenges to the Legal Process

First of all, the substance of the reforms had to be enacted. The abuse of children in the emerging factory system was addressed by a legislative programme beginning as early as 1802 and culminating in 1844[62] which imposed limits on the working hours of children in factories, introduced a minimum age for employment and provided the opportunity for education. In relation to the relief of the poor, the substance of the reform was the abolition of outdoor relief in money or goods and its replacement by indoor relief in workhouses and the introduction by the Poor Law Amendment Act 1834[63] of the principle of 'less eligibility'.[64] The sick, elderly and the very young would be cared for in the workhouses. As to the able-bodied poor, who had always constituted the principal problem, the level of poor relief was deliberately set at a level lower than that of a working man in order to ensure that the poor who were able to work would not choose poor relief in preference to labour. Thus only the genuinely destitute would accept poor relief. The workhouse, which was the only means of relief, was to act as a deterrent. The solution to the public health crisis was to ensure that working-class housing was better built and that there was adequate sewerage provision. To that end, and following Edwin Chadwick's inquiry, which reported in 1842,[65] a number of bills were put to Parliament culminating in the Public Health Act 1848.[66] The Act provided for the building and maintaining of sewers and drains, the provision of fresh water, the cleaning and paving of streets, the registration of slaughterhouses, the restriction on the use of cellars as dwellings and regulations as to burial grounds. Such improvements were to be financed by the raising of a local rate.[67]

In the sphere of land rights the decade from 1835 to 1845 was occupied with the formulation of a legislative solution to the problems of tithes, copyholds and inclosure. The challenge of the reforms was to arrive at a machinery to ensure full and fair compensation for the loss of any property rights. The first to be

---

[62] 42 Geo. III c. 73 (1802); 59 Geo. III c. 66 (1819); 6 Geo. IV c. 63 (1825); 1 & 2 Will. IV c. 39 (1831); 3 & 4 Will. IV c. 103 (1833); 7 & 8 Vict. c. 15 (1844).

[63] 4 & 5 Will. IV c. 76.

[64] See generally Fraser, *British Welfare State*, pp. 28–50.

[65] See Sir C. T. Carr, *Concerning English Administrative Law* (London: Oxford University Press, 1941), pp. 1–7.

[66] 11 & 12 Vict. c. 63.   [67] *Ibid.*, s. 86.

24   Legal Foundations of Tribunals in 19th-Century England

addressed was the tithe problem, and after considerable debate and various proposals, the legislature fixed on a programme of compulsory commutation. The Tithe Commutation Act 1836, 'an English Bill of deep and real importance',[68] provided for the abolition of the right to the traditional tenth of the gross produce, and its conversion to an annual rent charge regulated by the price of corn and calculated on the basis of seven years' average of titheable produce.[69] Despite a widespread demand for the enfranchisement of all copyholds, namely their conversion to one simple freehold tenure – in effect the complete abolition of the tenure – the legislature accepted the argument that enfranchisement had been hindered only by the want of a process by which the parties could arrive at a fair adjustment of their rights and, feeling that any more radical reform was impracticable, did no more than provide an accessible procedure to be used for those parties who so desired it.[70] The legislation provided machinery for the voluntary commutation of manorial rights in copyhold land, or the voluntary enfranchisement of those lands. The reason that enfranchisement was not made compulsory in 1841 – even though it was well understood that voluntary enfranchisement based on agreement would not suffice to abolish copyhold tenure in its entirety, an object which it was felt should be 'a national object'[71] – was that the customs were so numerous and varied that unlike tithe commutation no general rule could be formulated and applied and the cost of individual enfranchisement was considered prohibitive.[72] Inclosure followed the same model, and the legislation provided a purely procedural remedy, by making available a simpler and cheaper process whereby inclosure might be achieved by those parties who wished it.[73]

Though carried on by companies incorporated under private Acts of Parliament, with the financial burden of both obtaining the Acts and constructing and running the railway borne by

---

[68] John Croker (1836) 57 *Quarterly Review* 242–3.

[69] 6 & 7 Will. IV c. 71; see *Parl. Deb.*, vol. XXXIII, ser. 3, cols. 818 ff., 10 May 1836 (HC); *Ibid.*, cols. 882 ff., 12 May 1836.

[70] 4 & 5 Vict. c. 35. See too the amending Acts 6 & 7 Vict. c. 23 (1843) and 7 & 8 Vict. c. 55 (1844). It finally became compulsory in 1852 by 15 & 16 Vict. c. 51.

[71] *Report, Copyholds Enfranchisement, 1837–8* at p. 192.

[72] 'Third Report of the Real Property Commissioners', *HCPP* (1831–2) (484) xxiii 321 at p. 326.

[73] Inclosure Act 1845, 8 & 9 Vict. c. 118.

Challenges to the Legal Process

private individuals, the scale of railway enterprise and its parliamentary imprimatur gave it a semi-public character which curtailed the companies' freedom of action and made them susceptible to central control. The powers of railway companies were derived entirely from their founding Acts, and the view was that if they abused those powers, and used them oppressively or unfairly, then it was in the public interest that it should be investigated and remedied. The difficulties of competition and public safety were addressed through periodic regulation by public Act of Parliament in the wake of one of the most intensive and long-running periods of investigation by Select Committee and Royal Commission in the nineteenth century. Edward Cardwell's[74] Railway and Canal Traffic Act 1854 imposed two principal duties on the railway companies: that they should afford all reasonable facilities for the receiving and forwarding of traffic between one company's system and another, and should not give any undue preference to any particular person or commodity.[75] When the problem of amalgamation became acute in 1872 a Joint Select Committee was duly set up, and its recommendations formed the foundation of the Railway and Canal Traffic Act 1873.[76] However, the Committee felt the best it could do would be to recommend the provision of a more efficient machinery for the implementation of the 1854 Act, which it approved in its fundamental principles of railway regulation. The Committee's view was that if the Act had been properly implemented, it would have addressed the problems of railway regulation.[77]

Unlike the novel problems in social welfare, land tenure and railway communications, those in the fiscal field were rather an intensifying of difficulties that had long existed. The need for increased local and national revenue was addressed, as it always

---

[74] President of the Board of Trade.

[75] 17 & 18 Vict. c. 31 s. 2. See too Railway and Canal Traffic Regulation Bill 1854, *HCPP* (1854) (62) vi 1, cll. 5, 6. In practice the Act was of very limited success. Railway companies often acted in their own interests to prevent the shortest and most convenient route being available to the public, and the problem of charging unequal tolls continued.

[76] 36 & 37 Vict. c. 48.

[77] See generally the speech of Chichester Fortescue, President of the Board of Trade and chairman of the 1872 Joint Select Committee on Railways Amalgamation in *Parl. Deb.*, vol. CCXIV, ser. 3, cols. 229–40, 10 February 1873 (HC).

26 Legal Foundations of Tribunals in 19th-Century England

had been, by legislative demand. No new taxes were introduced, and the machinery for their collection remained broadly the same. Peel was convinced the solution to the 'great public evil' of the growing deficit lay in the reintroduction of income tax, and so he revived Pitt's income tax of 1799[78] as extensively modified in both principle and process by Henry Addington in 1803.[79] The reintroduction of the tax also allowed him the political space to reform the customs and excise, remove a number of those imposts, and promote his principles of free trade. Within income tax itself he addressed the problem of the failure fully to tax commercial income by introducing a new method of assessment. Furthermore, the assessed taxes continued to be levied, and the redemption of the land tax begun in 1798 continued apace. As to local rates, a new uniform mode of rating for the relief of the poor was introduced in 1836, when the basis of rating was fixed and defined to be on the net annual value of the hereditament rated, defined as the rent at which the same might reasonably be let from year to year, less taxation and the costs of maintenance,[80] and in 1862 legislation was passed with the same objective through the checking and revision of valuation lists.[81] This was regarded by contemporaries as a centralising measure.[82] In the second reading of the bill, the point was made that it took away the authority of the parish to arrive at their own assessments, and that the inhabitants were the best judges of what was a fair assessment.[83] It was argued in committee that 'it was an attempt by the Central Board in London to take into their own hands the management of all the local rates in England',[84] and was perceived in some quarters as a scheme which would drive the whole kingdom 'into an official valuation', at considerable cost.[85]

The reforms necessary to meet the social and economic challenges of the industrial revolution required not only the conception of the objectives, but also of the machinery to implement

---

[78] 39 Geo. III c. 13.   [79] 43 Geo. III c. 122.

[80] Parochial Assessments Act 1836, 6 & 7 Will. IV c. 96 s. 1.

[81] Union Assessment Committee Act 1862, 25 & 26 Vict. c. 103.

[82] *Parl. Deb.*, vol. CLXVII, ser. 3, col. 1334, 3 July 1862 (HC) *per* George Bentinck.

[83] *Ibid.*, vol. CLXV, ser. 3, col. 416, 17 February 1862 (HC); *Ibid.*, vol. CLXVII, ser. 3, col. 1330, 3 July 1862 (HC) *per* Joseph Henley.

[84] *Ibid.*, vol. CLXVII, ser. 3, col. 1330, 3 July 1862 (HC) *per* Frederick Knight.

[85] *Ibid.*, col. 1331 *per* Joseph Henley.

Challenges to the Legal Process

them. Implementation and enforcement were as important as substance if the evils were to be addressed by the new legislation. Indeed, it was arguably more important since it had to embody a strong centralised authority and control. Furthermore, the Victorians were possibly more concerned with the process than the principle and the machinery of implementation was of considerable importance to them. This was nothing new: when income tax was introduced in 1799, the principal objection was as to the inquisitorial nature of the tax administration machinery, rather than to the obligation itself.

Established local government, consisting of over 15,000 parishes, some 5,000 justices of the peace and 200 municipal authorities, was inadequate to meet the administrative challenge even though those were the traditional instruments by which such social and public legislation as existed was implemented. They were responsible for the administration of prisons and asylums, for the maintenance of roads and bridges, for policing and for the relief of the poor.[86] Although the justices of the peace were the expression of both government and law to the great majority of ordinary people, they were deficient in number, skill, vision and commitment to reform, and early attempts to place the enforcement of reforming legislation in their hands failed. They were too independent for any uniformity of implementation to be possible.[87] Municipal corporations suffered from corruption and apathy.[88] Even the makeshift special bodies set up for specific purposes such as improved public amenities and roads,[89] though often very successful, were symptomatic of this inadequacy rather than an effective policy for the future. Local government was incapable and distrusted.[90] It was recognised that the ultimate controlling and compelling authority had to be in London for the reforms to be carried out effectively, but central government was as unpromising as local government. In the 1830s only the Treasury, army,

---

[86] Lubenow, *Government Growth*, p. 16.

[87] See M. W. Thomas, 'The Origins of Administrative Centralisation' (1950) 3 *Current Legal Problems* 214 at 216–18, for the unsuccessful attempt at enforcement of the factory legislation by the justices of the peace.

[88] See Roberts, *Victorian Origins*, pp. 7–11.

[89] See Stanley and Beatrice Webb, *Statutory Authorities for Special Purposes*, English Local Government, vol. IV (London: Longmans. Green & Co., 1922), Chapter 4.

[90] Lubenow, *Government Growth*, p. 17.

28 *Legal Foundations of Tribunals in 19th-Century England*

navy and the courts of law were robust and efficient expressions of central government, a concentration that reflected the traditional limited conception of the role of the state. The rest was unsophisticated, weak and fragmented[91] and unable to provide the machinery required for the effective implementation of a policy that was necessarily one of centralisation and state interference.

In the face of a 'local, unco-ordinated and centrifugal'[92] administration, and despite an almost universal ideological abhorrence of state intervention, the Victorians created a centralised administrative infrastructure to administer their new legislative regimes.[93] They adopted the policy of creating, by statute, a number of ad hoc public and semi-public bodies, each explicitly designed to implement a specific statutory code.[94] The implementing organs were created by the reforming legislation itself. The new bodies were agencies of central government, or bodies subsidiary to them or created by them. They embodied the growth of the English administrative state and were of pragmatic rather than ideological provenance. Their political status varied considerably in their relationship with central government. Sometimes they constituted the department itself, sometimes a semi-independent organ attached to it, sometimes an entirely independent body, and were variously called boards, commissions, inspectorates or departments.[95] Whereas today one factor in the creation of tribunals is to resolve disputes in certain areas of activity where the government is content to allow decisions to be made independently of the department in question, the considerations of nineteenth-century legislators were different in nature and emphasis, notably as to the prominence of dispute-resolution, and the degree of independence of individual tribunals differed considerably. Boards were the traditional model and were particularly popular in the first half of the nineteenth century,[96]

---

[91] See Roberts, *Victorian Origins*, pp. 12–13; P. P. Craig, *Administrative Law*, 5th edition (London: Sweet and Maxwell, 2003), pp. 47–52.
[92] Thomas, 'Administrative Centralisation', 215.   [93] *Ibid.*, 214.
[94] Lubenow, *Government Growth*, p. 15.
[95] See Arthurs, *Without the Law*, pp. 103–31.
[96] See generally Craig, *Administrative Law*, pp. 52–6; F. M. G. Willson, 'Ministries and Boards: Some Aspects of Administrative Development since 1832' (1955) 33 *Public Administration* 43; Henry Parris, *Constitutional Bureaucracy* (London: George Allen and Unwin Ltd, 1969), pp. 82–93; Roberts, *Victorian Origins*.

Challenges to the Legal Process

and they generally enjoyed a large degree of independence from Parliament and ministers. They fell out of favour in the later years of the century largely because of this lack of responsibility, and the later history of administrative machinery is dominated by the development of ministerial responsibility.[97] There was an interchange of form, responsibility and control between boards, commissions and ministries throughout the nineteenth century.

The personnel of these organs were appointed and generally remunerated by central government and were accordingly civil servants. Their role was one essentially of policy-making, supervision and organisation while the work on the ground in the locality, the practical implementation of the legislative regime, was undertaken by paid functionaries appointed by them. It was understood that they would best be able to collect the local information and judge its nature and the weight to be accorded to it. In this way there was central supervision and local administration, a compromise between the government's desire for control and uniformity, and a traditional local demand for self-government. It was a compromise recognising that central executive power was most effective when it was applied locally, and appreciating its political sagacity. This duality characterised the development of the administrative state. The overall effectiveness of these bodies in implementing the new legislation has been widely examined by scholars.[98]

A permanent and overtly centralising inspectorate within the Home Office was created in 1833 to enforce the new factory regulations.[99] The four inspectors were empowered to enter mills and factories where children were employed, take evidence on oath,[100] give directions as to registers of daily work, issue regulations, and had the power of magistrates in relation to breaches of the law, including the right to fine or imprison those in breach.[101] They were to report periodically to the Secretary of

---

[97] Willson, 'Ministries and Boards', 47–8. See Roberts, *Victorian Origins*, pp. 128–9 for criticisms of the board system; Sir Norman Chester, *The English Administrative System 1780–1870* (Oxford: Clarendon Press, 1981), pp. 275–81; Parris, *Constitutional Bureaucracy*, pp. 80–105; Carr, *Administrative Law*, pp. 11–15.

[98] Notably by Professors Roberts and Lubenow: Roberts, *Victorian Origins*; Lubenow, *Government Growth*.

[99] Factories Act 1833, 3 & 4 Will. IV c. 103 s. 17.   [100] *Ibid.*

[101] *Ibid.*, ss. 32, 33, 38.

30 *Legal Foundations of Tribunals in 19th-Century England*

State.[102] These powers were shortly afterwards viewed as inappropriate and so curtailed.[103] The machinery whereby the new poor law was implemented was as important as the substance of the reform itself and considerably more radical. It recognised that for the new poor law to succeed it had to have a uniformity of administration and the control of a strong central body. It accordingly embodied the principle of centralised administration and while it did not eschew the justices of the peace altogether, it reduced their role considerably and in 1834 introduced a central and independent professional agency, the Poor Law Commissioners, with extensive powers to supervise the local administration of the law in the form of the framing of regulations, inspection, audit and administrative control.[104] Local administration was in the hands of elected Boards of Guardians, who administered poor relief in their allocated group, or union, of parishes. It comprised, therefore, local administration with central control. In administrative terms a central commission not acting under direct ministerial or parliamentary control and with wide powers was a radical development. While the Poor Law Commissioners were of considerable significance in the development of centralised administration, the extent of their originality and revolutionary nature has been challenged.[105]

So great was the problem of public health that it was clear to reformers such as Edwin Chadwick that central government intervention in some form was necessary, similar to that introduced to address the problems of poverty in 1834. The public health legislation followed a similar pattern and established central supervision with local administration.[106] A General Board of Health was formed on the model of the Poor Law Commissioners to superintend the execution of the Act.[107] It was established in order to improve the drainage, sewerage and water supply of the country's towns and cities. The General Board's prime function was regulatory and supervisory, with management and control in

---

[102] *Ibid.*, s. 45.   [103] Thomas, 'Administrative Centralisation', 227–8.

[104] 4 & 5 Will. IV c. 76. See generally Checkland (eds.), *Poor Law Report*, pp. 38–9; Sidney and Beatrice Webb, *English Poor Law Policy* (London: Longmans, Green and Co., 1910); Roberts, *Victorian Origins*, pp. 109–11. The commissioners were converted into a board under the presidency of a minister of the Crown in 1847 by 10 & 11 Vict. c. 109.

[105] Lubenow, *Government Growth*, pp. 180–1. See generally *Ibid.*, pp. 30–68.

[106] *Ibid.*, pp. 9–106.   [107] Public Health Act 1848, 11 & 12 Vict. c. 63 s. 4.

Challenges to the Legal Process

the hands of local boards. It could appoint officers and inspectors[108] and had power to direct a preliminary local inquiry as to water supply, drainage, sewerage, cleansing and paving and other environmental matters, if a sufficient proportion of local ratepayers demanded it.[109]

The debate as to the nature of the bodies best suited to implement the land rights legislation was extensive, though the tithe and copyhold legislation was novel in that the principle of systematic restructuring in those areas was new, and that made the acceptance of any proposed machinery less problematic. There was nevertheless a strong predisposition to putting the restructuring of land rights into the hands of the justices of the peace at Quarter Sessions, who, with their local knowledge, experience of land management and legal expertise, were the obvious body to administer the law. They were, however, rejected on the grounds of excessive formality, expense, lack of technical knowledge of the processes and the burden of other work.[110] They would also be unable to provide the sophisticated bureaucratic organisation necessary to complex restructuring. In the case of copyhold enfranchisement, for example, a staff would be needed to examine and ascertain all the customs of the manors, an expensive and skilled task.

When copyhold reform was first discussed by the Commissioners of Real Property in 1832, the bishops were asked which organ they felt would be best suited to carry out any enfranchisement. Most were against reference to the Court of Chancery on the grounds of expense and formality, and favoured instead a body of commissioners. The form they preferred, however, was one resembling arbitration, where the commissioners were local bodies, appointed by the parties, and confirming arrangements that the parties arrived at between themselves, rather than having the power to impose an enfranchisement against the wishes of the parties.[111] In the case of inclosure, however, the long tradition of locally and personally appointed commissioners in the nature of arbitrators was resistant to change. Accordingly the only

---

[108] *Ibid.*, ss. 5–7.   [109] *Ibid.*, s. 8.

[110] See the debate on Lord Althorp's proposal for the commutation of tithes, *Parl. Deb.*, vol. XVII, series 3, cols. 277–8, 18 April 1833 (HC).

[111] 'Third Report of the Commissioners of Real Property', *HCPP* (1831–2) (484) xxiii 321 at pp. 409–18.

32 Legal Foundations of Tribunals in 19th-Century England

common ground in the debate as to the machinery for inclosure was the recognition that the existing private bill machinery was unacceptable in delay and expense. It was ultimately agreed to place the commutation of tithes, the enfranchisement of copyhold tenure and the inclosure of common land into the hands of three new central temporary boards of commissioners: the Tithe Commissioners by the Tithe Commutation Act 1836, the Copyhold Commissioners by the Copyhold Act 1841[112] and the Inclosure Commissioners by the Inclosure Act 1845. It was felt that only a central public body would have the necessary authority and public confidence to implement the reforms, address the many points of detail and inquiry involved, and ensure the restructuring were properly conducted.[113] The admixture of central control and local administration was present in that the commissioners had the power to send their officers to the locality to carry out the restructuring. This was felt to constitute the cheapest, most accessible and most efficient method of implementing the legislation. Such bodies would address the specific needs of administration, keep careful and independent watch over the interests of smaller parties, and would soon build up an expertise which would of itself increase the efficiency of the implementation of the law. The statutory commutation of tithes was compulsory and centralised in both principle and process. The enfranchisement of copyhold land and the inclosure of common land were made neither mandatory nor exclusive, though where the processes were adopted they did import close control by central government.

In the field of railway regulation the choice of implementing organ was difficult and controversial. The railway interest was the greatest single commercial interest in the country throughout much of the nineteenth century and made the railways of outstanding economic, political and social significance. The powers of the railway companies affected most people in some way, either as users of the railway network or as investors. By 1881 the railway interest amounted in monetary terms to between £600

---

[112] Note that the Copyhold Commissioners were the Tithe Commissioners themselves, given the duty of the commutation and enfranchisement of copyholds, and when exercising this function they were to be known as the Copyhold Commissioners.

[113] *Minutes, Commons' Inclosure, 1844* qq. 4279–82.

Challenges to the Legal Process

million and £700 million of property.[114] The debate, both at the inception of the railways and when the issue of amalgamation was presented, was intense. The choice was between the regular courts, the Board of Trade and an independent commission. The novelty, complexity and sheer scale of railway enterprise, the magnitude of the financial interests involved, the considerable political influence of the railway companies and the prominence of any dispute-resolution function, were special features which greatly influenced the form which the implementing organ ultimately took and made the creation of acceptable machinery one of the most challenging issues in government in the nineteenth century.[115] They were also responsible for the time it took to resolve the question, for no less than six bodies were entrusted with the legislation between 1839 and 1888. In the 1840s a Parliament dominated by the railway interest was forced to accept that public safety and convenience demanded not only an insistence on the railway companies having a monopoly of conveying passengers on their lines, but also the placing of the railways under one controlling authority. Monopoly was acknowledged and approved, and was to be placed under proper supervision. The various evils which had been identified, and the context of powerful and wealthy organisations, called for firm action by Parliament. The solution proposed and adopted was the creation of a supervisory and controlling body to ensure the safety of the public and protect the interests of the users of the network, interests that were often opposed to those of the railway companies themselves. The inequality of the parties in railway matters was appreciated from the outset. An organ of the executive government was the preferred solution, annexed to the Board of Trade.[116] The Railway Department of the Board of Trade was

---

[114] *Minutes, Railways, 1881* q. 13,518 *per* James Grierson, general manager of the Great Western Railway Company, reading a paper previously prepared for the Board of Trade by the railway companies. It was said that there was nearly as much money involved in the railway interest as in the National Debt, with some £720 million invested in railways: see *Ibid.*, q. 15,305 *per* Charles Scotter, goods manager of the Manchester, Sheffield and Lincolnshire Railway Company.

[115] Geoffrey Alderman, *The Railway Interest* (Leicester: Leicester University Press, 1973), p. 15.

[116] 'Second Report from the Select Committee on Railways', *HCPP* (1839) (517) X 127; *Parl. Deb.*, vol. LIV, ser. 3, col. 894, 2 June 1840 (HC); Regulation of Railways Act 1840, 3 & 4 Vict. c. 97. See generally Parris, *Government and the*

34   Legal Foundations of Tribunals in 19th-Century England

created in 1840, primarily to inspect railways before they opened and inquire into accidents. This was replaced in 1846 by a short-lived board of commissioners constituting a separate department of the government.[117] With no debate in Parliament it was abolished in 1851, and its powers transferred back to the Board of Trade from whence it had come only five years before.[118] Its failure was due to its unpopularity with the railway companies and their preference for dealing with the Board of Trade.[119] Nevertheless, in the middle years of the 1840s, at the height of the railway boom, informed opinion urged the necessity of a department of the executive to supervise the railways. The implementation of the legislation was given, unsuccessfully, to the Court of Common Pleas in 1854 and, in 1873, to a specialised and independent statutory body known as the Railway and Canal Commissioners presided over by a High Court judge.[120] The substance of the law remained largely that of the 1854 Act. This was acknowledged as experimental, but there was a consensus that something had to be done to reassure the public that the railway companies would abide by the provisions of the regulating legislation.[121] It was not, however, regarded as revolutionary, and in many quarters did not merit a mention with respect to the machinery of implementation.[122] The commission was recast in 1888 and its jurisdiction increased.[123]

The earliest of these bodies, and potentially at least the model for them all and reflecting an early division of power between central control and local administration, were those created for the implementation of tax legislation. In taxation matters, efficient and expeditious machinery and procedure were, and always had been, all-important, for the consistency of revenue was as important as the yield. It was essential for the government to raise revenue and to enjoy a steady flow of revenue, and this depended on sound

---

Railways; Edward Cleveland-Stevens, *English Railways: Their Development and Their Relation to the State* (London: Routledge, 1915).

[117] Commissioners of Railways Act 1846, 9 & 10 Vict. c. 105.

[118] 14 & 15 Vict. c. 64.   [119] Parris, *Government and the Railways*, p. 112.

[120] Railway and Canal Traffic Act 1873, 36 & 37 Vict. c. 48.

[121] *Parl. Deb.*, vol. CCXIV, ser. 3, cols. 1042–53, 27 February 1873 (HC) *per* Chichester Fortescue.

[122] See for example the introduction to the Act in *The Practical Statutes* (London: Horace Cox, 1865–1900), pp. 57–8.

[123] Railway and Canal Traffic Act 1888, 51 & 52 Vict. c. 25.

Challenges to the Legal Process

administration. The Land Tax Act 1688 had required the implementing body to execute the Act speedily and effectively, 'so their Majesties service herein may not be delayed or hindered through any of their wilful neglect or default'.[124] No new bodies needed to be established in the Victorian period, for the machinery was already in existence: bodies of lay commissioners had been used to implement the direct taxes, notably aids and polls, since the seventeenth century, and were well-established institutions in English fiscal life.[125] Politically they operated under the authority of various boards within the Treasury. The commissioners appointed to implement the land tax and the assessed taxes, those involved with the redemption of the land tax and the appellate commissioners hearing land tax redemption appeals, the General Commissioners of Income Tax and the Special Commissioners of Income Tax, were familiar institutions. The earliest Land Tax Commissioners, on which the Assessed Taxes Commissioners and the General Commissioners were based, had been in existence since the seventeenth century. All these bodies administered the law, supervising the correct and full assessment to the tax and its collection, and resolving any disputes that arose in the course of that process. All save the Special Commissioners were independent bodies.

The rationale underlying the creation of these bodies for the administration of tax was articulated at the end of the eighteenth century when William Pitt introduced his new income tax and confined its administration into the hands of bodies of lay commissioners. The issues that were then of importance in taxation remained so in different spheres of activity and a different age. One of the reasons for choosing lay commissioners was that it was a familiar institution. Indeed, Pitt consciously used existing forms and processes to make his new and highly controversial income tax politically acceptable. The income tax of 1799 was the first tax to break with the fiscal tradition that taxes should be voluntary and was, as such, inquisitorial in nature and hugely unpopular.[126]

---

[124] 1 Will. & M. c. 20 s. 9 (1688). See too 4 Will. & M. c. 1 s. 10 (1692).

[125] See W. R. Ward, *The Administration of the Window and Assessed Taxes 1696–1798* (Canterbury: Phillimores, 1963), pp. 1–2.

[126] See William Phillips, 'The Real Objection to the Income Tax of 1799' (1967) *British Tax Review* 177; William Phillips, 'The Origin of Income Tax' (1967) *British Tax Review* 113 at 114–15; H. H. Monroe, *Intolerable Inquisition? Reflections on the Law of Tax*, Hamlyn Lectures 33rd series (London: Stevens & Sons, 1981); Stebbings, 'Secrecy in Income Taxation , 651.

36   *Legal Foundations of Tribunals in 19th-Century England*

The inquisitorial nature of the tax and the extreme sensitivity of public disclosure of private financial matters in the late eighteenth century called for machinery that was both efficient and sympathetic to popular concerns. Though a new body, they were unambiguously based on the Commissioners of the Land Tax. When Henry Addington recast the income tax in 1803, the General Commissioners were the primary local administrative body.

In the fiscal field, Sir Robert Peel's reintroduction of the income tax in 1842 after a suspension of some twenty-five years was an act of central government authority of equal power to those other more novel centralising reforms. He saw the political value of traditional forms and processes and looked to existing institutions for similar reasons. The existing machinery already embodied the principle of central control and local administration, but he added to it in the form of the allocation of extended powers to the Special Commissioners of Income Tax. This tribunal was a central body, an arm of the executive, which from 1842 had the power to assess the commercial wealth of the country to income tax. Their powers were extended to reassure the commercial community that their income could be assessed by a body quite independent from their competitors in trade, though not by one explicitly independent from the Inland Revenue.[127] The enlargement of their powers was a political and pragmatic initiative.

These various organs of the executive were not the only ones created in this dynamic period of British government. Of a similar political character[128] were the Ecclesiastical Commission created in 1836 to manage ecclesiastical property,[129] the Lunacy Commission of 1842 formed to supervise asylums,[130] the Charity Commission of 1853[131] and the Registrar of Births, Marriages and Deaths of 1836.[132] Like the Factory Inspectorate the Prison,[133] Mining[134] and Burial[135] Inspectors were created in the following twenty-five years as permanent bodies within the Home Office. Again the Colonial Land and Emigration Commission was created under the authority of the Colonial Office in 1839. In 1850 the

---

[127] *Parl. Deb.*, vol. LXII, ser. 3, col. 657, 18 April 1842 (HC).
[128] See Professor Roberts' classification: Roberts, *Victorian Origins*, pp. 93–5.
[129] Ecclesiastical Commissioners Act 1836, 6 & 7 Will. IV c. 77.
[130] 5 & 6 Vict. c. 84 (1842).   [131] 16 & 17 Vict. c. 137 (1853).
[132] 6 & 7 Will. IV c. 86 (1836).   [133] 5 & 6 Will. IV c. 38 (1835).
[134] 5 & 6 Vict. c. 99 (1842).   [135] 17 & 18 Vict. c. 87 (1854).

Challenges to the Legal Process

Marine Department was created with duties relating to merchant shipping, supervising the appointment and working conditions of masters, mates and seamen, and the condition of the ships. In 1854 a major Merchant Shipping Act was passed, another achievement of Edward Cardwell, which created a code for the regulation of the merchant marine.[136]

It was evident and foreseeable that a significant increase in such government interference in the private, professional and property affairs of individuals would give rise to disputes not only between individuals, but between the state and the subject.[137] Potentially these disputes varied considerably in nature and at the stage of occurrence. They could constitute a refusal to obey a statutory provision, objections to various administrative decisions made by the government agency itself or one of its subordinate officers at certain stages in the administrative process, or they could consist of a relatively formal appeal at the end of the process from a clear decision by the same tribunal, the same tribunal differently constituted, or a different tribunal altogether. They were all, however, disputes between the government, generally in the form of the commission itself, and a subject. The factory legislation clearly created a conflict between the state and parents who needed their children to work to contribute to a scanty family budget and again between the state and those mill and factory owners who resented any kind of limit or control on the way they conducted their enterprise. The disputes which would arise in the context of the public health legislation were primarily with respect to levels of compensation, damages and rates. The restructuring of land rights would inevitably give rise to disputes as to correct boundaries, disputes that had to be resolved in order that the legislation be implemented. Legislating for railway running powers and powers to use facilities was bound to give rise to differences between railway companies and those differences had to be resolved. Disputes in relation to tax were then, as now, primarily disputes as to the decision of the tax authorities to bring property into charge or to allow or deny various allowances and deductions. The disputes which are significant in the development of the

---

[136] 17 & 18 Vict. c. 104 (1854).
[137] See Inns of Court Conservative and Unionist Society, *Rule of Law* (London: Conservative Political Centre, 1955), p. 30.

38   Legal Foundations of Tribunals in 19th-Century England

modern adjudicatory administrative tribunal are those which were in the nature of an appeal by an individual aggrieved by a decision of an administrative officer where such dispute was determined by a separate body.

Dispute-resolution was an urgent necessity that had to be determined at the outset in order not only to ensure the smooth administration of the legislation, but also to reassure the public that any grievances they might have in a new and often controversial area of government activity would be clearly and unambiguously addressed in a publicly acceptable way. Fairness was a concern primarily insofar as it determined public confidence in the tribunal. Popular acceptance, if not approbation, was essential to the carrying out of government policy, and the protection of the individual through effective dispute-resolution provisions was central to popular acceptance. William Pitt had been aware some forty years earlier that a compulsory and inquisitorial tax imposed by central government would give rise to disputes between the individual and the taxing authorities, and that those disputes would have to be very carefully and sensitively provided for in order to make the tax acceptable to the public and to Parliament. When the new rating legislation was introduced in 1862, the bill was sent to every union in the country for their approval before it was debated in Parliament.[138] Provision for dispute-resolution posed a considerable challenge to the legislators in formulating their legislative schemes for reform, though not to the same extent as the challenge to the machinery of the political process to arrive at a method of implementation. Whereas the modern emphasis in tribunal creation is openness, fairness and impartiality,[139] the exigencies of the state in the nineteenth century required a method whereby disputes could be resolved quickly, cheaply, expertly and finally[140] since it was recognised that the opportunity of raising grievances and having them properly addressed was central to pacifying potentially hostile public opinion and achieving public support or, at least,

---

[138] *Parl. Deb.*, vol. CLXVIII, ser. 3, col. 729, 24 July 1862 (HL) *per* Duke of Newcastle.

[139] 'Report of the Committee on Administrative Tribunals and Enquiries', Cmnd 218 (1957), p. 5, paras. 23–5.

[140] *R.* v. *Bloomsbury Income Tax Commissioners* [1915] 3 KB 768 at 784 *per* Lord Reading CJ.

Challenges to the Legal Process

acquiescence. A means of dispute-resolution was essential to 'quieting the Minds' of potential objectors to the legislation.[141]

Provision had, therefore, to be made for dispute-resolution. The legislators and persons concerned in the various spheres of activity that came to be the subject of regulatory legislation considered different kinds of dispute-resolution, and their debates became increasingly reflective and penetrating as to the issues that were suitable for different kinds of dispute-resolution. The popular demand was for dispute-resolution that was neither too expensive nor too slow. It favoured 'quick justice, even if it is not of the highest'.[142] The primary objective of the state was the efficient implementation of the legislation, and in this context two dominant and special requirements of personnel and process were identified. The first was a composition ensuring specialist subject-specific expertise, with a supportive bureaucratic structure. The rules that had to be implemented were not as a whole those of the Common Law; they were novel rules that were often technical and promulgated in the context of a clear social policy.[143] Areas such as the restructuring of land rights were particularly technical in nature, and the implementation of the legislation, including the resolution of any disputes, would require a specialist knowledge of agricultural practice and land management to conduct a searching inquiry into the various claims. The safeguarding of the public safety and the efficient working of the railway system would require engineering skills and knowledge of railway management, while fiscal tribunals would need local knowledge of wages and conditions of business. Not only would the administration of the legislation require special technical knowledge, the disputes would in all likelihood be minor disputes of fact rather than principle or law, and might be very numerous. Many disputes in the railway sphere for example would be little more than

---

[141] The phrase was used in relation to the giving of powers of arbitration to the central organ established to regulate the railways and thereby 'quieting the Minds of Landed Proprietors': 'Minutes of Evidence before the Select Committee of the House of Lords (on Railways)', *HCPP* (1846) (489) xiii 217 q. 66 *per* George Webster, parliamentary agent.

[142] 'Appendix to the Report of the Departmental Committee on Income Tax, with Minutes of Evidence', *HCPP* (1905) (2576) xliv 245 at q. 1965 *per* Arthur Chamberlain JP, putting forward the views of the Birmingham Chamber of Commerce on income tax tribunals.

[143] Arthurs, 'Rethinking Administrative Law', 37.

40 *Legal Foundations of Tribunals in 19th-Century England*

disagreements as to the value of sometimes small parcels of land all over the country. Some questions of law would need to be resolved and, as with all disputes, legal skills would be desirable to ensure the proper and fair conduct of the resolution, though technical and legal skills were rarely found in the same person. The second requirement was for just and expeditious procedures. Disputes would need to be resolved promptly so as not to hinder the implementation of government policy, a matter of especial importance in the fiscal sphere, as the constant and reliable return of taxation revenue was as important, if not more important, than the actual amount raised.[144] In order to achieve the prompt settlement of disputes, the procedures had to be simple and relatively informal so as to ensure that the parties did not require legal representation. Furthermore, since the interference of central government in any field of activity which had hitherto been private invariably raised opposition, the dispute-resolution process had to be easily accessible and attractive to potential users, particularly where a new government policy was voluntary rather than compulsory. That meant it had to be inexpensive and this could be achieved by ensuring the process eschewed professional legal representation and by keeping the proceedings local. This brought the further advantage of geographical accessibility at a time when swift and inexpensive communication, though much improved by the construction of the railway network, was not yet available to all. The process had to be fair and impartial, with sufficient safeguards to ensure the confidence and support of the public, and, most importantly, had to be seen to be independent of the executive. Public confidence was of the utmost importance if the new policies were to gain sufficient acceptance, particularly when they interfered with private property rights. All these requirements were set in the context of a determination on the part of the legislators to keep litigation to an absolute minimum.[145]

[144] See for example the Land Tax Act 1688, where the bodies responsible for the raising and collecting of the land tax were to undertake their task quickly and effectively, 'so their Majesties service herein may not be delayed or hindered through any of their wilful neglect or default': 1 Will. & M. c. 20 s. 9.

[145] There was a general view that litigation should be reduced over the whole country. The ending of tithe litigation was an express aim of the Tithe Commission. Hence also the limitation of the right of appeal to the regular courts from such bodies: see below, Chapter 6.

Challenges to the Legal Process 41

A number of possibilities as to the allocation of dispute-resolution powers were open to the legislators of the early nineteenth century.[146] The most obvious was to call upon the judiciary to take these disputes as part of its constitutional role of adjudicating on and implementing the law and to hear and determine them in the regular courts. This approach had the considerable advantages of familiarity and authority. The regular courts of law were an established and ancient feature of British life and were familiar to everyone, even though the majority of the population had no personal experience of them.[147] The superior courts were organs of high status which carried respect and considerable authority, and whose independence from the executive was enshrined in the constitution. The judges were undoubtedly learned and independent, and their procedures were well established and tested over generations. And while the judges were skilled in weighing and handling evidence and applying the law, and might not be perceived as the best judges of fact, that was addressed by the tradition of the Common Law to leave matters of fact to be decided by a jury under the guidance of the judge. Indeed, it was accepted that laymen reflecting local values and knowledge were the best judges of matters of fact, and that the new legislation would be likely to give rise principally to disputes of that nature.

Nevertheless there were difficulties in entrusting the superior courts with the new legislation.[148] When the regulatory legislation began to emerge in the 1830s, the regular courts as a whole were still too confused. There were a large number of different courts, some archaic and anachronistic, many with overlapping or uncertain jurisdictions. The skills of the judges of the superior courts were problematic. They would not possess the technical knowledge deemed necessary to resolve disputes in the administration of specialist legislation, and indeed this had long been a concern in the commercial sphere. This was not, however, an insuperable problem since there was some tradition of specialist assessors in English law assisting judges in certain fields. The

---

[146] Professor Harry Arthurs establishes in a scholarly and convincing study the existence and importance of legal pluralism: Arthurs, *Without the Law*.

[147] Primarily because of the expense of litigation in the regular courts, but also because their jurisdictions still concerned primarily land.

[148] See generally Brian Abel-Smith and Robert Stevens, *Lawyers and the Courts* (London: Heinemann, 1967), pp. 459–68.

42   Legal Foundations of Tribunals in 19th-Century England

judges were not accustomed to deciding questions of fact, since the practice of the Common Law was to leave such issues to juries, but the juries themselves were not free from criticism.[149] They were expensive and time-consuming, and while they were generally adept at deciding simple issues of fact, they were not equipped to deal with technical issues of, for example, the settlement of disputed boundaries so necessary in inclosure, tithe and copyhold cases. There was also a growing perception that in the context of growing litigiousness, the superior courts of law should be reserved for the more important cases. It was also recognised that while the judges were accustomed to the analysis of legal problems, they were neither politicians nor administrators and so could not satisfactorily address the practical implementation of the legislation nor the underlying policy issues.[150] Furthermore, the regular courts were increasingly dominated by the rigorous doctrine of judicial precedent. Depending on their place in the judicial hierarchy, the courts had to decide according to precedents set by the superior courts, whatever the personal view of the judge in the case itself. It restricted the flexibility of the judges to respond to changing conditions. The new legislation would give rise to an unprecedented number of small disputes, and if they were deemed suitable to be given to the superior courts, there would be a need for more judges and accommodation, which would be a considerable expense. The judiciary was, in the 1830s, still very small: each superior Common Law court had its chief justice and three puisne judges, while the Court of Chancery had only relatively recently been increased by the appointment of a vice chancellor.

A far greater problem with the superior courts was one of procedure. The process in the superior courts of law was notoriously technical, complex, with demanding standards of proof and evidence, inflexible and slow and by its nature it demanded the involvement of lawyers at every stage: indeed, that was built into the process. That resulted in expense that often rendered the process inaccessible to all but the wealthiest litigant. In the railway context this would give the railway companies a considerable

---

[149] 'First Report of the Judicature Commissioners', *HCPP* (1868–9) (4130) xxv 1 at p. 18. See generally A. H. Manchester, *A Modern Legal History of England and Wales 1750–1950* (London: Butterworths, 1980), pp. 86–99.

[150] Arthurs, 'Rethinking Administrative Law', 19, 21.

Challenges to the Legal Process 43

advantage over the small private trader. So unsatisfactory was the formal legal process that even the judiciary itself was aware of its shortcomings. In 1828 the pragmatic and rational reformer Henry Brougham exposed the trouble, expense, delay, inconsistency and technicality that litigants in the superior courts of the Common Law had to endure.[151] The process was stultified by a dependence on form and a rigorous adherence to complex and detailed rules, exacerbated by fictions, verbosity and repetition.[152] He argued that this amounted to a denial of justice[153] and put forward comprehensive and pragmatic proposals for reform[154] to ensure swift and cheap administration of justice. He wanted to provide 'cheap justice, and near justice, and speedy justice' for the people of this country.[155] Procedures in the Court of Chancery were equally unsatisfactory, and were notorious following Charles Dickens' portrayal of the court in *Bleak House* in 1853. The process was described in Parliament as 'slow...nearly insensible',[156] and it was said that 'few entered the court of chancery without alarm, and...none escaped from it without suffering'.[157] Suits were lengthy, interested parties often died before determination, costs were so high that it was not unusual for a large proportion of the property in question to be consumed by them. There were attempts at reform in the 1850s to make it simpler and more flexible. The ponderous and formal nature of the process, the inherent opportunities for litigants to procrastinate, would not satisfy the government's desire for swift and efficient implementation of its policies nor the demands of the dynamic development of fields such as railway enterprise, and the need for professional legal assistance would make the resolution of even minor disputes prohibitively expensive. The legal year, with its

---

[151] *Parl. Deb.*, vol. XVIII, new series, cols. 127 ff., 7 February 1828 (HC).

[152] See 'First Report of the Common Law Commissioners', *HCPP* (1829) (46) ix 1; 'First Report of the Commissioners for Inquiring into the Process, Practice and System of Pleading in the Superior Courts of the Common Law', *HCPP* (1851) (1389) xxii 567. See generally The Law Society, *A Compendium of the Practice of the Common Law* (London: R. Hastings, 1847).

[153] *Parl. Deb.*, vol. XVIII, new series, col. 159, 7 February 1828 (HC); *ibid.*, ser. 3, col. 858, 17 June 1833 (HC).

[154] *Ibid.*, new series, cols. 127 ff., 7 February 1828 (HC).

[155] *Ibid.*, ser. 3, col. 891, 17 June 1833 (HL). Similar arguments were made in the debates on the Supreme Court of Judicature Bill in 1873, for example by the Attorney General in *ibid.*, vol. CCXVI, ser. 3, col. 643, 9 June 1873 (HC).

[156] *Ibid.*, vol. V, ser. 2, col. 1034, 30 May 1821 (HC) *per* M. A. Taylor.   [157] *Ibid.*

44 Legal Foundations of Tribunals in 19th-Century England

long vacations, fixed terms and assizes could not provide the uninterrupted settlement of large numbers of minor disputes necessary to the implementation of the new legislation. In short, the expense and delays inherent in the legal process were quite unsuited to a new dynamic industrial society. They were well known, and the courts rightly unpopular and distrusted because of them. Litigation was feared and avoided wherever possible. A Cornish farmer told the Select Committee on Commons' Inclosure in 1844 that he had always thought it was 'better to sacrifice the matter in dispute, if it is of small value, than to go to a court of law'.[158] It would do little to promote acceptance of controversial legislation if the sole avenue of dispute-resolution was to the superior courts at Westminster or on assize, and rendered inaccessible due to their expense and formality.

There was, furthermore, a reluctance on the part of many judges to implement new legislation which they did not regard as law at all. The judges of the superior courts in the nineteenth century perceived themselves to be the guardians of the law, members of an ancient, elite, intellectual and honourable profession, a perception strengthened by their reverence for the law itself. Accordingly they felt that the adjudication of small administrative factual disputes was beneath them or else highly technical and beyond the ability of the courts of law to determine. One of the most vocal in this respect was Lord Campbell who, representing the views of all but one of his brethren, protested against the use of the regular courts to implement regulatory railway legislation on the basis of the unsuitability of the work, arguing that the duties were not judicial duties at all.[159] Lord Bramwell too was a vigorous opponent on the grounds of lack of specialist knowledge and a reluctance to regulate competition.[160] In 1872 Thomas Farrer, the permanent secretary of the Board of Trade, suggested in relation to railway legislation that any tribunal created to implement it should be 'a body possessing the judicial power and the judicial experience of a court of law, with a

---

[158] *Minutes, Commons' Inclosure, 1844* q. 6141 *per* Ralph Cole.

[159] See below, pp. 54–6.

[160] See *Manchester, Sheffield & Lincolnshire Railway* v. *Brown* (1883), LR 8 App Cas 703 at 716–17 *per* Lord Bramwell; Abel-Smith and Stevens, *Lawyers and the Courts*, p. 112.

Challenges to the Legal Process

great deal of knowledge of the management of the railways, and with administrative experience'. 'I do not think', he continued,

> that a court of law can ever decide those cases; I mean questions as to the correspondence of trains and the minute arrangements of administration. A court of law is accustomed to decide an issue, yes or no; whether A wrongs B or not; but to decide a question of whether a railway company gives proper facilities or not to a particular town, or to a particular trade, or a particular class of passengers, is a question which is hardly fit for a court of law to decide.[161]

He thought it was difficult for a court of law to carry out any system of public policy as was contemplated by the Railway and Canal Traffic Act.[162] In 1873 Chichester Fortescue, the President of the Board of Trade, said he did not think 'the habits of the legal mind were best fitted to decide questions which were not questions of strict law, but of discretion, of administration, and of special knowledge directed to a special subject'.[163] And indeed Edward Cardwell himself had said in 1844 that courts of law were not suited to deciding certain questions arising under railway equal rate clauses, and he favoured a transfer of some jurisdiction of the regular courts in this respect to the executive government to provide a simpler and more direct remedy.[164]

The incompatibility of the work of the executive and that of the regular courts was highlighted in relation to the private bill committees. Their function was ultimately legislative and inquisitorial, but comprised some incidental duties of a judicial nature, notably the determination of contentious issues, and indeed the normal practice was for the parties to be represented by counsel, and for witnesses to be called and cross-examined. In its judicial function, however, this form of tribunal was open to criticism. The different sessions of Parliament meant that its composition of Members of Parliament fluctuated, and, while this was equally the case with juries, the former did not have the advantage of the legal issues in dispute being clearly defined at the outset and was often overwhelmed with a mass of evidence touching numerous issues of varying degrees of importance or clarity. Furthermore, the

---

[161] *Minutes, Railway Amalgamation, 1872* q. 7434. See too *Ibid.*, q. 7746.
[162] *Ibid.*, q. 7524.
[163] *Parl. Deb.*, vol. CCXIV, ser. 3, col. 1056, 27 February 1873 (HC) *per* Chichester Fortescue.
[164] *Minutes, Railways, 1844* qq. 4526–770. Ten years later, however, his Railway and Canal Traffic Act was to be implemented by the Court of Common Pleas.

46   Legal Foundations of Tribunals in 19th-Century England

chairmen of the committees did not control their committees according to recognised principles, but rather according to their own personal views of the public interest. It was well known that in railway matters in particular, such views frequently diverged considerably, a factor that it was impossible for applicants to address. The judicial duties, however, could not be isolated, and the regular courts were quite unsuited to the general nature of the work. It was too specialised, in that many questions required expert knowledge of railways or land management for example, and equally too general, in that many issues could not be reduced to clear legal questions.

The superior courts were not, however, the only regular courts in the legal system. Indeed it has been shown that before the nineteenth century most civil and criminal cases were decided in courts of local or special jurisdiction.[165] Legislation of 1846[166] created a system of local courts for the benefit of poorer litigants. These County Courts were described in 1869 as 'the poor man's Courts, where speedy justice could be had'.[167] They were part of a national network of local courts to process various small civil claims, staffed by professional judges, with the status of full courts of law of the regular legal system, and yet with procedures which were expeditious and relatively inexpensive. They appeared ideal as dispute-resolution bodies for the new reforming legislation of the first half of the Victorian period. They were not, however, selected for the purpose. They were not, of course, established in time to implement the legislation restructuring various land rights and were far too late for use in the fiscal sphere. They post-dated the new poor law, the factory legislation and the education reforms, but they were available to address disputes arising from the creation of the railways. By the time a new legislative regime was looking for a dispute-resolution body, the County Courts had been burdened with such an extensive jurisdiction in other fields, that little room was left for new business. For twenty-five years after their inception, successive Acts of Parliament increased their

---

[165] See generally Arthurs, *Without the Law*, Chapter 2.

[166] Recovery of Small Debts Act 1846, 9 & 10 Vict. c. 95. See generally Patrick Polden, *A History of the County Court 1846–1971*, Studies in English Legal History (Cambridge: Cambridge University Press, 1999).

[167] *Parl. Deb.*, vol. CXCVI, ser. 3, col. 1600, 11 June 1869 (HC) *per* Russell Gurney.

Challenges to the Legal Process

work not only in the value of litigation but also in its subject-matter, as for example under the Bankruptcy Act 1869.[168] Furthermore, the County Court judges were experts in law and legal process but did not possess the technical skills required to implement the new legislative schemes. Their processes, though simple in comparison to the superior courts, still required the participation of lawyers. Their principal advantage, in addition to the relative simplicity of their procedures, was their physical accessibility, but it did not suffice to attract the new dispute-resolution work.[169]

Another possibility within the regular court system was the concept of a specialist court. These too were ancient institutions and while not always courts of record, were an accepted part of the legal system. They were formed periodically to address specialist areas of law, particular classes of litigants, notably merchants, or specific geographical locations. Their personnel and procedures were suited to their particular jurisdictions. Specialist expertise would be inherent in the institution, and processes could be designed to suit the subject-matter. Furthermore, they could be situated in appropriate locations as necessary. The Mayor's Court of London, the Court of Passage at Liverpool, the Stannary Courts of Devon and Cornwall, the Admiralty Court of the Cinque Ports and the Salford Hundred Court at Manchester were a few examples of many.[170] Furthermore, from 1750 new Courts of Requests were being instituted by local Act of Parliament. These were small claims courts, mainly concerned with the recovery of debts, staffed by local merchants and acting without a jury.[171] For most people these busy courts constituted the usual form of civil justice.[172] In 1845 there were some 400 such courts hearing thousands of cases, and the numbers were increasing at the very time the legislators were searching for a solution to the

---

[168] 'Second Report of the Judicature Commissioners', *HCPP* (1872) (631) xx 217 at pp. 226–32; 32 & 33 Vict. c. 71.

[169] Though they were used as arbitrators under the Workmen's Compensation Act 1897, 60 & 61 Vict. c. 37, Schedule 2.

[170] See Arthurs, *Without the Law*, pp. 13–34; W. R. Cornish and G. de N. Clark, *Law and Society in England 1750–1950* (London: Sweet and Maxwell, 1989), pp. 29–30.

[171] See Cornish and Clark, *Law and Society*, pp. 30–1; Arthurs, *Without the Law*, pp. 25–49.

[172] Arthurs, *Without the Law*, p. 26.

48   *Legal Foundations of Tribunals in 19th-Century England*

dispute-resolution problem arising in respect of the new legislative regimes for social welfare reform, and were remarkably popular. They were created to address a problem resulting from an increasingly commercial society, namely the importance of credit, and they have been described as the civil equivalent to the summary jurisdiction of the justices of the peace on the criminal and administrative side.[173]

There were, however, arguments against this solution. The legislature was against the creation of new courts within the regular legal system – and all these specialised courts were permanent constituents of that system – and one of the principal recommendations of the Judicature Commissioners when they examined the state of the legal system in the 1870s was the reduction of courts of specialised jurisdiction. They understood that different types of litigation required different courts, but regarded these courts as 'exceptional and intermediate', and observed that 'if they did not exist no one would think of establishing them'.[174] They sought a more rational, uniform and organised system. There were other difficulties. The new legislative regimes might not create sufficient business to warrant the creation of a special court, and in some instances such as the restructuring of the rights in tithes, copyholds and common land, although there might be sufficient business in the short term, the finite nature of the work would require the closure of the court within a few years.

One institution with much to recommend it was the justice of the peace. Justices were an ancient institution having formed a familiar and important part of national life since the fourteenth century. They were undoubtedly part of the regular legal system, and as its lowest branch were well suited to handling large numbers of minor cases. Most importantly, however, they were the one branch of the regular legal system which was accustomed to handling purely administrative business alongside the judicial work of prosecuting and judging lesser criminal offences, and justices were already used on occasion to execute statutory law.[175] While they did not possess technical expertise in any

---

[173] Cornish and Clark, *Law and Society*, p. 31.

[174] 'Second Report of the Judicature Commissioners', *HCPP* (1872) (631) xx 217 at pp. 234–5. See too *Minutes, Railway Amalgamation, 1872* q. 7804 *per* Thomas Farrer.

[175] See for example *R.* v. *Glamorganshire Inhabitants* (1700) 1 Ld Raym 580.

Challenges to the Legal Process 49

particular field, they had extensive knowledge of their locality, a rudimentary knowledge of law and legal process, and in general a working knowledge of land management. These qualities would prima facie suit them for the task of administering the new land rights legislation. They were men of status within their communities, more so than juries, were accustomed to adjudication and decision-making and, importantly, acted without remuneration. Then, as now, they were a remarkably inexpensive legal resource. In comparison with the superior courts, their processes were relatively simple and inexpensive.

Their very position in the legal and social establishment, however, militated against their effective use. Their required landholding qualifications, their voluntary status and their high social standing in the community rendered them, as a body, conservative and independent in outlook. When much of the reforming legislation concerned the restructuring of land rights, increased taxation to support those in need through poverty, illness or misfortune, to expend money on rendering mines or factories safe or to carry out various public works, it was the propertied classes who were undermined by these reforms. The justices were in this respect the last people to select to implement often radical government policy. Furthermore, they were above all country landowners, and as such lacked the specialist skills to address that large proportion of the new legislation that concerned matters of commerce, industry and engineering, and more generally of urban life. They were also, like the County Court, busy with a considerable amount of business already, and as unremunerated laymen, could not be imposed upon at will. Neither were they a cheap solution. Despite their extensive administrative functions they were part of the regular legal system, and that brought with it certain costs.[176] And where they had been used in certain spheres in the past, they had on occasion shown a singular lack of success. The attempt to use them to administer the window tax in the early eighteenth century, for example, was less than satisfactory.[177]

---

[176] For the functions and procedures of the justices of the peace at the beginning of Victoria's reign see William Dickinson, *A Practical Guide to the Quarter Sessions*, 3rd edition (London: T.N. Talfourd, Baldwin and Cradock, and others, 1829).

[177] Ward, *Window and Assessed Taxes*, pp. 6–7.

50   *Legal Foundations of Tribunals in 19th-Century England*

The various institutions within the regular legal system of courts were solutions that embodied an approach of external and hierarchical control. An alternative in both approach and method was to look to the voluntary, consensual and wholly private institution of arbitration whereby persons submitted the matter in dispute to the judgment of arbitrators chosen by themselves. It was as well established as the regular courts of law and was of considerable importance throughout the nineteenth century as an alternative that met many of their inadequacies.[178] The general perception was that arbitration was less confrontational than litigation, engendering less friction between the parties. It was, in short, a more friendly and informal method of dispute-resolution. For this reason, and for its confidentiality, it was widely used in the commercial field, often to good effect. Since each party selected his own arbitrator, and the time and place for the process to take place were arrived at by agreement, the arrangement had the considerable advantage of engendering the feeling in the parties that the process was within their own control, a perception that might have gone a long way to promoting the acceptance of controversial government initiatives. It was favoured by those, such as Sir Robert Peel, who were ideologically opposed to compulsion. The process was relatively simple, and since the choice of arbitrator was within the hands of the parties, it allowed for the appointment of persons with the required expertise, whether technical or legal. Arbitrators could be leading members of the Bar in a particular field, or the leaders in a technical area such as the eminent engineer Sir William Cubitt.

Arbitration, however, was less than ideal. Its voluntary nature denied the device the necessary teeth to ensure the implementation of sometimes controversial legislation. As a consensual arrangement, if one party refused to invoke the process or abide by its outcome, a stalemate was quickly reached. Indeed it was rejected as a method of effecting the compulsory enfranchisement of copyhold for that reason in 1838.[179] It was by its nature a

---

[178] Cornish and Clark, *Law and Society*, p. 36; Arthurs, *Without the Law*, pp. 62–77; Lord Parker of Waddington, *The History and Development of Commercial Arbitration*, Lionel Cohen Lectures 5th series (Jerusalem: Magnes Press, 1959).

[179] Mr Freshfield had proposed a system of arbitration: see *Report, Copyholds Enfranchisement, 1837–8* at p. 199.

Challenges to the Legal Process

temporary body, which could not meet the demand for a permanent dispute-resolution organ that would help ensure uniformity and consistency in decision-making.[180] Furthermore, the element of personal control undermined the independence of the arbitrators, and in an institution with no external authority, the manipulation of the adjudicators was a well-known danger. There was a clear expectation that one's appointee would favour one. The arbitrators by their very nature also lacked the knowledge and the authority over the parties and witnesses required to ensure the proceedings were properly conducted. Neither was it necessarily an inexpensive process: arbitrators required remuneration, with an expert arbitrator commanding high fees, which he set himself according to his standing and the number and length of meetings. Where barristers were appointed as arbitrators, as was common, not only would they require high fees, but the nature of their profession meant they could not always give a continuous attention to an arbitration and the proceedings were often prolonged by their periodic absence on other work.[181] Neither did the process avoid the calling of witnesses and professional legal representation. In short, arbitration was often a process as lengthy and expensive as that in the formal courts of law and one, furthermore, which did not carry the safeguard of appeal to a higher body from a decision. Its shortcomings in the commercial sphere gave rise to an increased demand in the nineteenth century for specialised Tribunals of Commerce.[182]

None of the established institutions within the legal process was able to address the disputes between individuals and the state in the context of the reforming legislation entirely satisfactorily. The government could have accepted second best and employed any one of the established institutions, for in each the perceived disadvantages were balanced by some advantages and each was quite capable of taking on an adjudicatory role satisfactorily. Indeed, the Court of Requests, the County Court and the justices of the peace were all judicial bodies with comparable jurisdictions and a

---

[180] 'Minutes of Evidence before the Select Committee on Railway and Canal Bills', *HCPP* (1852–3) (736) xxxviii 447 at qq. 4523–46 *per* Rowland Hill, secretary to the Postmaster-General.

[181] See 'First Report of the Judicature Commissioners', *HCPP* (1868–9) (4130) xxv 1 at pp. 18–19.

[182] Arthurs, *Without the Law*, p. 57.

52 *Legal Foundations of Tribunals in 19th-Century England*

similar type of litigation and litigant. In some instances where political interests could best be served by continuity, familiarity or simply ease, existing institutions were regarded as adequate to cope with a new administrative scheme and its attendant dispute-resolution.

The regular courts were not always rejected as the means of resolving disputes at first instance in the context of regulatory legislation. The prime example of this was in relation to the regulation of the railways, and it illustrated powerfully the range of differing views as to the machinery appropriate to implement the new regulatory legislation where dispute-resolution was a prominent issue.[183] The substance of the legislation was that passengers and traders should enjoy the same facilities for travel over the whole country as they did over the lines of a single company. Edward Cardwell's proposed legislation of 1854 had three objectives: a statutory duty on railway companies to provide an integrated railway system permitting continuous and corresponding travel over the whole network; the enforcement of that duty by the regular courts of law; and the provision of expert assistance to the courts through a system of administrative arbitration. 'By enactment you will establish the right', he said. 'By decree of a court of justice, the violation of that right will be adjudicated. By arbitration the mode will be determined, in which complete effect can be given to the decision of that tribunal.'[184]

Cardwell first envisaged an arrangement that integrated the use of the regular courts of law and a department of the executive. Legislation would impose duties on the railway companies to provide continuous travel and not to show any undue preference. If the law were breached, the remedy lay with a regular court of law, but that court could use experts in the field to provide the administrative basis for its judgment. Those experts could consist either of the Board of Trade itself or of persons directly appointed by the court. They would proceed by way of arbitration, reflecting the consensus in the earlier Select Committees, to resolve disputes between railway companies and arrive at satisfactory arrangements to prevent injury and inconvenience to the shareholders

---

[183] See the account of Thomas Farrer in *Minutes, Railway Amalgamation, 1872* q. 7767.

[184] *Parl. Deb.*, vol. CXXXII, ser. 3, col. 594, 6 April 1854 (HC).

Challenges to the Legal Process

and the travelling public. His bill placed the Board of Trade at the centre of dispute-resolution in railway matters.[185] It was the prime instrument for the settling of all disagreements and disputes between railway companies and canal companies in general, for specific disputes as to the location of stations, and for the preliminary inquiry into, and hearing of complaints against, railway or canal companies. Though the courts of law were not eschewed entirely, arbitration by the Board of Trade in a form more robust than purely voluntary arbitration, was undoubtedly the chosen method of dispute-resolution.

It was clear even in relation to his original bill that Cardwell was all too aware of the power of the railway interest, and ultimately that power was to crush his proposal to give the Board of Trade extensive arbitral powers over railway matters. When the bill returned from committee a month or so later, it was radically different from its original, with all proposals to give such powers to the Board of Trade removed.[186] Instead the revised bill placed the regular courts at the centre of dispute-resolution. It provided that any person complaining of a breach of the duties laid down by the bill could apply by summary process to any single judge of a superior court, who would hear and determine the complaint. The court could call on the assistance of inquiries by experts such as engineers who would establish if such breach had taken place, and could then issue an injunction or impose penalties on defaulting companies.[187] The judges were empowered to make such regulations as may be necessary for their proceedings.[188] The solution proposed in the recast bill, therefore, was for a system lying someway between the regular courts and specialist lay tribunals, though with the emphasis firmly on the former.

There was support in the House of Commons for the original proposals, it being regarded not only as unrealistic to suppose individuals would be prepared to litigate in the courts against the powerful railway companies, but equally inappropriate to give to judges powers to regulate railway matters of which they had no knowledge and experience.[189] But the railway interest in the

---

[185] Railway and Canal Traffic Regulation Bill 1854, *HCPP* (1854) (62) vi 1, cll. 4–10, 13.
[186] *HCPP* (1854) (82) vi 13.   [187] *Ibid.*, cl. 3.   [188] *Ibid.*, cl. 4.
[189] *Parl. Deb.*, vol. CXXXII, ser. 3, cols. 1231–2, 4 May 1854 (HC) *per* Joseph Hume, and col. 1237 *per* Joseph Henley.

54 *Legal Foundations of Tribunals in 19th-Century England*

House of Commons proved too strong. It emerged that Cardwell had met with representatives of the railway companies, who had agreed with the principle of the bill in its imposition of duties on the companies, but had objected to the machinery of the Board of Trade, preferring an initial application to a court of law. They feared that regulation by the Board of Trade would necessarily be arbitrary and could affect the financial and commercial situation of the companies.[190] The Liberal lawyer William Atherton said that he 'certainly had objections to the bill as it originally stood, which entrusted these large powers to the Board of Trade; but those objections were obviated, when he found them entrusted to the judges of the land'.[191] Furthermore, it was argued, the procedure proposed in the revised bill was relatively cheap and easy, being by summary process to a single judge in chambers. The issue was, as succinctly stated by Lord Stanley in the House of Lords on the second reading of the final bill, that '[i]t was considered that there were two modes by which the rules might be carried into effect. The one was by the establishment of a separate and independent Board of the Executive Government, and the other by leaving it to courts of law, to whom all complaints should be made to enforce obedience to the laws that were prescribed.'[192]

The railway companies, however, faced robust opposition from the judges. Lord Campbell equally strongly approved of the principles of the bill but not the machinery. In a forceful speech on the second reading in the House of Lords, he made it clear he felt the task imposed on the judges was inappropriate and misconceived. 'The Act', he said, 'sought to turn the Judges of the courts of common law into railway directors.' The duties the Act proposed to impose on them had 'nothing at all to do with law'.[193] The judges were being asked to decide whether the railway companies had afforded all reasonable facilities for the receiving and forwarding of traffic and to ensure they had given no unreasonable preferences. In short, they had to decide if the companies had acted reasonably, and that would entail deciding issues such as when trains should start, the number of carriages, the fares and

---

[190] See Cleveland-Stevens, *English Railways*, pp. 198–9.
[191] *Parl. Deb.*, vol. CXXXII, ser. 3, col. 1242, 4 May 1854 (HC) *per* William Atherton.
[192] *Ibid.*, vol. CXXXIII, ser. 3, col. 595, 19 May 1854 (HL) *per* Lord Stanley.
[193] *Ibid.*, col. 596 *per* Lord Campbell.

Challenges to the Legal Process

so on. This, contrary to all legal principles, entailed the judges rather than juries deciding questions of fact, questions on which, he felt, they were not competent to pronounce.[194] Furthermore, his deliberate misreading of the clause allowing the judges to regulate their procedures as one allowing them to transfer these cases to Petty or Quarter Sessions, or pie-powder courts, revealed his view that such matters were the proper province of the lower courts, not of the superior judges, and in a later debate he expressly stated that a lay tribunal was the appropriate body.[195] Lord Campbell wanted nothing less than the remodelling of the bill to remove the provision for adjudication by the judges.

In further debate a week later Lord Lyndhurst said the issues the judges would have to determine were not of law, and so vague that there could be little uniformity of decision. He highlighted a practical problem, namely that as the Common Law judges were out on circuit twice a year for considerable periods, the duties would fall on the Equity judges who remained in London, and that their court was already notoriously overburdened with business. Any extra burden would negate the reforms recently enacted to render Chancery business more efficient. His solution, supported by Lord St Leonards and Lord Brougham, was to suggest the Court of Common Pleas as the sole tribunal for railway business, that court being the least burdened of all the superior courts of law.[196]

Lord Campbell, having had consideration of the bill postponed for some ten days to enable him to consult his fellow judges, returned to the House of Lords with his opposition undiminished. The judges, he said,

were unanimously of opinion that the duties which they were asked to undertake under the provisions of this Bill were not judicial duties; and the great majority of them stated they were not properly competent to perform those duties. That these were not judicial duties he thought there could be no question. Ordinarily, a Judge had to interpret the law, and the law was placed before him for that purpose; but by this Bill no law was laid before the Judges which they could interpret or enforce.[197]

---

[194] Ibid., cols. 596–8.
[195] Ibid., vol. CXXXIII, ser. 3, cols. 1137–8, 30 May 1854 (HL).
[196] Ibid., cols. 983–4, 26 May 1854 (HL).
[197] Ibid., col. 1136, 30 May 1854 (HL).

56   Legal Foundations of Tribunals in 19th-Century England

The duty to adjudicate on the reasonableness of facilities or preferences was too vague and left too much to their discretion. Nevertheless one judge, the Chief Justice of the Court of Common Pleas, Lord Jervis, maintained that despite the nature of the duties, his court could implement the legislation 'if they will take the trouble to work it'.[198] The acquiescence of Lord Jervis, coupled with the view expressed in the House of Lords that the Court of Common Pleas would be the only suitable regular court to implement the legislation, undermined Lord Campbell's stance and he had to capitulate. The Lord Chancellor felt justified by the novel state of affairs that the railways had created.[199] The Act received the royal assent a few weeks later,[200] the method of dispute-resolution in railway regulation thus being an entirely political decision.

As Lord Campbell and others had predicted,[201] and despite the summary process and the provision that the court could call upon the specialist assistance of an expert engineer or the Board of Trade,[202] the scheme failed. After only three years an amending bill was needed to provide an extra remedy to an aggrieved person, enabling him to complain to the Board of Trade, who could then call for evidence, and only if it felt there was a real grievance to direct the Attorney General to go to the Court of Common Pleas.[203] Although the bill did not become law, it reveals an appreciation that to oblige an aggrieved individual to seek his remedy in the Court of Common Pleas could be ruinous to such a party.[204]

The deficiencies of courts of law in dealing with this new kind of regulatory legislation were clearly revealed. The views on the quality of the court's decisions were mixed. With regard to decisions on the issue of undue preference, the decisions were regarded as sound and satisfactory in principle, but in relation to tolls and charges they were criticised as being erroneous through a

---

[198]   *Ibid.*, col. 1140 *per* Lord Stanley, reading a letter he had received from Lord Jervis.

[199]   *Ibid.*, col. 1138.

[200]   Railway and Canal Traffic Regulation Act 1854, 17 & 18 Vict. c. 31.

[201]   Ralph Littler QC said the Act of 1854 had little chance of success because the judges did not like it: *Minutes, Railways (Rates and Fares), 1882* q. 3999.

[202]   Railway and Canal Traffic Regulation Act 1854, 17 & 18 Vict. c. 31 s. 3.

[203]   *HCPP* (1857) (78 Session 2) iv 381.

[204]   *Parl. Deb.*, vol. CXLVI, ser. 3, cols. 1508–9, 14 July 1857 (HC).

Challenges to the Legal Process 57

lack of specialised knowledge.[205] It was said that the jurisdiction of the Court of Common Pleas under the Act of 1854 'had practically broken down'[206] and the legislation was so little used that it was rendered a dead letter.[207] An ultimately more material reason for the failure of the system was that it became clear that only the wealthiest traders with significant interests at stake had been able to do legal battle with the powerful railway companies.[208] The time, expense and subsequent damage to commercial relations made it impossible for traders in a small way of business to go to the court. They were left unprotected and often preferred to submit to their grievances. The popular view among the railway community was that 'the remedy was worse than the disease'.[209]

The nineteenth-century desire for the rationalisation of the legal system meant that the creation of a specialised court of law was a rare solution to the problems arising from new commercial conditions. One exception was its adoption as the preferred option in the case of bankruptcy in 1831. When the existing system of private bankruptcy administration was seen to be failing,[210] bankruptcy jurisdiction was removed from the Lord Chancellor and placed in a new and independent Court of Bankruptcy.[211] The administration of bankrupts' estates was put in the hands of the Official Assignees, who were officers of the court. This court-based system of bankruptcy administration itself came to fail,[212] again because an essentially administrative process had been given

---

[205] See the three cases discussed by Thomas Farrer in *Minutes, Railway Amalgamation, 1872* qq. 7503–9.

[206] *Minutes, Railways (Rates and Fares), 1882* q. 3016.

[207] *Report, Railway Amalgamation, 1872* p. 13. There were only two cases: *Caterham Railway Company* v. *the London, Brighton, and South Coast Railway Company and South Eastern Railway Company* (1857) 1 CB NS 410 and *Barrett* v. *the Great Northern Railway Company and Midland Railway Company* (1857) 1 CB NS 423, and both applications failed.

[208] *Ibid.*, p. 12.

[209] *Minutes, Railway Amalgamation, 1872* q. 1234 *per* Charles Clark, Liverpool merchant and chairman of the Liverpool Chamber of Commerce Railway Committee.

[210] *Parl. Deb.*, vol. CCLXXVII, ser. 3, col. 844, 19 March 1883 (HC); see too *ibid.*, cols. 848–9, 853.

[211] 1 & 2 Will. IV c. 56 (1831).

[212] 'Report from the Select Committee on the Bankruptcy Act', *HCPP* (1864) (512) v 1 and (1865) (144) xii 589 at p. 591. See too the speech of the Attorney General in *Parl. Deb.*, vol. CXCIV, ser. 3, col. 776, 5 March 1869 (HC).

58   *Legal Foundations of Tribunals in 19th-Century England*

to a judicial body to manage.[213] The administration of bankruptcy was outside the proper and ordinary scope of a court of law, and while initially the work had been well managed, fraud and corruption discredited the system, it lost popularity due to its high expense, excessive formality and inevitable publicity, and it was ultimately ripe for abolition. It appeared that such problems were inherent in formal courts of law.[214] Official supervision of such processes required a strong central body to direct policy, undertake appointments and maintain standards, and government intervention and involvement could provide that. Accordingly in 1883 the two functions were separated, with the judicial element of bankruptcy proceedings being conducted by the High Court, the administrative by the Board of Trade.[215]

Justices of the peace were retained for dispute-resolution purposes in some limited instances. Dispute-resolution was not regarded as a high priority within the new poor law system. The aim of the legislation was to reduce all litigation and especially settlement disputes by creating larger administrative areas so that the issue simply did not arise as often as it did when parishes were small and paupers moved easily between them. What litigation there still was remained as it was before, namely in the hands of the justices of the peace.[216] When in 1836 a uniform mode of rating for the relief of the poor was introduced, the rate was levied by the churchwardens and overseers of a parish, and allowed by the justices. The only appeal allowed was to the regular courts in the form of the justices in Special Session, who would hear and determine objections to the rate, and there was a further appeal to the justices in Quarter Sessions.[217] This administrative structure thus eschewed any innovative form for the resolution of disputes within the administrative process of rating. It furthermore

---

[213] In the second reading of the Bankruptcy Bill in 1883, Mr Serjeant Simon observed that in his view the Board of Trade and the court could not work together in the administration of bankruptcies. 'Here is thus', he said, 'the jarring of two authorities together': *Parl. Deb.*, vol. CCLXXVII, ser. 3, col. 872, 19 March 1883 (HC).

[214] 'Report of the Royal Commission on Bankruptcy', *HCPP* (1854) (1770) xxiii 1 at p. 20.

[215] Bankruptcy Act 1883, 46 & 47 Vict. c. 52. For the duties of the Official Receivers in bankruptcy see *Parl. Deb.*, vol. CCLXXVII, ser. 3, cols. 822–3, 19 March 1883 (HC); Bankruptcy Act 1883, 46 & 47 Vict. c. 52 ss. 66–70.

[216] Poor Law Amendment Act 1834, 4 & 5 Will. IV c. 76 s. 43.

[217] Parochial Assessments Act 1836, 6 & 7 Will. IV c. 96.

Challenges to the Legal Process

retained the justices in Quarter Session for the second-tier appellate stage. Justices of the peace were used in some respects in early railway enterprise, for example to give consent to a railway to cross a highway, to hear objections to the taking of land for temporary occupation during the construction of a railway, and to hear disputes as to the building of gates, bridges, culverts, fences and so forth.[218] Their duties were specific and local, and they were not conceived of as the primary method of dispute-resolution. And finally, the public health disputes were expressly to be addressed by the traditional dispute-resolution machinery, including the justices of the peace, a deliberate policy adopted in 1848 in preference to the giving of any general adjudicatory powers to the board.[219] Justices were also, though less obviously, employed to hear certain tax appeals. The Land Tax Redemption Appeal Commissioners had to be justices themselves, and heard appeals against the redemption of the land tax at Petty Sessions.[220]

Arbitration was also employed, sometimes in conjunction with the justices of the peace, and sometimes compulsorily, as a dispute-resolution technique that could promote state intervention, though attempts to establish it as the usual substitute for the regular courts was not entirely successful. The problems inherent in the arbitration process became particularly evident in the railway sphere. The preference for arbitration was one of the few unifying views held in the often acrimonious debate as to the form of the regulatory body for railway enterprise, since it retained control in the hands of the parties and allowed the inclusion of expert adjudicators. There was already an established tradition and culture of dispute-resolution by arbitration in this field, since the Railway Clearing House had its own system of internal and expert arbitration, settling disputed collisions for example, and this established practice was accordingly drawn upon. The substitution of the Board of Trade for the Railway Clearing House was understood. Robert Stephenson MP preferred the selection of

---

[218] Railway Clauses Consolidation Act 1845, 8 & 9 Vict. c. 20 ss. 36, 60, 69; see too Companies Clauses Consolidation Act 1845, 8 & 9 Vict. c 16 ss. 144, 147, 159.

[219] Public Health Act 1848, 11 & 12 Vict. c. 63 ss. 129, 135, 136; Public Health Act 1875, 38 & 39 Vict. c. 55 ss. 179–81 for arbitration provisions and ss. 268–9 for appeal to the Local Government Board. See generally Blake Odgers, 'Changes in Domestic Legislation', in Council of Legal Education (eds.), *Century of Law Reform*, pp. 141–8; Fraser, *British Welfare State*, pp. 51–71.

[220] 38 Geo. III c. 60 s. 121 (1798).

60   *Legal Foundations of Tribunals in 19th-Century England*

expert arbitrators by a department of the executive and with the approval of the parties.[221] It was thought this was sufficiently strong to exercise the necessary control primarily because the decisions of expert adjudicators would, it was suggested, be acceptable to the railway companies.[222] Earlier failures were often put down to insufficient specialist expertise. Others realised that any official arbitration had to be strong. One railway director said any power of arbitration 'should be compulsory, sharp, and decisive'.[223] Accordingly, just as many private railway Acts had made provision for dispute-resolution by arbitration in certain instances, so did the early public regulatory legislation, as with the negotiation of remuneration to be given to the railway companies for the carriage of mail.[224] For a time arbitration by the Board of Trade was a popular solution to settle disputes between railway companies, to hear the grievances of the public and to deal with the very wide range of disputes which this kind of activity gave rise to.[225] Some disputes were taken out of the hands of justices of the peace and given to arbitration by the Board of Trade.[226] Even when Edward Cardwell proposed this as his preferred method of implementation and dispute-resolution in railway matters, he acknowledged that pure voluntary arbitration was too weak a tool when great interests were at stake, and that a more robust form of it was necessary.[227] By the later years of the nineteenth century,

---

[221] 'Minutes of Evidence before the Select Committee on Railway and Canal Bills', *HCPP* (1852–3) (170) xxxviii 5 at q. 1094.

[222] *Ibid.*, q. 1233 *per* Captain Mark Huish, general manager of the London and North Western Railway Company.

[223] *Ibid.*, (736) xxxviii 447 at q. 4354 *per* Robert Roy, director of the Shrewsbury and Chester Railway, the Shrewsbury and Birmingham Railway Company and the Stour Valley Railway Company.

[224] Conveyance of the Mails by Railways Act 1838, 1 & 2 Vict. c. 98 s. 16. This was an instance where arbitration was deliberately retained by the Railway and Canal Traffic Act 1873, 36 & 37 Vict. c. 48 s. 19. Statutory compulsory arbitration was common throughout the nineteenth century. See Arthurs, *Without the Law*, pp. 99–103.

[225] See the evidence of Seymour Clarke, general manager of the Great Northern Railway, in 'Minutes of Evidence before the Select Committee on Railway and Canal Bills', *HCPP* (1852–3) (170) xxxviii 5 at qq. 421–33, 462–90, 555–624; Railway Companies Arbitration Act 1859, 22 & 23 Vict. c. 59.

[226] Railway and Canal Traffic Act 1840, 3 & 4 Vict. c. 97 ss. 10, 18–19. See too Regulation of Railways Act 1842, 5 & 6 Vict. c. 55 s. 11; Railway Clauses Consolidation Act 1845, 8 & 9 Vict. c. 20 s. 12.

[227] *Parl. Deb.*, vol. CXXXII, ser. 3, col. 1248, 4 May 1854 (HC) *per* Edward Cardwell.

Challenges to the Legal Process 61

however, arbitration as a dispute-resolution technique was perceived as slow, difficult and expensive. The arbitrators who were generally appointed were railway managers, who were so busy that they had insufficient time to give to the duties, and their decisions had no force of precedent.[228] It was felt that arbitration was of little use unless it could be effective and quick, which it was not.[229] It was generally very slow, with individual arbitrations often lasting months, and sometimes even years.[230] Delays were caused not only by the other engagements of the arbitrators, but by the deliberate obstructions and delays introduced by the railway companies when they did not agree, which was common. Such deliberate manipulation had the effect of postponing arbitrations indefinitely.[231] In the closing years of the nineteenth century, however, the use of conciliation and arbitration methods, popular in America, increased in settling railway grievances.[232] This came in the wake of the elevation of the Railway and Canal Commission to a full court of law in 1888, presided over by a High Court judge, and having formal procedures and legal representation. As the formality and attendant expense crept back into the processes of the commission, so its users sought a more flexible and informal mode of dispute-resolution. The conciliation clause was widely used in relation to small disputes, the commission itself taking the larger disputes. The conciliation clause, though a 'small weapon', was praised for bringing the railway companies and traders together, removing misunderstandings and generally arriving at a compromise over a disputed point.[233] Arbitration was often used to settle compensation, for example under the Land Clauses Consolidation Act 1845 where a

---

[228] *Report, Railway Amalgamation, 1872* p. 49.

[229] *Minutes, Railway Amalgamation, 1872* q. 403 *per* James Allport, general manager of the Midland Railway.

[230] *Ibid.*, at q. 3260 *per* Frederick Broughton, manager of the Mid-Wales Railway; q. 3679 *per* Charles Parkes, parliamentary agent; q. 4452 *per* James Allport; q. 7717 *per* Thomas Farrer.

[231] *Ibid.*, at q. 3828 *per* William Price, MP for Gloucester and chairman of Midland Railway Company; q. 4453 *per* James Allport; q. 4617 *per* Sir Edward Watkin, chairman of the Manchester, Sheffield and Lincolnshire, and the South Eastern Railway Companies.

[232] 'Minutes of Evidence before the Select Committee on Railway Rates and Charges', *HCPP* (1893–4) (462) xiv 535 qq. 373–82, 422–5 *per* Sir Courtney Boyle, permanent secretary of the Board of Trade.

[233] *Ibid.*, q. 7005 *per* James Beale, solicitor; qq. 624–5 *per* Sir Courtney Boyle.

62   Legal Foundations of Tribunals in 19th-Century England

landowner could choose it in preference to a jury to assess compensation for taking land for the railways.[234] It was also the method laid down by the Public Health Act 1848 for the resolution of disputes as to compensation.[235] Again the Workmen's Compensation legislation in 1897 made use of arbitration, for it provided that any disputes were to be resolved by means of an arbitration by the judges of the County Court,[236] and it was a favoured method under the building societies legislation.[237]

But recourse to established institutions of the regular legal system for dispute-resolution was the exception, principally because their defects were well known and their problems anticipated. On those occasions where they were used the outcome was generally not the efficient implementation and dispute-resolution which had been hoped for. As a general rule the legislators favoured the view expressed in 1844 by Major-General Pasley, the inspector-general of railways, that 'the best power of adjudicating is that which prevents unnecessary lawsuits',[238] and adopted none of the established organs of the legal system wholesale. They adopted neither regular courts nor justices of the peace, nor favoured specialist courts or private arbitration.

The reason they eschewed the organs of the legal system was because effective dispute-resolution was not the only, or even the principal, requirement. The duties required of a body to implement the new regulatory legislation were a mixture of legislative, administrative, judicial and policy functions, in varying proportions, and inextricably mixed. This admixture of functions made established institutions unsuitable or inappropriate. Had the legislature conceived of dispute-resolution as a discrete element in the process it laid down, it would have been recognised as a judicial function and entrusted, quite properly, to one of the regular courts of law. The legislature did not, and could not, isolate the function in this way. It regarded any dispute-resolution as no more than an element, albeit one of a judicial character, in a wider administrative process, and one which was too deeply embedded in the administrative nature and function of the organ

---

[234] 8 & 9 Vict. c. 18.   [235] 11 & 12 Vict. c. 63 ss. 123–8.

[236] Workmen's Compensation Act 1897, 60 & 61 Vict. c. 37, Schedule 2, s. 23; Abel-Smith and Stevens, *Lawyers and the Courts*, pp. 115–16.

[237] Building Societies Act 1874, 37 & 38 Vict. c. 42 s. 34.

[238] *Minutes, Railways, 1844* q. 2218.

Challenges to the Legal Process

to be perceived as a discrete, let alone a prominent, concern. From that perspective, quite apart from the various shortcomings of established legal institutions and of the policy of the legislature towards their rationalisation, the obvious solution was to bypass the regular courts of law and place the dispute-resolution function in the implementing body itself. The administrative machinery of the board possessed the advantages of flexibility, continuity and relative political neutrality, and this made it valuable not only as an administrative tool but also potentially ideally constituted for the new specialised purposes of dispute-resolution. This solution was, furthermore, consistent with constitutional theory: the implementation of the legislation was part of the administration of the country, and as such was a function of the executive, not the judiciary. Furthermore, when it was considered independently, it was appreciated that centralised dispute-resolution through the implementing administrative body would also serve to preserve central control over the entire administration of the law.[239] The concept of an alternative dispute-resolution body of a predominantly administrative nature was not new to English law and politics. The Court of Chancery, the King's Council, the Star Chamber were all at some point in their development examples of such organs.[240]

The debate was not, therefore, primarily as to how disputes should be resolved, but as to how the new centralising legislation could be administered in the cheapest, most efficient and most effective way and as to the nature of the body to be created in order to serve this overall function. Dispute-resolution played a part, but only a part, in the final solution. It has been seen that the policy was adopted from the very beginning to make appropriate provision in each particular case rather than to introduce a new general system. It appreciated the context of the dispute-resolution and accordingly the tribunals were the result of an extreme empirical approach to dispute-resolution, where provision was made for appropriate adjudication in each particular

---

[239] *Minutes, Commons' Inclosure, 1844* q. 23 *per* Revd Richard Jones, Tithe Commissioner, recommending use of legally qualified assistant commissioners to resolve disputes in the locality, as had been instituted under the Tithe Commutation Act.

[240] See Holdsworth, *History of English Law*, vol. XIV, p. 182; Wraith and Hutchesson, *Administrative Tribunals*, pp. 18–21.

64   *Legal Foundations of Tribunals in 19th-Century England*

situation. Subject-matter was so diverse, and the contexts differed so substantially, that such provision was regarded as essential. The task of designing these bodies was made easier because they were not perceived as courts of law. In the context of commercial litigation, for example, there was an agreed need for a new summary procedure in bodies staffed by men with commercial expertise, but no agreement could be reached as to the form such bodies should take, as to their composition, or as to the classes of case they should entertain. Whether the judges should be lawyers or laymen, the capacities and weight of each, the provision for remuneration, the rules of evidence to be adopted, legal representation and powers of appeal were all the subject of heated controversy.[241] But no consensus could be reached in 1874, because the implications of such a constitution in the context of courts of law and for the development of the law itself were too great. With ad hoc administrative bodies created for the purpose by individual statutes, however, a far greater degree of flexibility and design for the purpose was possible.

From the perspective of dispute-resolution only, the selection of the new ad hoc bodies to fulfil this function, even though lying outside the regular judicial system because of their administrative context, was consistent with the prevailing policy of the legislature in relation to regular litigation. 'It seems to us', said the Judicature Commissioners in 1868, 'that it is the duty of the country to provide tribunals adapted to the trial of all classes of cases, and capable of adjusting the rights of litigant parties in the manner most suitable to the nature of the questions to be tried.'[242] The objective was to use the courts 'to do the largest quantity of work in the simplest, most expeditious, and most efficient manner', and that could well import a diversion of inappropriate business from them to specialist organs.[243] It was accepted in the context of the regular courts that where the matter in dispute was small, it should be determined by a local tribunal with a simple procedure, and that such cases could not bear the expense of trial before the central

---

[241] 'Third Report of the Judicature Commissioners', *HCPP* (1874) (957) xxiv 1 at p. 7.

[242] 'First Report of the Judicature Commissioners', *HCPP* (1868–9) (4130) xxv 1 at p. 13.

[243] 'Second Report of the Judicature Commissioners', *HCPP* (1872) (631) xx 217 at p. 10.

Challenges to the Legal Process

superior courts.[244] While this could be perceived as an argument for consigning the new litigation to some inferior tribunal of the regular legal system, in practice it had a contrary effect. The process of rationalisation ultimately expressed in the Judicature Acts 1873 and 1875[245] followed profound reflection on the jurisdiction and methods of the regular courts and what was appropriate for them to undertake. From this perspective it was clear that a considerable amount of new small-scale litigation in specialist and unrelated fields, intimately connected with the administration of disparate and new reforming legislative regimes of an administrative character, were unlikely to fit into a new and rationalised legal system. Indeed, such litigation was of the very kind the legislators wanted to avoid in their pursuit of a reformed, free-flowing legal system. Furthermore, with a clear demarcation between tribunals with an administrative objective and those with a judicial one, reforms in one sphere did not necessarily impinge on practice in the other.

Most of the implementing organs of the executive, therefore, were given dispute-resolution powers,[246] though they varied considerably in their prominence within each body. At first the factory inspectors had very wide jurisdiction, including dispute-resolution powers,[247] but these were found inappropriate and their powers were gradually confined to the administrative. Throughout the voluminous debate in Parliament on all aspects of the poor relief and public health legislation, the location of dispute-resolution powers was a relatively minor consideration. Both legislative regimes, while administratively innovative in some ways and socially of immense significance, retained the traditional institutions of dispute-resolution in the form of arbitration and the justices of the peace. The central Poor Law and General Health Boards did have some dispute-resolution authority. The former had some judicial functions, though not expressly until 1851 when disputes between parishes as to questions of settlement, removal or chargeability could be referred to the Poor Law Board.[248] These dispute-resolution powers were,

---

[244] *Ibid.* [245] See Cornish and Clark, *Law and Society*, pp. 38–44.

[246] Professor Roberts identified sixteen new governmental departments in the mid-nineteenth century, and identified ten as having the power to hear and determine disputes: Roberts, *Victorian Origins*, p. 106.

[247] Factories Act 1833, 3 & 4 Will. IV c. 103.

[248] Poor Relief Act Continuance Act 1851, 14 & 15 Vict. c. 105 s. 12.

66   *Legal Foundations of Tribunals in 19th-Century England*

however, very specific, incidental and consensual in nature, resembling arbitration rather than adjudication. Only when a person was aggrieved by the proceedings of a local Board of Health as to the recovery of certain expenses could he appeal to the General Board of Health,[249] and the Public Health Act 1875 adopted the same approach.[250] The Local Government Board,[251] created by statute in 1871, took on a number of duties largely relating to the public health and the poor law. In these three areas of regulating legislation, dispute-resolution powers were not prominent, and the organs made little contribution to the development of the modern administrative tribunal as an adjudicatory body.

In other implementing bodies, however, the dispute-resolution powers were highly significant. The principle of an appellate dispute-resolution jurisdiction being given to the administrative bodies in the tax field was already well established. The various bodies of commissioners for fiscal purposes, namely the Commissioners of the Land Tax and for the Assessed Taxes, the General Commissioners and the Special Commissioners of Income Tax all had prominent appellate dispute-resolution functions, hearing appeals primarily against assessments to the tax in question. Dispute-resolution powers in the tax tribunals were thus familiar, and indeed were extended throughout the nineteenth century. It was anticipated that the bodies created to implement the land rights legislation would have a large number of disputes to resolve in the course of their work, with some, such as boundary disputes, being complex and potentially important matters. It was recognised that there was a need for machinery that could inquire into questions of law, questions of fact and questions of value cheaply and efficiently, attractive to the public and yet preserving to the legislature control to ensure the rights and interests of the poor were regarded.[252] Accordingly the three bodies of commissioners for the commutation of tithes, the enfranchisement of copyholds and the inclosure of common land were all given extensive and prominent dispute-resolution powers, and the need for such powers was a material element in the

---

[249] Public Health Act 1848, 11 & 12 Vict. c. 63 s. 120.
[250] 38 & 39 Vict. c. 55 ss. 179–80, 268–9. See too 35 & 36 Vict. c. 79 s. 32.
[251] See generally A. T. Carter, 'Changes in the Constitution', in Council of Legal Education (eds.), *Century of Law Reform*, pp. 122–5.
[252] *Minutes, Commons' Inclosure, 1844* q. 17 *per* Revd Richard Jones.

Challenges to the Legal Process 67

choice and structure of the implementing body. The debate on the Tithe Commutation Act throughout the early summer of 1836 reveals minimal objection to the method selected and no suggestion that the bypassing of the regular courts in the dispute-resolution aspect was unpopular.[253] This was so even in an area of traditionally bitter controversy and prodigious litigation.

In searching for an alternative, arbitration, the courts, juries, other commissioners and government departments[254] were all examined. The tradition of lay commissioners, however, meant that the concept was readily accepted for use in both an administrative and dispute-resolution capacity, but there were strong reservations as to the centralised nature of such a body. The strong tradition of arbitral commissioners in inclosure meant they were favoured for the resolution of disputes in preference to the court, even where the disputes were of a technical and potentially financially important nature.[255] It was suggested that there could be arbitration under the control of a central board, the latter having the power to appoint the arbitrator[256] or to review their decisions and thereby guarding against a lack of legal knowledge in the arbitrators. It was suggested a central board could itself act as arbitrators, acting as 'a sort of general public umpire, doing even justice' to all parties.[257] These suggestions were made by those who wanted to ensure that the elements of local and personal control were retained, and who would feel strongly the loss of their right to appoint their own commissioners or arbitrators for the conduct of inclosures, tithe commutation or copyhold enfranchisement.[258] The government's primary motive was to create a cheap and effective process, of which dispute-resolution

---

[253] *Parl. Deb.*, vol. XXXIII, ser. 3, cols. 882 ff., 12 May 1836 (HC); *ibid.*, cols. 906 ff., 13 May 1836 (HC); *ibid.*, cols. 1079 ff., 18 May 1836 (HC); *ibid.*, vol. XXXIV, ser. 3, cols. 592 ff., 17 June 1836 (HC); *ibid.*, cols. 857 ff., 24 June 1836 (HC); *ibid.*, cols. 973 ff., 27 June 1836 (HC); *ibid.*, cols. 1291 ff., 7 July 1836 (HL).

[254] *Minutes, Commons' Inclosure, 1844* q. 3432 *per* Thomas Woolley.

[255] *Ibid.*, at qq. 6136–58.

[256] *Ibid.*, q. 2587 *per* Charles Mickleburgh, land surveyor.

[257] *Minutes, Copyholds Bill, 1851* q. 1249 *per* James Cuddon, conveyancer and steward.

[258] Sir William Foster, a solicitor extensively involved with copyhold land as a steward of some 200 copyhold manors, approved of the appointment of the commissioners by the parties, taking as an example the cognate procedure for railway compensation under the Land Clauses Act: *ibid.*, qq. 536, 591, 592.

68   Legal Foundations of Tribunals in 19th-Century England

formed no more than a necessary element.[259] As has been seen, only boards of commissioners could achieve this, and when commissioners were adopted as the machinery for implementing the legislation, they were in the three areas of land rights restructuring given wide dispute-resolution powers.

In the regulation of railways the resolution of disputes between powerful private interests was particularly important and the search for an appropriate body correspondingly challenging. When the Joint Select Committee on Railway Companies Amalgamation identified the various disputes arising from the railway legislation and the need for their resolution, it observed that '[n]o existing institution possesses the necessary qualities. The Board of Trade has not the requisite judicial character or means of action; a Court of Law fails in practical knowledge and administrative facility; and a Committee of the Houses of Parliament has no permanence.'[260] The various lay organs entrusted with the duties from 1847 to 1853 were universally regarded as having failed, and the choice of the Court of Common Pleas to both implement the legislation administratively and resolve disputes from 1854 was equally unsuccessful. Experience suggested that the solution was a hybrid institution: a statutory tribunal with judicial processes, clear jurisdiction, expert lay members and legal advice. Accordingly a new supervisory and dispute-resolution body, the new Railway Commissioners,[261] was established with a summary power to adjudicate 'promptly, efficiently, and cheaply'.[262] Where legislation provided for the settlement of disputes by arbitration, the differences were to be referred to the commissioners instead. This machinery was shown to be more efficient and appropriate, and the principles of the 1854 Act were at last of general application.[263] It clearly showed that the right tribunal went a long way to ensuring the law's objective. Similarly, the Merchant Marine Board under the Merchant Shipping Act 1854 was given a

---

[259] *Parl. Deb.*, vol. LXXX, ser. 3, cols. 24–5, 1 May 1845 (HC) *per* Earl of Lincoln.
[260] *Report, Railway Amalgamation, 1872* p. 49.
[261] Railway and Canal Traffic Act 1873, 36 & 37 Vict. c. 48.
[262] *Parl. Deb.*, vol. CCXIV, ser. 3, col. 1056, 27 February 1873 (HC) *per* Chichester Fortescue.
[263] Henry Parris showed that within three years the commission had dealt with as many cases as there had been during the period 1854–73, and that by 1883 the total number of cases had risen to 110: Parris, *Government and the Railways*, p. 221.

Challenges to the Legal Process 69

number of dispute-resolution functions, primarily as a mediating body between ship-owners and pilot authorities, and settling disputes between seamen and their masters, and disputes as to elections to local marine boards.[264]

In local rating, new machinery was deemed necessary to carry out the reforms aimed at establishing a uniform mode of rating throughout the country. The task of rating property to the poor rate was left in the hands of the overseers, but their supervision and a power of revision was put in the hands of new Assessment Committees, composed of members of Boards of Guardians, on the basis that they 'would be the least inexperienced body to which that duty could be intrusted', and that with their local knowledge and experience, would 'be as competent and certainly a less expensive tribunal for deciding a question of that nature'.[265] The efficient implementation of the legislation would be promoted by self-interest, as the Board of Guardians consisted of the principal ratepayers and it was in their own interests to make a fair valuation. This pragmatic alliance of government policy and self-interest was used by the government at every opportunity. In relation to copyhold enfranchisement, for example, it had been hoped that as building speculations increased through the building of towns and railways, and builders found they could not sell with a copyhold title, they would be willing to seek enfranchisement under the first voluntary Act.[266] In both relevant knowledge and cheapness the new Assessment Committees improved upon the old method of dispute-resolution. There the only means of redress in the case of an incorrect valuation, itself often brought about by competing local interests, had been by appeal to the justices of the peace in Quarter Sessions, a process attendant with considerable expense and trouble, not least because legal representation was required. There was confidence in Parliament that the new committee was a competent and appropriate body to implement the new legislation effectively. 'The utmost care had

---

[264] 17 & 18 Vict. c. 104. See too the Elementary Education Act 1870 which gave the Education Department extensive judicial powers. It could, for example, hear appeals from decisions as to the extent of the school accommodation required in school districts and hear and determine disputes as to elections to school boards: 33 & 34 Vict. c. 75 ss. 9, 33; Prison Act 1877, 40 & 41 Vict. c. 21 ss. 9, 13, 14.

[265] *Parl. Deb.*, vol. CLXVII, ser. 3, col. 1332, 3 July 1862 (HC) *per* William Barrow.

[266] 'Fifth Report of the Copyhold Commissioners', *HCPP* (1846) (732) xxiv 101.

70   *Legal Foundations of Tribunals in 19th-Century England*

been taken in the framing of the measure', said a government spokesman, 'to provide against litigation and expense.'[267]

In creating these new bodies and in choosing to allocate to them the necessary dispute-resolution functions, the legislature was thus driven by essentially pragmatic motives and objectives. They were the result of a policy of administration rather than one of extra-judicial dispute-resolution springing from any idealistic rationale of comprehensive access to justice, though it was acknowledged that the inaccessibility of the private bill procedure made it almost impossible for poorer parties to uphold their property rights in cases of inclosure. It was, furthermore, politically expedient to create new bodies to administer the law and resolve disputes which arose in the course of it in order to arrive at a structure and process that achieved the various requirements of the reforms. In some instances the requirements overlapped. The need for expert personnel working to efficient procedures was common to both proficient administration and effective dispute-resolution, but the latter was a judicial function requiring legal expertise, a fair and impartial process, and public accessibility. And indeed, in demanding these the legislators and public were articulating what are now regarded as the clear indicia of an accessible legal system, namely an inexpensive, simple, effective, efficient and fair legal process, even if that were not the primary purpose for the establishment of the new bodies. It being evident that the established organs of the legal system were inappropriate, the legislature was freed from judicial conventions to create, by statute, a body that embodied the various qualities peculiar to the implementation of centralising legislation. Its necessary rejection of conventional judicial bodies paradoxically allowed it to endow the new body with those judicial characteristics it required for its own judicial function and which were suited to the overall purpose.

The essential character of these new bodies was reflected not so much in the terms used to describe them – which were generally 'commission' or 'board', terms that signified little more than an official authority of a public nature though did suggest it was not a purely judicial body[268] – but in the almost universal rejection of

---

[267] *Parl. Deb.*, vol. CLXVII, ser. 3, col. 1335, 3 July 1862 (HC) *per* C. P. Villiers.
[268] *Minutes, Railways (Rates and Fares), 1882* q. 1221 *per* J. H. Balfour Browne, barrister.

Challenges to the Legal Process

the appellation 'tribunal'. While that term did not have a clear meaning in law,[269] it was popularly restricted, throughout the late eighteenth and nineteenth centuries, to the courts of judicature and its avoidance suggested that the new bodies were not regarded as substitute courts, but as new creations with different functions. And when in the early years of the twentieth century the term came to be used more widely, it reflected not so much a change in its meaning, but a change in the institution itself. At first the new administrative organs heard and determined the disputes that arose from their own implementation of the regulations and the policy of their parent legislation. But as the structure of government developed in size and complexity, and as the pressures of ideology and material interests played their part, so administrative and judicial functions became more distinct. Routine administrative functions were consigned to the new elements of the executive machine that could now accommodate them, while the discrete dispute-resolution functions tended to remain with the original and increasingly independent body that ultimately became the modern administrative tribunal. Since by then these bodies had developed an expertise in determining these disputes, an adjudication that still required its own special procedures and skills, there was no question of removing it to the regular courts. The term tribunal thus became, and remains today, the appropriate description.

The challenge to the legislators was considerable. It lay in creating an administrative agency with the task of implementing effectively a legislative regime in diverse areas of government activity, but also of exercising judicial functions within that process equally efficiently but without the safeguards inherent in the ancient usage of the regular legal system. After all, unlike the regular courts, new bodies would have no tradition of public confidence in their proceedings. Despite serious criticisms as to procedures and some criticism of individual judges, the various organs of the regular legal system possessed all the in-built safeguards of an expert and ancient profession of high status, where judges had devoted their lives to the study of jurisprudence and the examination of evidence, with established and tested

---

[269] *Per* Fry LJ in *Royal Aquarium and Summer and Winter Garden Society Ltd* v. *Parkinson* [1892] 1 QB 431 at 446.

72   *Legal Foundations of Tribunals in 19th-Century England*

processes, independence and procedures to ensure any mistakes were corrected. The new bodies, on the other hand, satisfying the requirements of simple procedures and specialist knowledge would be comprised of adjudicators who were experts in their specific field of operation but not in law, with untried procedures and extensive discretionary powers. Jurisdiction, procedures, constitution and safeguards all had to be constructed and given coherent and meticulous statutory expression. The demand for informal and inexpensive procedures had to be balanced by sufficient safeguards to ensure acceptable standards of justice. Expert administrators had to possess judicial skills. The juxtaposition of functions raised considerable problems of independence, for a body conceived primarily as an instrument of central government to implement legislation pertaining to the administration of the country and yet with undoubted dispute-resolution functions had to have a demonstrable measure of independence from the executive to gain public confidence. There had to be a balance, however, between an independent machinery to gain public confidence, and sufficient control by the government over its policies. The challenge to the legal system lay in its accommodation of such a body. The resolution of these challenges, whether they were met by the creation of a bespoke tribunal or a ready-made one, the identification of its legal foundations and influences, its overall juridical nature and its place in the legal system are the subject of this book. Judicial functions were entrusted to the new tribunals because existing dispute-resolution techniques were inadequate, and because it was not evident that such functions were judicial in the accepted sense of the term at all. The purpose of this study is to reveal the legal foundations of the modern statutory tribunal, insofar as it is correct to use the term generically as an extra-judicial dispute-resolution body hearing and determining appeals against decisions of an administrative nature. The foundations sought are those in substantive law, in legal institutions and legal process; the search is for the doctrinal basis of the modern administrative tribunal.

2

THE IDEOLOGICAL AND THEORETICAL CONTEXT

The withholding from the regular courts of law of the dispute-resolution duties associated with the administration of the new reforming legislation of the early Victorian period was due to the various inadequacies of those bodies to take on novel and challenging functions. It was not, however, the most radical aspect of the legislation. The real novelty lay in the character of the legislation itself as interventionist, centralist and increasingly collective. It was interventionist in that it was founded on the principle of the state regulation of activities that had hitherto been regarded as private. It was centralist in that both in substance and in its machinery of implementation, including the embedded duty to hear and determine disputes arising in the course of its execution, it imported the control of the central government in Whitehall rather than in local government. This was either directly through an organ or agency of the executive based in London or through its own subordinate officers in the provinces. Finally it was collectivist in that it placed the wider good of the community above the interests of the individual.[1]

While it could correctly be stated that in 1900 government interfered hardly at all in the way people ran their daily lives, that assertion was relative: compared with the present day it was undoubtedly true, but compared with 1800 it was undoubtedly not.[2] Scholars now agree that the interventionist state was no twentieth-century phenomenon, but was formed in more than

---

[1] See generally W. R. Cornish and G. de N. Clark, *Law and Society in England 1750–1950* (London: Sweet and Maxwell, 1989), pp. 60–3.
[2] See generally A. T. Carter, 'Changes in the Constitution', in Council of Legal Education (eds.), *A Century of Law Reform* (London: Macmillan & Co. Ltd, 1901), pp. 117–26.

74 Legal Foundations of Tribunals in 19th-Century England

mere outline at a considerably earlier date.[3] From a largely passive role in maintaining the status quo, it has been seen that the state became an active force in reforming legislation and that such intervention was necessary because of the scale of the various challenges facing the early Victorians.[4] Only state intervention and central direction could achieve a system of continuous and uniform control, with clear and unquestionable authority and the necessary coercion and checks, and yet one which was both humane and efficient.[5] Without it, the implementation of laws that were undeniably necessary would inevitably fail. Accordingly the reforming legislation laid down one code for uniform application, and policy was developed by the commission or board created to implement it. The new poor law, the legislation relating to factories, public health and to railways, laid down regulations which were to apply uniformly and nationally with no local variation in substance. The land rights legislation laid down provisions for the national restructuring of rights in tithes and copyholds according to prescribed formulae. Lord John Russell, whose tithe bill eventually became law, wanted a single formula for commutation throughout the whole country, administered by one centrally appointed body of bureaucrats.[6] National taxation, such as the land tax, the assessed taxes and the income tax, was by its very nature an aspect of central government and its fundamental character as such was well established.

The lack of any real alternative within the existing government structure to administer the legislation and the absence of viable legal options to undertake the integral dispute-resolution function, resulted in the creation of those various central agencies

---

[3] See Michael Hill, *The State, Administration and the Individual* (London: Fontana/Collins, 1976), pp. 23–9; J. B. Brebner, 'Laissez Faire and State Intervention in Nineteenth Century Britain' (1948) 8 *Journal of Economic History Supplement* 59; M. W. Thomas, 'The Origins of Administrative Centralisation' (1950) 3 *Current Legal Problems* 214; Sir C. T. Carr, *Concerning English Administrative Law* (London: Oxford University Press, 1941), p. 8; Carol Harlow and Richard Rawlings, *Law and Administration*, 2nd edition (London: Butterworths, 1997), Chapter 1.

[4] Historians agree that state intervention was above all the result of industrialisation: David Roberts, *Victorian Origins of the British Welfare State*, reprint of Yale University Press edition 1960 (Hamden, CT: Archon Books, 1969), pp. 316–17; Brebner, 'Laissez Faire and State Intervention', 59.

[5] Thomas, 'Administrative Centralisation', 217–18.

[6] *Parl. Deb.*, vol. XXXIII, ser. 3, col. 882, 12 May 1836 (HC).

The Ideological and Theoretical Context 75

some of which, one hundred years later, were commonly called administrative tribunals. Though in their composition they varied in their degree of independence from the government,[7] their function was to exercise central executive control over the local implementation of the new legislation. They had to act under policy direction from Whitehall, and had to make periodical reports to the Secretary of State. In the case of inclosure, the only centralising feature was that of machinery, for that legislation did no more than provide a process for inclosure, but a central one which superseded the old machinery of inclosure by bodies of local commissioners.[8] And while the machinery of taxation was of all the implementing bodies the most local and independent, it did not escape central control in the shape of the government surveyor. All these bodies were, therefore, both the machinery and the expression of state interventionism and centralism.

This interventionist, centralist and collectivist legislation had not only a practical but also an intellectual provenance, and its characteristics were of considerable ideological significance. There were strong tensions between the legislation and traditional orthodox values.[9] The political and popular consensus throughout most of the nineteenth century was at best one of reluctant acceptance through absolute necessity with a slow and careful approach to reform, at worst one of intense dislike and suspicion. The English did not want centralised state intervention or the machinery that went with it. As *The Times* observed in 1893,

In all regions of life the area of freedom is being contracted. Everywhere appears an inclination to take out of people's hands the management of their own affairs. Everywhere the realm of the inspector and the commissioner and the *ex officio* tyrant of the vestry is widening.[10]

Their distrust stemmed from their adherence to certain dominant values and ideas that guided economic and social behaviour: to individualism, laissez-faire, localism and vested proprietary and professional interests. All these were eroded by the new legislation

---

[7] Some were composed of paid civil servants, some of independent or semi-independent members.

[8] Indeed the powers of the Inclosure Commissioners ultimately passed to the Board of Agriculture.

[9] Roberts, *Victorian Origins*, pp. 315–26.

[10] 'The Growth of Officialism', *The Times*, 5 April 1893, p. 3 col. d. See too 'Counterblast against Officialism', *The Times*, 1 June 1895, p. 11 col. e.

76   Legal Foundations of Tribunals in 19th-Century England

and the organs it spawned. The Victorians were committed to laissez-faire and loyal to local autonomy, but the ideological debate was fought against a background of the detailed exposure of the appalling social problems that had emerged from increased industrialisation, population and urbanisation. As humanitarians, Christians and patriots, their consciences and common compassion did not allow them to ignore the social and economic problems of the age once they had been revealed. From their moral and humanitarian perspective the Evangelicals, men such as William Wilberforce and Lord Shaftesbury, called passionately upon the government to address the evils which they found unacceptable. Ideological boundaries were fluid in the nineteenth century and no single political ideology promoted state interventionism as such,[11] though it was clear to most politicians that the evils could be addressed only through central government. The Whigs, Liberals and Tories were equally, though less forcefully, united in a humanitarian and orthodox Christian desire to achieve the same ends and adopted broadly similar approaches to the introduction of interventionist legislation.[12] Interventionism undermined the traditional values of the Tories, and while the Whigs were of a reforming tendency, they lacked the collective will to press through a radical programme of reform and tended to prefer compromise. The radical reformer Joseph Cowen supported the Bankruptcy Bill of 1883 which put the bankruptcy process into the hands of Official Receivers of the Board of Trade,[13] though he did so with considerable misgiving, since it was in his view yet another example of a rapidly growing system of central government invading every aspect of life, even of private affairs. He feared that any advantage arising from the reform could be outweighed by the disadvantages arising from the rapid and apparently unending 'net-work of officialism which was

[11] For an excellent analysis of the ideological background to the early Victorian administrative state, see Roberts, *Victorian Origins*, pp. 22–34, 95–104; William C. Lubenow, *The Politics of Government Growth* (Newton Abbot: David and Charles, 1971), pp. 23–5 and the authorities there cited.

[12] For politics of the railway bills of the 1880s see Geoffrey Alderman, *The Railway Interest* (Leicester: Leicester University Press, 1973), pp. 110 ff.

[13] Bankruptcy Act 1883, 46 & 47 Vict. c. 52. For the duties of the Official Receivers in bankruptcy see *Parl. Deb.*, vol. CCLXXVII, ser. 3, cols. 822–3, 19 March 1883 (HC); Bankruptcy Act 1883, 46 & 47 Vict. c. 52 ss. 66–70.

The Ideological and Theoretical Context

being thrown over the doings of private life'.[14] He condemned the Liberal party for having abandoned its original stance of resistance to the meddling of the state and accused it of having become 'the special supporter of officialism and centralization'.[15] His concern, and that of traditional Liberals, was that it would have the long-term effect of 'emasculating and enervating the population', rendering it inflexible.[16] He believed state intervention was justifiable only when human life was at stake, as in railways, mines or shipping, or when any section of the public was too weak to protect itself. It was beyond the remit of good government, he said, to 'protect grown men from the consequences of their own folly and carelessness'.[17] The Whigs and Liberals tended to be inconsistent in their approach to state intervention. So, for example, Edward Cardwell told the Commons in the debate on the merchant marine that 'the Government desire nothing so little as centralisation in this matter',[18] and yet not only was he responsible for the creation of a merchant marine department, he was the President of the Board of Trade who promoted, though unsuccessfully in 1854, the creation of a statutory tribunal for the railways.

This ideological ambivalence is characteristic of attitudes to state intervention. The early Victorians in general did not seek it, but in some instances they welcomed it and in others they opposed it vehemently. Furthermore, the complexity of the interrelationship of ideologies and politics, and the range of opinion, meant that individuals and parties did not hold consistent views on all issues that involved such central interference. It was not uncommon for one individual to hold differing views as to state intervention depending on its sphere of operation. Nassau Senior, for example, approved of the Poor Law Amendment Act 1834 but opposed the factory legislation. Victorian attitudes to legislative provision generally was characterised by a mixture of ideology and pragmatism;[19] legislation, it was said, should be tested 'by the

---

[14] *Parl. Deb.*, vol. CCLXXVII, ser. 3, col. 854, 19 March 1883 (HC).
[15] *Ibid.*, col. 857. [16] *Ibid.* [17] *Ibid.*
[18] *Ibid.*, vol. CXXIV, ser. 3, col. 1247, 7 March 1853 (HC).
[19] See generally Arthur J. Taylor, *Laissez-faire and State Intervention in Nineteenth-century Britain*, Studies in Economic History (London: Macmillan, 1972); Derek Fraser, *The Evolution of the British Welfare State* (London: Macmillan, 1973), pp. 91–114.

78   *Legal Foundations of Tribunals in 19th-Century England*

wants and necessities of the age ... by what was morally right and just, and what was expedient and practicable under the circumstances of the case'.[20] Nevertheless, in challenging the accepted ideology of the eighteenth century, it forced a reappraisal of the philosophical infrastructure to the relationship between the state and the individual.[21]

Intervention of the kind seen in the regulatory legislation of the 1830s and 1840s comprehensively breached John Locke's conception of the legitimate function of the state being limited to ensuring the individual rights of property, person and freedom. The philosophy of individualism, the belief that individual rights and freedoms should form the basis of society, was significant to the Victorians, and it underlay the importance they attached to self-help and to the responsibility of the individual to look after himself and his family. It was a characteristic widely recognised by contemporaries that the English guarded their individual freedoms jealously, particularly in the early years of the nineteenth century when the French revolution was still fresh in the popular and parliamentary mind. This independence was expressed in relation to numerous issues in the eighteenth and early nineteenth centuries, not least in the debate surrounding the introduction of the income tax in 1799. There the feature that gave rise to most resentment was not even the obligation to pay a new tax, but the invasion of individual privacy inherent in the duty to disclose personal financial matters to central government.[22] They believed in individualism but the necessity was for collectivism.

It was a natural concomitant of the importance attached to individual rights that the interference of central government in areas generally perceived to be the province of the private individual would be deeply felt. As a Tory magazine observed in 1836 in relation to the registration of births bill, 'there is nothing which renders a law so inoperative and a government so odious, as unnecessary and vexatious interference in matters of a private and

---

[20] *Parl. Deb.*, vol. CXCV, ser. 3, cols. 157–8, 5 April 1869 (HC), in relation to the Bankruptcy Bill of 1869.

[21] For the influence of ideas in the Victorian legal system, see Cornish and Clark, *Law and Society*, pp. 60–74.

[22] See C. Stebbings, 'The Budget of 1798: Legislative Provision for Secrecy in Income Taxation' (1998) *British Tax Review* 651.

The Ideological and Theoretical Context 79

domestic nature'.[23] Central control of such activity was perceived as tyrannical, as an undermining of fundamental freedoms and un-English. It was as such almost universally resented. Ideological objections were expressed loudly and consistently throughout the nineteenth century, most strongly by the Dissenters,[24] and the literature was prodigious. Of the earlier centralising measures, the poor law of 1834 and the public health legislation provoked the most vociferous objections,[25] though all instances of state intervention and centralisation during the whole of the nineteenth century gave rise to consistent and widespread opposition. It was not just the substance, but also the machinery of central state intervention that was resented. The various implementing agencies were almost all, at some point in their existence, referred to as 'star chambers', reflecting the public perception of such bodies as oppressive, tyrannical and unconstitutional. While ideological objections were valid and potent, in many cases those sections of the public who voiced such opinions about the new tribunals had a material interest in their operation that had been undermined, and this to some extent coloured their opinions.

The desire for uniformity was inherent in the new regulatory legislation, a feature that undermined the individual. In 1843 *The Times* observed that the legislation for the commutation of tithes involved 'the substitution of a centralizing, uniform, and negative machinery for the living principle which alone formed the ground for the original introduction of any law upon the subject, and which, therefore, and which alone, is now, or at any other time, capable of supporting it'. 'The modern system', it said, 'has simply no principle at all.' In this instance the objection was to making payments according to arbitrary statutory rules that failed to consider the situation of the individual – an argument which later came to be a common criticism of bureaucracy. 'We are convinced', it concluded, 'that the general practice of converting everything throughout the country into a level and uniform system, with a central commission at its head, is one which its oppressive and grievous injustice must sooner or later bring to

---

[23] (1836) 57 *Quarterly Review* 253.

[24] See for example the Dissenters' objection to government interference with education, Roberts, *Victorian Origins*, pp. 68–70, 260–4.

[25] For the influence of individualism in prison reform and the administration of the poor law, see *ibid.*, pp. 172–4 and 180–2.

80 *Legal Foundations of Tribunals in 19th-Century England*

that condemnation which its intrinsic perversity and impolicy so richly deserve.' Such legislation could be viewed only with suspicion, as partaking of 'this fashionable but mischievous quackery'.[26]

One aspect of the philosophy of individualism was the doctrine of laissez-faire in which the majority of Victorians believed. The influence of the doctrine, promulgated by classical economists such as Adam Smith, Ricardo and Malthus, was at its height in the 1830s at the very time centralising legislation was being enacted. It succeeded paternalistic mercantilism as the dominant ideology from the end of the eighteenth century, and was based on principles of non- or minimal interference by the state, a free market economy and the importance of self-interest.[27] It was primarily an economic doctrine, and as such its effects were particularly felt in those areas of commercial activity, notably railways. Railway history is dominated by the struggle between free enterprise and public control. The general view, shaped by laissez-faire ideology, was that the most effective way of regulating commercial affairs was by competition, and the universal expectation had been that this would be so in the case of railways. There was a clear reluctance to interfere with the early railway undertakings in which so much capital had been invested and so Parliament approached with great caution.[28] The problem was that it was necessary for the safety of the public to prohibit competition on the lines, but that tended to monopoly, and in the early days of the railways free competition on individual lines was not only permitted but insisted upon. Any person could run his engines and carriages on any line subject to the payment of a toll to the railway company that owned the line. Any owner of land adjoining a railway could construct branch lines to connect with the railway and could use the railway free of tolls. As the railway network grew at a rapid rate, it was clear that such a policy was impractical and could not be maintained if the public safety were to be ensured. Accordingly Parliament accepted that the railway

---

[26] *The Times*, 29 November 1843, p. 4 cols. b–c.

[27] For a discussion of the problems of definition and chronology, see Taylor, *Laissez-faire and State Intervention*, pp. 11–12 and 50–2. See too Fraser, *British Welfare State*, Chapter 5.

[28] 'Second Report from the Select Committee on Railways', *HCPP* (1839) (517) x 127 at p. 129.

The Ideological and Theoretical Context 81

companies should have a monopoly of conveying passengers. Similarly freedom of competition resulted in extensive railway amalgamations and ultimately in monopoly. Laissez-faire had failed; free competition had not secured a proper service at a fair price and neither had self-interest functioned in the railway context as it did in other commercial fields.[29] Though ideologically reluctant, Sir Robert Peel's government was forced to act in the public interest and to permit a degree of central interference with the railways. The legislative regulation of railways was frequently condemned as inhibiting freedom of action,[30] but the influence of laissez-faire was sufficiently strong not only to ensure vigorous debate on all railway regulation proposals, but also ultimately to keep railway enterprise firmly in private hands. It dominated the Royal Commission in 1865, but the Railway Commission created in 1873 was in clear though relatively mild opposition to that philosophy, largely due to changing public opinion as to the standards and services they demanded of railway enterprise.[31] From the 1880s, partly as a result of the growth of the party system in Parliament which kept the hitherto powerful railway interest in check,[32] state intervention, and accordingly an abandoning of laissez-faire principles, in railway matters grew significantly from mere supervision to intensive regulation and control,[33] stopping short of management until well into the following century.[34]

Laissez-faire proved equally unsatisfactory in taxation matters. The fiscal theories of Adam Smith and his opposition to taxation could not serve the needs of the new dynamic commercial society, and when governments adhered to them, as the Whigs did in the early years of the nineteenth century by granting widespread remissions of indirect taxation, the outcome was a near catastrophic deficit.[35] Despite its origins as an economic doctrine, it was given considerably wider scope by some adherents to

---

[29] *Report, Railway Amalgamation, 1872* pp. 29–30.
[30] *Parl. Deb.*, vol. CCCXII, ser. 3, col. 146, 14 March 1887 (HL) *per* Lord Brabourne.
[31] See Alderman, *Railway Interest*, pp. 31–2.
[32] See Henry Parris, *Government and the Railways in Nineteenth Century Britain* (London: Routledge and Kegan Paul, 1965), p. 214.
[33] See generally Alderman, *Railway Interest*, pp. 110–12, 153, 224–5.
[34] The British railway network was nationalised in 1948.
[35] See B. E. V. Sabine, *A Short History of Taxation* (London: Butterworths, 1980), pp. 120–1.

82 *Legal Foundations of Tribunals in 19th-Century England*

encompass all government activity including social issues,[36] and certainly the prevailing notion at the beginning of Victoria's reign was that social welfare could best be promoted by private enterprise. In areas of essentially social policy, it was the fundamental values underlying laissez-faire that inspired the rhetoric against state intervention. This opposition to state intervention as such was particularly clear in the case of the public health and educational reforms, and in these purely social issues, the principal cause for opposition was the undermining of local interests and authority. Traditional laissez-faire doctrine did not, however, exclude government intervention altogether, for even Adam Smith allowed for public works and institutions which no individual could undertake. Nassau Senior, a leading laissez-faire economist,[37] nevertheless ultimately believed that

[t]he only rational foundation of government ... is expediency – the general benefit of the community. It is the duty of a Government to do whatever is conducive to the welfare of the governed ... [T]he most fatal of all errors would be the general admission that a Government has no right to interfere for any purpose except the purpose of affording protection.[38]

Indeed, he became instrumental in the reform of the poor law to provide a centralised administration for poor relief, and was appointed a Poor Law Commissioner.

John Stuart Mill,[39] despite his clear adherence to the fundamental doctrine of laissez-faire, addressed the role of government more directly. He based his argument against government interference on the maxim that individuals were the best judges of their own interests and accordingly wanted to keep state intervention in the lives of individuals to a minimum. 'Letting alone, in short, should be the general practice: every departure from it, unless required by some great good, is a certain evil.'[40] However, he

---

[36] Taylor identifies 'extremes of definition', and observes that 'one man's *laissez-faire* is another man's intervention', Taylor, *Laissez-faire and State Intervention*, pp. 11–12.

[37] He was professor of political economy at Oxford.

[38] Quoted from Nassau Senior's *Lectures* by Marian Bowley, *Nassau Senior and Classical Economics* (London: George Allen and Unwin Ltd, 1937), p. 265.

[39] Jose Harris, 'John Stuart Mill (1806–73)', in *Oxford Dictionary of National Biography* (Oxford: Oxford University Press, 2004), vol. XXXVIII.

[40] John Stuart Mill, *Principles of Political Economy*, People's Edition (London: Longmans, Green and Co., 1891), Chapter 11, s. 7, p. 573.

The Ideological and Theoretical Context 83

believed that certain exceptions were justifiable, on the grounds that they were essential to a civilised state and that the benefits to society as a whole would be immense, and in this he included the education of the people, the care of the incapable and the young, the relief of the poor, the carrying out of certain public works, factory legislation and colonisation.[41] The classical economists, therefore, were not committed to laissez-faire to the extent of a complete rejection of state intervention, though it did have a restraining influence and most regarded state intervention as permissible only on the grounds of necessity, and to be strictly circumscribed by it, requiring explicit justification in each instance. All the measures addressing the problems arising from the industrial expansion of the late eighteenth and early nineteenth centuries were breaches of the doctrine of laissez-faire, the first to be identified as such being the initial statutory regulation of factories, namely the Health and Morals of Apprentices Act 1802.[42] The doctrine, however, significantly limited its scope by insisting on state intervention with individuals' working hours only on the basis of an overriding social need. Similarly with the new poor law of 1834, where reformers strove to achieve the minimum interference with a free market economy through the establishment of the workhouse test and principle of less eligibility.

The doctrine's precise influence on and relationship with state intervention have been subject to profound and scholarly debate.[43] Though strictly an ideal, an aspiration, and despite its original promoters allowing some flexibility in it in terms of state intervention, it broadly had the effect of strengthening the conventional opposition to centralising legislation and limiting its scope. It resulted primarily in a reluctance by government to intrude into the private affairs of individuals, and explains the vehement opposition to legislative measures which undermined that policy.[44] Implicit in it, therefore, was an exclusion of

---

[41] *Ibid.*, Chapter 11, ss. 8–16, pp. 575–91. This view was not shared by hard-line adherents of laissez-faire.

[42] 42 Geo. III c. 73. It was identified as 'the first breach made in the bastions of *laissez-faire*' by Thomas, 'Administrative Centralisation', 215.

[43] See generally P. P. Craig, *Administrative Law*, 5th edition (London: Sweet and Maxwell, 2003), pp. 56–8; Brebner, 'Laissez Faire and State Intervention', 59; Taylor, *Laissez-faire and State Intervention*; Henry Parris, *Constitutional Bureaucracy* (London: George Allen and Unwin Ltd, 1969), pp. 268–71.

[44] For example, income tax.

84 Legal Foundations of Tribunals in 19th-Century England

centralised government and an accompanying bureaucracy. The popular view of laissez-faire was less sophisticated and most did not look beyond its fundamental tenet of non-interference. It was vigorously promoted by the *Westminster Review* and the influential *Economist*,[45] among others, and called for resistance to government interference and vigilance over any infringement of property rights. *The Economist* included commissions in its condemnation of 'engrossing centralisation'.[46] There were undoubtedly tensions between the pervasive ideology of laissez-faire and the humanitarian insistence that social evils had to be addressed and could only be effectively dealt with by state intervention.

The role of the school of thought deriving from Jeremy Bentham[47] with its diverse views, emphases and internal tensions, variously known as Benthamism, Utilitarianism or Philosophic Radicalism,[48] has been vigorously debated by scholars for many years.[49] One view is that its influence was negligible, another is that it was a dominant force, and yet again that its impact is impossible of ascertainment. Professor A. V. Dicey, who himself preferred individualism to collectivism, famously characterised the period 1825 to 1870 as the great age of 'Benthamism or individualism',[50] believed that Bentham's influence in law reform was 'potent',[51] and stated that '*laissez-faire* ... was practically the most vital part of Bentham's legislative doctrine'.[52] Indeed Bentham himself adhered to the personal freedom of the individual and the

---

[45] From its foundation in 1843 until 1859.

[46] *The Economist*, 10 July 1847, p. 780 (vol. 5).

[47] F. Rosen, 'Jeremy Bentham (1748–1832)', in *National Biography*, vol. V.

[48] See generally John Plamenatz, *The English Utilitarians*, 2nd edition (Oxford: Blackwell, 1958).

[49] Oliver MacDonagh, 'The Nineteenth Century Revolution in Government: A Reappraisal' (1958) 1 *Historical Journal* 1 at 52. See too Henry Parris, 'The Nineteenth Century Revolution in Government: A Reappraisal Reappraised' (1960) 3 *Historical Journal* 1 at 17; Lubenow, *Government Growth*; Fraser, *British Welfare State*, Chapter 5; Roberts, *Victorian Origins*, pp. 29 ff.; Taylor, *Laissez-faire and State Intervention*, pp. 32–8; Jeremy Bentham, 'A Fragment on Government' (1776) and 'An Introduction to the Principles of Morals and Legislation' (1789), in Wilfrid Harrison (ed.), *A Fragment on Government and An Introduction to the Principles of Morals and Legislation* (Oxford: Blackwell, 1948).

[50] A. V. Dicey, *Lectures on the Relation between Law and Public Opinion in England during the Nineteenth Century*, 2nd edition (London: Macmillan and Co., 1914), p. 63 and Lecture VI.

[51] *Ibid.*, p. 126.   [52] *Ibid.*, p. 147.

The Ideological and Theoretical Context 85

principles of laissez-faire and disliked the new administrative bodies created by government. He was highly critical of boards[53] and was essentially opposed to state intervention. Like the classical economists, however, his view of laissez-faire comprised a number of necessary exceptions that allowed for state intervention if that were the means whereby his utilitarian objective of the greatest happiness of the greatest number could be achieved. He thus also promoted some collective ideas.

Bentham and his followers looked to the efficiency and effectiveness of laws and institutions. This inevitably led to their support of centralisation, for in many instances only central agencies could ensure the reform, control, uniformity and efficiency they demanded. Certainly Bentham's disciples, promoting the pragmatic and rational philosophy of Utilitarianism, saw the limitations of laissez-faire,[54] and, though individualists,[55] appreciated the value and indeed the necessity of the close involvement of a strong and efficient central government in the reforms of the first half of the nineteenth century. In the context of any state intervention being kept to an absolute minimum necessary to achieve their aims, they put forward their arguments in a rational, practical and convincing way, and, along with the Evangelicals, have been identified as the 'creative minority' in the growth of the administrative state.[56] John Stuart Mill developed Bentham's original philosophy and accepted the need for centralised state intervention, but feared the consequent increase in power of government agencies. In *On Liberty* in 1859, he reaffirmed though circumscribed the principle of individual liberty. Edwin

---

[53] John Bowring (ed.), *The Works of Jeremy Bentham*, 11 vols. (Edinburgh: William Tait, 1843), vol. IX, pp. 214–19. See too L. J. Hume, *Bentham and Bureaucracy* (Cambridge: Cambridge University Press, 1981), pp. 136–7.

[54] See Fraser, *British Welfare State*, p. 94 on John Stuart Mill.

[55] The extent to which Jeremy Bentham was a collectivist, and the complexities and contradictions of ideologies, is analysed by Brebner, 'Laissez Faire and State Intervention', 59; see too MacDonagh, 'Nineteenth Century Revolution', 52; J. D. Chambers, *The Workshop of the World*, 2nd edition (Oxford: Oxford University Press, 1968), pp. 130–9; Thomas, 'Administrative Centralisation', 214. For the influence of Bentham in the field of law reform see Michael Lobban, *The Common Law and English Jurisprudence 1760–1850* (Oxford: Clarendon Press, 1991), pp. 185–9.

[56] See Roberts, *Victorian Origins*, p. 318; Thomas says of the Benthamites that 'the centralisation of authority was inherent in their philosophy of government': Thomas, 'Administrative Centralisation', 222.

86 *Legal Foundations of Tribunals in 19th-Century England*

Chadwick, a lawyer who was Bentham's private secretary and his ideological disciple, was instrumental in the promotion and organisation of the major centralising reforms in relation to factories, the poor law and public health. His methods were of the essence of Benthamism, comprising thorough investigation, empirical analysis, report, and centralising reform supported by inspection.[57] He was an outstanding and perceptive administrator who saw the need for state intervention, provided it as a solution to the pressing needs of his time, but believed it should be strictly delimited and focused on the task in hand.[58] Like all Benthamites he did not believe in sweeping centralisation for its own sake, but as a tool to be selectively and carefully though strongly employed when circumstances proved that it was essential. His personal contribution to the welfare reforms of the early Victorian period was immense, and constituted the foundation of the English administrative state.

Benthamite influence was equally strong in the Tory factory legislation of 1833 and in the Whig legislation for poor relief in 1834 and public health in 1848. The fundamental tenet of Utilitarianism was unmistakably reflected in measures such as the Inclosure Act 1845, and indeed in all the legislation restructuring the land rights in tithes, copyholds and common land. These reforms were Benthamite in character in that they promoted a greater freedom of dealing with real property and an inexpensive and efficient enforcement of rights, and any reallocation of real property rights to achieve those ends was in sympathy with this ideology. Nevertheless the inclosure measure in particular, centralist in policy and machinery,[59] gave rise to vociferous ideological criticism in Parliament, primarily from the radical party, which included such prominent Benthamites as Joseph Hume. There was no blanket acceptance of centralising legislation; it was minutely scrutinised and justified even by those disposed to reform. In the case of the Inclosure Act 1845 the distance between the government and the constitution of the implementing body was perceived as too close. It provided that the presiding Inclosure Commissioner was to be the Chief

---

[57] See generally Chambers, *Workshop of the World*, pp. 130–45.
[58] See Roberts, *Victorian Origins*, pp. 31–2.
[59] See *Report, Commons' Inclosure, 1844*.

The Ideological and Theoretical Context 87

Commissioner for Woods and Forests.[60] In that capacity his duty was to administer the landed property of the Crown, and so he would be interested in the matters he would have to decide upon in the matter of inclosure of commons. Charles Buller, a Liberal and a Radical Reformer, said that the great objection was that such extensive powers should be placed in the hands of a government body forming part of the administration of the day.[61] To entrust to such a body the power to decide whether millions of acres of commons and waste lands should be inclosed or not was to give the government a great power over the landed property of the country and over people who were not landholders. 'Was it constitutional', he said, 'that such power should be placed in the hands of the minister of the day, who was obliged to depend for the tenure of his office on the votes of a majority of that House?'[62] There was a tension between the permanency of landed property and the transience of political tenure. The Tithe Commissioners, who had been suggested in earlier inclosure bills to be suited to taking on the task of implementing a general inclosure legislative regime, were not open to such criticism, as they were not removable on a change of government and so were not as overtly susceptible to political bias, though of course they were just as much an organ of central government. Joseph Hume, the leader of the Radicals, also objected to the composition of the commission, but was also critical of the measure in the extent to which it protected the poor. He believed the report of the Select Committee on Commons' Inclosure in 1844 had been one-sided in favouring the landed proprietors, and had left the poor commoners unconsidered.[63] Another criticism of having a minister of the Crown (the Commissioner of Woods and Forests) as chairman of the Inclosure Commissioners was that it would undermine ministerial responsibility. Thomas Wakley,[64] another Radical Reformer, doubted whether any real responsibility would attach to the minister in that capacity, and equally the government could exert such influence as it wished to ensure its chosen measures

---

[60] 8 & 9 Vict. c. 118 s. 1.
[61] *Parl. Deb.*, vol. LXXXII, ser. 3, cols. 32–3, 4 July 1845 (HC).
[62] *Ibid.*, col. 33.   [63] *Ibid.*, cols. 23–4.
[64] W. F. Bynum, 'Thomas Wakley (1795–1862)' in *National Biography*, vol. LVI. Wakley was a medical journalist, politician, founder of *The Lancet* and Radical Reformer.

88 *Legal Foundations of Tribunals in 19th-Century England*

were passed, while the minister would hide behind the body of commissioners and deny that it was his individual act.[65] Certainly in relation to the enfranchisement of copyhold, it was accepted that the tenure had some advantages, but only to the individual and not to the public at large, suggesting that a private benefit was to be sacrificed to the public good. The passage of the land rights legislation through Parliament reveals the close scrutiny to which all such legislation was subjected even by politicians of a reforming and Benthamite tendency, ever vigilant to guard against an oppressive state and yet pragmatic in reform. Indeed, the predominance of ideology or pragmatism in any given instance determined contemporary attitudes to state intervention. With the Utilitarians' critical and demanding approach to established institutions allied to their acceptance of central state intervention in appropriate circumstances, they were not opposed on ideological grounds to the giving of dispute-resolution functions to the new ad hoc organs of government.

When the traditional consciousness of individual rights and duties was intensified by the philosophy of self-interest inherent in laissez-faire, the outcome was a positive cultural promotion of self-help and one that furthermore had a strong religious and moral dimension. Both John Stuart Mill's *On Liberty* and Samuel Smiles' *Self-Help* were published in 1859, and reflected the prevailing culture of the family and the public good, of the responsibility of the individual and of thrift and self-reliance. This concept of self-help was a central tenet of Victorian moral, religious, social and economic life. It constituted the means whereby an individual earned his place in, and made his contribution to, the society in which he lived and worked, and as such was not just a material duty, but a moral one. State intervention ran contrary to this, and, reinforced by the ethos of competition in Charles Darwin's *Origin of Species*, also published in 1859, gave rise to an inherent popular objection, particularly in business circles, to the interference of the state in private affairs. It was widely feared that the consequences of state intervention were dangerous in that it could teach men 'to rely for protection in their commercial dealings not on their own prudence, but on the watchfulness of a

---

[65] *Parl. Deb.*, vol. LXXXII, ser. 3, col. 42, 4 July 1845 (HC).

The Ideological and Theoretical Context 89

paternal Government'.[66] Men should 'mind their own business'.[67] In the debate on the companies winding-up bill in 1890 it was maintained that 'the object of wise statesmanship ought always to be to cultivate principles of self-dependence, and cultivate principles of self-reliance, and not to teach the people to trust to the management of the Government'.[68]

In addition to the powerful undermining influence of individualism and laissez-faire, that of localism was immensely strong.[69] The historic emphasis on local self-government, whose institutions were perceived as enshrining the liberties of the English people, was threatened by the growth of a centralised administration. It was particularly important to the Tories who consistently argued for the retention of local control. After all, it was generally the Tories who occupied those very local offices that were being undermined, notably the justices of the peace. For some opponents of state intervention, the undermining of local autonomy was the essential issue. Joshua Toulmin Smith,[70] who founded the Anti-Centralisation Union in 1854, was totally opposed to all government by commission. For him government was either local self-government or centralised control and they sat at opposite extremes; the first was good, the second comprehensively evil.[71] He called centralisation 'mere charlatan legislative experiments', and 'a miserable but mischievous abortion'.[72] This practical and emotional attachment to traditional local institutions was sufficiently strong to shape many of the administrative reforms in the first half of the nineteenth century. In the early years of regulatory legislation, it was usual for reform to be approached initially on a local basis. For example at the inception of the railway network the problems were treated as local issues, until it was realised that this approach was unrealistic and ineffective for what was clearly

---

[66] Edward Stanhope (Conservative) in *ibid.*, vol. CCLXXVII, ser. 3, col. 843, 19 March 1883 (HC).

[67] *Ibid.*, vol. CXCV, ser. 3, col. 162, 5 April 1869 (HC).

[68] *Ibid.*, vol. CCCXLVI, ser. 3, col. 844, 4 July 1890 (HC).

[69] See Fraser, *British Welfare State*, p. 109.

[70] L. T. Smith rev. H. C. G. Matthew, 'Joshua Toulmin Smith (1816–69)', in *National Biography*, vol. LI.

[71] Lubenow, *Government Growth*, pp. 89–95. See Joshua Toulmin Smith, *Government by Commissions, Illegal and Pernicious* (London: S. Sweet, 1849).

[72] Joshua Toulmin Smith, *Centralization or Representation? A Letter to the Metropolitan Sanatory Commissioners*, 2nd edition (London: S. Sweet, 1848), pp. v, viii.

90   *Legal Foundations of Tribunals in 19th-Century England*

coming to be a national problem. It was not surprising that the Tory Peel should retain justices of the peace as the basis for his fiscal tribunal to implement the restored income tax. The Poor Law Amendment Act 1834 retained local Guardians of the Poor but created a central and independent Poor Law Commission to supervise them and establish unions of parishes. Compromises between state intervention and local control gave some reforms a particular, and not always successful, character. In public health, local opposition was such that it prevented effective centralisation.[73] Many reforms were reduced to a matter of mere inspection by central government of local bodies, with local bodies enjoying considerable autonomy. When Viscount Morpeth brought in the public health bill in 1848 he said that central control was to 'provide indispensable preliminaries, ... suggest useful methods, ... check manifest abuses, but ... leave the execution and detail of the requisite proceedings to local agency and effort'.[74]

This was also the case with the poor law, but the degree of central control in fact increased invidiously throughout the century through the domination of full-time expert officials and the increased subjugation of the Guardians, just as the surveyor gradually increased in dominance over the General Commissioners of Income Tax in the fiscal sphere. Broadly, however, the outcome was an institution that combined central control and local administration, and the fiscal, land rights and social welfare commissions of the early nineteenth century all reflected that essential nature. Indeed, it has been argued that the weight of localism triumphed in that it limited central state intervention by keeping a significant degree of power in local agencies.[75]

The deep attachment felt by the majority of the English to their local institutions was one aspect of the value they put on tradition. Another was the veneration of the Common Law. This was the ideology of the eighteenth century, epitomised by Sir William Blackstone in his *Commentaries on the Laws of England* published between 1765 and 1769. The Common Law was seen as a considered and practical body of law constructed over many generations by learned judges on the basis of human experience and with

---

[73] Fraser, *British Welfare State*, pp. 64–7, 108–10.
[74] *Parl. Deb.*, vol. XCVI, ser. 3, col. 389, 10 February 1848 (HC).
[75] Lubenow, *Government Growth*, pp. 180–1, and see too pp. 30–68. See Taylor, *Laissez-faire and State Intervention*, pp. 55–9.

The Ideological and Theoretical Context 91

the implicit assent of the people. It was coherent, familiar and understandable. State intervention was based entirely on statute law. There was no tradition of legislation, and it was a type of lawmaking which was still relatively unknown. It was perceived as an arbitrary form of law, which did not fully consider legal principles and which imposed uniformity with no consideration of the individual.[76] This was a potent and negative influence in the context of state intervention.

Individualism and localism both contributed to the influence of vested interests on the implementation of the new regulatory legislation of the 1830s onwards. It has been said that in factory legislation, 'opposing forces of individualism and collectivism came into sternest conflict',[77] with parents and mill owners both strenuously resisting and bitterly opposing the statutory limitations imposed on the labour of children in the factories. Both regarded the legislation as impinging on personal freedoms and the rights of the individual. The most powerful vested interests were those of property, and were very dear to Tory hearts. While occasionally material interests resulted in the acceptance of centralising legislation, notably the submission to the new poor law because it was promised that it would have the effect of reducing the poor rate, vested interests generally hindered the implementation of the statutory codes. Private interests in property were staunchly defended, and where the state intervention consisted of an interference with such rights the tension between traditional views as to the sanctity of private property, particularly land, and government policy was all too clear The early public health legislation was significantly delayed as a result of opposition from those whose material interests were affected, notably property owners who were required to build drains and sewers, whitewash slaughterhouses or undertake other mandatory improvements.[78] Private property interests were central to the early debate on the regulation of railways, and Parliament certainly feared giving too much inappropriate power to a central government department in this respect. The proposal to give jurisdiction to the Board of Trade to hear appeals by owners of lands adjoining a railway

---

[76] See Lobban, *English Jurisprudence*, pp. 2, 17, 24, 54
[77] Thomas, 'Administrative Centralisation', 215.
[78] Roberts, *Victorian Origins*, p. 25; Lubenow, *Government Growth*, p. 89; Fraser, *British Welfare State*, pp. 61–3.

92 *Legal Foundations of Tribunals in 19th-Century England*

against deviations was condemned as a dangerous precedent,[79] but justified by necessity, by pragmatism.[80] Nevertheless it was given legislative effect by the Railway Clauses Consolidation Act in 1845.[81] The commutation of tithes, enfranchisement of copyhold and inclosure of common land all, to some degree, undermined property rights.[82] The Common Fields Inclosure Act 1846, for example, which was permissive in both principle and process, originally provided that two-thirds of the proprietors in value alone could compel the others to inclose against their will. This was condemned by the Tory press and the 'habitual and constitutional vigilance' of the House of Lords was praised for ensuring this was amended to be two-thirds of the proprietors in value and in number. It was observed that had the original been a Tory bill, there would have been accusations of 'aristocratical oppression'.[83] Again in relation to tithe commutation, the Tories pressed numerous amendments in the Commons, amendments which were accepted by the government because, according to the *Quarterly Review*, the bill was 'an *English* bill of deep and real importance, and the English gentry, even the few radicals who may be reckoned in that class, would not permit great and permanent interests to be made the plaything of faction – a tub to be tossed and lashed about by the *tail* of the leviathan'.[84] In 1852 the Lord Chancellor was in favour of enfranchising copyhold land 'if it were possible to do so without trespassing too much on the rights of property'.[85] The tensions in these instances, however, were diffused by a combination of an undeniable evil, an evident public benefit and the possibility of full financial compensation, all in the context of an overall lightening of the burdens on landownership. Where the prime aim of official intervention was to remedy a public social evil, and where it involved the undermining

---

[79] *Parl. Deb.*, vol. LXXVII, ser. 3, col. 1161, 25 February 1845 (HC) *per* Fox Maule.
[80] *Ibid.*, col. 1161 *per* Lord Granville Somerset. See too *ibid.*, vol. LXXVIII, ser. 3, cols. 50–1, 27 February 1845 (HC) *per* Colonel Sibthorp.
[81] 8 & 9 Vict. c. 20 s. 12.
[82] These were not the only areas of landowner activity in which central government intervened during the first half of the nineteenth century. See discussion of the Public Money Drainage Act 1846 in David Spring, *The English Landed Estate in the Nineteenth Century: Its Administration* (Baltimore: Johns Hopkins Press, 1963), Chapter 5.
[83] (1836) 57 *Quarterly Review* 255–6.
[84] *Ibid.*, 242–3. [85] *Parl. Deb.*, vol. CXXI, ser. 3, col. 1105, 25 May 1852 (HL).

The Ideological and Theoretical Context　　93

of private interests which did not lend themselves to financial compensation, as for example the poor law and the factory legislation,[86] the driving force of ideology was stark and opinion, though often mixed,[87] was more polarised.

The various professions objected to legislative reform: engineers, lawyers and medical doctors all objected, fearing the undermining of their professional interests. The Board of Health gave rise to objections from a number of groups, not only the medical profession.[88] While the centralising reforms of the first half of the nineteenth century tended in the main to increase the work of lawyers rather than diminish it, and so give little cause for widespread active resistance, the situation was quite different in the later years of the century. When in the 1880s a number of proposals were made to put trust administration, bankruptcy, some aspects of conveyancing and company winding up in the hands of government departments, there was a furious backlash from the Law Society on behalf of the solicitors' profession.[89] Similarly certain groups watched their interests closely. Those of the church were guarded by churchmen within Parliament and by the Tories who were ideologically committed to protecting them. In the early years of the century the interests of the church were closely identified with those of the state, and one widely held view was that the utmost caution should be shown towards any interference with the propertied interests of the church, lest it should undermine the state. A lay titheholder in 1816 warned landholders 'that when they venture, directly or indirectly, to attack the right to this species of property, they shake every other'.[90] Where ecclesiastical interests in property were concerned, ideological conflict between reformers and traditionalists was inevitable. It was clearly seen in relation to the commutation of tithes, though the evils of tithes were so clear to everyone that the church ultimately agreed with commutation and gained from improved relations with the public and the removal of one perceived abuse that had only encouraged calls for its disestablishment.

---

[86] Legislation which increased the burdens of ownership.
[87] Fraser, *British Welfare State*, Chapter 5.
[88] Roberts, *Victorian Origins*, pp. 267–70.
[89] C. Stebbings, ' "Officialism": Law, Bureaucracy and Ideology in Late Victorian England', in Andrew Lewis and Michael Lobban (eds.), *Law and History*, Current Legal Issues (Oxford: Oxford University Press, 2003), vol. VI, p. 317.
[90] 'A Lay Titheholder', Letter (1816) 86 *Gentleman's Magazine*, Pt II, 311.

94 *Legal Foundations of Tribunals in 19th-Century England*

One of the most powerful and distinctive interest groups in the nineteenth century was the railway interest. It has been said that it 'represented big business at its most ruthless and at its most highly organized'.[91] This group resisted central government control, for after all they had paid heavily in terms of money, time and effort to obtain their private Acts of Parliament, and were naturally hostile to any subsequent attempt at government interference which they regarded as undermining their legitimate statutory authority. The group was responsible for blocking the establishment of Cardwell's special tribunal for railway disputes in 1854, and it lessened the rigour of the legislation of 1873. When the railway regulation bill was in committee in 1873, it was subject to criticism from a number of quarters. Joshua Fielden objected to the extent of the powers given to the commissioners over an interest as extensive and important as that of the railways. He thought the liberties of the country were threatened, that this was an unwarranted interference with railway management, that the legislative power of Parliament was undermined, and that it amounted to nothing less than the beginnings of placing the entire railway system under the management of central government. It was, he said, the thin end of the wedge.[92]

The ideological dislike of state interference was intensified when the interference was compulsory. As it denied freedom of choice, it was an issue that always had a direct bearing on ideological perceptions, and challenged adherents of individualism, laissez-faire and localism, and exacerbated the undermining of vested interests. Indeed, the reason why income tax was so unpopular was not only that it was invasive, but also that it was compulsory, in a fiscal climate where taxes had hitherto been essentially voluntary.[93] At one extreme there was the view that compulsion was acceptable if it was for the public good,[94] but the orthodox view was that compulsion was to be avoided if at all possible. A voluntary approach to regulating legislation was

---

[91] Alderman, *Railway Interest*, p. 224. See generally T. R. Gourvish, *Railways and the British Economy 1830–1914* (London: Macmillan, 1980), pp. 54–6.

[92] *Parl. Deb.*, vol. CCXV, ser. 3, cols. 351–6, 31 March 1873 (HC).

[93] See William Phillips, 'The Origin of Income Tax' (1967) *British Tax Review* 113 at 118 ff.; B. E. V. Sabine, *A History of Income Tax* (London: George Allen and Unwin Ltd, 1966), p. 31.

[94] For example, James Stewart, the secretary to the Copyhold Commissioners. See *Report, Copyholds Bill, 1851* pp. 140–1.

The Ideological and Theoretical Context 95

consistent with the freedom of the individual inherent in laissez-faire and Benthamism. In some instances the issue could be sidestepped if there were practical reasons why the reforming legislation could not be made compulsory. In the case of the enfranchisement of copyhold, for example, it was well understood that voluntary enfranchisement based on agreement would not suffice to abolish copyhold tenure in its entirety. Nevertheless it was not made mandatory in 1841 because the customs were so numerous and varied that unlike tithe commutation no general rule could be formulated and applied and the cost of individual enfranchisement by commissioners was considered prohibitive.[95] Some Whigs believed that enfranchisement should not be made compulsory because in contrast to tithes, copyhold tenure had some clear advantages.[96] Underlying such pragmatic considerations, however, there were deeply held ideological objections to compulsory legislation. The common distrust of centralised government could only be exacerbated by compulsory administration. In the case of tithe commutation, the Tories found themselves unable to accept the coercive element in the legislation,[97] the church was uncomfortable about it, and even Lord John Russell himself, whose bill it was which ultimately became law, had reservations in this respect.[98] Sir Robert Peel was particularly opposed to compulsion, and spoke against it in relation to both tithes[99] and copyholds. He preferred a consensual approach in the nature of an arbitration. Though compulsion was accepted in relation to tithe commutation, the Act gave every opportunity for voluntary settlement first, and the policy of the commissioners was to seek to achieve voluntary commutation and only in case of intransigence to proceed to the compulsory provision. This astute masking of compulsion by a permissive cloak was responsible

[95] 'Third Report of the Real Property Commissioners', *HCPP* (1831–2) (484) xxiii 321 at p. 326.

[96] A view expressed by Sir James Graham MP in *Ibid.*, at p. 399. He was a Conservative who inclined to the Liberal party: Michael Stenton (ed.), *Who's Who of British Members of Parliament*, 4 vols. (Hassocks: Harvester Press, 1976), vol. I, p. 163.

[97] Sir Robert Peel objected to compulsion in both tithe commutation and copyhold enfranchisement.

[98] *Parl. Deb.*, vol. XXXIV, ser. 3, col. 1350, 7 July 1836 (HL), and *ibid.*, vol. XXXIII, ser. 3, cols. 507–8, 2 May 1836 (HC). Lord John Russell's tithe bill was similar to Sir Robert Peel's, though differed on the point of compulsion.

[99] *Ibid.*, vol. XXXIV, ser. 3, cols. 973–4, 27 June 1836 (HC).

96   Legal Foundations of Tribunals in 19th-Century England

for the outstanding and exceptional success of tithe commutation, though it was acknowledged that it had been a 'great experiment', not so much in form as in its compulsory nature.[100] Both schemes, however, unambiguously imposed a mandatory recasting of the property rights involved under the supervision and policy direction of a central board of commissioners in London. In the field the process was supervised by central Assistant Commissioners but the actual work was undertaken by valuers who were appointed by the parties themselves. This element of local control and of voluntaryism, sufficed to diffuse the intense popular resentment of compulsory legislation, and the restructuring of land rights was effected with remarkable success.[101]

Compulsion was rejected in relation to the enfranchisement of copyholds for the reasons mentioned above, and the Act of 1841 imposed no general legal compulsion to enter into any arrangement. In that sense, however, the legislation was deceptive. It was recognised when the Act was passed that the objective of national copyhold enfranchisement could not be achieved through voluntary agreement, and that a mandatory element was essential, but there was an ideological division between those who wanted compulsion and those who did not. A two-tier plan was adopted, whereby initial legislation would first provide a process for voluntary enfranchisement, and a later enactment would make it compulsory. The plan was identical to that for tithe commutation, except that the two stages were articulated in separate statutes rather than in one.[102] In spirit, if not in the letter, therefore, the 1841 Act was as mandatory in its centralisation as the Tithe Commutation Act 1836. Furthermore, there was an element of compulsion in the process in that the majority of the tenants could bind the minority to enter into commutation, though not an enfranchisement. This compulsion was of particular concern, since not only was the outcome a significant alteration of the rights of both lord and tenant, but one which involved the tenant in a

---

[100] *Minutes, Commons' Inclosure, 1844* q. 3431 *per* Thomas Woolley, land agent and Assistant Tithe Commissioner.

[101] See Eric J. Evans, *Tithes and the Tithe Commutation Act 1836*, Standing Conference for Local History, 3rd revised edition (London: Bedford Square Press, 1997), p. 18; 'Report of the Tithe Commissioners for England and Wales for 1840', *HCPP* (1840) (215) xxviii 139 at p. 141.

[102] *Report, Copyholds Enfranchisement, 1837–8* at p. 192.

The Ideological and Theoretical Context 97

revised financial outlay and this could bear hardly on the smaller and poorer copyholders. When commutation and enfranchisement did occur under the 1841 Act it appears that both parties benefited from the application of the statutory powers and the outcome was regarded as fair compensation. The lord was compensated for the loss of his manorial rights by a rent charge calculated to take individual circumstances into account, while the tenant's land rose in value when it became freehold and was freed from liabilities in respect of improvement and demands from the lord. When enfranchisement was made compulsory on the demand of lord or any tenant in 1852 the hardship of the individual uncooperative copyholder was avoided by making enfranchisement compulsory only at the next death or alienation,[103] and by giving a choice as to payment in gross or by rent charge, an arrangement which was regarded as a fair compromise.[104] In practice the compromise as to compulsion attempted by the copyhold legislation was a mistake. The Act of 1841 introduced uncertainty and confusion and failed to achieve either commutation or enfranchisement. Tenants were unwilling to enfranchise because they knew a compulsory measure would soon be passed, under which they might, they believed, receive better terms.[105] As a result the process provided by the Act was very rarely used,[106] and only after enfranchisement was made compulsory in 1852 did it gather momentum.[107]

Most opposition to the centralising legislation and its implementing organs was unequivocally ideological and consisted of a distrust of a policy of centralisation with its corresponding reluctance to relinquish any element of local self-government and a dislike of government by boards.[108] There were, however, many other specific objections, some principled, some ethical, some

---

[103] 15 & 16 Vict. c. 51 s. 1.

[104] *Ibid.*, s. 7; *Parl. Deb.*, vol. CXXI, ser. 3, cols. 1104–5, 25 May 1852 (HL).

[105] 'Seventh Report of the Copyhold Commissioners', *HCPP* (1849) (1039) xxii 97.

[106] It was said there had been only 400 enfranchisements and two commutations under the 1841 Act: *Parl. Deb.*, vol. CXXI, ser. 3, cols. 1103–4, 25 May 1852 (HL).

[107] 'Twelfth Report of the Copyhold Commissioners', *HCPP* (1854) (1730) xix 147.

[108] See Roberts, *Victorian Origins*, pp. 127–36.

98   Legal Foundations of Tribunals in 19th-Century England

practical, though even the latter often disguised an ideological opposition to state intervention.[109]

One did not need to be ideologically opposed to state interference to appreciate the importance of the independence of the implementing bodies, both from the matter in hand and from the political influence of the government. Some commentators feared partiality in decision-making. Henry Aglionby, for example, said that compensation for compulsory enfranchisement of copyhold would be acceptable to him if the sum were fixed by a competent and fair tribunal, by which he meant 'such a tribunal as a commission formed of gentlemen under government, who would have no interest in it, and who would have nothing but equity to consult'.[110] The appointment of a government body certainly addressed the problem inherent in arbitration and personally appointed commissioners as to bias towards one of the parties, but potentially replaced it with bias towards the government view. Where one of the parties was the government, as in taxation, the problem of independence was one of some moment. This was an issue that became increasingly important as the complexity of government and administrative practices grew. It was particularly striking in the sphere of income taxation, where by the end of the nineteenth century the traditional safeguard to the taxpayer – the General Commissioners of Income Tax – had become in many instances little more than the tool of the bureaucracy. It was all the more remarkable in this instance because such domination was not intended by the legislation. Indeed, the statute expressly provided that control and responsibility were in the hands of the General Commissioners while the role of the government official, the surveyor, was merely supervisory. It was, however, an almost inevitable result of the practical working of the system. The surveyor dominated the administrative and the adjudicatory functions of the General Commissioners. The complexity and intricacy of the law and practice of income tax, as well as the growth in volume, came to result in the task of assessment to income tax surpassing the intellectual and physical ability of the lay commissioners. The bureaucrat stepped in, and with the time

---

[109] See H. W. Arthurs, *'Without the Law': Administrative Justice and Legal Pluralism in Nineteenth-Century England* (Toronto and Buffalo: University of Toronto Press, 1985), p. 134.
[110] *Minutes, Copyholds Bill, 1851* q. 1562.

The Ideological and Theoretical Context 99

and expertise acquired from his full-time office, his familiarity with tax practice and accountancy and real knowledge of the tax affairs of individuals, the commissioners were no match for him. This knowledge and expertise could be exploited to achieve policy objectives. Bureaucratic dominance in the administration of income tax was due to the exceptionally specialised nature of the subject-matter and the composition of the implementing body, but it was a danger inherent in the practice of all administrative organs exercising judicial powers.

There was a question, occasionally articulated, whether it was morally right to deny parties the right to sustain their rights before a court of law if they were prepared to incur the expense, but on the whole pragmatism dominated such issues and the convenience and ease of dispute-resolution by inferior and primarily administrative bodies were preferred. There was, however, a real tension between the desire for a cheap and expeditious process and a reluctance to allow rights as important and potentially valuable as property rights being determined by a central board and its appointees rather than the courts of law.[111] This tension was increasingly marked the larger the sum in question. The reluctance to allow decisions to be made by lay commissioners and the demand for dispute-resolution to be put in the hands of the regular courts increased according to the importance of the matter in hand. This was seen in relation to boundary disputes in the restructuring of land rights, particularly where minerals were concerned, and in virtually all disputes concerning railways. This underlying concern found expression in the demand for some legal input at some stage in the process, as assessors, first instance adjudicators, or via rights of appeal to the courts of law.[112]

Practical objections were significant. By the end of the century, despite some successes, fifty years of state intervention in many spheres of human activity had revealed its deficiencies. Most importantly, it had had time to fail, and the practical problems of bureaucracy had become evident. While it was still believed that the interference of the state with the private business of individuals should be kept to a minimum, in the later nineteenth century public opinion became increasingly directed towards a

---

[111] *Minutes, Commons' Inclosure, 1844* qq. 2577–84, 4679, 4684–6.
[112] *Ibid.*, q. 2580 *per* Charles Mickleburgh, land surveyor.

100 *Legal Foundations of Tribunals in 19th-Century England*

resentment of the effects of centralisation rather than its principle. Every instance of state intervention inevitably gave rise to a bureaucracy: the commissioners had assistants, clerks and a host of other officials; the systems they administered were detailed and spawned supplementary regulations, rules, policies, directives, circulars and instructions. It was an objection to the inevitable bureaucracy that arose in the wake of centralist policies. It was expressed as an antipathy towards 'officialism',[113] a disparaging term for bureaucracy, itself a word that had not then acquired its modern popular derogatory sense. The objections to the developing bureaucracy were many and various.[114] They included an adherence to processes rather than substance,[115] an inflexibility among bureaucrats,[116] a perception that existing systems were adequate,[117] concerns as to the danger of misconduct by officials dealing with significant amounts of money,[118] the likelihood of patronage giving rise to a suspicion of political expediency[119] and, above all, a fear of the financial cost to the individual and to the state.[120]

Concern for the civil expenditure of government and a determination to keep it within bounds was a very real issue for successive Victorian administrations. Despite the undoubted expense inherent in the implementation of law by the courts, many feared the expense involved in setting up new commissions, costs that would translate into increased taxation. A bureaucratic infrastructure was a necessary element of these commissions and the salaries of commissioners,[121] their assistants and subordinate officers, and the costs of the premises and the running of the offices, were paid for out of national taxation. There was, however, no need

---

[113] See generally Stebbings, 'Officialism', 317; 'The Growth of Officialism', *The Times*, 5 April 1893, p. 3 col. d.

[114] The best and worst of civil service practice and personnel in the nineteenth century are depicted in Anthony Trollope's fictitious account of Victorian tribunals in *The Three Clerks*, first published in 1858.

[115] 'The Evils of Bureaucracy', *The Times*, 17 October 1866, p. 10 col. c.

[116] *Ibid.* See too *Minutes, Railway Amalgamation, 1872* q. 3864 *per* William Price, Member of Parliament for Gloucester and chairman of the Midland Railway Company; *Parl. Deb.*, vol. CCCXLVII, ser. 3, col. 25, 17 July 1890 (HL) *per* Lord Herschell on the second reading of the companies winding-up bill.

[117] *Parl. Deb.*, vol. LXV, ser. 3, col. 1082, 5 August 1842 (HC). [118] *Ibid.*

[119] *Ibid.*, col. 1141, 8 August 1842 (HC). See too *ibid.*, vol. CCLXXVII, ser. 3, cols. 903–4, 19 March 1883 (HC) *per* William Grantham.

[120] *Minutes, Commons' Inclosure, 1844* q. 1320; 'Report of the Royal Commission on Bankruptcy', *HCPP* (1854) (1770) xxiii 1 at p. 20.

[121] Though not all commissioners were remunerated: see below, pp. 141–2.

The Ideological and Theoretical Context   101

to have specialised buildings as with the regular courts of law. Local buildings of suitable size and formality were used, notably local government buildings, hotels, offices, and courtrooms that were not in use, and while that cost would be borne by central government, it was considerably lower than the cost of specialised and permanent buildings. Concerns as to cost were particularly prevalent in relation to commissions entrusted with an open-ended task. The work of the Tithe and Copyhold Commissions was finite, since the processes were compulsory and a time would come where all tithes had been commuted and where copyhold tenure had been finally extinguished. However, Colonel Charles Sibthorp,[122] a traditional Tory and outspoken opponent of centralisation, said he had 'no great predeliction for Commissioners' and believed most of the country agreed with him. He objected strongly to their cost, citing the Poor Law Commissioners and the Tithe Commissioners as bodies costing the country hundreds of thousands of pounds and achieving very little for it.[123] In 1846, though he objected to railways as a threat to traditional values of life and property and so supported their regulation, he opposed the establishment of the Railway Commissioners on the basis of expense and patronage.[124] Objections to the creation of Assessment Committees for rating valuations in 1862 consisted primarily of fears as to the expense of valuations, though the centralising nature of the proposals, 'jobbery'[125] and interference with local self-government were also significant.[126] When it was realised that few cases were going before the Railway Commission of 1873, its cost of £10,000 a year in salaries was condemned as being disproportionate to the amount of business it conducted.[127]

---

[122] J. A. Hamilton rev. John Wolffe, 'Charles Sibthorp, 1783–1855', in *National Biography*, vol. L.

[123] *Parl. Deb.*, vol. LXXXII, ser. 3, col. 18, 4 July 1845 (HC), in the debate on the inclosure of commons and waste lands bill. In his view of the Tithe Commissioners he was in the minority. It was generally accepted that they were a highly successful institution.

[124] *Ibid.*, vol. LXXXVIII, ser. 3, col. 929, 21 August 1845 (HC).

[125] *Ibid.*, vol. CLXVII, ser. 3, col. 1334, 3 July 1862 (HC) *per* Sir Lawrence Palk.

[126] *Ibid.*, vol. CLXVIII, ser. 3, col. 17, 8 July 1862 (HC) *per* J. A. Turner.

[127] It seems that the Railway and Canal Commissioners had even touted for business by public advertisement: see *Minutes, Railways, 1881* q. 13,518 *per* James Grierson, general manager of the Great Western Railway Company, reading a paper previously prepared for the Board of Trade by the railway companies, and the advertisement itself at q. 16,474.

102 *Legal Foundations of Tribunals in 19th-Century England*

A concern closely allied to that of cost was abolition. Ideological resistance to state intervention was undoubtedly stronger if it took a permanent form,[128] and it was increasingly realised that once a government agency had been established, it was very difficult to abolish it if it proved to be a failure. This concern had been expressed in relation to the early commissions for tithes, copyholds and inclosures. While they were limited to five years by statute, it was tempting – because of the convenience – to impose new cognate duties on them. So, for example, the Tithe Commissioners were made the Copyhold Commissioners as well, and when a new Inclosure Commission was created rather than giving the work to the Tithe Commissioners, it was argued that to create a new commission was 'perfectly superfluous, and worse than useless'.[129] In this way, early on, ostensibly temporary government organs were effectively made permanent, to the concern of many. When asked whether he would be in favour of the appointment of the Tithe Commissioners as Commissioners of Inclosure, one witness before the Select Committee on Commons' Inclosure said that he would 'feel the greatest possible jealousy of Commissions, if there were a tendency to keep them alive by feeding them with fresh duties before they had quite discharged the old ones'.[130] Even the express provision of temporary existence, however, was regarded with some scepticism, not least because of the experience of the income tax. This had been introduced as a temporary tax in 1799, had been suspended for some twenty-five years and reintroduced in 1842 and would not be suspended again, and so the General and Special Commissioners of Income Tax were in practice, though not in theory, a permanent institution. In the debate on the Inclosure Commissioners, Viscount Palmerston observed that Colonel Sibthorp clearly had difficulty in believing that that commission would be limited to five years, doubtless because of the experience with the income tax.[131] By the end of the nineteenth century the perception

---

[128] F. M. G. Willson, 'Ministries and Boards: Some Aspects of Administrative Development since 1832' (1955) 33 *Public Administration* 43 at 49.

[129] *Parl. Deb.*, vol. LXXXII, ser. 3, col. 35, 4 July 1845 (HC) *per* Charles Buller.

[130] *Minutes, Commons' Inclosure, 1844* q. 1320 *per* Thomas Lewis.

[131] *Parl. Deb.*, vol. LXXXII, ser. 3, col. 41, 4 July 1845 (HC), in the debate on the inclosure of commons and waste lands bill. This was a rare reference to one tribunal in the context of another in a different field of activity.

The Ideological and Theoretical Context 103

was that official institutions, being artificially sustained by government, and, not, like private enterprise, subject to the control of market forces, were self-perpetuating organs. In 1905 the Law Society said the view was too often taken that it was better to pay officials salaries 'for doing a little work unnecessarily than pensions for doing nothing at all'.[132] This was exacerbated by the inherent resilience of a strong *esprit de corps*, resulting from a small coherent body with common interests under a strong central authority.[133] The spectre of having to pension off the large number of officials which the new schemes involved, in the event of a need to close them down, added to already considerable fears as to the cost of the expanding bureaucracy and raised the added fear that to avoid such costs, voluntary systems could be made compulsory and thus justify their existence.

Individualism, laissez-faire, localism and vested interests pervaded government and society in the nineteenth century. The fundamental dislike of the Whigs and Tories of any increase in central government power, along with the firm belief of the latter in the value and efficacy of local government, kept the new central bodies strictly restricted in their powers and duties. But while the dominant ideologies limited the scope of government interference, they failed to prevent it altogether.[134] Pragmatism won over ideology, and the public view was one of noisily unwilling acceptance. Government intervention gathered apace in an astonishingly wide field of activity to address pressing problems for the rest of the nineteenth century. The influence of laissez-faire in its broadest sense gradually weakened as practical problems of immense importance presented themselves to Victorian governments. As A. V. Dicey observed, 'sincere believers in *laissez faire* found that for the attainment of their ends the improvement and strengthening of governmental machinery was an absolute necessity'.[135] By the close of the century the individualist imperative had long been undermined and collectivism dominated.

---

[132] Law Society, *Report of the Special Committee on Officialism* (London: Law Society, 1905), p. 40.

[133] See *The Times*, 17 October 1866, p. 10 col. c.

[134] Fraser, *British Welfare State*, pp. 103 ff. purports to resolve the paradox between the reality of centralisation in the nineteenth century and the prevailing ideologies that ran contrary to it.

[135] Dicey, *Law and Public Opinion*, p. 306.

104 *Legal Foundations of Tribunals in 19th-Century England*

The state intervened in the private affairs of its citizens, even at the cost of individual freedom, for the common good.

The complex and conflicting political, social and religious ideologies of the 1830s gave rise, however haltingly and inefficiently, to the early statutory tribunals. Their form was dictated by practical considerations, their powers largely by ideological ones. Whatever their limitations and weaknesses, and whatever the degree of ultimate success in achieving the suppression of glaring social evils, it was these bodies which were endowed with dispute-resolution powers. Political ideologies were challenged considerably earlier than legal ones. While the desirability and appropriateness of increased state intervention formed a topic of intense political debate from the 1830s until well into the next century, that of the placing of judicial functions in the hands of organs of the executive staffed by government appointees only became the object of serious examination in the closing years of the nineteenth century. Until then, the dispute-resolution functions of the new bodies were so confined by their administrative objectives that they were not naturally perceived as judicial functions at all. Where the general political debate touched on dispute-resolution at all, it was in that context. For example, arguments that central boards would not be able to judge the value of evidence in the locality was a common argument to support local control in a variety of spheres.[136] The preference for arbitration rather than tribunal adjudication was an expression of dislike and distrust of official interference and a statement of independence, while the favour shown to dispute-resolution by the justices of the peace or privately appointed commissioners was an assertion of local control and support for traditional institutions. Similarly, arguments in favour of leaving dispute-resolution in the hands of the regular courts were in opposition to interventionist policies, since the courts were perceived as independent of central government, indeed as a major safeguard to the rights of free Englishmen. While ideologically the retention of the regular courts would have been less challenging, such ideological concerns did little more than contribute to the retention of the regular courts and traditional institutions in some specific instances. They were insufficient to overcome practical requirements and prevent

---

[136] See for example *Minutes, Commons' Inclosure, 1844* qq. 4003–4.

The Ideological and Theoretical Context 105

the establishment of the principle of dispute-resolution by the newly created agencies, particularly since public, politicians and, with their emphasis on the efficiency of institutions for their purpose, Utilitarians, were united in criticising established methods of dispute-resolution. Bentham and his followers valued highly the ability of each person to enforce his legal rights. Bentham himself promoted a new 'natural' mode of adjudication process,[137] and concerned himself with all aspects of the regular courts and their procedures.[138] He favoured informal and swift process coupled with a wide judicial discretion.

The granting of dispute-resolution powers to organs of the executive challenged accepted constitutional theories. Nineteenth-century legal theory was dominated by the doctrine of the rule of law[139] on which was based the constitutional theory of the separation of powers.[140] The separation of powers was drawn from Montesquieu's analysis of the English constitution in his *L'Esprit des lois* published in 1748[141] and the influence of John Locke.[142] Refined and developed after the revolution, it subjugated the Crown and made Parliament supreme. Legislation was put into the hands of Parliament, administration in the hands of the executive, and adjudication, being the state's power to decide controversies between its subjects or itself and its subjects, into the hands of the courts. The theory demanded that functions and personnel should remain in their appropriate organ and be

---

[137] See generally William Twining, *Theories of Evidence: Bentham and Wigmore* (London: Weidenfeld and Nicolson, 1985).

[138] See generally Gerald J. Postema, *Bentham and the Common Law Tradition* (Oxford: Clarendon Press, 1986).

[139] For analysis of the meaning of the term, see Sir William Wade and Christopher Forsyth, *Administrative Law*, 9th edition (Oxford: Oxford University Press, 2004), pp. 20–42; H. W. Arthurs, 'Rethinking Administrative Law: A Slightly Dicey Business' (1979) 17 *Osgoode Hall Law Journal* 1 at 3; W. Burnett Harvey, 'The Rule of Law in Historical Perspective' (1961) 59 *Michigan Law Review* 487.

[140] See Sir Ivor Jennings, *The Law and the Constitution*, 5th edition (London: University of London Press Ltd, 1959), pp. 18–28.

[141] Charles Louis de Secondat, Baron de Montesquieu, *De l'esprit des lois*, 1748 (Paris: Librairie Garnier Frères, 1949), Livre xi, Chapitre vi 'De la Constitution d'Angleterre'. See Jennings, *Law and the Constitution*, pp. 18–28; C. K. Allen, *Law and Orders* (London: Stevens and Sons Ltd, 1947), pp. 6–18.

[142] See generally M. J. C. Vile, *Constitutionalism and the Separation of Powers* (Oxford: Clarendon Press, 1967), pp. 76–118.

106 *Legal Foundations of Tribunals in 19th-Century England*

clearly differentiated.[143] Dispute-resolution bodies outside this framework were rejected.[144] The administration of justice was the purpose of the regular courts of law, their principal and proper function in which they were to be supreme. They, and they alone, were constitutionally permitted to do justice. Their adjudicatory power was, therefore, an end in itself. They were created to exercise it, and in so doing were exercising the judicial power of the state, and they constituted the judicial system. This was so even where the court in question was one of limited jurisdiction, whether the limitation was geographical, monetary or of subject-matter. Those limitations left the purpose of the court unchanged: resolution of the dispute before it was its sole object. Not only did the judicial power of the state belong to the courts of law, but certain jurisdictions belonged to specific courts.[145] Where the function was a judicial one, in the sense of the finding of facts and the application of legal rules to the facts so found through certain established procedures, the effect of the strict application of the rule of law was that only the regular courts could undertake this function. There was more flexibility with respect to the mere ascertainment of facts, a function that was comfortably left to lesser bodies, notably juries. The constitutional presumption, however, was that the regular courts of law were the appropriate bodies for the resolution of disputes.

It is clear that this doctrine could potentially undermine the new executive bodies with dispute-resolution functions, for in the exercise of such powers, the new tribunals undoubtedly performed an essentially identical function. In resolving the disputes that arose between parties in the course of implementing a new legislative regime, the tribunal had to find the facts and apply the statutory rules to them. Although at most 'a respectable ideal',[146] the doctrine of the separation of powers was dominant throughout the nineteenth century. For most of that time, however, it was not

---

[143] The theory was not, and could not be strictly adhered to in practice, and a number of exceptions still exist today.

[144] See R. E. Wraith and P. G. Hutchesson, *Administrative Tribunals* (London: George Allen and Unwin, 1973), pp. 22–4.

[145] See for example *Brown* v. *Trant* (1701) 2 Vern 426 and counsel in *Williams* v. *Steward* (1817) 3 Mer 472 at 487.

[146] Sir C. T. Carr, *Concerning English Administrative Law* (London: Oxford University Press, 1941), p. 18. See 'Report of the Committee on Ministers' Powers', *HCPP* (1931–2) (4060) xii 341 at pp. 354–5.

The Ideological and Theoretical Context

regarded as relevant to the dispute-resolution functions of the commissions, and the extent to which they were legitimate in constitutional terms was not queried. This was consistent with the view that these bodies were organs of the executive and that any dispute-resolution functions they had were integral to their primary administrative function and not an aspect of the judicial power of the state. Even in the tax sphere, one of the earliest fields of activity to which dispute-resolution bodies outside the court system had been accorded,[147] although there were expressions of discontent as to the usurpation of the regular judges,[148] the administrative nature of the subject-matter, and its fragmentation, largely concealed the breach of the rule of law.

As the nineteenth century progressed, and these established organs began to transfer their administrative functions to the developing departments of the central government, and newly created ones were endowed with predominantly judicial powers, so the doctrine of the separation of powers with its implicit independence of the judiciary from the executive, sat increasingly uneasily with the progressively more prominent and exclusive adjudicatory powers of the commissions. This, allied to the ever-growing number of such bodies, eventually penetrated a consciousness dulled by the gradual and insidious growth of tribunals on an ad hoc and subject-specific basis, an approach which not only contributed to the inhibition of any developing principles of form or conduct, but which also masked the considerable collective extent of extra-judicial dispute-resolution. In the closing years of the nineteenth century, though the time had not yet come where the traditional rule of law was considered to be under threat,[149] there began a realisation of the extent, and the legal implications, of allocating extensive dispute-resolution powers to

---

[147] Commissioners of Customs and Excise had been given dispute-resolution powers as early as the seventeenth century: 12 Car. II c. 23 (1660).

[148] Sir William Wade draws attention to the definition of excise in Johnson's *Dictionary*, where it was described as 'a hateful tax levied upon commodities, and adjudged not by the common judges of property, but wretches hired by those to whom excise is paid': Wade and Forsyth, *Administrative Law*, p. 907. See too Sir William Blackstone, *Commentaries on the Laws of England*, 1783 edition printed for W. Strahan and T. Cadell, London and D. Prince, Oxford, 4 vols. (New York: Garland Publishing Inc., 1978), vol. IV, p. 281.

[149] Sir William Holdsworth, *A History of English Law*, 17 vols. (London: Methuen & Co. Ltd, 1964), vol. XIV, pp. 186–7.

108 *Legal Foundations of Tribunals in 19th-Century England*

semi-independent commissions in preference to the regular courts of law.

The perception that the tribunals' dispute-resolution functions were undermining the rule of law was first articulated, though in general terms, by Professor A.V. Dicey in his *Introduction to the Study of the Law of the Constitution* in 1885.[150] According to Dicey and to the accepted legal theory of his age, the rule of law in essence stressed and embodied the supremacy of the 'ordinary' courts of law and the 'ordinary' law and legal procedure in the settlement of disputes and the imposition of punishment or loss.[151] Although Dicey did not, in that study,[152] expressly discuss the many well-established administrative tribunals that were exercising dispute-resolution functions around him, an omission for which he has been forcefully criticised,[153] it was clear that his theories undermined them. If the regular courts had the theoretical[154] monopoly of dispute-resolution, the tribunals that had proliferated throughout the nineteenth century, not being courts, were left with no theoretical anchor and were, indeed, in breach of the rule of law. He felt that the objection to giving government functions that should belong to the courts was obvious. 'Such transference of authority', he said, 'saps the foundation of that rule of law which has been for generations a leading feature of the English Constitution.'[155] He did not regard the law which those bodies administered as law at all and viewed the discretion which these tribunals were empowered by their parent Acts to exercise as the direct opposite of law.[156] By implication, tribunals were no more than 'persons in authority', and the law they administered

---

[150] Richard A. Cosgrove, 'Professor Albert Venn Dicey (1835–1922)', in *National Biography*, vol. XVI; A. V. Dicey, *Introduction to the Study of the Law of the Constitution*, E. S. C. Wade (ed.), 10th edition (London: Macmillan, 1959).

[151] Dicey, *Law of the Constitution*, pp. 202–3; Jennings, *Law and the Constitution*, pp. 305–17.

[152] See however the introduction to the 8th edition in 1931, pp. xxxviii–xl.

[153] Arthurs, *Without the Law*, p. 95; Jennings, *Law and the Constitution*, p. 55; Wade in his edition of Dicey, *Law of the Constitution*, pp. cxv–cxvii; Parris, *Constitutional Bureaucracy*, pp. 258–66.

[154] They certainly did not have a practical monopoly of dispute-resolution: see Arthurs, *Without the Law*. Arthurs states his pluralist theory of law at Arthurs, 'Rethinking Administrative Law', 13.

[155] A. V. Dicey, 'The Development of Administrative Law in England' (1915) 31 *Law Quarterly Review* 148 at 150.

[156] Dicey, *Law of the Constitution*, p. 188. See Arthurs, 'Rethinking Administrative Law', 22–5.

The Ideological and Theoretical Context 109

'wide, arbitrary, or discretionary powers of constraint'.[157] In short, they breached a fundamental constitutional principle.[158] Their position was tolerable in legal theory only because of the control exercised over them by the regular courts through judicial review and appeal.

Dicey wrote at the height of state interventionism and centralisation, with increasing collectivism and after a lifetime of new tribunals. Though his views have been subject to profound and scholarly analysis, their weaknesses and inconsistencies exposed[159] and the terms 'ordinary law' and 'ordinary courts' shown to be untenable,[160] he nevertheless reflected the orthodox views of his contemporaries. His *Introduction to the Study of the Law of the Constitution* was well received,[161] and his theories had wide support among the public particularly because he explained complex issues clearly and lucidly. These views were, unsurprisingly in view of the undermining of their interests, shared by the majority of lawyers.[162] Dicey disliked collectivist and regulatory legislation, and it has been shown that many judges were of the same mind.[163] Dicey's view dominated among legal theorists and constitutional lawyers, a domination that was to endure until well into the twentieth century.[164]

---

[157] Dicey, *Law of the Constitution*, p. 188.

[158] *Ibid.*, pp. 183–205.

[159] Arthurs, 'Rethinking Administrative Law', 8 ff. and 24 ff.

[160] Notably by Arthurs, *ibid.*

[161] *Ibid.*, p. 4 n. 15, and quoting F. Frankfurter, 'Discussion of Current Developments in Administrative Law' (1938) 47 *Yale Law Journal* 515 at 517. See the favourable review in (1885) 1 *Law Quarterly Review* 502.

[162] Harlow and Rawlings, *Law and Administration*, pp. 29–66 (Red Light Theories). Arthurs points out that Maitland had reservations but that Holdsworth supported him: Arthurs, 'Rethinking Administrative Law', 4 n. 15.

[163] Arthurs, 'Rethinking Administrative Law', 17–22. See Brian Abel-Smith and Robert Stevens, *Lawyers and the Courts* (London: Heinemann, 1967), p. 112 for judicial attitudes to railway regulation.

[164] Notably by Lord Hewart, *The New Despotism* (London: Ernest Benn Ltd, 1929). Note that Dicey ultimately had to accept that state intervention was inevitable: Dicey, 'Development of Administrative Law', at 150. The post-war period was to see the analysis and widespread criticism of Dicey's views. For a full discussion of the orthodox and alternative theories see Harlow and Rawlings, *Law and Administration*, pp. 29–90.

3

COMPOSITION AND PERSONNEL

The regular courts of law had been rejected as the instruments of implementation of the new regulatory legislation on the grounds of expense, formality and the lack of specialist technical knowledge in the judges. The only alternative was a predominantly lay personnel. Because the new bodies were perceived as essentially administrative in nature, a proposed composition of laymen, even with some dispute-resolution functions, did not cause alarm to the legal establishment. Indeed, the sanguine attitude of the legislature to lay composition is revealing of the true nature of the new bodies. The use of laymen was also a well-known feature even of the regular legal system, through the institution of the justices of the peace.[1] The innovative and specialised legislation of the nineteenth century was often controversial and, as such, demanded progressive and positive implementation by tribunals composed of members with imagination and ability. The calibre of the personnel was fundamental to the authority, efficacy and ultimate success of each tribunal, particularly where the processes were voluntary, as with the land rights tribunals, and informal, as with all the tribunals. A high calibre of commissioner and subordinate staff gave weight to the decisions of the tribunals in all spheres, provided a safeguard to the parties and, crucially, gave them confidence.

There was therefore a constant and consistent demand for a dispute-resolution body made up of persons in whom the parties would have confidence. This was indispensable, because it meant that the parties would be prepared to use the tribunals, and that was an essential step in the public acceptance of a possibly

---

[1] See J. P. Dawson, *A History of Lay Judges* (Cambridge, MA: Harvard University Press, 1960).

Composition and Personnel 111

unpopular legislative regime. As Viscount Palmerston observed in relation to the Inclosure Commissioners in 1845,

the object was to inspire confidence in that tribunal. If persons, who were ignorant and ill-informed, entertained apprehensions with regard to the constitution of the Commission, and such persons were those who would most probably entertain them, then the Bill must necessarily fail in its purpose, as applications would not be made for the exercise of the power which it was intended to create.[2]

One reason for the outstanding success of the tithe commutation of the 1830s and 1840s was due to the skill of the Tithe Commissioners and their assistants. Commissioner William Blamire was particularly praised as being an efficient administrator, and for his conciliatory approach and scrupulous fairness.[3] There was, furthermore, a direct correlation between the confidence felt by the public in the quality of the tribunals' decisions and the number of appeals to the regular courts. If a tribunal was perceived as incompetent, then that induced the losing party to go to the regular courts and prolong the litigation. The prime requirement, therefore, was for men of 'firmness, integrity, ability, and high character'.[4] When William Pitt introduced the General Commissioners of Income Tax to implement his new tax in 1799, he sought 'persons of a respectable situation in life; as far as possible removed from any suspicion of partiality, or any kind of undue influence; men of integrity and independence'.[5] In many cases, the parent Act of a tribunal required the appointment of 'fit' persons.[6] The central tribunals were small, generally three in number, and were composed of men of high calibre and qualification. Indeed, Edwin Chadwick had hoped to be appointed a Poor Law Commissioner, but he was perceived as being of an insufficiently high social standing, and was appointed their secretary instead.[7]

---

[2] *Parl. Deb.*, vol. LXXXII, ser. 3, cols. 40–1, 4 July 1845 (HC).

[3] Eric J. Evans, *The Contentious Tithe* (London: Routledge and Kegan Paul, 1976), p. 137.

[4] *Parl. Deb.*, vol. XXXIV, ser. 3, col. 859, 24 June 1836 (HC) per Henry Goulburn, speaking about the commutation of tithes.

[5] *Parliamentary History*, vol. XXXIV, col. 6, 1798 (London: T. C. Hansard, 1819).

[6] See for example Poor Law Amendment Act 1834, 4 & 5 Will. IV c. 76 s. 1.

[7] See David Roberts, *Victorian Origins of the British Welfare State*, reprint of Yale University Press edition 1960 (Hamden, CT: Archon Books, 1969), pp. 137–202 for the qualities and characters of civil servants.

112 *Legal Foundations of Tribunals in 19th-Century England*

The first demand of the new tribunals was that their members possess the same moral rectitude as was required of the judges of the regular courts. There did not, however, exist the clear and rigorous training, nor the well-established practices for appointment, such as were found within the legal profession to provide the personnel of the courts. Neither did the tribunals possess the same formal processes to provide a procedural safeguard to the interests of the parties, and accordingly the personnel of the tribunals took on a new importance. Furthermore, without the anonymity afforded by ancient establishment, the members of the new tribunals would be visible and prominent as individuals, particularly since the numbers were so small. In order to ensure that men of the highest calibre were appointed to the tribunals, the legislature looked to two familiar and traditional techniques: the oath and the property qualification.

Just as the judges of the regular courts had to take the judicial oath whereby they bound themselves under God to do right to all people without fear or favour, affection or ill will, so the commissioners of the statutory tribunals of the nineteenth century invariably had to take similar oaths under which they bound themselves to act in a judicial manner. They underlined the probity, honesty and impartiality with which the commissioners would carry out their duties. The oath varied remarkably little between tribunals, being generally to execute their powers 'faithfully, impartially, and honestly, according to the best of [their] skill and judgment'. The oath to act judicially was the only one required of the Tithe and the Inclosure Commissioners and their assistants[8] and was an attenuated version of the older oath taken by inclosure commissioners from the eighteenth century under their private inclosure Acts, whereby each had to swear that he would 'faithfully, impartially, and honestly, according to the best of [his] Skill and Ability, execute and perform the several Trusts, Powers, and Authorities vested and reposed in [him] as a Commissioner, by virtue of [the relevant Inclosure Act] according to Equity and good Conscience, and without Favour or Affection, Prejudice or Partiality, to any Person or Persons whomsoever'.[9] The oath to act judicially was taken by the Commissioners for the

---

[8] 6 & 7 Will. IV c. 71 s. 9; 8 & 9 Vict. c. 118 s. 8 and, for the valuer's oath, s. 38.
[9] 41 Geo. III c. 109 s. 1.

Composition and Personnel

Redemption of the Land Tax and the Land Tax Redemption Appeal Commissioners,[10] and the Assistant Commissioners under the Triple Assessment Act 1798 swore to 'faithfully execute the office' and to act 'to the best of [their] knowledge and judgment'.[11] Every Poor Law Commissioner under the parent legislation of 1834 swore that he would 'faithfully, impartially, and honestly, according to the best of [his] skill and judgment, execute and fulfil all the powers and duties of a Commissioner under [this Act]'.[12] In some oaths the importance of the commissioners' appellate jurisdiction was stressed by making express mention of the duty to act judicially in relation to appeals.[13]

Sometimes the oath addressed anticipated particular dangers. A prominent example was the requirement to take an oath of non-disclosure of information by the commissioners for the new income tax in 1799. It was a point of particular sensitivity in relation to this new impost and so necessary to give the public more confidence in a tax perceived to be inquisitorial and invasive.[14] Accordingly the various bodies of tax commissioners, and all their subordinate officers, took oaths of non-disclosure of any personal information pertaining to a taxpayer's fiscal affairs that they acquired in the course of the performance of their duties.[15] Though in practice these oaths were scrupulously taken and apparently respected,[16] their effect in law was limited, and so their value in ensuring both secrecy and judicial behaviour must be doubtful. Penalties were laid down for acting without having taken the oath,[17] but as these were promissory oaths, namely oaths relating to an intention to do, or not to do, something in the

---

[10] 38 Geo. III c. 60 s. 5.   [11] 38 Geo. III c. 16 s. 60.

[12] 4 & 5 Will. IV c. 76 s. 11.

[13] For example the oaths taken by the commissioners under the Inhabited House Duty 1779, 19 Geo. III c. 59 s. 14; Servants Duties Act 1785, 25 Geo. III c. 43 s. 18; Horses and Carriages Act 1789, 29 Geo. III c. 49 s. 12.

[14] 39 Geo III c. 13 s. 22 (1799); 43 Geo. III c. 122 ss. 30, 233, Schedule F (1803). See C. Stebbings, 'The Budget of 1798: Legislative Provision for Secrecy in Income Taxation' (1998) *British Tax Review* 651.

[15] 39 Geo. III c. 13 ss. 22, 34, 35, 105, 106 (1799); 43 Geo. III c. 122 s. 30 and Schedule F (1803). See too *Lee* v. *Birrell* (1813) 3 Camp 337; Income and Property Taxes Act 1842, 5 & 6 Vict. c. 35, Schedule F.

[16] 5 & 6 Vict. c. 35 ss. 19, 38, Schedule F; DRO 337B add2/TAXATION/Income Tax 7.

[17] The penalty was £100, 39 Geo. III c. 13 s. 22. The same penalty was laid down by the Triple Assessment Act 1798, 38 Geo. III c. 16 s. 60 which was incorporated into the 1799 Income and Property Taxes Act by reference.

114 *Legal Foundations of Tribunals in 19th-Century England*

future, their breach would not result in a prosecution for perjury.[18] It would seem that until 1889 when it became a criminal offence to disclose tax information to unauthorised persons,[19] the only sanction for breaching the oath was a moral or religious one. Neither did these oaths carry much public conviction in the tax sphere. One taxpayer observed in the 1870s that he did not doubt the commissioners were honourable men, 'but even honourable men did not at all times exercise sufficient prudence and keep secrets'. Another felt that it was all very well to be told that the commissioners had to take an oath of secrecy, 'but he discovered that some people could swallow an affidavit as easily as he could a pill'. He 'very much questioned whether matters connected with his business would not ooze out, and if they did it would cause him much annoyance and perplexity'.[20]

The integrity and impartiality of commissioners was supported more robustly by a statutory property qualification, in an age where the cultural perception was that the ownership of property indicated the moral worth of the individual, and that accordingly wealth equated with honesty and probity. This was particularly important in the case of the fiscal tribunals, where the members had to be seen to enjoy a sufficiently high status to command the respect and trust of the taxpayers that their affairs would not be disclosed, to ensure that as far as possible the commissioners were independent and incorruptible, and to ensure that they were able to undertake onerous duties without payment. Accordingly the only formal qualification for acting as a tax commissioner, whether for the land tax, the assessed taxes or the income tax, was a material one, namely the ownership of property of a certain value.

The imposition of a property qualification on tax commissioners drew heavily on established practices, since the only qualification of justices of the peace was that they had to own land yielding at least £100.[21] The first Land Tax Act 1688 required its

---

[18] Prosecution for perjury would lie for most assertory oaths, where a matter of fact was falsely affirmed or denied. See Thomas Wood, *An Institute of the Laws of England*, 5th edition, 1734 (New York: Garland Publishing, 1979), p. 412; *The Times*, 20 December 1798.

[19] Official Secrets Act 1889, 52 & 53 Vict. c. 52.

[20] These comments were made in the context of a local rebellion against income tax in Devon, as reported in the *Exeter and Plymouth Gazette*, 13 January 1871 and 1 December 1871.

[21] 5 Geo. II c. 18 (1731); 18 Geo. II c. 20 (1744).

Composition and Personnel 115

commissioners to have real estate to the value of £100,[22] and that of 1797 required possession of a freehold, copyhold or leasehold estate of the clear yearly value of £100, or be heir to such an estate worth £300.[23] The Land Tax Redemption Commissioners had to satisfy the same requirements,[24] and the requirements were unchanged when the Land Tax Commissioners were given duties under the assessed taxes legislation.[25] So revolutionary and unpopular was the new income tax in 1799, and yet so pressing the need for its success, that overt care was taken in the appointment and qualification of the commissioners.[26] The property requirements of the General Commissioners of Income Tax were much higher than those demanded of the Land Tax Commissioners, being broadly set at £10,000 of personal estate in the counties and cities, or three times the landed qualification of the Land Tax Commissioners.[27] The qualifications of the appellate tribunal, the Commissioners of Appeal, were set even higher at double the qualification for the General Commissioners.[28] In their case the requirements were enormous: personal estate of £20,000, or six times the landed qualifications of the Land Tax Commissioners. The object was to give greater confidence to any taxpayer who wished to appeal against his assessment. It was highly unlikely, observed Pitt of his new commissioners, that such men would 'wantonly abuse their trust' or 'indulge in idle or injurious curiosity'.[29] When Henry Addington recast the income tax in 1803, he retained the principle of selection and the traditional property-based qualification. The commissioners were to be selected from the Land Tax Commissioners as before,[30] were to be 'fit and proper' to act in the capacity of General Commissioners, and were to satisfy the property qualifications laid down by the Act, namely

---

[22] 1 Will. & M. c. 20 s. 7. This was omitted in the Land Tax Act 1692, which instead required its commissioners to have paid a certain sum under a poll tax Act of the same session. See 4 Will. & M. c. 1 s. 51 (1692).

[23] 38 Geo. III c. 5 s. 92. To ensure that no one acted without being duly qualified, a monetary penalty of £50 was laid down for each offence by 39 Geo. III c. 5 s. 96 and 38 Geo. III c. 48 s. 1.

[24] 38 Geo. III c. 60 s. 4 (1797).

[25] Houses and Windows Duties Act 1747, 20 Geo. II c. 3 s. 6; Servants Duties Act 1777, 17 Geo. III c. 39 s. 7; Inhabited House Duty Act 1778, 18 Geo. III c. 26 s. 10; Horses and Carriages Duties and Taxes Management Act 1785, 25 Geo. III c. 47 s. 11; Triple Assessment Act 1798, 38 Geo. III c. 16 s. 45.

[26] 39 Geo. III c. 13 ss. 11–15, 23, 24.   [27] *Ibid.*, s. 23.   [28] *Ibid.*

[29] *The Times*, 4 December 1798.   [30] 43 Geo. III c. 122 s. 3.

116 *Legal Foundations of Tribunals in 19th-Century England*

land to the value of £200 per annum, personal estate of £5,000, or any property yielding £200 per annum.[31] These requirements were kept unchanged when the income tax was revived after a twenty-five-year suspension in 1842.[32] Penalties were imposed on commissioners acting without being qualified.[33]

The statutory qualifications required of commissioners accurately reflected the social status of the persons ultimately appointed. The property qualifications of the tax commissioners, true to their model of the justices of the peace, served to maintain the status quo in relation to the position that the landed gentry held in the lay administration of justice in the country. The permitted qualification through the ownership of personal estate, particularly in the cities, opened the ranks of lay justice to the new commercial fortunes. Most General Commissioners were also justices of the peace and Land Tax Commissioners, and were almost invariably considerably involved in civic life. The tax tribunals constituted a self-perpetuating civic elite as a result of their appointment and renewal from their own ranks. Under the private inclosure bills of the eighteenth century, the office of commissioner was repeatedly filled by the same people, and thus became in the nature of a profession.[34]

The property qualifications, however, addressed not only quantum but also location. Justices of the peace had to be resident in the districts over which they were given jurisdiction, and the land they were required to own had to be in that county. Land Tax Commissioners similarly had to satisfy their landownership requirement with at least half being in the district for which they were appointed,[35] and at least a third of the landed qualification of General Commissioners of Income Tax needed to be in the district for which a commissioner was to act.[36] The residency requirement was retained for the General Commissioners in 1803, though somewhat obliquely, through their selection from among the Land Tax Commissioners, who did have to satisfy an express residency requirement, and by requiring no more than half of a

---

[31] *Ibid.*, s. 12.   [32] 5 & 6 Vict. c. 35 ss. 4, 5, 6.

[33] For example, see Houses and Windows Duties Amendment Act 1748, 21 Geo. II c. 10 s. 3; 39 Geo. III c. 13 s. 27 (1799).

[34] E. C. K. Gonner, *Common Land and Inclosure*, 2nd edition (London: Frank Cass & Co Ltd, 1966), p. 90 n.

[35] 38 Geo. III c. 48 s. 2 (1798).   [36] 39 Geo. III c. 13 ss. 25, 26 (1799).

Composition and Personnel

117

landed qualification to be in the area for which a commissioner was appointed.[37] When the income tax was revived in 1842 a landed property qualification was retained, though it no longer needed to be in the district for which a person had been appointed.[38] Additional Commissioners, however, had to be resident in the district.[39] In practice most General Commissioners lived in the district to which they were appointed. If they did not, it could cause problems with the daily administration of the tax. In 1860, for example, in Stafford, the clerk had a crisis of personnel. He had eight commissioners. Three resided in Scotland or abroad, two resided at some distance from Leek and could rarely act, and the remaining three were aged over seventy and could not easily act. The clerk complained to the Board of Inland Revenue that '[t]he want of gentlemen residing in the town to sign papers on non-meeting days' caused very real problems in the transaction of routine business.[40]

Though the purpose in requiring local property ownership was not articulated in the legislation, it was to ensure that the tribunal members possessed specialist knowledge in the form of familiarity with local economic and commercial conditions. It was peculiar to the lay tax tribunals, and reflected their close connection with the institution of the justices of the peace. No expert knowledge of any kind was required of a magistrate. It was considered that he would judge well enough by the light of common sense. In tax, however, it was regarded as of essential importance in arriving at correct assessments to ensure knowledge of local people and local economic conditions, of the level of wages in particular trades, and of profits in particular individuals. It was a real aid to correct assessment when trade was still small scale and local,[41] but its real value declined as the scale of trade and industry grew and tax administration became more complex.[42] Despite the diminishing value of local knowledge in the tax sphere, however, it remained central to legislative policy, though more as an expression of local

---

[37] 43 Geo. III c. 122 s. 17.   [38] 5 & 6 Vict. c. 35 s. 14.   [39] *Ibid.*, s. 16.

[40] TNA:PRO IR 40/1052, Meeting of the Land Tax Commissioners for the County of Stafford, 1860.

[41] See *Minutes, Income and Property Tax, 1852* qq. 3268, 3275.

[42] *Minutes, Income Tax, 1919* q. 552. See generally C. Stebbings, 'Popular Perceptions of Income Tax Law in the Nineteenth Century: A Local Tax Rebellion' (2001) 22 *Journal of Legal History* 45.

118 *Legal Foundations of Tribunals in 19th-Century England*

control so as to ensure the acceptance of measures that were centralising in nature. It ensured that local interests were represented in the implementation of certain controversial measures and went some way to satisfying the enduring desire for localism.

The selection of tribunal members from the local community, however, brought with it the danger of partiality and so raised doubts as to their independence. The strength they derived from being selected from the taxpayers themselves was equally their weakness. As local laymen possessing only regional knowledge in addition to good characters judged by the possession of material wealth, the tax commissioners were intended to be independent and divorced from the executive. In reality, their qualifications rendered this apparent independence vulnerable. The independence from government of the General Commissioners in hearing appeals was of essential importance to the success of the tribunals in terms of public acceptance not only of the tribunals, but of the legislation they were seeking to implement.

The dissatisfaction felt by many taxpayers in the 1870s with the appellate jurisdiction of the General Commissioners[43] stemmed from a perception that the General Commissioners, possessing only imprecise and inadequate local knowledge, were ill-equipped to carry out their adjudicating functions and were inevitably unduly influenced in this respect by the government official in the district, the surveyor. This of course meant that an appeal against assessment or surcharge was viewed as futile, being an appeal against the Crown in effect determined by a paid Crown official, and as going against the principles of English justice. It was because of the perceived inadequacy of local knowledge as the basis of determining tax appeals, and the undoubted superior knowledge of the surveyor that he was perceived as the real power in the appeals process. This perception reflected the reality. The surveyor's entire working life was dedicated to the administration of tax according to the statutory provisions and he gained a complete mastery of a complex and increasingly technical area of activity. Part-time, unremunerated and busy commissioners, even if they were conscientious, could not expect to equal this

---

[43] See for example *Exeter and Plymouth Gazette*, 1 November 1872, where it was described as 'one of the greatest evils ... one of the vilest Courts that an Englishman could have to submit to'.

Composition and Personnel 119

knowledge and experience. The surveyor was also expected to ensure a measure of uniformity in the administration of tax across the country and accordingly was not well disposed to local variations in practice. Much depended on the calibre, attitude and dedication of individual panels of commissioners, but in general the commissioners did take a great deal of notice of the views of the surveyor at the appeal hearings, and rarely disagreed with him.[44] This perceived lack of independence from the executive was often resented by taxpayers, particularly in the 1870s when the income tax abolition movement was at its height.

The resentment and suspicion felt by the taxpayers was exacerbated by its intensely personal dimension. The lay income tax tribunals were composed of local men of standing with some knowledge of business and commerce, being generally themselves in some form of trade, or in some profession, or having retired from one. It was inherent in the system of lay commissioners, as both administrators and adjudicators, that a taxpayer's neighbour, friend, commercial or political rival would have access to the details of his private tax affairs. Not only was this regarded as an unacceptable invasion of privacy,[45] it raised the specific fear of commercial bias. Taxpayers resented disclosing financial information about themselves for fear the commissioners might use it to undermine their trade in pursuance of a commercial grudge or simply for commercial gain.[46] Though there is evidence to suggest that such partiality or disclosure was rarely, if ever, known,[47] such perceptions illustrate that there was little public confidence in the statutory safeguards of property qualifications and oaths to ensure that General Commissioners of calibre and integrity were appointed. The personal dimension, and to some extent the influence of the surveyor, constituted the price taxpayers had to pay for lay involvement in the assessment process, which in turn – in theory at least – kept the government at a distance and acted as a safeguard to the taxpayer.

---

[44] *Minutes, Income and Property Tax, 1852* q. 2469.

[45] *Minutes, Income Tax, 1919* q. 555. One surveyor giving evidence in 1852, however, maintained that such disclosure was not a problem, and that taxpayers preferred the system of lay assessing and adjudicating: *Minutes, Income and Property Tax, 1852* q. 1561.

[46] *Minutes, Income Tax, 1919* qq. 7148, 8190.

[47] *Minutes, Income and Property Tax, 1852* q. 3271.

120 *Legal Foundations of Tribunals in 19th-Century England*

Local knowledge had traditionally been implicit in the appointment of inclosure commissioners under private Acts of Parliament, but in those instances their independence was severely compromised by their methods of appointment. Traditionally the commissioners were appointed by the parties: one for the landowner, one for the lord of the manor and one for the church. The general perception reflected the reality that this method of appointment was abused, and that each commissioner watched over the interests of the party to whom he owed his appointment.[48] This was a clear feature of arbitration, but it was accepted in that context as the entire arrangement was based on agreement, implying notions of compromise and the voluntary foregoing of rights. In private inclosures it was not overt, but was perceived as ensuring the security of the appointing party's own interests. Accordingly this right was highly valued,[49] and the proposal in 1845 that a central board of commissioners should appoint Assistant Commissioners and send them into the locality to supervise the inclosure was met with some resistance as potentially undermining individual property rights. There were good reasons too for appointing a local commissioner, namely to ensure that he knew the area, the property, the parties and their 'liability to discordance', a commissioner who would 'come fairly and amicably to the consideration of the questions which would be submitted to him'.[50] On the other hand, a policy of local commissioners brought with it the potential for bias, just as it did in tax matters, to which danger the public was very much alive, a danger which would be obviated by the appointment of a centrally appointed commissioner from London.[51] There was thus some tension as to the most effective and acceptable composition of the new Inclosure Commissioners.

---

[48] *Minutes, Commons' Inclosure, 1844* q. 3624; W. E. Tate, *The English Village Community and the Enclosure Movements* (London: Gollancz, 1967), p. 109. Under the provisions of the Common Fields Inclosure Act 1836, 6 & 7 Will. IV c. 115 s. 3 the commissioners were appointed by a majority of the parties interested.

[49] *Minutes, Commons' Inclosure, 1844* q. 2968 *per* Richard Banks, solicitor.

[50] *Ibid.*, q. 1525 *per* John Higgins, an experienced commissioner of inclosures under the Common Fields Inclosure Act 1836; *Ibid.*, qq. 3979, 3984 *per* Wedd Nash, retired lawyer and farmer.

[51] *Ibid.*, qq. 3437, 3459 *per* Thomas Woolley, land agent and Assistant Tithe Commissioner; *ibid.*, q. 6158 *per* Ralph Cole, farmer.

Composition and Personnel

Yet another advantage of locally appointed commissioners was that of the power of self-interest if it were properly channelled. The tribunals formed under the Union Assessment Committee Act 1862[52] were composed of members of local Boards of Guardians, on the basis that they 'would be the least inexperienced body to which that duty could be intrusted', and that with their local knowledge and experience, would 'be as competent and certainly a less expensive tribunal for deciding a question of that nature'.[53] They were to have some practical knowledge of rating matters. As was later to be observed in the course of litigation, the members of the Assessment Committees were 'experts and have expert assistance, and they may be assumed to be capable of appreciating the real point and seeing what ought to be done'.[54] This object was promoted by self-interest, since the Board of Guardians consisted of the principal ratepayers and it was in their own interests to make a fair valuation.

Other tribunals required knowledge more specialised than a mere familiarity with a geographical area, knowledge that was essential for the administration of the statutory regime in question. Specialist, technical or practical knowledge was a major motive force behind the development of statutory tribunals, in that it constituted one of the principal shortcomings of the regular courts of law. Though the exact proportions of these skills, and whether they should all be looked for in the commissioners themselves, or merely in the subordinate officers, were matters of debate, the consensus was that there should be a combination of specialist skills. These could be practical knowledge, legal knowledge, business knowledge or local knowledge, or a combination of one or more. The nature and extent of the special knowledge and other skills required depended on the subject-matter with which the tribunal was concerned.

In some cases the specialist knowledge was reflected in the composition of the tribunal itself, with a requirement that one or more of the members be qualified in a particular way. In others, it was accepted that the specialisation would be acquired by the

---

[52] 25 & 26 Vict. c. 103.

[53] *Parl. Deb.*, vol. CLXVII, ser. 3, col. 1332, 3 July 1862 (HC) *per* William Barrow.

[54] *Gateshead Union Assessment Committee v. Redheugh Colliery Ltd* [1925] AC 309 at 325 *per* Viscount Finlay.

122 *Legal Foundations of Tribunals in 19th-Century England*

members through experience of the work. The three land rights tribunals established in the 1830s and 1840s to commute tithes, enfranchise copyholds and inclose land were examples of the latter. The three Tithe Commissioners appointed by the government and the Archbishop of Canterbury to supervise the commutation of tithes and the enfranchisement of copyholds were required by their parent Act only to be 'fit persons',[55] as were the Inclosure Commissioners. There was no property or other qualification. However, when they were appointing their Assistant Commissioners, they were to look for particular qualities that they felt necessary to undertake the challenging work of implementing the legislation in the field. They sought robust, imaginative, competent, practical men who were nevertheless sensitive to the conciliatory spirit of the legislation and in whom the parties concerned would have confidence. In practice they looked for men experienced in agricultural matters, perhaps as land agents, valuers, surveyors or practical country gentlemen, and as a result of many years of active inclosure, such men were available. Sound local knowledge was regarded as indispensable,[56] and their respect for and understanding of local issues was partly responsible for their success.[57]

The most efficient commissioners under the private inclosure Acts of the eighteenth century had been men with knowledge of farming or surveying who had gained inclosure experience by being appointed in many such processes.[58] When the settling of disputes arising in the course of tithe commutation was being debated, this same admixture of experience and practical knowledge was acknowledged as the most desirable qualification. William Blamire proposed a local board composed of a number of Assistant Commissioners, two of whom should be barristers of a certain standing, and men of practical experience in such matters, being farmers or surveyors. He was concerned for their independence, and maintained they should have no interest in the issue to be determined.[59] Sir Robert Peel, however, favoured the use of valuers to determine disputes, as under the inclosure legislation, with

---

[55] Tithe Commutation Act 1836, 6 & 7 Will. IV c. 71 s. 1.
[56] Evans, *Contentious Tithe*, pp. 138–9; *Minutes, Commons' Inclosure, 1844* q. 209 *per* William Blamire.
[57] Evans, *Contentious Tithe*, p. 139.   [58] Gonner, *Common Land*, pp. 74–5.
[59] *Parl. Deb.*, vol. XXXIII, ser. 3, col. 886, 12 May 1836 (HC).

Composition and Personnel

123

recourse to 'some man of weight and character' as umpire if they did not agree.[60] The valuation in an inclosure had to be made by someone with good farming experience who was able to judge the realistic yield of land and, accordingly, its value. But in the course of the debate as to the Inclosure Commissioners the power given to valuers to adjudicate on claims was regarded as unacceptable, the task being of such importance that it should be addressed by men of considerable experience rather than 'mere land agents'.[61] Status was regarded as an important factor in the determination of disputes. An attorney and banker giving evidence to a Select Committee on inclosure in 1844 said that the commission should include 'a highly eminent engineer' and 'a very good man of business, who combined with that knowledge of land and its interest'.[62]

The various land rights commissioners quickly built up considerable experience in their sphere of operation a quality that was acknowledged by the courts on numerous occasions. In relation to a disputed inclosure in 1862, which came to court in that year, Erle J remarked on the 'abundance of experience' that the commissioners had in the technical aspects of inclosure.[63] When the enfranchisement of copyhold tenure was being debated in the late 1830s, it was decided that the matter should be put in the hands of the Tithe Commissioners because they had wide experience in an analogous field and were familiar with the machinery necessary to adjust the rights of parties interested in copyholds.[64]

There were some fiscal tribunals where the need for a similar degree of specialist knowledge was acknowledged and the inefficiency of mere local knowledge recognised. With respect to the taxation of commercial income the legislature suggested that more might be needed, but in the event its provision was inadequate. The first provisions in William Pitt's legislation of 1799 were the more robust: the sensitivity of taxing commercial income was

---

[60] *Ibid.*, col. 908, 13 May 1836 (HC).

[61] *Per* Lord Worsley, *ibid.*, vol. LXXXII, ser. 3, col. 22, 4 July 1845 (HC).

[62] *Minutes, Commons' Inclosure, 1844* qq. 6576–8 *per* Thomas Salt, attorney and banker at Shrewsbury.

[63] *Church* v. *Inclosure Commissioners* (1862) 11 CB NS 654 at 680. The issue was whether an interest in brick earth should be taken into account when calculating the statutory assents and dissents to a proposed inclosure.

[64] *Report, Copyholds Enfranchisement, 1837–8* at p. 192.

124 *Legal Foundations of Tribunals in 19th-Century England*

addressed by the appointment of a separate tribunal, the Commercial Commissioners, with specialised personnel. Though like all lay tax commissioners the Commercial Commissioners had to satisfy a high property qualification,[65] they were to be selected by and from the commercial community to deal entirely, exclusively and secretly with its income. In London the Commercial Commissioners were the leading and wealthiest merchants.[66] The emerging industrial centres of the midlands and north of England were to have fewer commissioners according to the extent of the trade and manufacturing activity in the centre concerned.[67] Commercial knowledge was thus not expressly required, but was implicit in the machinery of appointment. It was more explicit in relation to their assistants, since these had to be persons who in their opinion would be 'best able to judge of the amount of the reputed income' of the taxpayers being considered by the commissioners.[68] When the taxation of commercial income was put in the hands of the Additional Commissioners in 1803, the mercantile quality of the tribunal composition was ensured only through the special provision for appointment in mercantile centres.[69] Their formal qualifications remained those only of residency and property. In practice, however, Additional Commissioners were usually local businessmen, often retired, or active merchants or bankers.

When the Special Commissioners of Income Tax were given appellate powers in 1842, as civil servants they did not have to satisfy any property or residency requirements. In practice they came from the ranks of functionaries in the Inland Revenue with considerable experience of tax administration. There was some demand for the appointment of at least one chartered accountant to the tribunal,[70] and the importance of specialist accounting knowledge in the preparatory stages of tax appeals was widely acknowledged.[71] The accumulated experience and expertise of the

---

[65] 39 Geo. III c. 13 ss. 111, 114, 23, 24.   [66] *The Times*, 20 May 1800.

[67] 39 Geo. III c. 13 s. 111.

[68] *Ibid.*, s. 98. They too had to satisfy the same property requirements as the General Commissioners: *ibid.*, s. 114.

[69] 43 Geo. III c. 122 ss. 6, 7.

[70] *Minutes, Income Tax, 1919* q. 13,719 *per* G. F. Howe, presiding Special Commissioner.

[71] *Ibid.*, q. 15,994 *per* A. M. Bremner, barrister, on behalf of the General Council of the Bar of England.

Composition and Personnel

Special Commissioners of Income Tax, intensified by a measure of internal specialisation,[72] were soon recognised as outstripping those of their lay colleagues. A. M. Bremner, barrister, appearing before the Royal Commission on the Income Tax in 1919, reflected on his own long experience of the tax tribunals and made it clear that when he had a case which presented particularly difficult problems of law which necessitated reference to provisions of the income tax legislation and decided cases, he would always be confident that if appearing before the Special Commissioners they would know and understand the issue.[73] He felt no such confidence before the General Commissioners and so always advised taxpayers whose cases turned on difficult points of law to appeal to the former.[74]

But it was in relation to railway regulation that the need for specialist knowledge was paramount. The railway companies wanted an independent, permanent and fixed tribunal of high standing which would have the confidence of the railway companies and the public through its specialised knowledge of railway management.[75] Specialised knowledge was required in order to interpret badly drawn statutory provisions in a more enlightened way than a court of law was able to do, in an area where the subject-matter was often highly technical. Even when the Railway Department was a purely administrative body scrutinising railway bills and reporting on them to Parliament it was clear that specialist engineering expertise was essential. When asked what kind of body would give confidence to the railway companies, a railway engineer in 1846 replied that it was any board of appropriate ability: 'what they are afraid of', he said, 'is ignorance; they are not afraid of knowledge'.[76] Robert Stephenson MP, son of George Stephenson and himself a leading railway engineer, believed any central board of control should be constituted of men with

---

[72] *Minutes, Income and Property Tax, 1852* qq. 545, 620 *per* John Fuller, Special Commissioner; 'Minutes of Evidence before the Select Committee on Inland Revenue and Customs Establishments', *HCPP* (1862) (370) xii 131 q. 405 *per* Charles Pressly, chairman of the Inland Revenue Department.

[73] *Minutes, Income Tax, 1919* q. 15,921. [74] *Ibid.*

[75] *Minutes, Railway Amalgamation, 1872* qq. 91–4 *per* William Cawkwell, general manager of the London and North Western Railway.

[76] 'Minutes of Evidence before the Select Committee on Railway Acts Enactments', *HCPP* (1846) (590) xiv 5 at q. 1599 *per* John Hawkshaw, engineer of the Manchester and Leeds Railway Company.

126 *Legal Foundations of Tribunals in 19th-Century England*

engineering, commercial and local knowledge.[77] Though the Court of Common Pleas was given sole jurisdiction over questions of railway facilities and undue preference in 1854, provision was made for the assistance of an engineer or barrister. The court was permitted to appoint expert engineers or other specialists to inquire into the case and thereby assist them in arriving at their determination.[78] In practice it seems that the court interpreted this provision as requiring the experts to assist the court by acting as witnesses to one party or another.[79] The use of expert witnesses, however, was problematic. There was, it seems, a greater danger of partisanship where expert witnesses were called by the parties, for there was a greater tendency for a witness to favour his party's cause in the giving of his evidence.

The use of expert assessors to assist the superior courts of law in specialist cases was a familiar feature of the legal system. It reflected the accepted policy against the creation of more special courts of law, and the adjudication of all disputes before the regular courts of general jurisdiction. The Elder Brethren of Trinity House were regularly called in to assist the judge in the Court of Admiralty with questions of navigation, in the Wreck Commissioners' Court and in arbitrations, and indeed the Judicature Act of 1873 contained full provisions for the trial of technical cases in the High Court, if need be, by a judge sitting with skilled assessors in preference to the appointment of a specialist judge.[80] This solution was also preferred to the creation of a special tribunal of commerce in the last quarter of the nineteenth century. In their third report in 1874 the Judicature Commissioners accepted that the courts of law lacked the specialist technical and practical knowledge needed to adjudicate properly upon commercial cases, and felt that the provision of assessors would achieve all the perceived advantages of a specialist tribunal. They drew short, however, of permitting such assessors to have any say in the decision itself; that was to be left entirely to the judge.[81] In

---

[77] 'Minutes of Evidence before the Select Committee on Railway and Canal Bills', *HCPP* (1852–3) (170) xxxviii 5 at qq. 1072–4.

[78] Railway and Canal Traffic Regulation Act 1854, 17 & 18 Vict. c. 31 s. 3.

[79] See R. E. Wraith and P. G. Hutchesson, *Administrative Tribunals* (London: George Allen and Unwin, 1973), p. 26.

[80] 36 & 37 Vict. c. 66 s. 56.

[81] 'Third Report of the Judicature Commissioners', *HCPP* (1874) (957) xxiv 1 at pp. 8–9.

Composition and Personnel 127

practice, however, assessors were not widely used, partly because of their cost and enduring fears of partisanship.[82]

Despite the provision for expert assistance, ultimately the Court of Common Pleas was found to be inadequate in its implementation of the railway legislation, being unable for example to decide whether the railway companies could indeed make arrangements with each other or not to ensure the free forwarding of traffic. The Joint Select Committee of 1872 proposed 'a court constituted of persons specially acquainted with the subject' to settle disputes over running powers and rates without the difficulty associated with recourse to the regular courts.[83] Not only was their expert knowledge necessary to enable the disputes to be settled, it was also necessary to fulfil another envisaged function of the tribunal, which was to assist and advise Parliament in railway legislation to ensure it was 'more harmonious and satisfactory'.[84] The Railway and Canal Traffic Act 1873 showed a real commitment to specialised lay expertise, both in the composition of the tribunal itself – since of the three persons of high standing who were to make up the tribunal, one member was to be skilled in railway management – and in the power given to the commissioners to appoint one or more assessors to assist them in the exercise of their jurisdiction.[85] Thomas Farrer, the permanent secretary of the Board of Trade, had said in evidence that one of the members should be 'some person of technical knowledge, like the knowledge of a railway manager or of a railway director' and probably also 'some experienced engineer'.[86] The commissioners themselves found the presence of a member skilled in railway matters to be invaluable, and believed that it led to a higher quality of evidence from the witnesses, as the latter were confident their evidence was being understood. Even some lawyers agreed that it was essential for specialist experts to be members of the tribunal. Robert Baxter, a solicitor who was also a coal owner, giving evidence before the Select Committee on Railways in 1881,

---

[82] See *Minutes, Railways (Rates and Fares), 1882* qq. 1495–6 *per* Edward Pember QC.

[83] *Report, Railway Amalgamation, 1872* p. 48.   [84] *Ibid.*, at p. 49.

[85] 36 & 37 Vict. c. 48 s. 23. The clause was not present in the first version of the bill, but was added in committee: see first version in *HCPP* (1873) (34) iv 325, cl. 19; second version, *HCPP* (1873) (121) iv 341, cl. 22. See too *Report, Railway Amalgamation, 1872* p. 49.

[86] *Minutes, Railway Amalgamation, 1872* q. 7435.

128 *Legal Foundations of Tribunals in 19th-Century England*

said: 'Now the law is particularly unwise in mercantile transactions; there is a special incapacity in the legal mind to grasp the requirements and particularities of mercantile transactions, and if you send those questions to this court you have not got any very wise trader there, and therefore it is a court commanding no respect in that matter.'[87] However, Ralph Littler QC, when putting forward his model for a reformed Railway Commission in 1882, favoured assessors as the best means of ensuring technical knowledge before the court. He said they never became out of touch with their field of expertise as they were currently engaged in it, and they could not dominate the court because they were always different. He thought assessors should consist of engineers and traffic managers, men of eminence who, for example, had been presidents of their chambers of commerce, and men of integrity and knowledge, who should be moderately rewarded for their services.[88]

There were, however, arguments against having lay specialists as members of the tribunal itself.[89] A common objection was that as soon as they served full time on a tribunal and left the practice of their trade or profession, their knowledge became outdated and obsolete. This was perceived as a particular danger in areas of rapid development such as the railways. The most potent objection, however, was expressed by Edward Pember QC, a barrister with wide railway experience, in 1882. He condemned specialist lay adjudicators as 'apt to be partisans', with no legal training and generally no judicial aptitude, for that skill did not follow from a man's success, however great, as a trader or railway manager.[90] This objection went to the heart of the ethos of the statutory tribunals, which were necessarily conceived as fundamentally lay bodies, with membership depending not on any legal knowledge, but on technical expertise or familiarity with a geographical area. Nevertheless, the lesson long learned in arbitration, that experts in the subject-matter of a dispute were often not sufficiently

---

[87] *Minutes, Railways, 1881* q. 9313. See too the evidence of Samuel Laing, secretary to the Railway Department of the Board of Trade, experienced counsel before Railway Committees, Member of Parliament and chairman of a railway company: *Minutes, Railways, 1844* q. 257.

[88] *Minutes, Railways (Rates and Fares), 1882* qq. 3921–5.

[89] See *ibid.*, q. 1339 *per* J. H. Balfour Browne, barrister, where a preference is expressed for expert witnesses.

[90] *Ibid.*, at q. 1496.

Composition and Personnel 129

conversant with the rules of legal procedure or evidence, and that the proceedings suffered from the introduction of irrelevant or unacceptable evidence,[91] was remembered. An attorney in 1844 told a Select Committee inquiring into inclosures that he wanted 'an eminent lawyer to control the law of the thing'.[92] This was a widely held view: that if a judge or lawyer presided over a tribunal, he could keep a much stricter control over evidence and proceedings than a layman, and could thereby keep the length, and thus the cost, of proceedings down.

It was accepted that no dispute-resolution body could function effectively without access to some degree of legal expertise. Only lawyers were accustomed to sifting evidence and judging its value from an independent and neutral perspective, with special knowledge acquired in a formalised and disciplined way with the natural and rigorous assessments inherent in a well-established profession. The degree of legal expertise within a tribunal, or the provision for access to it, were questions of some moment in the formative period of each statutory tribunal. There was an underlying anxiety about giving too much discretion and power to settle legal rights to a tribunal composed of untrained laymen, but it was accepted that legal expertise need constitute only one element, and possibly a minor one, in the composition and personnel of the tribunal. In the context of a court of law, however, the emphasis was quite different. A lay composition was the fundamental block to the establishment of the Tribunal of Commerce in 1874. Despite its objectives and proposed composition, that organ was unambiguously conceived as a court of law. As a body administering justice, the orthodox view was that it was imperative that it should be composed of, or at least presided over by, men learned in the law. It would be making decisions on commercial questions of principle, and those should be uniform and constitute clear precedents for commercial conduct, for otherwise it would lead to 'confusion and uncertainty in the administration of the law'.[93] Merchants, it was feared, 'would be too apt to decide questions that might come before them ... according to their own

[91] 'First Report of the Judicature Commissioners', *HCPP* (1868–9) (4130) xxv 1 at p. 13.
[92] *Minutes, Commons' Inclosure, 1844* q. 6578 *per* Thomas Salt.
[93] 'Third Report of the Judicature Commissioners', *HCPP* (1874) (957) xxiv 1 at p. 8.

130 *Legal Foundations of Tribunals in 19th-Century England*

views of what was just and proper in the particular case'.[94] Accordingly, while the desirability of the contribution of commercial men was accepted, it could not be allowed to dominate the composition. 'Commercial questions', maintained the Judicature Commissioners, 'ought not to be determined without law, or by men without special legal training.'[95] Legal training was essential to determining cases according to the rules of law and judicial precedent. In relation to the statutory tribunals, however, the perspective was otherwise. Specialist expertise above all was necessary to administer the new legislation, and legal input was, to varying degrees, merely desirable and helpful, particularly in the dispute-resolution context. Accordingly different solutions were suggested, debated and ultimately adopted, ranging from the compulsory membership of one or more legally qualified commissioners, of more or less eminence, to informal legal advice from a clerk not even required to be so qualified by statute. The unifying principle, however, was that there was at least some degree of legal expertise available to the tribunal in its deliberations.

The potential legal dimension of the work of the land rights tribunals was particularly evident, with the complexity of the law of real property being well known, and consequently the issue of the extent of desirable legal skill was hotly debated in their formation. While it was desirable for even lay commissioners in these tribunals to have some knowledge of property law[96] to deal with routine issues, it was understood that however well versed they were in the technical processes of tithe commutation, copyhold enfranchisement or inclosure, and even if they had a rudimentary knowledge of property law, they would inevitably on occasion have to address matters of considerable challenge in an area of law well known for its archaic technicality and extreme complexity. While calls for at least one Inclosure Commissioner to be 'a very eminent lawyer, of deep reading, and of many years' experience'[97] were regarded as excessive, and even provision of a permanent lawyer on the staff was considered generous, the necessity for

---

[94] *Ibid.*   [95] *Ibid.*

[96] *Minutes, Commons' Inclosure, 1844* q. 5760 *per* Walter Coulson, the draftsman of the commons' inclosure bill.

[97] See *ibid.*, evidence of Thomas Salt, q. 6577, and at q. 6583 where he maintained that 'one thorough-paced lawyer is indispensable'. See too *Parl. Deb.*, vol. LXXXII, ser. 3, col. 41, 4 July 1845 (HC).

Composition and Personnel

direct access to high-quality legal advice was accepted and expressly provided for.

In both tithe commutation and inclosure, boundaries were often disputed and their definition was an essential prerequisite to both processes. When tithe commutation under the 1836 Act began it was soon found that the Assistant Commissioners were generally unable to deal efficiently with the difficult issues of law that presented themselves in the resolution of the disputes as to the right to tithe and in most boundary disputes, which by the Act they were bound to resolve. Questions of the admissibility, reliability and relevance of evidence in such disputes were found to be beyond them,[98] as they themselves admitted.[99] The Tithe Commissioners had to apply to the Lords of the Treasury for permission to appoint legally qualified assistants, and it was granted only two years after the passing of the principal Act.[100] The object was to ensure an effective machinery for the carrying out of tithe commutation at a reasonable cost. One of the objections to the appointment of a permanent lawyer-commissioner was that of expense. No lawyer would be prepared to act unpaid, and a competitive salary was regarded as excessive. As was observed in parliamentary debate, 'it was the duty of the Government, in cases like the present, to get the best man at the cheapest rate'.[101] The appointments were made from barristers and recorders in the localities, who would undertake the business in their own areas for the remuneration of an ordinary Assistant Commissioner. The central commission in this way made savings on travel expenses and were able to appoint lawyers who need not, and could not, give up their general practices permanently for the remuneration offered. The Tithe Commissioners looked for 'gentlemen of respectable legal attainments, and who are fitted to grapple with the difficulties of the cases referred to them'.[102]

Similarly the Inclosure Act 1845 made provision for the appointment of a legally qualified Assistant Commissioner, but

---

[98] *Minutes, Copyholds Enfranchisement, 1837–8* at q. 17.
[99] *Minutes, Commons' Inclosure, 1844* qq. 2577, 4035–6.
[100] *Minutes, Copyholds Enfranchisement, 1837–8* q. 13. Specialist Assistant Commissioners were to be barristers. See for example *Re Dent Tithe Commutation* (1845) 8 QB 43.
[101] *Parl. Deb.*, vol. LXXXII, ser. 3, col. 47, 4 July 1845 (HC).
[102] *Minutes, Copyholds Enfranchisement, 1837–8* q. 16.

132 *Legal Foundations of Tribunals in 19th-Century England*

had learned the lesson not only of its own past in the form of the difficulties which the Inclosure Commissioners under private inclosure Acts had experienced in the resolution of boundary disputes,[103] but also of the Tithe Commissioners. As with tithes, the general view was that boundary disputes were better resolved by a lawyer rather than a lay commissioner or a jury, and accordingly the parent Act of the commission made provision for it. The Act provided that a specialist Assistant Commissioner, being a practising barrister of at least five years' standing, could be appointed as assessor to assist the valuer in the determination of a contested claim or objection, and when he was appointed the determinations of the valuer were to be made in accordance with his advice.[104] The decision to make the appointment lay with the valuer himself or with the persons interested in the inclosure. The provision went some way to meeting the criticism that a valuer was of insufficient status and experience to adjudicate on disputed claims, and served to give the parties more confidence in the dispute-resolution aspect of the inclosure procedure.

In tithe commutation and inclosure the legally qualified Assistant Commissioners were brought in not so much because of their knowledge of tithe or inclosure law, but for their more general legal skills relating to the admissibility of evidence, its weighting and the inferences to be drawn from it. It was felt that 'to know what is legal evidence is a science requiring a large portion of a life, and can only be attained by gentlemen at the bar'.[105] Though possibly experienced in inclosure law, country surveyors and farmers were insufficiently skilled as judges of evidence. In tithe commutation the legally qualified Assistant Commissioners were retained only in relation to disputes involving legal rights where the evidence was likely to be particularly complex, notably determining boundary disputes and modus[106] disputes. Indeed disputes of this kind generally involved such a substantial amount of written and oral evidence, as well as a complexity of subject-matter, that a trained legal mind was regarded as indispensable. In 1846, for example, a tithe commutation for the

---

[103] See *Minutes, Commons' Inclosure, 1844* qq. 258 ff.
[104] 8 & 9 Vict. c. 118 s. 35.
[105] *Minutes, Copyholds Enfranchisement, 1837–8* qq. 6577, 6579 *per* Thomas Salt.
[106] A modus was a private arrangement that converted the exact tenth of produce into the right to receive a fixed annual sum or a fixed amount of produce.

Composition and Personnel 133

parish of Barlaston in Staffordshire was hindered by a dispute between the landowners and the incumbent as to the existence of a number of moduses. The landowners alleged moduses on certain hay crops, milch cows, wood fuel, garden produce, swarms of bees, honey and colts, which the incumbent denied. A meeting was called under the provision of the 1836 Act and was heard at a local inn. The incumbent and the major landowners were legally represented, while the smaller landowners appeared in person. The evidence was voluminous, complex and technical, and consisted entirely of proceedings in two earlier suits in the Exchequer and Chancery on the claims to the moduses in question. Though the suits concerned the same subject-matter and were based on the same evidence, the outcomes were contradictory. The Assistant Commissioner had to read, digest and understand this litigation leading to decrees of courts of competent authority and the judgments that were, even by the standards of the day, regarded as 'elaborate'. Though a barrister, the Assistant Commissioner was in a difficult position. He reported that to give effect to the two contradictory decrees must 'be to do a manifest absurdity' and the consequent recital would 'appear very indecent upon the fact of it'. He concluded that he had no option but to disregard one or other decision, or disregard both and rehear the entire matter. 'I do not think it decorous', he said 'in an Assistant Tithe Commissioner to pretend to decide between Mr Baron Alderson and Vice Chancellor Knight Bruce, nor that it would be consistent with public convenience to give operation to both of these decisions.' He asked the board to take the opinion of the law officers. The law officers observed that it was not for the commissioners to 'constitute themselves a superior court of appeal to revise those decisions', and that 'a little care in drawing the recitals may avoid all indecency which is apprehended'. He was told that he was not bound by the decisions, but that he should merely take them into consideration and that one decision was, in the circumstances, to be given greater weight. The Assistant Commissioner held a further meeting on this basis and 'after much negotiation' arrived at an award that was acceptable to all parties.[107]

The lay character of the tribunals sometimes informed the limits of their jurisdiction, as in the case of the Tithe Commissioners.

---

[107] TNA:PRO IR 18/9249 (1846–3).

134   *Legal Foundations of Tribunals in 19th-Century England*

In 1839 Alderson B, in holding that the jurisdiction of the Tithe Commissioners was limited to deciding suits pending in court only if those questions impeded the making of an award, observed that he could not 'presume that the Legislature would ever have dreamed of giving jurisdiction to the Tithe Commissioner to determine nice questions depending on equity pleading, or evidence affecting not only the validity of moduses but other important questions. I cannot think that such matters were meant to be decided by persons who have, generally speaking, received no legal education.'[108]

The new specialised tribunal for railway regulation replacing the Court of Common Pleas in 1873, known as the Railway and Canal Commission, consisted not only of railway experts, but also of a person with 'the legal and judicial experience and habits of a judge'.[109] He was to be an eminent lawyer,[110] and the new tribunal was perceived as 'a mingled court of law and trading, the law preponderating'.[111] However, the directors and shareholders of railway companies showed considerable animosity to the commission in the years immediately following its introduction, arguing that it was not protecting their interests sufficiently strongly and expressing a want of confidence in the legal members of the commission. Edward Pember QC, a barrister with considerable experience of railway matters, believed the commission had failed largely through its composition.[112] In his view, and the view of other lawyers, the legal element in the cases before the commission predominated, concerning questions of law and the interpretation of the legislation, and yet this was not reflected by its composition where the legal commissioner was in the minority. Another barrister with a railway practice was Richard Webster QC, and he too believed the commission had failed because it was not presided over by a lawyer. All judicial and quasi-judicial proceedings in his experience, he observed, were best conducted 'where the head and governing mind ... is a legally-trained mind'.[113] Sir Frederick Peel, the first chairman of the commission,

---

[108] *Girdlestone v. Stanley* (1839) 3 Y & C Ex 421 at 423.
[109] *Minutes, Railway Amalgamation, 1872* q. 7435 *per* Thomas Farrer.
[110] *Report, Railway Amalgamation, 1872* p. 49.
[111] *Minutes, Railways, 1881* q. 9313 *per* Robert Baxter.
[112] *Minutes, Railways (Rates and Fares), 1882* qq. 1489–93.
[113] *Ibid.*, at q. 1640.

Composition and Personnel 135

disagreed and said that the questions his tribunal heard were not so dominated by legal issues, just the implementation of the 1854 Act, so bearing in mind the object of that legislation, the questions which the commissioners had to address were questions of fairness, reasonableness and the adequacy of arrangements.[114]

Lawyers and railway companies demanded that the three commissioners should be replaced with a single judge of equal standing, rank and remuneration to a High Court judge.[115] The companies believed that a single judge could decide virtually all the cases coming before him, but that if a case did happen to be of particular technical difficulty, it would be a simple matter to extend to his court the power given to the High Court of Justice by the Judicature Act of appointing a skilled assessor to sit with him.[116] This view, which in effect called for a return to the adjudication of 1854, was not, however, shared by either the individual traders or the general public, and in 1882 a Select Committee recommended that the composition of the commission remain unchanged.[117]

In 1887 the House of Lords debated the question whether a judge should be appointed at the head of the Railway Commission. The personnel of that commission had always been an issue of prime importance, essentially because the magnitude of the interests in question were such that the railway companies in particular wanted the confidence which only a high-status composition could give them. With considerable financial interests at stake they wanted the highest quality of decision-making, and they were probably also conscious that their means were such as to permit the purchase of the best legal advice and that they were likely to win their cases on points of law. To deny them that right was to undermine their dignity and status. As Lord Grimthorpe observed at the second reading of the Railway and Canal Traffic Bill of 1887, even 'the common pickpockets and burglars have a right to be tried by the best Judge in England, and a woman with

---

[114] *Ibid.*, at qq. 2969, 2972–3.

[115] *Ibid.*, at q. 1495 *per* Edward Pember QC.

[116] *Minutes, Railways, 1881* qq. 13, 518 *per* James Grierson, general manager of the Great Western Railway Company, reading a paper previously prepared for the Board of Trade by the railway companies.

[117] 'Report from the Select Committee on Railways (Rates and Fares)', *HCPP* (1882) (317) xiii 1 at p. 13; see too *Minutes, Railways (Rates and Fares), 1882* q. 1336 *per* J. H. Balfour Browne.

136 *Legal Foundations of Tribunals in 19th-Century England*

an action for breach of promise could appeal through all the Courts on points of law'.[118] The Lord Chancellor, Lord Halsbury, however, opposed the proposal for a permanent judge on the commission, on the basis that the judges were already over-committed and that specialist expertise was required; legal expertise could be acquired through the medium of appeals.[119] The traders too opposed the idea of a permanent professional judge for fear that it would render the tribunal prohibitively expensive to them.

The Prime Minister in 1887 favoured a panel of expert laymen rather than a judge, at least insofar as issues of policy were concerned, and the real issue was the function of the tribunal itself. If the sole purpose of the Railway Commission were the determination of questions of law, then the regular courts were the obvious tribunal. But, he said,

In the determination of those questions some element of policy must be introduced. In the interpretation of the principles laid down in the exercise of the powers and discretion of the Commission there was an element of policy of a grave character in which the balance had to be held fairly between the two great and important interests of the trader and the Railway Companies – a policy which required knowledge of a special kind that Judges, with all their omniscience, did not possess in a greater degree than other subjects of Her Majesty. For those reasons it seemed to him that it was wise to provide that the expert element should predominate in the Court.[120]

Ultimately, however, the railway companies succeeded in their demands. Legislation of 1888 reformed the commission primarily by altering its composition to include a judge of the High Court as a new, permanent and presiding commissioner to replace the former legal commissioner.[121] The other members were to be appointed on the recommendation of the Board of Trade, and one was to have experience of railway business.[122] In composition, therefore, the tribunal most closely resembled a court of law, and indeed it was provided that it should sit at the Royal Courts of Justice when in London and was commonly called a court. Under its constitution the judge always sat, even where no questions of law were at issue, and where any question of law occurred, the

---

[118] *Parl. Deb.*, vol. CCCXII, ser. 3, col. 162, 14 March 1887 (HL).
[119] *Ibid.*, col. 1748, 29 March 1887 (HL).
[120] *Ibid.*, col. 1750 *per* Marquess of Salisbury.
[121] Railway and Canal Traffic Act 1888, 51 & 52 Vict. c. 25 s. 4.   [122] *Ibid.*, s. 3.

Composition and Personnel

137

opinion of the judge was to prevail.[123] This was a change from the 1873 legislation where the legal member had to abide by the decision of the majority, even on a question of law. This had also meant that the expert legal opinion was unknown to the parties, but this was remedied in 1888 when it was provided that the commissioners should deliver separate judgments, as the regular courts did, rather than one joint and necessarily majority view. In practice, however, it seems that even when judgments were collective, they generally concealed no overruling of the expert legal opinion, for the view of the legal member on a legal question almost invariably prevailed.[124]

Where neither a commissioner was required to be legally qualified, nor was provision made for direct access to legal advice, other means had to be found to deal with those occasions on which such advice was necessary. The tax tribunals illustrated the range of possibilities. Alone among the fiscal tribunals, the Commissioners of Appeal for the Redemption of the Land Tax were expressly permitted to seek professional legal advice if they had any doubts as to the correct resolution of the appeal before them. They could call upon a barrister of at least five years' standing.[125] These commissioners were, unusually, required to be justices of the peace as well,[126] but the provision allowing them to call on legal experts suggests that their status as such was required not for any legal expertise but rather for their local knowledge and possibly their social standing. The Special Commissioners of Income Tax, who were given judicial functions in 1842, were generally experienced Inland Revenue officials and men with other, often legal, training. The legal element in their work became so dominant that in 1919 it was suggested that the Special Commissioners 'should be drawn like any other judicial tribunal from the ranks of the legal profession',[127] though this was rejected.[128] In the case of the majority of fiscal tribunals, however, statute demanded qualification only by property ownership and residence, and there was no formal

---

[123] *Ibid.*, s. 5.

[124] *Minutes, Railways (Rates and Fares), 1882* q. 2990 *per* Sir Frederick Peel.

[125] 38 Geo. III c. 60 s. 121 (1798); 42 Geo. III c. 115 s. 157 (1802).

[126] 38 Geo. III c. 60 s. 120 (1798).

[127] *Minutes, Income Tax, 1919* q. 24,099 *per* Randle F. W. Holme, solicitor, on behalf of the Law Society.

[128] 'Report of the Royal Commission on the Income Tax', *HCPP* (1920) (615) xviii 97 at p. 184, para. 360.

138 *Legal Foundations of Tribunals in 19th-Century England*

legal expertise included within their structure. All were empowered by their parent legislation to appoint a clerk.[129] Though his statutory functions were invariably laid down as purely ministerial, comprising the receipt, filing, copying and storage of the key documentation,[130] the position developed into a more substantive contribution to the legal process of the tribunal. The tax commissioners came to look to their clerk for legal advice, both substantive and procedural, and the clerk often became as dominant as the surveyor.[131] There was a similar development in relation to the clerk of the justices of the peace, and since the tax commissioners were often also justices of the peace, the parallel development is unsurprising. Despite the key role as legal adviser to the tribunal, the qualification to act as a clerk to all the direct tax commissioners remained throughout the nineteenth century as merely to be a 'fit person' in the view of the appointing commissioners.[132]

In the everyday running of the land rights tribunals too the clerks took on the role of adviser to lay adjudicators in matters of law and procedure. Where the subject-matter of the tribunal was largely legal in nature, as in the land rights tribunals, and where the members were all laymen, there was a considerable risk that the tribunal would be dominated by a forceful and able clerk. The commissioners in private inclosures were often largely controlled by their clerk, generally a local solicitor, and commonly influential and the promoter of the inclosure bill for a wealthy client. One of his principal duties was to give a sound opinion if a legal question arose,[133] but he often conducted the whole inclosure through his mastery of its detail. Ostensibly matters of judgment such as the value of the land were left to the commissioners themselves.[134] The professional clerk was particularly influential when the private lay Inclosure Commissioners had to determine boundary disputes. It

---

[129] 38 Geo. III c. 5 s. 14 (1797).

[130] 1 Will. & M. c. 20 s. 10 (1688); 4 Will. & M. c. 1 s. 12 (1692); 38 Geo. III c. 5 ss. 14, 15 (1797); 38 Geo. III c. 16 s. 78 (1798).

[131] See 'Appendix to the Report of the Departmental Committee on Income Tax, with Minutes of Evidence', *HCPP* (1905) (2576) xliv 245 qq. 1978, 2014 *per* Arthur Chamberlain JP, putting forward the views of the Birmingham Chamber of Commerce on income tax.

[132] See for example the Taxes Management Act 1803, 43 Geo. III c. 99 s. 9 and the Taxes Management Act 1880, 43 & 44 Vict. c. 19 s. 41.

[133] *Minutes, Commons' Inclosure, 1844* qq. 3803, 3808.

[134] *Ibid.*, q. 4536 *per* Robert Graham, attorney and solicitor.

Composition and Personnel 139

was a well-known danger. In the debate surrounding the establishment of a Tribunal of Commerce in 1874, it was observed that where in France a commercial tribunal was composed of lay merchants advised by a legally qualified greffier, that officer dominated the tribunal and was the most important person in it, despite having no formal vote, resulting in the anomaly that the person who in effect decided the case did not have the formal responsibilities of a judge.[135] Such professional domination was the inherent danger of lay tribunals.

The clerk was just one of a number of subordinate officers which the commissioners were empowered to appoint by their parent legislation. Since the central boards of commissioners acted in an essentially supervisory role, the legislation invariably made provision for the appointment of a number of subordinate officers to undertake the practical work of the administration of the legislation.[136] With the commissioners and their subordinate officers, all appointed directly or indirectly by the commissioners themselves,[137] the tribunals comprised a number of layers of authority and competence. The land rights tribunals' structures comprised commissioners, their assistant commissioners, valuers and assessors or apportioners. The Assistant Commissioners were the ones who implemented the law in practice, and were central to the process. All subordinate officials had significant functions, but the extent of any dispute-resolution function differed as to the tribunal, being very prominent in the land rights tribunals and in some fiscal tribunals,[138] and less so in the railway tribunals. They reported back to the central commissioners in London, who directed policy and gave advice to their assistants as to how to proceed in individual cases. Inclosure valuers had very wide powers, both administrative and adjudicatory, greater indeed than in tithe commutation or copyhold enfranchisement, but they were firmly under the control of the commissioners who had the authority to remove them.[139] Tithe commutation required not

---

[135] 'Third Report of the Judicature Commissioners', HCPP (1874) (957) xxiv 1 at p. 8.

[136] See for example the Poor Law Amendment Act 1834, 4 & 5 Will. IV c. 76 s. 7.

[137] Tithe Commutation Act 1836, 6 & 7 Will. IV c. 71 s. 4; Copyhold Act 1841, 4 & 5 Vict. c. 35 s. 4.

[138] Notably under the Triple Assessment Act 1798, 38 Geo. III c. 16 s. 56.

[139] Inclosure Act 1845, 8 & 9 Vict. c. 118 s. 128.

140 *Legal Foundations of Tribunals in 19th-Century England*

only the Assistant Commissioners to undertake the process in the locality, but also valuers, apportioners and mappers, the calibre of whom was often subject to criticism. The problem was that inexperienced or ignorant subordinate officers were often appointed, either because of a shortage of such expertise, or because the landowners insisted on particular individual appointments. In 1839 the Tithe Commissioners wearily accepted this fact, observing that if they employed persons in whom the landowners had no confidence, 'discontent, appeals, and, consequent on these, very heavy expenses both to the public and individuals would follow, which must entirely destroy the harmony and contentment which have hitherto marked the progress of Commutations'.[140] In many instances the appointment of valuers for tithe commutation was taken very seriously and the duties required of them clearly enunciated. In the tithe commutation of the parish of Newton St Cyres in Devon in 1842, two valuers were proposed to carry out the apportionment, and their appointment was agreed subject to the approval of their prices by the landowners. The valuers were given clear instructions and time limits.[141]

In the fiscal tribunals, which were the most independent and so differed from other tribunals in the nature and extent of central control, there were assessors and collectors as well as a clerk. Early land tax legislation provided that the assessors, whose task it was to make the valuation of the property and assess it to the tax, were to be appointed from the leading inhabitants of the area and were to be 'able and sufficient', summoned by precept and subject to a penalty if they refused to serve.[142] They were equally liable to a penalty if they were found to be guilty of fraud or abuse in the carrying out of their duties.[143] Those chosen by the commissioners, therefore, had little choice as to whether to act or not. The collectors were, in the case of the land tax, appointed by the assessors. In their execution of the various assessed taxes and the triple assessment the Land Tax Commissioners of the eighteenth century were to appoint assessors and

---

[140] 'Report of the Tithe Commissioners for England and Wales', *HCPP* (1839) (108) xvi 335 at p. 337.
[141] TNA:PRO IR 18/1419.
[142] 4 Will. & M. c. 1 s. 8 (1692); 38 Geo. III c. 5 s. 19 (1797).
[143] 38 Geo. III c. 5 s. 19 (1797).

Composition and Personnel 141

collectors,[144] whose only qualifications were that they should be resident in the district in question, and, sometimes expressly and sometimes implicitly, fit and responsible persons in the eyes of the commissioners. Some had to give security.[145] The income tax legislation gave the commissioners the duty and power to appoint assessors and collectors.[146] The Railway Commissioners were empowered under the legislation of 1873 to appoint and dismiss two Assistant Commissioners to act under their direction, and their functions were clearly defined to include the making of inquiries and reports and the undertaking of arbitrations at the direction of the commissioners. The assistants possessed all the powers of entry, inspection, summoning and examining witnesses, requiring documents and administering oaths.[147] They could also appoint and remunerate such officers as they thought fit.[148]

Most commissioners, with the notable exception of the local tax commissioners,[149] were remunerated. With their intense concern to keep government expense to a minimum, the remuneration of the new tribunal members was always an issue of debate. The Poor Law Commissioners were paid £2,000 pa, and it was clear from their inception that the Tithe Commissioners were to be paid, though there was some dispute as to the source of their remuneration. The proposal was that they would be paid out of the consolidated fund, on the basis that as the issue of tithe commutation was 'a great national question', the nation should bear the cost. Others believed that the parties interested in the settlement of the tithe question should bear the cost.[150] Ultimately they were entitled by their governing legislation to a maximum salary of £1,500 pa paid from public funds.[151] Inclosure Commissioners appointed under private arrangements were

---

[144] Houses and Windows Duties Act 1747, 20 Geo. II c. 3 ss. 6 9; 20 Geo. II c. 42 s. 2 (1747); Houses and Windows Duties Amendment Act 1748, 21 Geo. II c. 10 s. 23; Servants Duties Act 1777, 17 Geo. III c. 39 ss. 9, 14; Inhabited House Duty Act 1778, 18 Geo. III c. 26 ss. 12, 18; Horses and Carriages Duties and Taxes Management Act 1785, 25 Geo. III c. 47 ss. 19, 25; Triple Assessment Act 1798, 38 Geo. III c. 16 s. 44.

[145] For example, collectors under the Houses and Windows Duties Amendment Act 1748, 21 Geo. II c. 10 s. 23.

[146] 43 Geo. III c. 122 s. 28 (1803); 43 Geo. III c. 99 s. 9 (1803).

[147] 36 & 37 Vict. c. 48 s. 21.   [148] *Ibid.*, s. 24.

[149] Special Commissioners of Income Tax were remunerated.

[150] *Parl. Deb.*, vol. XXXIV, ser. 3, col. 857, 24 June 1836 (HC).

[151] Tithe Commutation Act 1836, 6 & 7 Will. IV c. 71 s. 7

142 Legal Foundations of Tribunals in 19th-Century England

remunerated, but only one of the three new central Inclosure Commissioners was to be remunerated.[152] The Railway Commissioners under the legislation of 1873 were to be well remunerated out of public funds. Each commissioner was to receive up to £3,000 pa, and each of the two Assistant Commissioners up to £1,500 pa.[153] The Special Commissioners of Income Tax were paid a fixed salary of £600 pa[154] in 1851 and by 1920 they were being paid £1,200 a year for the presiding commissioner and between £850 and £1,000 pa for the others.[155] They were paid an allowance of 2 guineas a day when out on circuit for the purpose of hearing appeals.[156] The other tax commissioners, however, were unpaid, and in that followed the justices of the peace, whom they resembled in so many other ways. Justices of the peace had always performed their judicial and administrative functions without remuneration, viewing them as a civil and social duty and an honour to perform. Their functions were assigned by the executive to men who were sufficiently rich and sufficiently disinterested to devote their leisure to the public service.

Whatever variation there was in the remuneration of the commissioners themselves, provision was invariably made in the legislation for the remuneration of subordinate officials. The Assistant Tithe Commissioners, for example, received by statute a maximum allowance of £3 a day, and the secretary not more than £800 pa.[157] Clerks to Inclosure Commissioners under private bills were paid in the region of 3 guineas a day.[158] The clerk to the Land Tax Commissioners was to be paid by poundage,[159] as were the collectors and the receivers-general.[160] Under the Triple

---

[152] Inclosure Act 1845, 8 & 9 Vict. c. 118 s. 6; Common Fields Inclosure Act 1836, 6 & 7 Will. IV c. 115 s. 9 allowed the commissioners a maximum of 3 guineas a day, including expenses.

[153] 36 & 37 Vict. c. 48 s. 22.

[154] *Minutes, Income and Property Tax, 1852* q. 160 *per* Charles Pressly.

[155] *Minutes, Income Tax, 1919* q. 13,609 *per* G. F. Howe.

[156] 'Minutes of Evidence before the Select Committee on Inland Revenue and Customs Establishments', *HCPP* (1862) (370) xii 131 q. 121 *per* Charles Pressly.

[157] Tithe Commutation Act 1836, 6 & 7 Will. IV c. 71 s. 7. Assistant Inclosure Commissioners were to be paid a maximum of 3 guineas a day, and all reasonable expenses to be paid out of the consolidated fund: 8 & 9 Vict. c. 118 ss. 6, 7.

[158] *Minutes, Commons' Inclosure, 1844* qq. 3897–9.

[159] 1 Will. & M. c. 20 s. 10 (1688); 4 Will. & M. c. 1 s. 12 (1692); 38 Geo. III c. 5 s. 14 (1797).

[160] 1 Will. & M. c. 20 s. 10 (1688); 4 W. & M. c. 1 s. 11 (1692); 38 Geo. III c. 5 ss. 13, 14 (1797).

Composition and Personnel 143

Assessment Act 1798 the remuneration of the clerk to the Assistant Commissioners was a central matter, and there was express provision that it should be no more than attorneys or solicitors would charge for like work.[161] The clerks to the commissioners themselves were to be paid such sum as the commissioners should direct, with the agreement of the Treasury, not exceeding $1\frac{1}{2}$d in the $£$,[162] while clerks to the General Commissioners of Income Tax were paid 2d in the $£$.[163]

All the commissioners were appointed either directly or indirectly by the Crown. Though they varied in their degree of independence from the executive, their provenance, their remuneration by central government and their mixed administrative and adjudicative functions, seriously compromised the public perception of their independence where an appeal was against an administrative decision of the executive. There were exceptions, of course, where the government was not involved in a dispute as a party. In such cases, notably where disputes were between railway companies, tribunal members appointed by the government were actively welcomed as impartial adjudicators.[164] In general, however, the independence of the statutory tribunal was undermined by their composition and functions. This was in contrast to the regular courts of law, for although individual judges were criticised on occasion for their political allegiances, the existence and implementation of the doctrine of the separation of powers, and the public perception of it, ensured that the judges were generally regarded as entirely independent of the executive.[165] In his introduction to his second edition of *Law and Public Opinion in England*, Professor Dicey argued that unlike the judges, government officials exercising even adjudicatory functions could not be entirely independent of the government.[166] The perception was,

---

[161] 38 Geo. III c. 16 s. 78 (1798).

[162] *Ibid.*, s. 79; *Minutes, Income Tax, 1919* qq. 13,599–603 *per* G. F. Howe.

[163] 'Report from the Select Committee on Inland Revenue and Customs Establishments', *HCPP* (1862) (370) xii 131 qq. 179, 180 *per* Charles Pressly.

[164] *Minutes, Railway Amalgamation, 1872* q. 4506 *per* Sir Edward Watkin, chairman of the Manchester, Sheffield and Lincolnshire Railway Company and of the South Eastern Railway Company.

[165] See generally A. H. Manchester, *A Modern Legal History of England and Wales 1750–1950* (London: Butterworths, 1980), pp. 79–83.

[166] A. V. Dicey, *Lectures on the Relation between Law and Public Opinion in England during the Nineteenth Century*, 2nd edition (London: Macmillan and Co., 1914), p. xliii. See Arthurs' criticism of Dicey's analysis, and a comparison of

144 Legal Foundations of Tribunals in 19th-Century England

therefore, that the judges protected personal freedoms, with the implication that government officials did or could not. It was certainly an argument in the debate as to the constitution of the new tribunals that the appointment of legally qualified commissioners or assistants, to decide tithe boundary disputes for example, would introduce an element of impartiality and protection of individual rights.

The two extremes of status were seen in the tax tribunals: General Commissioners of Income Tax were independent, unpaid, part-time lay members appointed essentially by Parliament,[167] while Special Commissioners of Income Tax were full-time civil servants appointed by the central government with a background either in the Inland Revenue itself or private legal practice, were based in London, remunerated out of an annual vote of Parliament, and were pensionable under the Civil Superannuation Acts. Furthermore, the members of the government department later known as the Board of Inland Revenue were themselves ex officio Special Commissioners, and as late as 1891 a judge observed that 'practically the Special Commissioners are identical with the Board of Inland Revenue'.[168] The land rights and Railway Commissioners were centrally appointed and remunerated, but were independent and answerable only to Parliament. It was undoubtedly the case that when commissioners were remunerated, there was a stronger tendency to view them as government officials. Indeed when the composition of the Tithe Commissioners was being debated, they were referred to as the 'Government Commissioners'.[169] Whether they were independent though government-appointed men possessing certain required qualities or government officials who would soon acquire them, the question of their independence was a pervasive issue in

---

the qualities of judges and administrators, in H. W. Arthurs, 'Rethinking Administrative Law: A Slightly Dicey Business' (1979) 17 *Osgoode Hall Law Journal* 1 at 34–6.

[167] They were chosen by the Land Tax Commissioners from among their number, and the Land Tax Commissioners were appointed by naming in each new Parliament's Name Act until the Act 32 & 33 Vict. c. 64 (1869), when the names of qualified persons were to be published in the *London Gazette*.

[168] *Special Commissioners* v. *Pemsel* (1891) 3 TC 53 at 99 *per* Lord Macnaghten, though he was speaking in a primarily administrative context.

[169] *Parl. Deb.*, vol. XXXIV, ser. 3, col. 859, 24 June 1836 (HC) *per* Henry Goulburn.

Composition and Personnel 145

the nineteenth century, affecting many aspects of the tribunals' nature and work. It was not, however, the dominant issue it was to become in the next century, because the work of the tribunals was accepted as being primarily administrative in nature with any adjudicatory function being purely ancillary to that function.

The independence of the commissioners in their adjudicatory function was raised particularly in relation to the tax tribunals, because of all the areas of activity in which tribunals were concerned, it was the one of constant and paramount concern to any government. While the implementation of railway regulation, land rights reconstitution and other social welfare legislation was highly desirable, the raising of tax revenue was imperative. The fact that the General Commissioners of Income Tax were not government officials was highly valued by taxpayers wishing to appeal against their tax assessments, and this was a factor in resisting the occasional calls for their abolition.[170] Accordingly when their independence was undermined by the domination of their judicial proceedings and decision-making by the greater knowledge and experience of the government official, there was widespread public resentment.[171] The domination undoubtedly existed, principally because the lay, part-time and unremunerated nature of the General Commissioners led to their being insufficiently informed and knowledgeable about income tax in general and individual taxpayers' financial affairs in particular, and so tended to accept the assessments of the surveyor unquestioningly. Since the surveyor was the representative of the Crown, a common feeling was that he was primarily motivated to secure as high a revenue as possible. And yet this was not the case with the Special Commissioners, despite a professional background and training which they shared with the Crown representative who appeared before them in appeal hearings,[172] and their strong and unambiguous intimacy with the Board of Inland Revenue, the government department whose function was the direction and control of the machinery and systems necessary to raise the revenue. There was a largely uncritical acceptance of their avowed impartiality and public confidence in the tribunal was high

---

[170] *Minutes, Income Tax, 1919* at q. 8280 *per* William Cash, on behalf of Institute of Chartered Accountants.

[171] See Stebbings, 'Popular Perceptions of Income Tax Law'.

[172] *Minutes, Income Tax, 1919* q. 23,891 *per* Randle F. W. Helme.

146 *Legal Foundations of Tribunals in 19th-Century England*

throughout the nineteenth century.[173] The Special Commissioners said they made every effort to stress their independence, impartiality and concern for the truth, and in the opinion of one Special Commissioner this perception was beginning to become established by the close of the century.[174] A Special Commissioner in 1906 said his tribunal was 'actually independent in every way of the Inland Revenue in the consideration of appeals, and we do our utmost to convey that fact to the public'.[175] The Special Commissioners themselves saw no tension in the same persons acting as administrators and adjudicators,[176] though in practice ensured as far as possible that the commissioners who made an administrative decision did not subsequently hear any appeal against it.[177] It was only in the following century that the admixture of administrative and judicial functions came to be perceived as unacceptable, and was ultimately addressed.[178]

[173] See the evidence of G. O. Parsons, the secretary to the Income Tax Reform League, who said in 1919 that he felt the taxpayer received 'the best of treatment': *ibid.*, q. 1853. This confidence proved to be enduring. See 'Report of the Committee on Ministers' Powers', *HCPP* (1931–2) (4060) xii 341 at pp. 432–3.

[174] See 'Minutes of Evidence before the Select Committee on Income Tax', *HCPP* (1906) (365) ix 659 at q. 2709 *per* Walter Gyles, Special Commissioner.

[175] *Ibid.* See too *Minutes, Income Tax, 1919* qq. 13,582; 13,588 *per* G. F. Howe.

[176] *Minutes, Income Tax, 1919* q. 13,781 *per* G. F. Howe. Other commentators did, however. See *ibid.*, (288–6) 269 at qq. 23,891; 24,017 *per* Randle F. W. Holme.

[177] *Ibid.*, (288–4) 627 at q. 13,782 *per* G. F. Howe.

[178] The administrative functions of the Special Commissioners of Income Tax were finally abolished in 1964, though it was first recommended in 1920.

4

JURISDICTION AND FUNCTIONAL POWERS

The tribunals of the first quarter of the nineteenth century were created in order to implement certain statutory regimes in a variety of spheres of human activity and concern, and were created by the statutes themselves. The nature of their duties was determined by the character of the legislation they were called on to implement and the statutory provision governing their creation, and so by their very nature their duties and functions varied considerably in their detail. However, whether their purpose was to make assessments to tax, to convert tithes to money payments, or copyhold land to freehold land, to value land for the poor rate or to regulate the railways, in principle they were strikingly similar. Their purpose was an administrative one, in the sense of the management of public affairs, and the enabling powers they exercised were largely administrative in nature. In order to execute their predominantly administrative function, it has been seen that there had to be some mechanism whereby any grievances, objections or disputes an individual might have could be raised and settled. When hearing and determining disputes, their function was a judicial one in the sense of resolving disputes on their merits by the establishment of facts and the application to those facts of legal rules. A common feature of these tribunals, therefore, was that they invariably combined functions that are today recognised as essentially administrative in nature with others which were primarily judicial. The stage in the administrative process at which the dispute-resolution might occur differed between tribunals, as did the balance of administrative and judicial powers, with the latter having a greater prominence and importance in some spheres than others. Taking jurisdiction in the wider and looser sense as synonymous with power rather than in the strict sense of the exercise of judicial authority, it was this

148 *Legal Foundations of Tribunals in 19th-Century England*

composite and internally incompatible jurisdiction that characterised tribunals and ultimately made their placement in both governmental and legal systems so problematic.[1] That the jurisdiction of the tribunals should be combined in this way was inevitable in view of their purpose and genesis. The admixture of functions was inherent and necessary, for the purpose of the tribunals was to administer a statutory regime and resolve any disputes which arose in the course of that implementation, and their powers reflected that objective. It was also novel, in that while there was a long tradition of giving administrative functions to judicial bodies, notably the justices of the peace, their functions were internally distinct and did not possess the feature of functional integration.

All the tribunals of the nineteenth century possessed these dual powers to a greater or lesser extent. The distinction between administration and judicial activity was often hard to draw, though purely ministerial functions could generally be identified. In the fiscal tribunals, which first in time and in clarity exhibited this mixed extra-judicial jurisdiction, a clear pattern of administrative and adjudicative functions could be discerned. When lay commissioners were appointed by an Act of 1797[2] to administer the land tax, a tax levied on personal property, employments and land,[3] the statute laid down the necessary administrative powers and structures to execute it. The Act stated that commissioners would be responsible 'for the better assessing, ordering, levying and collecting' of the tax 'and for the more effectual putting ... in execution' of the Act.[4] Their primary stated function and the determinant factor in their jurisdiction was therefore to execute the land tax, to supervise and co-ordinate the assessment to and collection of the duty. Their authority was thus both delimited and primarily administrative in nature. Their practical administrative duties of valuing, assessing and collecting were to be

---

[1] See below, pp. 295–314. [2] 38 Geo. III c. 5.

[3] See generally W. R. Ward, *The English Land Tax in the Eighteenth Century* (London: Oxford University Press, 1953). The Land Tax Act 1797 granted an aid to the Crown of some £2 million, with set quotas for each county, to be raised by a levy of 4s in the pound on personal property, employments and an equal pound rate on land: 38 Geo. III c. 5 ss. 6, 2.

[4] The wording was virtually identical to that in an Act of 1688 granting an aid to the Crown for the defence of the realm, 1 Will. & M. c. 20 s. 7, and in the Act of 1692 granting an aid in order to carry on the war against France, 4 Will. & M. c. 1 s. 7.

Jurisdiction and Functional Powers 149

undertaken by their subordinate officers, with assessors making the assessments and collectors undertaking the collection process.[5] There was no express requirement for any formal 'approval' by the commissioners of the assessments,[6] which would have been a reinforcement of their essentially administrative function of responsibility for correct assessment of the tax, though it was implicit in the requirement that they sign and seal the assessments.[7] The commissioners' ultimate control over the administration of the tax in 1797 was, however, confirmed by their statutory duty to summon the collectors and to examine them on oath so as to 'assure themselves of the full and whole Payment' of the sum charged on the district in question.[8] This was entirely inquisitorial and administrative, to check the actual sum levied by the Act had been duly raised and collected. When the Land Tax Commissioners were given the additional burden of executing the various assessed taxes, imposed on a large number of luxury items from the seventeenth century,[9] the governing legislation similarly stated that they were appointed 'for the better execution of [the] act, and for the ordering, raising, collecting, levying, and paying' of the sums raised.[10] Again, their function was expressly and unambiguously administrative in nature. The procedures the commissioners were to follow in doing this were set out by statute, and followed the usual pattern of supervising and controlling the subordinate assessors undertaking the practical work of assessment, the verification of the assessments by the commissioners' examination and inquiry, their formal allowance of the assessments, and collection by the collectors.[11] When finally the Land

---

[5] 38 Geo. III c. 5 s. 8. Cf. 1 Will. & M. c. 20 s. 7 (1688) and 4 Will. & M. c. 1 s. 8 (1692). In 1797 the commissioners had lost the power given to some of their predecessors to summon a taxpayer whom they believed had not been properly assessed. In 1692 they had been able to do so and to examine him 'by all lawful Ways and Means' as to his estate and its value (4 Will. & M. c. 1 s. 9), but the Act of 1797 left this to the assessors.

[6] Unlike earlier legislation: 1 Will. & M. c. 20 s. 8 (1688); 4 Will. & M. c. 1 s. 9 (1692).

[7] 38 Geo. III c. 5 s. 8.   [8] *Ibid.*, s. 22 and cf. 1 Will. & M. c. 20 s. 26 (1688).

[9] See generally W. R. Ward, *The Administration of the Window and Assessed Taxes 1696–1798* (Canterbury: Phillimores, 1963).

[10] The foundation of their jurisdiction over the many different assessed taxes lay in those Acts imposing taxes on houses and windows. See 20 Geo. II c. 3 s. 6 (1747). See Ward, *Window and Assessed Taxes*, pp. 8–9. See too 20 Geo. II c. 2 (1747).

[11] 20 Geo. II c. 3 ss. 6–10 (1747).

150 *Legal Foundations of Tribunals in 19th-Century England*

Tax Commissioners were entrusted with the execution of the Triple Assessment Act in 1798,[12] their jurisdiction was unchanged in its primarily administrative character. By its very nature, that tax left little room for the exercise of discretion, since it consisted of a straightforward multiplying of certain assessed taxes already determined. Accordingly the function of the commissioners was essentially that of supervising the correct calculation of the sum due on the basis of settled figures provided by central government and the making out of individual schedules of charge.[13]

In their administration of the various taxes, the Land Tax Commissioners were invariably given certain adjudicatory functions. The Land Tax Act itself made provision for the hearing of appeals by the commissioners. It provided that

all Questions and Differences which shall arise touching any of the said Rates, Duties and Assessments ... or the collecting thereof, shall be heard and finally determined by the said Commissioners, in such manner as by this Act directed, upon Complaint thereof made to them by any Person or Persons thereby grieved.[14]

The provision therefore embraced appeals against assessments and the other specific instances of adjudication and made it clear that their power was a general power to resolve disputes that arose in the course of the administration of the land tax.[15] Their powers of adjudication were thus expressly contained within the context of the administrative function.[16] The commissioners' statutory appellate adjudicatory jurisdiction was founded on the direction to 'hear and determine' disputes. The hearing and determination of appeals was the commissioners' primary adjudicatory task, but they also had to settle differences occurring in the levying of the tax by distress and sale,[17] between landlord and tenant as to the

---

[12] 38 Geo. III c. 16. By s. 45 this Act too was to be administered according to the procedures, rules and methods laid down for other taxes under the management of the Commissioners for the Affairs of Taxes.

[13] *Ibid.*, s. 48.   [14] 38 Geo. III c. 5 s. 23.

[15] See for example *Re Glatton Land Tax* (1840) 6 M & W 689 where this provision was regarded as providing the proper remedy for the double rating of land. This adjudicatory and appellate jurisdiction was no innovation, powers similar in nature and scope being found in the seventeenth-century land tax legislation: see 1 Will. & M. c. 20 s. 17 (1688); 4 Will. & M. c. 1 s. 20 (1692).

[16] Note that in the Land Tax Act 1688 the commissioners were to certify the tax raised into the Court of Exchequer under their signature and seal, after all appeals have been determined by them: 1 Will. & M. c. 20 s. 8.

[17] 38 Geo. III c. 5 s. 17.

Jurisdiction and Functional Powers

deduction of the land tax out of rents,[18] and as to the assessment of some non-exempt charity land.[19] Similarly in their administration of the assessed taxes, the Land Tax Commissioners were empowered to hear and determine the appeals of persons who felt themselves aggrieved by being over-rated by the assessors.[20] The commissioners were also given a broader adjudicatory power to settle 'all questions and differences that shall arise' in relation to the tax.[21] Again, in the course of their administration of the triple assessment, if a person was aggrieved by any assessment on the basis of a miscalculation, he could appeal to the commissioners, who were required to hear and determine the complaints.[22] They were empowered to 'compute and ascertain the sum justly to be charged', a provision which places their appellate power firmly in the context of assessment, and amend the assessment accordingly.[23] Similarly in specific instances, as for example when a joint occupation of a house was not reflected in the assessment,[24] provision was made for the hearing and determination of the issue by the commissioners.[25]

The Land Tax Commissioners thus possessed both administrative and adjudicatory functions, but when William Pitt introduced his legislation for the redemption of the land tax in 1798,[26] he adopted a different approach and separated the functions between two specialised bodies. The distinction was only superficially significant, for the administrative context of the adjudicatory jurisdiction remained. He created a new tribunal, the Commissioners for the Redemption of the Land Tax,[27] whose functions were exclusively administrative and consisted of contracting for the sale of the land tax and the consequent exoneration of the land[28] in return for a purchase of a stated amount

---

[18] *Ibid.*, s. 18.   [19] *Ibid.*, s. 28.

[20] The Act laid down the procedure to be followed: 20 Geo. II c. 3 s. 12 (1747).

[21] *Ibid.*, s. 21.

[22] 38 Geo. III c. 16 s. 54 (1798). By s. 56 the commissioners could nominate the Assistant Commissioners to hear appeals.

[23] *Ibid.*, s. 54.   [24] *Ibid.*, s. 53.   [25] *Ibid.*

[26] 38 Geo. III c. 60. The object of the legislation was to make the land tax set in 1797 perpetual, to be raised by an equal pound rate, but subject to redemption and purchase. For contemporary debate as to Pitt's scheme, whereby the tax could be discharged by a single payment, see *Parliamentary History*, vol. XXXIII, cols. 1434–54, 9 May 1798 (London: T. C. Hansard, 1819).

[27] Though they were to be selected from the ranks of Commissioners of the Land Tax: 38 Geo. III c. 60 s. 4 (1798).

[28] *Ibid.*, s. 17.

152 *Legal Foundations of Tribunals in 19th-Century England*

of government stock which was then to be transferred to the Commissioners for the Reduction of the National Debt.[29] The commissioners were described as 'merely servants of the Crown for the purposes of the act',[30] their task being to contract to sell or redeem the land tax for the highest possible price according to the statutory provisions for the public advantage.[31]

Where a person was aggrieved by the decision of the Redemption Commissioners, they could appeal to a separate body of appellate commissioners, composed of Commissioners of the Land Tax who were also justices of the peace.[32] They were required to hear and determine at Petty Sessions the appeal of any person aggrieved by a determination of the Redemption Commissioners in relation to any right or benefit of preference in, or any right of redemption of, any land tax to be sold by the Act, or with respect to the sale, mortgage or charging of any land for the purpose of redemption, where the consideration for the sale of the land tax did not exceed £500 of stock.[33] By expressly stating, albeit widely, the determinations which could be subject to appeal in this way, the legislation impliedly limited the scope of the appellate power.[34] While the jurisdiction of the appellate commissioners was exclusively adjudicatory, it was expressly limited to the adjudication of disputes arising in relation to the redemption. This division of administrative and adjudicatory duties between two separate bodies was maintained when the various Land Tax Redemption Acts were consolidated in 1802.[35] Nevertheless the adjudicatory powers were clearly still subordinate to, and subsumed by, the primary administrative function.

The same arrangement was adopted by Pitt when almost contemporaneously he introduced the new tax on income. While the income and property tax of 1799[36] was innovative in substance, it

---

[29] So much stock in the 3 per cent Consols as would produce a dividend exceeding the amount of the land tax redeemed by one-tenth: *ibid.*, s. 9.

[30] *Williams* v. *Steward* (1817) 3 Mer 472 at 506.

[31] *Ibid.*, at 504 *per* Lord Eldon.   [32] 38 Geo. III c. 60 s. 120 (1798).

[33] *Ibid.*, s. 121. When the sum in question exceeded £500 of stock, an aggrieved party had to appeal to the Court of Chancery or Exchequer: 38 Geo. III c. 60 s. 121 (1798).

[34] See counsel's argument in *Williams* v. *Steward* (1817) 3 Mer 472 at 491 in relation to the appeal provision in the consolidating Act 1802, 42 Geo. III c. 116 s. 197.

[35] 42 Geo. III c. 116.

[36] 39 Geo. III c. 13. By s. 36 the powers, rules, procedures and methods contained in the Triple Assessment Act and the other Acts relating to taxes under the

Jurisdiction and Functional Powers 153

was utterly traditional in machinery and in the nature of the jurisdiction with which the commissioners entrusted with the execution of the legislation were endowed. In the first instance those commissioners, formally called the Commissioners for the General Purposes of the Income and Property Tax Act, were entrusted with purely administrative powers. Since the legislation required a taxpayer to submit a sum which he maintained was 10 per cent of his income according to the rules in the Act to be used for calculation, the initial practical work of assessment in the hands of assessors was less demanding and less inquisitorial than with earlier taxes, and consisted of collecting the names of persons chargeable to tax and their statements. Accordingly the substantive administrative function of making the actual assessments rested with the commissioners, and they did so either on the basis of the statements if they believed them, or as a result of their own inquiries. The jurisdiction of the General Commissioners was limited to the ministerial act of arriving at the assessment, and was thus entirely administrative. It was also undoubtedly inquisitorial in nature.

As with the redemption of the land tax, the appellate jurisdiction for income tax was placed in the hands of a quite separate and higher body, the Commissioners of Appeal, whose sole function it was. In the familiar language of formal dispute-resolution, those commissioners were empowered to meet 'for the purpose of hearing and determining Appeals to be made by virtue' of the Act,[37] the jurisdiction extending to complaints by taxpayers aggrieved by assessments made upon them by the General Commissioners[38] and complaints by the surveyor. In determining these appeals they were given wide investigative powers in order to obtain information 'as they shall think necessary for ascertaining the due Proportions which such Party or Parties assessed ought to pay by virtue of this Act'.[39] This procedural provision was one that indicated the jurisdiction itself, though adjudicatory, was inquisitorial in nature, and underlined the primary purpose of the appeal as a step in the determination of the correct amount of tax payable.

management of the Commissioners for the Affairs of Taxes were to extend to this latest fiscal legislation.

[37] 39 Geo. III c. 13 s. 16 (1799). The Act laid down the process to be followed.
[38] *Ibid.*, s. 64.　　[39] *Ibid.*

154 *Legal Foundations of Tribunals in 19th-Century England*

This period of relative jurisdictional clarity within the income tax tribunals ended when Henry Addington recast the tax in 1803[40] and abolished the appellate commissioners. He transferred their powers to the General Commissioners, who then came to constitute both the supreme assessing body, as before, and also the supreme appellate body. The introduction by the same legislation of the schedular system, whereby income was taxed according to its source, introduced a further fragmentation of jurisdiction. The assessments were made by the General Commissioners, or by a new body of Additional Commissioners appointed from the General Commissioners, or by certain public officials, with the assistance of assessors and powers of investigation, depending on the source in question.[41] Not only were the General or Additional Commissioners to make the assessments, they possessed other administrative tasks such as the allowance or disallowance of exemptions and abatements.[42] The administrative functions of the General Commissioners were, therefore, extensive. Despite possessing the supreme assessing power, either directly or through the Additional Commissioners, the General Commissioners were constituted the only appellate body by the legislation of 1803. The appellate adjudicatory jurisdiction was superimposed on the administrative assessing function in the same hands, and the two were no longer distinct. Thus appeals from assessments under Schedules A and B were heard by the General Commissioners, who were the very men who had made the initial assessments. If a taxpayer felt aggrieved by any assessment of his commercial income made on him by the Additional Commissioners he could appeal to the General Commissioners, who were to hear and determine the appeals accordingly.[43] The context, however, remained the same: the commissioners' primary function was to

---

[40] 43 Geo. III c. 122.

[41] See *ibid.*, s. 31 (Schedules A and B, ownership and occupation of land); *ibid.*, s. 66 (Schedule C, annuities and dividends); *ibid.*, s. 84 (Schedule D, profits from any property, profession, trade or vocation); *ibid.*, s. 75 (Schedule E, public offices, employments, pensions and annuities). The Act made provision for an alternative assessment of commercial income by a system of referees, as a concession to the mercantile community's demand for secrecy in the taxation of their incomes: *ibid.*, ss. 110–24.

[42] *Ibid.*, ss. 198, 199.

[43] *Ibid.*, s. 144. The appeal procedure was the one of general application under the 1799 Act.

Jurisdiction and Functional Powers 155

implement the income tax legislation, and any appeal was merely the final step in the assessment to income tax.[44] There were no major changes to the legal basis of the appellate jurisdiction of the General Commissioners during the century.[45]

The Special Commissioners of Income Tax were given a limited administrative jurisdiction when they were created in 1805,[46] consisting of determining claims principally by charities to exemptions from tax on the ownership of land and on tax on the interest on government bonds. They also had power to assess dividends from the public funds when a taxpayer neglected to make a proper return to the local commissioners or where he had made a special arrangement.[47] When Sir Robert Peel reintroduced the income tax in 1842, one of the few major changes he made to Pitt's and Addington's legislation was to extend the Special Commissioners' administrative and adjudicatory jurisdiction considerably. Though their administrative duties still consisted mainly of examining and deciding upon various claims,[48] they now had a new power of assessment and an appellate adjudicatory function in relation to commercial income.[49] Taxpayers were given the option of being assessed either by the local commissioners or by the Special Commissioners. They made the assessments on the basis of the taxpayers' returns and the inquiries of the surveyor. In practice their power of assessment was relatively little used.[50] Later in the century

[44] Income and Property Taxes Acts 1806 (46 Geo. III c. 65 ss. 126–35) and 1842 (5 & 6 Vict. c. 35 ss. 118–26) reproduced in almost identical language the appeal provisions of the 1803 Income and Property Taxes Act and by reference incorporated the management Act of 1803 too.

[45] Taxes Management Act 1880 (43 & 44 Vict. c. 19) reproduced the wording of the 1803 Act almost exactly in s. 57(6)(7)(8).

[46] 45 Geo. III c. 49 s. 30.

[47] For a comprehensive account of the functions of the Special Commissioners, see J. Avery Jones, 'The Special Commissioners from Trafalgar to Waterloo' (2005) *British Tax Review* 40 and J. Avery Jones, 'The Special Commissioners after 1842: From Administrative to Judicial Tribunal' (2005) *British Tax Review* 80.

[48] 45 Geo. III c. 49 ss. 30, 37, 73–85 (1805); see A. Hope-Jones, *Income Tax in the Napoleonic Wars* (Cambridge: Cambridge University Press, 1939), pp. 23–8; A. Farnsworth, 'The Income Tax Commissioners' (1948) 64 *Law Quarterly Review* 372.

[49] *Parl. Deb.*, vol. LXII, ser. 3, cols. 657–8, 18 April 1842 (HC) *per* Sir Robert Peel. See Income and Property Taxes Act 1842, 5 & 5 Vict. c. 35 ss. 130–1.

[50] *Minutes, Income and Property Tax, 1852* q. 806 *per* Edward Welsh, surveyor of taxes for the City of London.

156 Legal Foundations of Tribunals in 19th-Century England

they acquired other assessing functions with respect to railway companies and railway employees.[51]

Their judicial appellate duties were limited, but ultimately came to dominate their work in importance. A taxpayer who had been assessed to income tax on his commercial income, whether by the Additional or the Special Commissioners, could elect to appeal against the assessment to the Special Commissioners.[52] Their appellate jurisdiction was considerably wider in Ireland, where they heard all appeals against all assessments, that country not having the infrastructure of General Commissioners.[53] In fact in Ireland there was the possibility of a further appeal from their decision, to the Board of Inland Revenue and an assistant barrister.[54]

The parent legislation of the fiscal tribunals laid down the matters of which they could take cognisance, their jurisdiction in the strict sense of the term. The nature of their jurisdiction was, however, informed in some instances by their procedure. The character of their methods as inquisitorial or adversarial was in certain instances evidence as to the nature of their appellate jurisdiction as administrative or judicial. This was particularly so in relation to the assessed taxes and the income tax, where the appellate jurisdiction was to allow an assessment to 'stand good' unless – and only then – it could be shown by the evidence before the tribunal that it should be varied. This provision was found in all the assessed taxes Acts, and in the Taxes Management Act 1803.[55] It confined the appellate jurisdiction to an adversarial expression, and confirmed the adjudicatory nature of the appellate power and the limits placed on the initiative that the commissioners could take in exercising it. It suggested that in hearing and determining appeals against assessments, the function of the commissioners was not to investigate the financial affairs of the taxpayer de novo to ascertain the correct amount of tax in fresh and absolute terms, but rather to decide whether, on the evidence before them, the assessment should, in the usual phrase, 'stand

---

[51] 23 & 24 Vict. c. 14 ss. 5, 6 (1860).   [52] 5 & 6 Vict. c. 35 s. 131.

[53] 'Minutes of Evidence before the Select Committee on Inland Revenue and Customs Establishments', *HCPP* (1862) (370) xii 131 qq. 408–9 *per* Charles Pressly, chairman of the Inland Revenue Department.

[54] *Ibid.*, q. 408.   [55] 43 Geo. III c. 99 s. 26.

Jurisdiction and Functional Powers   157

good'.[56] Accordingly they were given the power to increase or reduce the assessment as they thought fit in the light of the evidence presented to them.[57] A procedure that demanded fresh inquiry would have strengthened the administrative role of the appellate jurisdiction. Even, however, when the legislation directed the commissioners to compute the sum properly to be charged, as in the triple assessment and the early income tax, this did not necessarily import a fresh and searching inquiry at the appellate stage.[58] Even if the tribunals were exercising their appellate jurisdiction adversarially, and so arguably in a manner resembling the regular courts, its significance in relation to the juridical nature of the tribunal was limited. The adversarial or inquisitorial exercise of powers was an essentially procedural issue not touching the essential jurisdiction of the tribunal as administrative. It merely emphasised the appellate nature of the jurisdiction, the inquisitorial assessment having taken place at an earlier stage. Where tribunals survived, as in the case of the General Commissioners of Income Tax, the adjudicatory power became increasingly separated from the administrative one, both procedurally and functionally, the latter being placed in the hands of a government functionary. Even when this development took place, however, the general context of the appellate jurisdiction, which was clearly administrative in nature, remained unaffected.

The nature of the appeals heard by the fiscal tribunals can be discerned with varying degrees of accuracy, depending largely on the records kept by the tribunals of their proceedings, and the existence of a right of appeal to the regular courts. Not being courts of law themselves, their decisions were reported only if they went to appeal to the regular courts. The records of the proceedings of General Commissioners of Income Tax survive by chance. The clerk was usually a local solicitor, and if he retained

---

[56] Houses and Windows Duties Amendment Act 1748, 21 Geo. II c. 10 s. 8; Taxes Management Act 1803, 43 Geo. III c. 99 s. 26.

[57] Houses and Windows Duties Act 1747, 20 Geo. II c. 3 s. 12, and the amending Act 1748, 21 Geo. II c.10 s. 8.

[58] The Triple Assessment Act empowered the commissioners to 'compute and ascertain the sum justly to be charged'. The Income and Property Taxes Act 1799 directed the Appeal Commissioners to ascertain the 'due proportions' a taxpayer should pay: 39 Geo. III c. 13 s. 64. But 'justly' and 'due' could mean justly or due in absolute or in relative terms (ie as in the sum he ought to pay, or as in the assessment not needing alteration on the evidence before the tribunal).

158 *Legal Foundations of Tribunals in 19th-Century England*

the records, and if the papers of the firm happened to find their way into a public record office, an indication of the nature of the appeals can be gleaned from them. Their value is limited however; generally speaking the substance of the appeal was not recorded, and only the decision is to be found, namely whether the assessment has been confirmed, reduced or increased. Where an issue has been taken on appeal to the regular courts of law, however, a fuller picture of the tribunals' adjudicatory jurisdiction is seen because the commissioners' initial determination, from which the appeal lies, is laid down in the report. Thus with the assessed taxes, where a right of appeal by case stated existed from 1748,[59] a comprehensive view of the exercise of their adjudicatory jurisdiction survives. Where, as in the land tax and the income tax prior to 1874, the decisions of the tribunal were final, complete knowledge of the practice of the tribunals' appellate jurisdiction is lacking.[60] The Special Commissioners did not keep reports of their decisions until the closing years of the following century.

The first of the new centralised regulatory bodies of the emerging welfare state was the Poor Law Commission of 1834. Its stated function was to carry the Poor Law Amendment Act 1834 into execution, and to do this it was granted a mixed jurisdiction, though with a balance heavily favouring the administrative. It had broad powers, notably administrative, and a significant legislative power, but a relatively small and unimportant judicial power.[61] Its administrative powers, exercised at local level by their appointed assistants, consisted of ensuring that the new parochial unions were formed, boards of guardians appointed and workhouses built, and thereafter largely of inspecting, inquiring, advising, reporting and appointing officials. Most importantly, it had the power to make rules and regulations applicable to the management and control of the new legislation, it being understood that the necessary detail of such rules made them inappropriate for Parliament itself to draft.[62] These rules addressed the

---

[59] 21 Geo. II c. 10 s. 10.

[60] Some information is found in the reports arising from judicial review.

[61] See generally David Roberts, *Victorian Origins of the British Welfare State*, reprint of Yale University Press edition 1960 (Hamden, CT: Archon Books, 1969), pp. 106–18.

[62] S. G. and E. O. A. Checkland (eds.), *The Poor Law Report of 1834* (Pelican Books, 1974), p. 417.

Jurisdiction and Functional Powers 159

management of the poor, the superintendence and government of workhouses, the appointment of local officers and general directions to implement the law, but they had to be approved by Parliament.[63] The commissioners could lay down rules regarding virtually any aspect of the management of the poor, and those rules had to be obeyed by the Guardians of the Poor.

The Act of 1834 did not expressly allow the Poor Law Commissioners to hear and determine disputes that arose in the course of their implementation of the legislation. Indeed, the general view was that the Poor Law Board, as it became in 1847, was 'not a judicial body'.[64] However, in 1848 the commissioners could determine questions arising as to the cost of relief of a pauper between parishes,[65] and in 1851 were given the power to arbitrate questions of settlement, removal or chargeability arising between parishes or unions.[66] The real significance of the Poor Law Commission, like the General Board of Health, lay in its administrative functions, since its formal judicial functions were strictly circumscribed,[67] highly specific and essentially consensual. As such, its contribution to the development of the modern adjudicatory statutory tribunal was limited.

The tribunals created in the 1830s and 1840s to restructure certain private property rights in the public interest, however, were given extensive dispute-resolution powers. The Tithe Commissioners of 1836,[68] the Copyhold Commissioners of 1841[69] and the Inclosure Commissioners of 1845[70] were similar to each other not only in chronology, but in subject-matter, purpose and

---

[63] Poor Law Amendment Act 1834, 4 & 5 Will. IV c. 76 s. 17.

[64] 'Minutes of Evidence before the Select Committee on Private Bill Legislation', *HCPP* (1863) (385) viii 205 q. 549 *per* George Rickards, counsel to the speaker.

[65] Poor Relief Act 1848, 11 & 12 Vict. c. 110 s. 4.

[66] Poor Relief Act Continuance Act 1851, 14 & 15 Vict. c. 105 s. 12.

[67] The Poor Law Board did settle disputes informally by giving advice on disputed points.

[68] Tithe Commutation Act 1836, 6 & 7 Will. IV c. 71. The leading scholarly works in this field are Eric J. Evans, *Tithes and the Tithe Commutation Act 1836*, Standing Conference for Local History, 3rd revised edition (London: Bedford Square Press, 1997); Eric J. Evans, *The Contentious Tithe* (London: Routledge and Kegan Paul, 1976). See too Roger J. P. Kain and Hugh C. Prince, *The Tithe Surveys of England and Wales* (Cambridge: Cambridge University Press, 1985); W. R. Cornish and G. de N. Clark, *Law and Society in England 1750–1950* (London: Sweet and Maxwell, 1989), pp. 141–4.

[69] Copyhold Act 1841, 4 & 5 Vict. c. 35.

[70] Inclosure Act 1845, 8 & 9 Vict. c. 118.

160 *Legal Foundations of Tribunals in 19th-Century England*

function. It followed that their jurisdiction and their consequent juridical character were similar. The first tribunal of this nature to be created, and itself an early example of the genre, was the Tithe Commission. It was introduced to effect the compulsory commutation of tithes and rid the country of the evils of the payment of tithes in kind. Commissioners were to be appointed 'to carry [the Tithe Commutation Act] into execution',[71] an express and limited function which was administrative in nature. When in 1841 the Copyhold Commission was created to implement the legislation for the commutation of manorial rights in copyhold land and the voluntary enfranchisement of those lands – the evils that flowed from such land being regarded as long ripe for reform – it was superimposed on the Tithe Commission. The Tithe Commutation Act was taken as the model, and with similar objects, powers and duties the juridical nature of both tribunals was naturally very similar. The expressed function of the Copyhold Commissioners was to carry the legislation into execution.[72] In 1845 a general Inclosure Act was passed, to facilitate the inclosure of common lands.[73] This Act followed the same pattern as the tithe commutation and the copyhold legislation, with commissioners charged with the execution of the legislation.[74] The various land rights commissioners were to carry their legislation into effect through the appointment of various subordinate officers, to whom they had full power of delegation, through the supervision of these officers, the settling of any disputes that arose in the course of the process, and the formal certification of the final scheme. Within this wide remit, the commissioners possessed powers and duties, which were a mixture of the administrative or managerial and the adjudicatory, though dominated by the former.

The administrative process in tithe commutation differed from that in the fiscal tribunals, primarily because commutation was, initially at least, voluntary rather than mandatory, and because it consisted of two distinct decisions, each of equal importance, rather than the single decision as to assessment which characterised the fiscal process. The policy of the Act being to encourage a voluntary agreement to commute wherever possible,

---

[71] 6 & 7 Will. IV c. 71 s. 1.   [72] 4 & 5 Vict. c. 35 s. 1.   [73] 8 & 9 Vict. c. 118.
[74] *Ibid.*, s. 1.

Jurisdiction and Functional Powers 161

it allowed complete freedom to the parties to arrive at the arrangement they wished,[75] and then all that was required was the approval of the commissioners to ensure the probity of the agreement. If the statutory provisions for due representation of the landowners and tithe owners had been complied with, and the commissioners were satisfied that there had been no fraud or collusion, this approval would be accorded to the agreement and the commissioners would confirm it by signing and sealing, which rendered the agreement binding on the persons interested in the land and tithes.[76] Their administrative jurisdiction in relation to a voluntary commutation, therefore, consisted essentially of supervision and final confirmation. The practical administrative work of implementation of a voluntary agreement to commute tithes was in the hands of the valuer appointed by the parties. He had to apportion the agreed rent charge among the lands in the parish.[77] Voluntary commutation thus comprised the agreement and the apportionment, and both were in the hands of the parties themselves.

Where, however, agreement could not be reached, commutation was imposed.[78] This mandatory commutation, albeit after voluntary commutation had proved impossible to achieve, was the steel in the measure and the feature that distinguished the tithe commutation legislation from that for copyhold enfranchisement and inclosure. The considerable administrative task of calculating the tithe values and arriving at an appropriate permanent commutation into rent charge payments – known in a compulsory commutation as an award and the compulsory equivalent of the voluntary agreement – was undertaken by the Tithe Commissioners, though in practice they did so by delegating their powers to their Assistant Commissioners.[79] The commissioners had to confirm and allow the final award.[80] The second stage, the

---

[75] As long as it satisfied the statutory requirement of consent of at least two-thirds in value of the landowners and tithe owners to the sum to be paid to them instead of tithes: 6 & 7 Will. IV c. 71 ss. 17, 27.

[76] Ibid., s. 27. The statistics contained in the commissioners' annual reports show that the great majority of voluntary tithe commutation agreements were confirmed by the commissioners.

[77] 6 & 7 Will. IV c. 71 s. 33.   [78] Ibid., s. 36.

[79] Ibid., ss. 36–44. By s. 53 the apportionment of the rent charge would then be made by valuers appointed by the landowners, as in the case of voluntary agreements.

[80] Ibid., s. 52. Note the terminology, suggestive of arbitration though in the context of a compulsory adjustment of land rights.

162 *Legal Foundations of Tribunals in 19th-Century England*

apportionment, was undertaken by the valuer appointed by the parties,[81] though if the apportionment were not completed within six months, the commissioners would undertake the task themselves.[82] Once the apportionment was final, the commissioners were to confirm and allow it.[83] In relation to a compulsory commutation, therefore, the commissioners' administrative functions were directly or indirectly onerous.

Copyhold commutation was to be achieved by converting the lord of the manor's rights in copyhold land into a rent charge; enfranchisement was the conversion of copyhold land into freehold with appropriate monetary compensation for the loss of the lord's manorial rights. The difficulty in both cases was to adjust the claims of the lord and the tenant in the light of significant local and customary variation. In supervising and controlling these processes, the commissioners were exercising an administrative function. Within that context, however, their duties and powers were, as with taxes and tithes, mixed in nature. Unlike the tithe commutation process, however, the commutation and enfranchisement of copyholds under the 1841 Act was entirely voluntary and based on agreement. That inevitably gave the commissioners' statutory function a character more akin to that of arbitrators rather than adjudicators. Their jurisdiction was wholly directed towards arriving at an agreement to commute the manorial dues into a rent charge or a fine and the confirmation by them of that agreement. The practical work was undertaken by the valuer, with the commissioners' role, though more substantive in the implementation of the agreement, being essentially one of supervision, organisation, control and instruction. In relation to their confirmation of the agreement, however, they had to satisfy themselves that the agreement should properly be confirmed, and their jurisdiction extended to making inquiries and requiring satisfactory proof to that effect.[84] Once the valuer had completed his administrative work of valuation, the commissioners had to draw up a schedule of apportionment.[85] Thereafter the lands were discharged from the payment of the lord's rents, fines and heriots, and a rent charge and fixed fine were to be paid in

---

[81] *Ibid.*, s. 53.   [82] *Ibid.*, s. 54.

[83] *Ibid.*, s. 63. The confirmation was described by counsel in *Re the Appledore Tithe Commutation* (1845) 8 QB 139 at 148 as 'an act merely ministerial'.

[84] Copyhold Act 1841, 4 & 5 Vict. c. 35 s. 23.   [85] *Ibid.*, ss. 31, 32.

Jurisdiction and Functional Powers 163

lieu.[86] Where the parties chose to enfranchise the copyhold land, namely convert it to freehold tenure and give monetary compensation to the lord for the loss of his dues, the consent of the commissioners to any agreement was necessary, as was their formal confirmation of it.[87] The commutation provisions of the Act were to apply.

While chronologically the final tribunal to be created to restructure the land rights was the Inclosure Commission of 1845, it was in fact the prototype, having been known since the seventeenth century, though then as private commissioners created by private Inclosure Acts rather than as a central board under the provisions of a public general Act. The first Act of general application to these private commissioners was the Inclosure Clauses Consolidation Act 1801.[88] Because of the nature of the legislation as a clauses consolidation measure, it did not lay down the function of the commissioners, but gave them certain powers and duties from which their overall nature can be deduced. Their jurisdiction was primarily administrative, with powers to survey and value the land in question,[89] receive the claims, and any objections to claims,[90] to build roads,[91] to make the division and allotments, and to draw up the final and binding award.[92] Under another voluntary inclosure measure in 1836,[93] private Inclosure Commissioners were given an extensive administrative jurisdiction to carry out the inclosures of certain common lands. With their authority based in the agreement of a majority of interested parties, the commissioners could make the allotments, award compensation for standing crops, direct the course of husbandry, determine boundaries, allow exchanges and direct fencing, ditching and drainage. When the Inclosure Act 1845 created a central process through a board of Inclosure Commissioners in London, the commissioners themselves were to receive applications for inclosure from interested parties,[94] but it was their subordinate officers, the Assistant Commissioners, who initially undertook the practical administrative work in the field. In this

---

[86] *Ibid.*, s. 36.   [87] *Ibid.*, s. 56.   [88] 41 Geo. III c. 109.

[89] *Ibid.*, s. 4. See generally E. C. K. Gonner, *Common Land and Inclosure*, 2nd edition (London: Frank Cass & Co. Ltd, 1966).

[90] 41 Geo. III c. 109 s. 6.   [91] *Ibid.*, s. 8.   [92] *Ibid.*, s. 35.

[93] Common Fields Inclosure Act 1836, 6 & 7 Will. IV c. 115.

[94] 8 & 9 Vict. c. 118 s. 25.

164 *Legal Foundations of Tribunals in 19th-Century England*

the process resembled that of tithe commutation. Thus it was the Assistant Commissioners who inspected the land, inquired into the correctness of the claims and generally decided whether or not to recommend to the central board of commissioners that an inclosure should be permitted to take place. If any objection to the proposed inclosure were raised, the Assistant Commissioner could 'hear' it, but not determine it; he had to take it into account in his report to the Inclosure Commissioners.[95] The commissioners decided whether or not to allow the inclosure, and if there were sufficient support by the persons interested,[96] it would go ahead.[97] The inclosure process was thus based on the agreement of the parties and the assessment of the public interest by the commissioners. Once the decision had been made that an inclosure should take place, the onerous and practical task of dividing and allotting the land had to begin. As with tithes and copyholds, this was undertaken by a valuer,[98] though in inclosures he played a key role. He had the widest administrative powers to make water courses, tunnels and bridges and to alter roads, and his was the central decision as to the allotment of the land.

All the land rights tribunals were given the necessary jurisdiction to settle any disputes that arose in the course of the restructuring process. If any disputes arose during the voluntary tithe commutation process, these could be referred to arbitration,[99] in keeping with the permissive nature of this form of commutation. The commissioners' adjudicatory powers were applicable principally within the context of a compulsory commutation, and consisted of hearing and determining any objections at each of the two distinct stages of the process: the award as to the total sum to be paid by way of rent charge in lieu of the tithes, and the apportionment of that rent charge among the lands of the parish. They did not, therefore, hear and determine an appeal against one single and final decision, as the fiscal tribunals did. In this way their adjudicatory powers were more clearly integrated into the administrative commutation process. This, and the requirement that the final commutation scheme be formally certified by the commissioners to have any validity,

---

[95] *Ibid.*, s. 26.

[96] *Ibid.*, s. 27 required the consent of the owners of two-thirds in value of the land. See *Church* v. *Inclosure Commissioners* (1862) 11 CB NS 664.

[97] 8 & 9 Vict. c. 118 s. 27.   [98] *Ibid.*, s. 33.   [99] 6 & 7 Will. IV c. 71 s. 24.

Jurisdiction and Functional Powers

characterised their primary function as unambiguously administrative in character. Their adjudicatory powers ensured that all disputes arising in the course of the commutation would be settled, and any objections heard. It was a familiar format, being seen subsequently in the other commissions involved with the restructuring of land rights, and already familiar from the earlier fiscal tribunals.

The Tithe Commissioners were given the jurisdiction to hear and determine any disputes that arose in the making of the award, including those subject to a suit pending in a court of law.[100] Indeed, all such suits had to be determined before the award could be made.[101] These adjudicatory powers were delegated to the Assistant Commissioners, though the Tithe Commissioners themselves had an adjudicatory function, in that if a party was dissatisfied with the decision of the Assistant Commissioner and felt he had come to an erroneous decision on the evidence, he could appeal to the tribunal in London. It would be for him to show the Assistant Commissioner had come to the wrong conclusion, and the tribunal would come to a decision on the basis of the evidence collected by the assistant. If the tribunal felt the evidence was insufficient, the assistant would be required to take further evidence in the locality on the point in question.[102]

The Act specifically mentioned disputes as to the right to tithe, the existence of a modus or of a customary payment, or claims to exemption. Their decision was to be final and conclusive.[103] The extent of the jurisdiction with which this provision endowed the commissioners was judicially considered three years after the passing of the Act in the case of *Girdlestone* v. *Stanley*[104] and was given a restrictive interpretation. In the course of a tithe commutation, the Assistant Tithe Commissioner had to resolve a number of important questions as to the validity of certain moduses and customary payments, which were the subject of a suit pending in the Court of Exchequer. He maintained he could

---

[100] *Ibid.*, s. 45.

[101] Determined by the court or by the commissioner: see *ibid.*, s. 450 and *Re Crosby Tithes* (1849) 13 QB 761.

[102] *Minutes, Commons' Inclosure, 1844* q. 23 *per* Revd Richard Jones, Tithe Commissioner.

[103] Tithe Commutation Act 1836, 6 & 7 Will. IV c. 71 s. 45. It was, however, subject to appeal to the regular courts: *ibid.*, s. 46.

[104] (1839) 3 Y & C Ex 421.

166 *Legal Foundations of Tribunals in 19th-Century England*

not arrive at the award until the issues had been resolved. The question arose whether the commissioner could decide those questions under the provision in the Act which empowered him to hear and determine any suit pending which touched the right to any tithes, the existence of a modus or customary payment, or the boundary of land whereby the making of an award was hindered. Alderson B held he could not. The statute allowed the commissioner only to decide the right underlying a suit pending if that suit actually impeded him in the making of the award, and not otherwise. As the tithes that were subject to the court proceedings were already due, they could not form part of the commutation, and so were not impeding the commissioner in the making of his award. To decide otherwise, he said, would be to give the commissioner too wide a jurisdiction, allowing him, for example, to determine boundaries whether or not the lands in question were subject to tithes. He could not believe that Parliament intended to give such a jurisdiction to a lay tribunal such as this, and so he placed a 'rational limit' on the words of the Act.[105] The judge accepted that in the course of the commutation the commissioner might well have to determine the same issues as the court as to the validity of these moduses and customary payments for the purposes of the future commutation into a rent charge, and that he had concurrent jurisdiction to do so, but that was a different question. The decision of the court in *Girdlestone* v. *Stanley*[106] made it clear that the jurisdiction of the Tithe Commissioners to adjudicate was limited to the context of the commutation, and was, therefore, a judicial power which was intended to serve, and did serve, an administrative purpose. Their power to determine disputes as to moduses, customary payments and boundaries was limited to the administrative process of tithe commutation, and so confirmed the juridical nature of the Tithe Commission as an administrative, and not a judicial, tribunal.

Once the commissioners had arrived at an award, they were empowered to hear and determine objections to it and amend it as they saw fit before it could be formally confirmed.[107] When the apportionment was similarly arrived at, they were in the same way to hear and determine objections to it and amend it if they saw

---

[105] *Ibid.*, at 424. [106] *Ibid.*
[107] Tithe Commutation Act 1836, 6 & 7 Will. IV c. 71 ss. 51, 52.

Jurisdiction and Functional Powers 167

fit[108] prior to formal confirmation.[109] In *Re the Appledore Tithe Commutation* in 1845,[110] objections were raised to an apportionment. The valuer appointed to make the apportionment of the rent charge charged certain pasture land leased from the church with a sum in lieu of grain and corn tithes on the basis that it was likely that it would be ploughed up after commutation. The lessee objected on the basis he did not intend to apply for the necessary licence to cultivate the land. The Assistant Commissioners heard the objections in the locality and decided to confirm the apportionment, as did the Tithe Commissioners themselves at Somerset House. The commissioners were held to be acting properly and within their jurisdiction in doing so, and so a prohibition would not issue.[111] The case illustrates the judicial nature of the commissioners' function in hearing and determining such objections. They had to sift and weigh a considerable amount of conflicting evidence adduced by the parties, deciding questions of fact, weighing up different opinions and deciding questions of law.[112] They had to decide whether there was a tendency in the district to plough the land, which was a question of fact. They had to decide whether it was likely that the lands in question would be converted from pasture to arable after commutation, which was a question of opinion; and they had to decide what in law constituted waste.

The commissioners decided a variety of disputes in the course of a commutation, often as to the existence of moduses[113] and frequently as to boundaries. Both were among the most complex and important which Assistant Commissioners had to address. They had to decide thousands of miles of boundaries, largely because in remote and mountainous areas the boundaries between parishes were not well defined, and so gave rise to disputes. Such disputes were common, often bitter and always lengthy.[114] The Assistant Commissioners had to make detailed inquiries, examine witnesses and consider plans and proofs.[115] Richard Jones, one of

---

[108] *Ibid.*, s. 61.   [109] *Ibid.*, s. 63.   [110] (1845) 8 QB 139.

[111] It is unfortunate that the report states only the bare decision. It seems the judges had prepared a written judgment, which was then lost.

[112] See for example the dispute as to moduses in TNA:PRO IR 18/9249 (1846–8).

[113] *Earl of Stamford and Warrington* v. *Dunbar* (1844) 12 M & W 414.

[114] For an example of a boundary dispute before the regular courts, see *Evans* v. *Rees* (1839) 10 A & E 151.

[115] See for example the settling of the boundary between the parishes of Seaton, Beer and Colyton in Devon in 1841: TNA:PRO TITH 1/16.

168 *Legal Foundations of Tribunals in 19th-Century England*

the Tithe Commissioners, described the work of one of his legally qualified Assistant Commissioners in settling disputes as to moduses and boundaries. The assistant had decided some 148 disputes between 1836 and 1844, and his work was highly regarded when judged by the few number of appeals from his decisions.[116] In the year after the passing of the Tithe Commutation Act their jurisdiction in this respect was increased. The original Act of 1836 allowed them to settle a difference as to any boundaries where it hindered the making of an award. An Act of 1837 gave them the power to settle disputed boundaries,[117] and legislation of 1839[118] and 1840[119] extended these powers further to settle disputed parochial boundaries. The interrelationship of these various enactments was complex and their jurisdiction uncertain with conflicting judicial interpretations.[120] Whether the commissioners could properly adjudicate on boundaries which divided counties as well as parishes was a question of some moment and judicial division in the mid-1840s.[121] The issue depended on close scrutiny and careful construction of the statutory provisions,[122] a task that lay Assistant Tithe Commissioners found challenging.[123]

In *Re Dent Tithe Commutation* in 1845,[124] an Assistant Commissioner[125] ascertained the boundaries of the township of Dent under the provisions of the Tithe Commutation Amendment Act 1837.[126] His award was ultimately quashed for want of jurisdiction on the face of the award because it did not show that the boundary dispute was part of the commutation process, and because there was a procedural error as to the calling of the parochial meeting. However, the case clarified the nature of the jurisdiction of the Tithe Commissioners under the various provisions relating to boundary disputes, stating that the power under the Act of 1837 was restricted to ascertaining old and

---

[116] *Minutes, Commons' Inclosure, 1844* q. 23.
[117] Tithe Commutation Amendment Act 1837, 7 Will. IV & 1 Vict. c. 69 s. 2.
[118] 2 & 3 Vict. c. 62.   [119] 3 & 4 Vict. c. 15.
[120] See the evidence of Revd Richard Jones in *Minutes, Commons' Inclosure, 1844* qq. 3297 ff.
[121] See *Re Ystradgunlais Tithe Commutation* (1844) 8 QB 32.
[122] See Lord Denman CJ's exercise in statutory interpretation in *Re Dent Tithe Commutation* (1845) 8 QB 43 at 56–7.
[123] See for example the modus dispute at TNA:PRO IR 18/9249 (1846–8).
[124] (1845) 8 QB 43.   [125] He was a barrister.   [126] 7 Will. IV & 1 Vict. c. 69 s. 2.

Jurisdiction and Functional Powers

existing boundaries, while that under the Act of 1839[127] allowed the drawing of new ones. More significantly, however, Lord Denman CJ made it clear that the power to settle boundaries given by the Act of 1837 was given solely to facilitate the final commutation of tithes, and so should be exercised before the commutation took place. Just as with the general provision in the principal Act giving the commissioners jurisdiction to settle disputes, their adjudication as to boundaries was limited by the administrative context of the tithe commutation.

The Copyhold Commissioners were also given adjudicatory powers in the context of commutation. As with a voluntary commutation of tithes, any disputes as to entitlement to, or value of, manorial rights, or as to boundaries, could be referred to arbitration.[128] The commissioners' adjudicatory powers were limited to the hearing and determination of objections to the valuer's valuations,[129] even though they closely supervised and controlled the valuer.[130] Their function was judicial in that it was adjudicatory and appellate.[131] However, in a provision almost identical to that in the Tithe Commutation Act, the commissioners were given the wider power to hear and determine disputes pending concerning the right to manorial dues.[132] Their decision was binding and conclusive on all parties who had received notice, but was subject to appeal.[133]

The process of arriving at any successful inclosure necessitated dispute-resolution powers, since most inclosures threw up disputes as to boundaries and disputed rights to allotments of commons. Disputes would arise, for example, where the parties wanted to fix boundaries to their sheep-walks,[134] and there were also disputes as to usage.[135] These disputes were often difficult to resolve, claims to rights of pasturage being particularly

---

[127] 2 & 3 Vict. c. 62 s. 34. [128] Copyhold Act 1841, 4 & 5 Vict. c. 35 s. 21.
[129] *Ibid.*, s. 29.
[130] This is no different from the General Commissioners supervising assessors or Assistant Commissioners, and yet hearing appeals against their decisions.
[131] The commissioners would then amend the valuations if they saw fit: Copyhold Act 1841, 4 & 5 Vict. c. 35 s. 29.
[132] *Ibid.*, s. 39. [133] *Ibid.*, s. 40.
[134] See for example TNA:PRO ED 27/5672 (1859).
[135] *Minutes, Commons' Inclosure, 1844* q. 2619 *per* Charles Mickleburgh, land surveyor and valuer.

170 *Legal Foundations of Tribunals in 19th-Century England*

challenging,[136] and one private inclosure commissioner observed that he had had fifty-six disputed claims in one inclosure.[137] For this reason both private and public Inclosure Commissioners' jurisdiction included this authority. Under the Act of 1801 they were given jurisdiction to settle specific disputes strictly within the inclosure process. They were to hear and determine objections to the building of roads 'to the best of their Judgment',[138] though in so doing they were to adjudicate with any justices of the peace at the meeting and were given jurisdiction to settle parish boundary disputes.[139] Under the measure of 1836 they could hear and determine any disputes with regard to the division or allotment of the land[140] and again in some instances their first-tier dispute-resolution jurisdiction was shared with the justices at Quarter Sessions.[141] Under the 1845 Act the dispute-resolution jurisdiction was not exclusively in the central commissioners. The valuer, unusually, had such powers. He could hear and determine contested claims, though he could be assisted in that regard by a legally trained Assistant Commissioner.[142] The valuer could allow or disallow them 'as to him shall appear just'. His determination was final, unless a dissatisfied party requested that the claim be heard by the commissioners.[143] In that case, the commissioners were to hear and determine the claim in the normal way,[144] and unless challenged in the regular courts, their decision was final. In the same way the commissioners or their assistants were to adjudicate in objections to the final allotment, prior to confirmation by them in the usual way.[145] The jurisdiction of the commissioners to adjudicate in inclosure disputes was, therefore, retained as a high-status appeal coming above the valuer but below the regular courts. Only in relation to disputed boundaries was the adjudication a matter only for the commissioners.[146]

The three land rights tribunals all possessed considerable administrative and judicial powers, and in all the administrative

---

[136] *Ibid.*, q. 2627.   [137] *Ibid.*, q. 2620.

[138] Inclosure Clauses Consolidation Act 1801, 41 Geo. III c. 109 s. 8.

[139] *Ibid.*, s. 3.

[140] Common Fields Inclosure Act 1836, 6 & 7 Will. IV c. 115 s. 15.

[141] *Ibid.*, s. 53.   [142] 8 & 9 Vict. c. 118 s. 35.   [143] *Ibid.*, s. 48.

[144] *Ibid.*, s. 55.   [145] *Ibid.*, s. 104.

[146] *Ibid.*, s. 39. If a party was dissatisfied with the determination of the commissioners in this respect, they could ask that the matter be put to a jury, or be removed to the Queen's Bench.

Jurisdiction and Functional Powers

function dominated. They were each created in order to perform an administrative function, just as the fiscal tribunals were. When they adjudicated, they did so to serve and achieve this overarching function, and when they strayed from these confines, they were subject to the remedial jurisdiction of the regular courts. When they adjudicated it was in response to an expression of dissatisfaction with an earlier administrative decision, either their own or that of a subordinate officer, and the adjudication invariably occurred before the final confirmation which marked the achievement of the process. Their jurisdiction was limited not only by its overall administrative purpose, but also by an express provision that they could not determine any question of title to the land in question.[147] That could only be done 'in due course of law'.[148]

One tribunal which had functional characteristics in common with both the fiscal tribunals and the land rights tribunals was the Assessment Committee. These bodies, created by the Union Assessment Committee Act 1862,[149] formed part of the machinery for the implementation of the poor law. The system of poor relief was based on the levying of a rate on property. Some mechanism was needed whereby the property in question was valued for the purposes of rating, and whereby objections to the valuations could be addressed. When in the middle of the century there was a demand for a more uniform method of arriving at these valuations, legislation introduced a new form and basis of rating. The Parochial Assessments Act 1836[150] provided that all rates were to be made on the net annual value of the property, namely the market rent when let from year to year with appropriate deductions.[151] It laid down the form in which the rates were to be made, empowered the Poor Law Commissioners to order new valuations and put the task of making the valuation in the hands of the overseer or churchwarden under the authority of the justices of the peace. Under legislation of 1862 the actual valuations were again made by the parish overseers in a specified form.[152] They

---

[147] Copyhold Act 1841, 4 & 5 Vict. c. 35 s. 43; Inclosure Clauses Consolidation Act 1801, 41 Geo. III c. 109 s. 7; Common Fields Inclosure Act 1836, 6 & 7 Will. IV c. 115 ss. 15, 19; Inclosure Act 1845, 8 & 9 Vict. c. 118 s. 49.
[148] Inclosure Act 1845, 8 & 9 Vict. c. 118 s. 49.   [149] 25 & 26 Vict. c. 103.
[150] 6 & 7 Will. IV c. 96.   [151] Ibid., s. 1.
[152] Union Assessment Committee Act 1862, 25 & 26 Vict. c. 103 s. 14.

172 *Legal Foundations of Tribunals in 19th-Century England*

were to prepare a list of the rateable property in their parishes, with their values, and to 'transmit the same' on completion to a new organ, the Assessment Committee.[153] The function of the Assessment Committee of a union was expressed by the Act to be 'the investigation and supervision of the valuations ... and ... the performance of such said acts and duties' as the statute laid down.[154] In common with the fiscal and land rights tribunals, the expression of this function covered duties that were both administrative and judicial in nature.

The Assessment Committees' primary function was an unambiguously administrative one, namely to supervise the valuation of property in the parish as the foundation of the levying of an appropriate poor rate and to approve the valuation list. The duty of the overseers was, in the same way as that of the assessors under the income tax legislation, clearly administrative. They were to carry out the ministerial task of valuing the property. The precise nature of the duty of the Assessment Committee was not elaborated in the statute, and so the extent of its task was unclear. Whether the duty to supervise and investigate amounted to no more than a formal transmission of the list to the committee and its rubber-stamping, or a meaningful examination of the correctness of the valuations, was unclear. The later provision for the appointment of a surveyor by the committee to check valuations suggests the latter. This issue was raised in Parliament by Joseph Henley, who sought a clarification of the extent of the committee's discretion. His view was that the committee should exercise its own judgment on a valuation before it sent it to the parish to be appealed against,[155] though others thought it should be sent straight to the parish 'instead of being cavilled over by the assessment committee'.[156] Whatever the extent of the committee's duty in the investigation and supervision of the valuation list, it was of an administrative nature, with the committee functioning as assessors rather than adjudicators. Having thus ascertained the correctness of the overseer's valuations so as to satisfy the statutory provisions and make any necessary alterations, the committee

---

[153] *Ibid.*, s. 17.

[154] *Ibid.*, s. 2. See generally the judgment of A. L. Smith J in *Churchwardens and Overseers of West Ham* v. *Fourth City Mutual Building Society* [1892] 1 QB 654.

[155] *Parl. Deb.*, vol. CLXVIII, ser. 3, col. 238, 11 July 1862 (HC).

[156] *Ibid.*, col. 238 *per* William Deedes.

Jurisdiction and Functional Powers 173

returned the list to him, and the list would be deemed the valuation in force for the parish in question.

While the Assessment Committees had the clear administrative function of supervising, investigating and approving the valuation of property by the overseer, the statute provided that they were to perform such other acts as the statute should specify, and one of these was to hold meetings to hear and determine objections to the valuation list. Though not the hearing of an appeal in the strict sense of the term, it was an express adjudicatory power. If a parish or any person felt themselves to be aggrieved by any valuation on the grounds that it was unfair, or incorrect, or omitted a rateable hereditament, an appeal would lie to the committee having given written notice of the objection in due time, before the list was formally approved.[157] This new power to appeal against a valuation before the rate had actually been made was regarded as one of the real benefits of the legislation. The purpose was to give the Assessment Committee the opportunity to correct any error in the list before the expense of a formal appeal to the Quarter Sessions took place. The committee had to hold meetings to 'hear and determine' the objections, with or without adjournment.[158] It was empowered, even if no objection had been made, to alter the valuation of any hereditament in the list, to insert omitted properties and make any necessary amendments. This function, with its judicial terminology, was clearly adjudicatory and it was repeatedly argued before the courts of law that the committee acted in a judicial capacity.[159] The jurisdiction of the Assessment Committees to hear and determine objections to the valuation list was discussed in the case of *R. v. Justices of London* in 1897.[160] The committee could hear objections to the valuation list only if proper notice according to the statute had been given to the committee, namely in writing specifying the ground of the objection. The court, as was usual with statutory jurisdictions,

---

[157] 25 & 26 Vict. c. 103 s. 18. See too Union Assessment Committee Amendment Act 1864, 27 & 28 Vict. c. 39 s. 1.

[158] 25 & 26 Vict. c. 103 s. 19. See *R. v. Assessment Committee of St Mary Abbotts, Kensington* [1891] 1 QB 378.

[159] See counsel's argument in *R. v. Assessment Committee of St Mary Abbotts, Kensington* [1891] 1 QB 378 at 379 and 381.

[160] [1897] 1 QBD 433.

174   *Legal Foundations of Tribunals in 19th-Century England*

construed this narrowly[161] to mean that when the committee heard an objection to the list, its jurisdiction was limited to entertaining only the objections specified in the notice of objection, unless the party supporting the valuation list consented otherwise. What was clear, however, was that the committee's adjudicatory power was integral to the administrative process, since the overseers who prepared the list would send it to the Assessment Committee who, after hearing objections, would approve the list with or without alterations and send it back to the overseers, when it became the basis on which the rate would be levied.

The complexity and range of issues, both administrative and adjudicatory, involved in the regulation of the developing railway network demanded a comprehensive jurisdiction in the regulating body. There was considerable debate as to the powers such a body should be given, and in the 1830s when the network was still under construction, it was questioned whether the new body should examine estimates for construction, take over from juries the task of valuation of land, inspect lines and bridges and control the companies' powers to take land for temporary purposes of construction. The jurisdiction of the first railway department of the Board of Trade under the Regulation of Railways Act 1840[162] was almost entirely administrative, being essentially supervisory and directed to ensure the public safety. It was to call for accounts, review bye-laws, enforce all the Acts of Parliament relating to railways and appoint inspectors of railways. In its administrative jurisdiction it largely took over from the justices of the peace. The function of the new Railway Commissioners proposed by a Select Committee of the House of Lords in 1846 was to control the initiation and management of the railway companies and the policy of railway communication in the public interest. All the powers and duties of the Railway Department of the Board of Trade were transferred to the new Commissioners of Railways[163] but in addition they were to have the power to ensure the railway companies did not exceed the

---

[161] In *Redheugh Colliery Ltd* v. *Gateshead Assessment Committee* [1924] 1 KB 369 at 387 Atkin LJ observed that 'The jurisdiction ... is purely statutory, and it is to my mind undesirable to depart from the plain meaning of the statute.'
[162] 3 & 4 Vict. c. 97.
[163] Commissioners of Railways Act 1846, 9 & 10 Vict. c. 105.

Jurisdiction and Functional Powers

175

powers given to them in their Acts of incorporation. The commission's primary functions were superintendence, information and guidance. The governing legislation did not, however, set out in detail its powers. A bill purporting to regulate its proceedings in 1847[164] was ultimately withdrawn under pressure from the railway directors.

It was always understood that the management and regulation of the network would bring with it the need to resolve a variety of disputes in its course, but the approach adopted by the legislature in giving dispute-resolution powers to the various railway bodies created in the mid-nineteenth century was supremely cautious. It was felt that such bodies should not deal with issues between the railway companies and the public, such as claims for compensation or accidents, because the regular courts provided for such disputes. At first the justification for allowing any dispute-resolution powers to a tribunal that was unequivocally part of the executive was public safety, but it soon became clear that it could usefully be widened, albeit on a voluntary basis.

The first body in 1840 had just one adjudicatory function, namely to decide disputes between railway companies as to where openings should be made for branch lines, a power which had hitherto been in the justices of the peace,[165] and the Board of Trade had power to act as arbitrator in some disputes.[166] Two years later this power was extended to allow the Board of Trade to resolve disputes between railway companies who could not agree how to share a terminus or line.[167] Furthermore, many of the powers given to the Board of Trade, such as the power to take land compulsorily for public safety purposes, gave rise to disputes, and they were solved by arbitration by the board.[168] This power to act as an arbitrator in disputes between railway companies fell short of a legislative power to adjudicate. It was limited to recommending and advising, and its decisions were not binding. When the new Railway Commission was proposed in 1846

---

[164] *HCPP* (1847) (65) iii 415.
[165] Regulation of Railways Act 1840, 3 & 4 Vict. c. 97 s. 18.   [166] *Ibid.*, s. 19.
[167] Regulation of Railways Act 1842, 5 & 6 Vict. c. 55 s. 11.
[168] See example in *Minutes, Railways, 1844* qq. 261–76 per Samuel Laing, and at qq. 968–72 on a dispute as to bye-laws. See Henry Parris, *Government and the Railways in Nineteenth Century Britain* (London: Routledge and Kegan Paul, 1965), pp. 38–41.

176 Legal Foundations of Tribunals in 19th-Century England

one of its functions was to address technical standards of construction and issues of notice for the protection of private interests, to assess the extent of any private injury and to arbitrate between the landowners and the promoters in any disagreement. One aspect of their jurisdiction would be to inquire into compliance of railway companies with the parliamentary standing orders and allow alterations to the deposited plans, thought in some quarters to be 'a judicial kind of function',[169] or again a legislative one that was the proper province of Parliament.[170] It was undoubtedly inquisitorial in nature, investigating matters to save time and expense before proceeding to the private bill committees. In the course of this it would settle the numerous disputes that inevitably arose. For example, questions and disputes arose between companies as to the situation and control of joint stations where a number of lines terminated in one place, and such issues were otherwise resolved by the private bill committees, at great expense to all concerned. It was also seen that such a body could advantageously deal with all complaints made against railway companies, and the bill of 1847 purported to give the commissioners power finally to decide disputed compensation, to hear objections to proposed railways, and to settle disputes between railway companies and the Postmaster-General,[171] though the last was removed by the subsequent version of the bill, where traditional arbitration was preferred.[172] The power in the Board of Trade to settle disputes between railway companies having coterminous lines[173] was transferred to the commissioners, though it was voluntary in nature.[174]

---

[169] 'Minutes of Evidence before the Select Committee of the House of Lords (on Railways)', *HCPP* (1846) (489) xiii 217 q. 217 *per* James St George Burke, parliamentary agent.

[170] *Ibid.*, qq. 220–2, 335; *ibid.*, q. 529 *per* Robert Stephenson, engineer; *ibid.*, q. 847 *per* John Shiell, solicitor.

[171] 'A Bill for regulating the Proceedings of the Commissioners of Railways, and for amending the Law relating to Railways', *HCPP* (1847) (65) iii 415, cll. 18, 19, 34, 55.

[172] 'A Bill for regulating the Proceedings of the Commissioners of Railways, and for amending the Law relating to Railways (No. 2)', *HCPP* (1847) (442) iii 451, cl. 51.

[173] Under s. 11 of 5 & 6 Vict. c 55.

[174] 'A Bill for regulating the Proceedings of the Commissioners of Railways, and for amending the Law relating to Railways', *HCPP* (1847) (65) iii 415, cll. 79, 80.

Jurisdiction and Functional Powers 177

In 1854 the regulation of the railway network was recast and reformed by the Railway and Canal Traffic Act.[175] The implementation of the new legislation was given to the Court of Common Pleas, to the dismay of Lord Campbell and most of his fellow judges who objected to the ministerial nature of the duties imposed on them.[176] The Act imposed a duty on railway companies to make arrangements for receiving and forwarding traffic without unreasonable delay and without partiality.[177] There were two elements to the new duties placed on railway companies: to provide facilities for the free forwarding of traffic between railways all over the country wherever the several companies' stations or lines were close, and to ensure the fair and equal treatment of different classes of traffic and traders so that none was given a preferential service. If a railway company breached these duties, the court was to hear and determine any complaint, and issue an injunction to restrain the company from continued violation.[178] It was this jurisdiction that the judges argued was ministerial rather than judicial. Lord Campbell maintained that

The Judges, and himself among them, felt themselves incompetent to decide on these matters. He had spent a great part of his life in studying the laws of his country; but he confessed he was wholly unacquainted with railway management, as well as the transit of goods by boats; he knew not how to determine what was a reasonable fare, what was undue delay, or within what time trucks and boats should be returned.[179]

In speaking of the duties placed on the railway companies by the legislation, Cockburn CJ said that the policy was to afford accommodation on equal terms to the whole of the public. 'The policy and the justice of such a requirement', he continued,

are manifest, it being obvious that the powers of a railway company, and its monopoly, under the impossibility of all competition, might otherwise be converted into a means of very grievous oppression ... Such being plainly the intention of the Legislature, and this court having been constituted the tribunal by which any injustice or inequality in the working of the railway system as between the companies and the public is to be redressed, we must endeavour to prevent any injustice either in the rate of charge or the degree of accommodation afforded, at the same time that we

---

[175] 17 & 18 Vict. c. 31.   [176] See above, pp. 54–6.

[177] 17 & 18 Vict. c. 31 s. 2. See Railway and Canal Traffic Regulation Bill 1854, *HCPP* (1854) (62) vi 1, cll. 5, 6.

[178] 17 & 18 Vict. c. 31 s. 3.

[179] *Parl. Deb.*, vol. CXXXIII, ser. 3, col. 1137, 30 May 1854 (HL).

178 Legal Foundations of Tribunals in 19th-Century England

carefully avoid interfering, except where absolutely necessary for the above purpose, with the ordinary rights which ... a railway company, in common with every other company or individual, possesses, of regulating and managing its own affairs, either with regard to charges or accommodation, or to the agreements and bargains it may make in its particular business.[180]

The Court of Common Pleas had considerable difficulty in exercising its jurisdiction satisfactorily. In *Caterham Railway Company* v. *the London, Brighton, and South Coast Railway Company and South Eastern Railway Company* in 1857[181]the Caterham Railway Company complained that the London, Brighton and South Coast and the South Eastern Railway companies were showing an undue preference to a company owning a branch line from their trunk line. It was alleged that the parent companies charged higher rates to convey passengers to the Caterham Railway Company's branch line terminus than they did to convey passengers to the terminus of a third company's branch line, when the distances involved were the same in each case. This was held not to be an undue preference, because all the passengers travelling to the Caterham Railway Company's terminus paid the same rate. The fact that passengers going to another terminus could do so at a lower rate was not an instance of undue preference. However, the court upheld another complaint to the effect that there was no convenient covered station at the Caterham junction though there were covered stations at all other places on the line, and this amounted to a denial of 'reasonable accommodation' under the Act. In its judgment the court observed that the Act conferred 'very extensive powers' on it, 'powers which may be exercised for the benefit of the public, but which may also be exercised to the great detriment of those who are engaged in carrying on railway concerns; and therefore the court should be very cautious'.[182] In *Barrett* v. *the Great Northern Railway Company and the Midland Railway Company* in the same year[183] the court held that to justify its interference to enforce the running of through trains on a continuous railway line, it had to be shown that the public convenience required it and that it could reasonably be done. On that occasion the court refused to interfere

---

[180] *Baxendale* v. *Great Western Railway Company* (1858) 5 CB NS 309 at 351–2.
[181] (1857) 1 CB NS 410. [182] *Ibid.*, at 419 *per* Cresswell LJ.
[183] (1857) 1 CB NS 423.

Jurisdiction and Functional Powers

where a passenger could purchase through tickets on a through line, though on a longer route; neither he nor the public was seriously inconvenienced.

It some cases of alleged undue preference, the court was often equally divided and unable to determine whether the preference was undue or not in the context of the interests of the railway company and of the public.[184] In *Ransome v. the Eastern Counties Railway Company* in 1857[185] the court found that the railway company had shown undue preference to one coal merchant by charging him considerably less to transport his coal by rail than another, rival, coal merchant was charged. In determining whether there has been undue preference, or undue prejudice, the court said that it could take into consideration not just the interests of the parties using the railway, but also the fair interests of the railway company itself, and entertain such questions as whether the company could carry larger quantities, or for longer distances, at lower rates per ton per mile, than smaller quantities, or for shorter distances, so as to derive equal profits to itself. Cresswell J said that in taking into account the fair interests of the railway the questions raised 'assume a very complicated and difficult character, and are such as we feel but little qualified to decide'.[186] In *Baxendale v. the Great Western Railway Company* in 1858[187] the court held that the company was prohibited from giving a preference to a paper manufacturer in the rates it charged for carrying his large quantity of paper simply because that customer had agreed to use the company for the carriage of other goods. To charge unequal rates depending on whether a customer agreed with the company to use its facilities for other business was undue preference under the Act. This case was followed in *Palmer v. the London and Brighton Railway Company* in 1871[188] where a railway company refused to allow the trader's goods into their station after a certain time at night for dispatch that same night,

---

[184] According to the editors of *Practical Statutes* 1873, p. 57.
[185] (1857) 1 CB NS 437.
[186] *Ibid.*, at 452. This decision was followed in *Oxlade v. the North Eastern Railway Company* (1857) 1 CB NS 454 and *Nicolson v. the Great Western Railway Company* (1858) 5 CB NS 366. In *Harris v. the Cockermouth and Workington Railway Company* (1858) 3 CB NS 693 at 715 Crowder J said that 'undue preference is not to be confined to the mere desire to benefit the individual'.
[187] (1858) 5 CB NS 309; (1862) 12 CB NS 758. [188] (1871) 40 LJ CP 133.

180 *Legal Foundations of Tribunals in 19th-Century England*

but would let its own vans in. The court held this was undue preference under the 1854 Act.

When it was accepted that the legislation of 1854 had failed through want of enforcement by the Court of Common Pleas, and a new tribunal was proposed in its stead, the Joint Select Committee on Railway Companies Amalgamation of 1872 had in mind a mixed jurisdiction of administrative and judicial functions. In so doing it observed that 'questions concerning the fairness of charges are matters of administrative policy rather than simple questions of law, and would be better dealt with by a special tribunal'.[189] It was recognised that the new commissioners would be doing more than dispute-resolution; they were there also 'to build up a policy, to create a code on which they should legislate'.[190] Some of the commission's functions were clearly administrative, such as ensuring the publication of rates and fares so that parties would know whether they were being treated unfairly,[191] deciding on the reasonableness of through rates[192] and approving working agreements between railway companies, the last function having been transferred to the commission from the Board of Trade.[193] It also had the power to make general orders for the regulation of its proceedings and its implementation of the railway legislation.[194]

The tribunal's principal jurisdiction, however, continued to consist of the implementation of the Act of 1854 and the adjudication of complaints of its violation.[195] The commissioners were given full power to decide all questions whether of law or of fact[196] in settling all complaints of unfairness between traders or districts and resolving any disputes with regard to the interchange of

---

[189] *Report, Railway Amalgamation, 1872* p. 48.
[190] *Parl. Deb.*, vol. CCXV, ser. 3, col. 358, 31 March 1873 (HC) *per* Gabriel Goldney.
[191] Railway and Canal Traffic Act 1873, 36 & 37 Vict. c. 48 s. 14. See *Pelsall Coal and Iron Co. Ltd* v. *London and North Western Railway Company* (1889) 23 QBD 536.
[192] 36 & 37 Vict. c. 48 s. 12 (1873).
[193] *Ibid.*, s. 10. These were powers under the Railway Clauses Consolidation Act 1863, 26 & 27 Vict. c. 92, Pt III.
[194] 36 & 37 Vict. c. 48 s. 29 (1873).
[195] *Ibid.*, s. 6, being violations of s. 2 of the 1854 Act and of s. 16 of the Regulation of Railways Act 1868, 31 & 32 Vict. c. 119, or any other amending or implementing Act.
[196] 36 & 37 Vict. c. 48 s. 25 (1873).

Jurisdiction and Functional Powers

traffic, through rates, charges for the use of stations, sidings, warehouses and servants and new branch lines. The jurisdiction was extended to include the affording of facilities by railway companies to through traffic at through fares from one company to another,[197] and giving effect to this duty was to be an important element of their jurisdiction. The commissioners were also given the power to resolve disputes arising as to terminal charges not fixed by Parliament and to decide on a reasonable sum for loading, delivery and so forth,[198] and, at the option of the railway company only, to resolve any dispute under the Act between it and the Postmaster-General.[199] Other adjudicative jurisdiction consisted of the arbitration of various disputes. Some disputes between railway and canal companies were by statute to be referred to arbitration, and where there was no designated arbitrator, the task was to fall to the commission.[200] From its inception the Railway Commission heard few cases, but it was often said that an efficient railway tribunal had very little to do. Its success could not be measured simply by the number of cases it heard, for part of its role was to undertake administrative and regulatory functions and to act as a deterrent to wrongdoers in the railway community. Sir Frederick Peel, the first chairman of the Railway Commissioners, said that aggrieved persons had been deterred from bringing their grievances to the commission by the expense of litigating with the companies, and also because the limits of the commission's jurisdiction and the meaning of the Act were not always clear.[201]

When the Railway Commission of 1873 was succeeded by the Railway and Canal Commission of 1888, the principal difference was in personnel, which reform led to the constitution of the commission as a full court of record.[202] The new commission succeeded to all the jurisdiction which the Railway Commission had had under the 1873 Act,[203] and so was to give effect to the 1854 duties as to facilities and equal treatment. It was to hear complaints as to the contravention of certain provisions in private Acts,[204] could decide disputes as to the legality of tolls and

---

[197] *Ibid.*, s. 11. [198] *Ibid.*, s. 15.
[199] *Ibid.*, s. 19. The normal method of dispute-resolution in this case was to be arbitration.
[200] *Ibid.*, s. 8. [201] *Minutes, Railways (Rates and Fares), 1882* q. 2974.
[202] Railway and Canal Traffic Act 1888, 51 & 52 Vict. c. 25 s. 2. [203] *Ibid.*, s. 8.
[204] *Ibid.*, s. 9.

182 *Legal Foundations of Tribunals in 19th-Century England*

rates,[205] and was given a new power to award damages.[206] Like the Court of Common Pleas and the Railway Commission, the Railway and Canal Commission heard relatively few cases, partly because the Board of Trade dealt with a number of disputes as to the reasonableness of rates under the conciliation clause of the 1888 Act, cases which otherwise would have come before the commission. By the beginning of the following century, it was found that the commission was sitting only a few days in the year, though proposals to extend its jurisdiction and act rather like a public prosecutor in the railway field, investigating violations and initiating proceedings, were resisted.[207] The commissioners encountered similar problems in applying the 1854 Act, and in 1890 Wills J observed that '[t]he path of decision in matters of railway traffic is so thorny, and the consequences of unnecessary deviation may be so far-reaching, that I think it more than usually desirable not to take one step outside the path that must be trodden in the particular case under consideration'.[208] In 1894 in a case on the provision of through facilities the same judge observed that '[w]e sit here, not to enforce a pedantic and useless compliance with the letter of the section, but to remedy practical grievances'.[209] He thus found that where a railway company closed a station for passenger traffic at which there was a substantial amount of traffic without providing an equivalent, it was in breach of its statutory obligation to provide reasonable facilities for the forwarding and delivery of traffic.

It was clear that in their practical implementation of their statutory regimes the new tribunals exercised a wide administrative and adjudicatory jurisdiction. The latter was conceived as part of the administrative process and was circumscribed by it, existing and interacting in order to serve it. Despite this undoubted administrative context – a feature that was to have a fundamental effect on the status and place of the tribunals in the legal system – if the adjudicatory function were taken in isolation,

---

[205] *Ibid.*, s. 10.   [206] *Ibid.*, s. 12.

[207] 'Minutes of Evidence taken before the Departmental Committee appointed by the Board of Trade to consider the law relating to Railway Agreements and Amalgamations', *HCPP* (1911) (5927) xxix Pt 2, 51 at q. 13,762 *per* Claude Andrews, solicitor to the London and North Western Railway Company.

[208] *Winsford Local Board* v. *Cheshire Lines Committee* (1890) 24 QBD 456 at 460.

[209] *Darlaston Local Board* v. *London and North Western Railway Company* [1894] 2 QB 45 at 50.

Jurisdiction and Functional Powers   183

it was undoubtedly judicial in its essentials. Whether the adjudication was as to an objection raised in the course of the administrative process or a more formal appeal once a stage of the administrative process had been completed, it still consisted of the hearing and determination of a dispute, on its merits, by finding facts and applying legal rules. This essential nature of even a subsidiary component element in the overall jurisdiction demanded a process with special features to ensure fair and high-quality adjudication.

5

PROCEDURE AND PRACTICE

The new regulatory legislation of the nineteenth century was rarely popular. It undoubtedly and invariably addressed a clear and acknowledged evil, and as such was welcomed by that sector of society with humanitarian beliefs its members were prepared to act on, and by that sector which suffered under the evils the legislation was designed to remove. There remained, however, a large proportion of the public who had no real ideological or practical interest in the efficient implementation of the legislation, and others whose private interests were actively undermined by it. The government was thus faced with indifference or antipathy, and yet the prompt and effective implementation of the new policies embodied in the legislation was a social, economic or political necessity. To persuade the public to embrace the new legislation, the implementing bodies had to be attractive, and that meant easily accessible in terms of simplicity, cheapness, speed and proximity. The procedures had to be seen to ensure fairness, though the evidence suggests that the public were prepared to some extent to sacrifice the quality of justice if they could have the procedure they wanted. The Victorian age was one which valued individual independence and privacy and as such was particularly concerned with the machinery of implementation of the new legislation, often even more than with its substance. As was observed in relation to the new Railway Commission proposed in 1872, and reflecting popular views on the desirable attributes of the tribunal process, its proceedings were to be 'as simple and inexpensive as is consistent with giving due notice and hearing questions openly and fairly'.[1] The consensus was that there should be as little legal involvement as possible, a 'simple familiar

---

[1] *Report, Railway Amalgamation, 1872* p. 49.

Procedure and Practice

manner'[2] and something 'short, sharp, and decisive'.[3] The need for bodies operating such procedures was central to the creation of the statutory tribunals. As with their constitution their procedures had to be carefully and imaginatively conceived. Their popular acceptance lay at the heart of the effectiveness of the tribunals themselves, for it was in this very respect that the regular courts of law had proved deficient and rendered themselves unusable in the new conditions of early nineteenth-century government control.

The established procedures of both the regular courts of law and to some extent the arbitral bodies had been found wanting in this respect, but their experience was revealing. The principal deterrent to litigation was the expense. The new tribunals could mitigate the expense of litigation by the simple expedient of abolishing court fees and placing the entire expense of the process in the hands of the state. This was almost invariably done, and gave critics of the commission system more reason to complain as to the burden on the country. It was the exception rather than the rule that fees had to be paid, and the notable exception was the Railway Commission. But the long experience of the judicial process had made it clear that the expense of all judicial or quasi-judicial procedures was principally due to the need for the involvement of lawyers at some stage in the process, and partly to its geographical location. The expedition of the process was dependent on the degree of formality and, again, the location of the process. The need and the opportunity were there for legislators to design new, informal and swift procedures that addressed novel political and social needs. It constituted a considerable challenge. Procedures had to be established which were so simple and informal that they did not require the involvement of the legal profession, that ensured the process was not protracted and yet were clear and precise. It had long been understood that precision and clarity were often inconsistent with brevity.[4] Furthermore,

---

[2] *Minutes, Railway Amalgamation, 1872* q. 3270 *per* Frederick Broughton, manager of the Mid-Wales Railway.

[3] 'Minutes of Evidence before the Select Committee on Railway Rates and Charges', *HCPP* (1893–4) (462) xiv 535 at q. 4649 *per* Samuel Boulton, partner in a London firm of timber merchants and vice president of the London Chamber of Commerce.

[4] See 'First Report of Commissioners inquiring into the Practice and Proceedings of the Superior Courts of the Common Law', *HCPP* (1829) (46) ix 1 at p. 7.

186 *Legal Foundations of Tribunals in 19th-Century England*

they had to be formal enough to make it clear to the parties that the adjudication was serious and official. As a solicitor observed in 1911, the process should not be 'too conversational'.[5]

The design of appropriate procedures was challenging in two principal ways. The legislators had first to address the inherent tension of a mixed jurisdiction of administrative and judicial functions. The integration of the adjudicatory with the administrative, however, demanded unusual and somewhat conflicting procedures, with the former arguably requiring higher and more open standards of conduct and a swifter process than the latter. The entire process, however, was a continuous one with an administrative purpose and its procedures, like its jurisdiction, had to serve that objective. The overall administrative process contained judicial elements that were more or less discrete depending on the tribunal in question. In some instances, notably the land rights tribunals and the Assessment Committees, the adjudicatory element consisted of a stage in the administrative process where objections to a proposal or a decision were made by aggrieved parties and heard and determined by the tribunal. Sometimes the adjudicatory element was more clearly defined and was unambiguously appellate in nature, as with the fiscal tribunals where there was a clear appeal against an identifiable administrative decision and constituted a new and distinct stage in the process. In some instances, as with the railway tribunals, the notion of a complaint to be resolved permeated the entire proceedings. A common feature, however, was that they were adjudicatory functions, and to that extent judicial, but it was recognised that the more the procedures resembled judicial procedures, the slower they became. Because the judicial function was ancillary to the administrative function in the early statutory tribunals, the procedures were inquisitorial in their overall nature, with adversarial procedures predominating only in the dispute-resolution elements of the process. Even where the dispute-resolution element was distinct, as in the case of appeals against tax assessments, the process was fundamentally one in which the commissioners had to judge between two arguments put to them

---

[5] 'Minutes of Evidence taken before the Departmental Committee appointed by the Board of Trade to consider the Law relating to Railway Agreements and Amalgamations', *HCPP* (1911) (5927) xxix Pt 2, 51 at q. 6930 *per* William Calthrop Thorne, solicitor to the Mersey Docks and Harbour Board.

Procedure and Practice 187

rather than to seek out the truth on their own initiative, but the same tribunal was inevitably involved in the investigation in its administrative capacity.

The second challenge was that while simple and informal procedures were desirable to achieve fast and cheap implementation, they could not be allowed to undermine acceptable standards of fairness and efficiency. Despite the deep-seated and acknowledged faults of the judicial process, it was at least well established, tested and known. It was also recognised as possessing, however imperfectly, inherent safeguards for the administration of justice. These safeguards of formal evidence, the conduct of proceedings, legal representation and strict requirements of process were built into their procedures to ensure a fair trial and the impartial conduct of adjudication. In theory whatever was not guaranteed in this way through the procedures was ensured through the training and standards of an honourable profession and the constitutional independence of the courts of law. While these too were not without fault, on the whole they did provide an extra degree of protection. The new tribunals had none of these advantages, and so the design of procedures, which gave the public confidence in their effectiveness and even-handedness, was of the utmost importance. It was undoubtedly the case that the more informal the procedures, the less rigour was introduced into the process and so the greater the risk of a miscarriage of justice. The legislators had to strike a balance between the desire for the highest quality of justice and the achievement of their administrative ends.

The tribunals, being new creatures of the age, were unable to call on ancient usage to supply guidance as to procedures, and they were therefore entirely dependent on, and constrained by, the provisions of their parent legislation.[6] It was thus for the legislators to conceive, develop and then express the necessary procedures in statutory form. This did have some advantages, for with a clean sheet and fresh minds, no constraints of tradition or of judicial form, and with a clear objective to attain, the tribunals could be given procedures to achieve the desired cost-effectiveness, speed and security. Furthermore, the task of the

---

[6] *R. v. Assessment Committee of St Mary Abbotts, Kensington* [1891] 1 QB 378. See too *R. v. Mansel Jones* (1889) 23 QBD 29.

188 *Legal Foundations of Tribunals in 19th-Century England*

legislators was facilitated by the context of a more general movement for the reform of court procedures that prevailed in the first half of the nineteenth century, and the mood of popular and parliamentary opinion was in favour of a simplification of the litigation process. The Utilitarians were particularly concerned with the reform of procedures in the regular courts so as to enable each individual to establish and enforce his legal rights. Bentham himself examined closely matters of evidence, process, jurisdiction and constitution of the courts.[7] There was a continuous programme of legislation from the 1830s simplifying the procedures in the superior Common Law courts by introducing uniform methods of starting actions, reducing or removing technicalities and fictions[8] and introducing a new system of accessible local courts.[9] It culminated in the complete recasting of the system of superior courts and a uniform code of procedure outlined in the schedule to the Supreme Court of Judicature Act 1873, the latter going far towards achieving the 'cheapness, simplicity, and uniformity of procedure'[10] which had been desired some forty years before. The reforms in the earlier years of the century were not radical and were limited in their scope and effectiveness, but they constituted a considerable step towards the facilitation of the administration of justice in the regular courts.[11] The climate, therefore, was propitious.

The procedures were laid down in the parent Acts, sometimes in meticulous detail as to the administrative process, but rarely exhaustively and usually giving only broad guidance as to certain

---

[7] See A. V. Dicey, *Lectures on the Relation between Law and Public Opinion in England during the Nineteenth Century*, 2nd edition (London: Macmillan and Co., 1914), pp. 205–6.

[8] Uniformity of Process Act 1832, 2 & 3 Will. IV c. 39, provided for a uniform writ of summons; Real Property Limitation Act 1833, 3 & 4 Will. IV c. 27. See too Common Law Procedure Acts 1852 and 1854 (15 & 16 Vict. c. 76; 17 & 18 Vict. c. 125). For the simplification of pleading, see Sir William Holdsworth, 'The New Rules of Pleading of the Hilary Term, 1834' (1923) 1 *Cambridge Law Journal* 261. See the speech of Henry Brougham as he then was on the state of the courts of law in *Parl. Deb.*, vol. XVIII, new series, cols. 202–12, 7 February 1828 (HC).

[9] Recovery of Small Debts Act 1846, 9 & 10 Vict. c. 95.

[10] *Parl. Deb.*, vol. CCXIV, ser. 3, col. 337, 13 February 1873 (HL) *per* the Lord Chancellor.

[11] See generally Baron Bowen, 'Progress in the Administration of Justice during the Victorian Period', in *Select Essays in Anglo-American Legal History*, 3 vols. (Boston: Little, Brown & Co., 1907), vol. I, pp. 516–57.

Procedure and Practice

key matters, notably the summoning and examination of parties and witnesses, the extent to which legal representation was allowed, and the production of documents. Other details were sometimes included, such as the required quorum, whether majority decisions were allowed and rights of appeal. Other than this provision, tribunals tended to have no special instructions to follow as to their procedures other than the most general and apparently informal guidance from the central government department where appropriate. These statutory procedures were thus extant from the inception of the tribunal and tended to remain unchanged during the life of the tribunal, though their practical application evolved. The overall process addressing both their administrative and their dispute-resolution functions was dictated by the demands of the task of the tribunal, whether for example it was to commute tithes, assess taxes or regulate railways. In the fiscal field the tribunals were subject not only to their own substantive legislation but also to the overarching regulatory Acts which later became known as Taxes Management Acts.[12] These Acts were essentially procedural in nature.

In the fiscal, land rights and rating tribunals, the processes began as pure administration, with no element of adjudication necessary at their inception. Within their particular subject areas they differed little, with the fiscal tribunals and the land rights tribunals both having recognisably characteristic procedures within their cognate groups. In the fiscal tribunals, whose process was directed at making correct assessments to tax and collecting it, the procedures were all similar despite the differences between the various taxes. The process generally began with a meeting of the commissioners to appoint the subordinate assessors, who then would ascertain who was liable to pay the tax. The assessors would go into the field to make the assessments to the tax in question or to collect the lists, statements and declarations required under the various taxing statutes.[13] When the assessors had done their work, they would return the assessments[14] or the statements to the commissioners who would meet to examine them and, in the case of assessments, require the assessors to

---

[12] 38 Geo. III c. 16 s. 45 (1798).

[13] 39 Geo. III c. 13 ss. 38, 39 (income tax of 1799); 43 Geo. III c. 122 ss. 105–9 (Schedule D of income tax of 1803).

[14] 43 Geo. III c. 122 s. 143 (1803) (Schedule D assessments under 1803 Act).

190 *Legal Foundations of Tribunals in 19th-Century England*

verify them on oath.[15] If they suspected any undercharging in any assessment or valuation[16] or any omission in any statement they would summon and examine the taxpayer,[17] sometimes on oath,[18] make general inquiries, require further information,[19] and when they were satisfied they would then make[20] or amend[21] the assessment as appropriate. In the case of special assessments of commercial income by the Special Commissioners of Income Tax, the assessments were made by the commissioners on the basis of a report by the surveyor based on that official's knowledge and the return made by the taxpayer to the assessor. The commissioners would then sign and formally allow the assessments,[22] and collection could then take place by the subordinate collectors who would have been appointed at the beginning of the process. The purely administrative functions were chronologically distinct from the adjudicatory ones, since the appeals would follow the formal arrival at the assessment.

The general procedures of the land rights tribunals shared a similar nature dictated by the cognate nature of their subject-matter. The underlying philosophy of the tribunals, at least in the first instance, was one of a voluntary restructuring of the land rights in question. The procedures reflected this, and were characterised by a number of consecutive meetings of the commissioners and all interested parties, designed to arrive at a voluntary agreement between the parties and to give every opportunity for objection and the resolution of those objections. In this sense the administrative procedure, and indeed the adjudicatory functions, were more akin to arbitration procedures than to the adversarial

---

[15] 20 Geo. II c. 3 (1747) s. 7 (houses and windows duties).

[16] As in the income tax under Schedules A and B of 1803: 43 Geo. III c. 122 s. 43.

[17] As in the window tax and all the assessed taxes and the income tax of 1799: 39 Geo. III c. 13 s. 57.

[18] As with the Additional Commissioners assessing income tax under Schedule D of the 1803 legislation: 43 Geo. III c. 122 s. 136.

[19] As in the window tax and all the assessed taxes and the income tax of 1799: 39 Geo. III c. 13 s. 52.

[20] 39 Geo. III c. 13 ss. 51, 57 (income tax of 1799); 43 Geo. III c. 122 s. 47 (Schedules A and B assessments under income tax of 1803).

[21] 20 Geo. II c. 3 s. 9 (houses and windows duties of 1747).

[22] As in the window tax and all the assessed taxes. See too the procedures for the assessment and collection of the tax on houses imposed in 1778: 18 Geo. III c. 26 s. 20. For the 1799 income tax see 39 Geo. III c. 13 s. 63. Commissioners allowed the assessments made by the assessors under Schedule E of the 1803 Act: 43 Geo. III c. 122 ss. 184, 187.

Procedure and Practice 191

and so more confrontational process adopted by the regular courts of law.

In the case of a voluntary commutation of tithes, the aim was to get the interested parties to arrange matters between themselves and the procedures left it in the hands of the parties themselves as far as possible.[23] The objective was to arrive at an agreed valuation of the tithes between the parties, at a meeting called for the purpose and with a prescribed representation of landowners and tithe owners, and then to appoint a valuer to make the apportionment of the sum among the lands of the parish according to rules agreed by the parties, or in default to the rules contained in the Act.[24] Where the commutation was compulsory, the process consisted first of arriving at an award, namely the valuation of the tithes, a task which was undertaken nominally by the commissioners though in practice delegated to their assistants, according to detailed rules laid down in the Act.[25] Secondly they had to effect an apportionment, namely the allocation of that sum among the lands of the parish, which task was undertaken by a valuer appointed at a special meeting by the parties under the supervision of the Assistant Commissioner.[26] Similarly, in the commutation of manorial dues under the copyhold enfranchisement legislation, where the aim was to convert the lord's dues into an annual rent charge, a fine on death or alienation, or a combination of both,[27] a meeting was to be called of the lord and tenants of the manor for the purpose of reaching an agreement as to the terms of the commutation with rules as to adequate representation of parties interested.[28] The copyhold agreement then needed to be carried out, and as with tithe commutation the task was put into the hands of a valuer appointed by the parties,[29] though closely supervised by, and under the instructions of, the commissioners who now played a more proactive role. He was to make the necessary valuations, apportionments and schedules, largely on the basis of information provided by the stewards of the manors. The valuer and the steward were to provide the commissioners

---

[23] See Marquess of Lansdowne in *Parl. Deb.*, vol. XXXIV, ser. 3, cols. 1293–4, 7 July 1836 (HL).
[24] Tithe Commutation Act 1836, 6 & 7 Will. IV c. 71 ss. 32–5.
[25] *Ibid.*, ss. 36–44.   [26] *Ibid.*, s. 53.
[27] Copyhold Act 1841, 4 & 5 Vict. c. 35 ss. 14, 15.   [28] *Ibid.*, s. 13.
[29] *Ibid.*, s. 24.

192 *Legal Foundations of Tribunals in 19th-Century England*

with such valuations, apportionments or schedules as they should require.[30] Once the valuer had completed his work, the commissioners were to draw up a schedule of apportionment detailing the liability of the various lands and landowners,[31] and were to confirm it,[32] marking the successful achievement of the commutation.

The Inclosure Commissioners' task was to arrive at a fair allocation of newly inclosed lands on the basis of existing rights in common land, and they too did so by arranging for a survey of the land, and a true valuation of the land once it had been inclosed, which tasks were carried out by professional surveyors and valuers, and then to proceed to making the allotment. Once they had so divided the land, they embodied their decision in an award. Unlike the tithe and the copyhold procedures, there was a clear model available to the new Inclosure Commission of 1845, since there were established practices under the parliamentary private bill process and the Inclosure Clauses Consolidation Act 1801.[33] However, the reasons for the creation of a new tribunal had been entirely procedural, since the old process had required the consideration of each inclosure by a committee of each of the two Houses of Parliament and had been prohibitively expensive. The new procedure was simple and cheap and resembled that in tithe and copyhold commutation. It was initiated by the owners of at least one-third in value of the land applying on a standard pre-printed form to the commission in London. If the commissioners thought it might be expedient to proceed with the inclosure, they would send an Assistant Commissioner to the locality to inspect the land, make inquiries and call a meeting to hear any preliminary objections.[34] If he reported favourably,[35] a provisional order for inclosure which included all the detail of the proposal and which was deposited in the locality for public inspection would follow. The Assistant Commissioner would thereafter hear assents and dissents, and if the proportion of the former sufficed, he would confirm the inclosure.[36] At that point the valuer took

---

[30] *Ibid.*, ss. 25, 27.   [31] *Ibid.*, s. 31.   [32] *Ibid.*, s. 32.

[33] Or even earlier, see E. C. K. Gonner, *Common Land and Inclosure*, 2nd edition (London: Frank Cass & Co. Ltd, 1966), p. 93.

[34] Inclosure Act 1845, 8 & 9 Vict. c. 118 s. 25.   [35] *Ibid.*, s. 26.

[36] *Ibid.*, s. 27. The process is seen in the case of *Church* v. *Inclosure Commissioners* (1862) 11 CB NS 664.

Procedure and Practice

over to value the claims and make the allotments.[37] The process drew to a close with the Assistant Commissioner hearing objections in general.

Whether the tithe commutation was voluntary or compulsory, both stages of agreement or award, and apportionment, were subject to formal confirmation by the commissioners, just as the fiscal commissioners signed and allowed assessments. Once the Assistant Commissioner had heard all objections and arrived at a satisfactory conclusion, he would submit a draft award and apportionment for confirmation by the Tithe Commissioners in London.[38] The report he sent the central board was always detailed. Sometimes a printed form was used containing a number of questions as to requirements of notice, details of the interests, the proving of evidence, the number and nature of objections and the opinion of the Assistant Commissioner on the desirability of the award or apportionment.[39] The commutation agreement in the copyhold process also had to be confirmed by signing and sealing by the commissioners,[40] and this confirmation made the agreement binding on the parties interested. Until the point of formal confirmation the role of the Copyhold Commissioners in the process was organisational and supervisory, but a more substantive function was envisaged in relation to confirmation. The statute provided that the commissioners were to inquire and require satisfactory proof that the agreement should be confirmed.[41] The Copyhold Commissioners also had to confirm the schedule of apportionment,[42] that act marking the successful achievement of the commutation. In the inclosure of common land the process of inclosure was brought to a close by the signing of the award by the Inclosure Commissioners. The requirement that the tribunals confirm the final achievement of the process after any necessary adjudication had taken place was another indication that all dispute-resolution undertaken by the tribunal was firmly placed within an overall scheme of administration.

---

[37] 8 & 9 Vict. c. 118 s. 33.

[38] See for example the proceedings for the tithe commutation for Brampford Speke in Devon in 1841, TNA:PRO IR 18/1116 (1841).

[39] See for example the Assistant Commissioner's report of the commutation of tithes in Swavesey in Cambridgeshire, TNA:PRO IR 18/13644 (1838).

[40] Copyhold Act 1841, 4 & 5 Vict. c. 35 s. 23.   [41] Ibid.

[42] Ibid., s. 32.

194 *Legal Foundations of Tribunals in 19th-Century England*

The Assessment Committees of 1862 followed similar procedures. The purpose of the legislation was to ensure the correct and uniform valuation of all property to the poor rate by appointing a new tribunal to supervise and if necessary revise the valuation lists prepared by the overseers. This relatively straightforward and recurrent task was reflected in the simpler nature of its procedures. The overseers of the parish made and signed a list of all the rateable property in the parish and its annual value[43] according to legislative provisions as to the method of valuation. After a period to allow for public inspection, this valuation list was to be transmitted to the Assessment Committee,[44] and after the committee had heard and determined any objections to the list,[45] and directed that any further valuations, corrections and amendments be made,[46] the list was again to be deposited for public inspection before being formally approved by the committee.[47] At that point the list became the list in force and the basis for the raising of the rate.

The procedures of railway regulation differed from those of the fiscal, land rights and rating tribunals in that the process was adjudicatory from its inception, the objective of the tribunals being primarily to hear and determine complaints of infringements of the statutory duties placed on the railway companies. The preference was always to allow tribunals to settle their own procedures,[48] and so not only were the tribunals constituted to implement the railway regulation legislation given the power to create their own procedures standing outside their parent Acts, their procedures were more obviously judicial in nature. When Edward Cardwell proposed, contrary to his initial preference, that the regular courts implement the Railway and Canal Traffic Act in 1854, he instituted a relatively cheap and easy procedure. Complaints were to be addressed to any single judge of the superior courts in chambers.[49] The Act itself provided that on a complaint being made, the Court of Common Pleas would hear and

---

[43] Union Assessment Committee Act 1862, 25 & 26 Vict. c. 103 s. 14.

[44] *Ibid.*, s. 17.   [45] *Ibid.*, ss. 18, 19.   [46] *Ibid.*, s. 20.   [47] *Ibid.*, s. 21.

[48] As with the Railway Commissioners of 1846: see 'A Bill for regulating the Proceedings of the Commissioners of Railways, and for amending the Law relating to Railways', *HCPP* (1847) (65) iii 415, cl. 87.

[49] 'A Bill (as amended in Committee) for the Better Regulation of the Traffic on Railways and Canals', *HCPP* (1854) (82) vi 13, cl. 3.

Procedure and Practice 195

determine the complaint and could make inquiries through engineers or barristers or other experts and could issue a writ of injunction if the complaint was upheld.[50] The court, like all courts of law, had the power to regulate its own procedures and could 'make all such general rules and orders as to the forms of proceedings and process, and all other matters and things touching the practice and otherwise in carrying this act into execution ... as they may think fit'.[51] Similarly, but unusually among lay statutory tribunals, the Railway Commissioners of 1873 and of 1888 were given the power to make general orders for the regulation of their proceedings and their implementation of the railway legislation, though they had to be approved by the Lord Chancellor and laid before both Houses of Parliament.[52] Their procedures were the most judicial of the tribunals, emphasised by the provision that where the Act or the orders did not expressly provide for a particular case, the general principles of practice in the superior courts of law could be adopted and applied at the discretion of the commissioners.[53] They were, however, to conduct their proceedings in such manner as was convenient to the speedy dispatch of business,[54] and their general orders introduced considerable flexibility into their proceedings and left much to their discretion. In their first annual report after their creation in 1873 they observed that they had revised the rules in order 'to simplify and expedite' their procedures, to which end they had dispensed with the writ of summons and with requiring the corporate seal to be attached to all documents.[55] Before the formal proceedings began, for example, the Act permitted the commissioners to give the company complained of the opportunity to make any observations concerning the complaint,[56] in other words to communicate with the parties before the hearing of the case, a provision

---

[50] Railway and Canal Traffic Regulation Act 1854, 17 & 18 Vict. c. 31 s. 3.

[51] *Ibid.*, s. 4.

[52] Railway and Canal Traffic Act 1873, 36 & 37 Vict. c. 48 s. 29; Railway and Canal Traffic Act 1888, 51 & 52 Vict. c. 25 s. 20.

[53] General Ord. 54, printed after the Railway and Canal Traffic Act 1873 in *The Practical Statutes* (London: Horace Cox, 1865–1900), 1373.

[54] 36 & 37 Vict. c. 48 s. 27.

[55] *Annual Report of the Railway Commissioners for 1873*, TNA:PRO MT 68/28. See too *Annual Report of the Railway and Canal Commissioners for 1890*, TNA: PRO MT 68/29.

[56] General Orders made under the Railway and Canal Traffic Act 1873 (36 & 37 Vict. c. 48) Ord. 14.

196 Legal Foundations of Tribunals in 19th-Century England

later criticised as an improper function of a judicial body.[57] They had the power to dispense with pleadings,[58] could hold a preliminary meeting in person or by correspondence to alter the usual mode of proceeding,[59] and dispense with viva voce examination of witnesses.[60]

The location of the proceedings was an issue of considerable importance in making any tribunal accessible to the public. The inconvenience and expense to a litigant of proceedings in London had been a major complaint against the regular courts for years. The cost to the parties of taking themselves and their witnesses to the capital, and remaining there for the possibly long duration of the trial, rendered much litigation prohibitively expensive. It was costly not just in terms of having to pay for board and lodging, but also in lost earnings for the period of the trial. The distance a litigant had to travel to recover a small debt – in some instances some fifty miles to recover a debt of less than 40 shillings – was one of the problems that gave rise to the creation of the County Courts in 1846. An ancient tenet of the administration of the Common Law in England, however, was that of the circuit, of itinerant judges bringing justice to the people twice each year. The concept was originally introduced in order to ensure a knowledgeable uniformity and consistency in the application of law, free from the influence of local faction. Even though the original purpose of the circuit system was essentially political, it did accustom the people to the availability of central justice in their own locality, and so any centralised tribunal was not necessarily and automatically perceived as inaccessible. With respect to traditional litigation, where it was important to reduce expense and prevent delay, where the cases were contentious, small and simple and could by their nature be speedily disposed of, it was accepted that they should be heard and determined as near as possible to the localities of the parties, and this was the underlying premise of the County Courts. Where the jurisdiction was primarily administrative, however, it was frequently maintained, as in the case of the location of a Court of

---

[57] *Minutes, Railways (Rates and Fares), 1882* q. 1371 *per* J. H. Balfour Browne, barrister.

[58] General Orders made under the Railway and Canal Traffic Act 1873 (36 & 37 Vict. c. 48) Ord. 17.

[59] *Ibid.*, Ords. 28 and 29.   [60] *Ibid.*, Ord. 35.

Procedure and Practice 197

Bankruptcy,[61] that the relevant tribunal should be stationary and in London, the argument being that it should be near the machinery of the parent executive department. There was thus some tension as to location in relation to tribunals exercising a jurisdiction that was primarily administrative and yet incorporated a clear dispute-resolution function. Furthermore, in some instances such as the land rights, fiscal and rating tribunals, the political importance of localism and the practical necessity for local knowledge made the situation of the tribunal an issue of considerable importance.

When the tribunals to restructure tithes, copyhold tenure and common land were established in the 1830s and 1840s, the importance of an easily accessible location and its effect of keeping the cost of summoning witnesses to a minimum were clearly recognised. While the commissioners themselves were based in London, the practical tasks in the field were undertaken by their assistants, and they worked on their investigations and adjudications in the locality in question. The primary concern was to establish a convenient location for the geographical area the tribunal was serving.[62] It was maintained in the context of tithe commutation, for example, that the tribunal 'should go from place to place where the matters in question were to be settled',[63] and the legislation itself provided that disputes were to be heard and determined at a place 'in or near the Parish'[64] and objections heard at 'some convenient Place'.[65] Under one general inclosure provision the meetings for conducting business were to be held in one of the parishes or townships where lands were to be inclosed, or within seven miles of the boundary of one of them.[66]

In taxation matters the accepted model for 200 years was local assessment and appeal, with central control, and so the essential and obvious geographical structure of the administration was to have local tribunals and not a centralised one in London. The close relationship between the system and that of the justices of

---

[61] 'Report of the Royal Commission on Bankruptcy', *HCPP* (1854) (1770) xxiii 1 at p. 41.

[62] Inclosure Act 1845, 8 & 9 Vict. c. 118 s. 55, 'some convenient place'.

[63] *Parl. Deb.*, vol. XXXIII, ser. 3, col. 886, 12 May 1836 (HC) *per* William Blamire.

[64] Tithe Commutation Act 1836, 6 & 7 Will. IV c. 71 s. 44.   [65] *Ibid.*, s. 51.

[66] Common Fields Inclosure Act 1836, 6 & 7 Will. IV c. 115 s. 7.

198 *Legal Foundations of Tribunals in 19th-Century England*

the peace also necessarily presupposed a local tribunal. Being local appointments, the assessment to tax took place on a local basis, and the adjudicatory functions within the assessment process were equally local. Accordingly the Triple Assessment Act 1798 specified the appeals location as 'the usual place of holding parochial meetings'.[67] The General Commissioners of Income Tax, who numbered in their thousands and whose appointment required local residence, sat in hundreds of small divisions throughout the country. They, like the Land Tax Commissioners, were the expression of a clear legislative policy of local tax administration, with centralised control in the form of the government surveyor. The Land Tax Redemption Appeal Commissioners, being justices of the peace, heard appeals at their local Petty Sessions.[68] Rating for the relief of the poor was equally local in its fundamental conception, and the Assessment Committees were essentially parochial creatures. The rating legislation, therefore, provided that the adjudicatory function should be exercised in a local venue.[69]

The Special Commissioners of Income Tax, on the other hand, constituted a notable exception in the localism of the fiscal tribunals and were an unambiguously central tribunal based in London. Their duties, however, extended over the whole country, and since the commissioners numbered only three[70] it was clear that they could only hear cases outside the capital if they went on circuit. The Income and Property Taxes Act 1842 gave them an appellate jurisdiction over commercial income provided that they would hear any appeal 'in the District in which such Appellant shall be chargeable',[71] and so 'for the convenience of taxpayers' they went on circuit all over the country solely to hear appeals.[72] They went out on circuit usually once, sometimes twice, a year, depending on the circumstances,[73] totalling some

---

[67] 38 Geo. III c. 16 s. 63.

[68] Land Tax Redemption Consolidation Act 1802, 42 Geo. III c. 116 s. 197.

[69] Valuation of Property (Metropolis) Act 1869, 32 & 33 Vict. c. 67 s. 63 provided that appeals were to be heard in 'any room maintained out of the proceeds of any rate levied wholly or partly in the metropolis'.

[70] Excluding the members of the Board of Inland Revenue who were appointed ex officio.

[71] 5 & 6 Vict. c. 35 s. 130.

[72] 'Report of the Royal Commission on the Income Tax', *HCPP* (1920) (615) xviii 97 at p. 184, para. 358.

[73] *Minutes, Income and Property Tax, 1852* q. 1106 *per* James Dickens, Special Commissioner.

Procedure and Practice

three to four weeks annually.[74] As a rule taxpayers had to have their appeals heard in their own location. When a taxpayer who could appear before the Special Commissioners in his own district of Newcastle only at 'great inconvenience' to himself asked to appear before them in London, the Board of Inland Revenue refused. He was firmly told by the board that his assessment by the Special Commissioners would be discharged, but a fresh assessment would be made by the local commissioners, and any subsequent appeal would be heard locally.[75] It seems, however, that there was a measure of flexibility and that the board made every effort to enable taxpayers to appeal to the Special Commissioners. There are many examples of the board informing taxpayers that they could appeal to the Special Commissioners against an assessment made by the General Commissioners even though the appeals had already been heard in their district, and could do so by attending at the office in London.[76]

Unlike the judicial circuits, the Special Commissioners' itinerary was not fixed. Their provincial sittings depended on which districts gave rise to appeals, but they tended to go only to the main towns and cities. The 130 appeals to be heard in 1849, for example, entailed two or three days of appeal hearings in London and visits to twenty-seven towns and cities in England, from Truro to Newcastle.[77] In 1863 they attended thirty-nine centres in England from Plymouth to Liverpool. In most places they heard just one appeal, but in major centres they heard more, though still not a large number. In Plymouth for instance they heard five, and in Manchester nine. The greatest number was heard in Somerset House, where they heard forty-one. The Special Commissioners made considerable use of the new uniform penny post in their procedures. Rowland Hill had introduced the system in 1840, at the height of the formative period of the new

---

[74] 'Minutes of Evidence before the Select Committee on Inland Revenue and Customs Establishments', *HCPP* (1863) (424) vi 303 at q 2511.

[75] TNA:PRO 1R 86/1, Board Minute, 13 May 1843.

[76] See for example TNA:PRO 1R 86/1, Board Minutes, 4 December 1845 and 30 December 1845.

[77] *Minutes, Income and Property Tax, 1852* qq. 1068–71 *per* James Dickens. The places visited were Bury, Norwich, Lynn, Leicester, Derby, Doncaster, Leeds, Normanton, York, Whitby, Newcastle, Manchester, Liverpool, Wolverhampton, Birmingham, Kidderminster, Worcester, Gloucester, Stroud, Clifton, Newport, Swansea, Taunton, Plymouth, Truro, Bath and Slough.

200 Legal Foundations of Tribunals in 19th-Century England

tribunals. Instead of letters being paid for by the recipient on the basis of distance and the number of sheets used, with a single letter sent a short distance costing 4d, all letters were to be charged by weight at the flat rate of 1 penny per half ounce, whatever the distance. The facility of fast, reliable and cheap postage enabled some appeals to be settled without recourse to personal attendance at a hearing, and accordingly cut down considerably on the potential expense to individual taxpayers, notably in not having to take time away from their business or profession. From the first days of the Special Commissioners' appellate jurisdiction, they endeavoured to settle as many appeals by correspondence as possible, particularly for districts where very few appeals were listed.[78] The General Commissioners, the Poor Law Board and the later Local Government Board all made similarly extensive use of the postal service to settle appeals.

When the regulation of railways was allocated to the Court of Common Pleas, it was clearly located in London. When the Railway Commission was created in 1873 the legislation provided that the commissioners should 'sit at such time and in such places ... as may seem to them most convenient for the speedy despatch of business',[79] and a similar provision was found in the Act of 1888.[80] Since no application was made in an English case for the commission to sit anywhere other than in London, the location of the tribunal in the capital was not perceived as a material objection. When the location of a new tribunal was being debated in 1882, one commentator favoured the capital, observing that he looked 'to London as being the Omphalos of all business', and as such 'the most convenient place practically for all parties'.[81]

The precise place for the meeting of the tribunal within the locality could not be set by the statutes, though the importance of an easily accessible place was recognised. The appropriateness of accommodation, the desirability to strike a balance between the formality necessary to engender respect for the proceedings and sufficient informality so as not utterly to intimidate the litigants, was to be questioned only by a later age,[82] and so the suitability of

---

[78] TNA:PRO IR 86/2, Board Minute, 8 October 1850.
[79] 36 & 37 Vict. c. 48 s. 27.   [80] 51 & 52 Vict. c. 25 s. 5.
[81] *Minutes, Railways (Rates and Fares), 1882* q. 1553 *per* Edward Pember QC.
[82] The appropriateness of the General Commissioners using the premises of the Inland Revenue was officially questioned by the Royal Commission on the

Procedure and Practice 201

meeting in inns, hotels or government offices was rarely noted. The primary concern was to establish a convenient location in the geographical area the tribunal was serving.[83] Most parent Acts were silent, though some specified the appeals location as 'the usual place of holding parochial meetings',[84] or again, any public room.[85] The Assistant Tithe Commissioners nearly always held their meetings to hear objections in an inn,[86] a common practice simply because inns often constituted the largest rooms in the area other than the private houses of the gentry. Occasionally meetings were held in the parish church.[87] General Commissioners of Income Tax usually sat in a local hotel[88] or used the same courtrooms as those used by the justices of the peace. The Special Commissioners heard appeals at their own offices in London, variously at Broad Street, Lancaster Place, the Old Jewry, Somerset House and Kingsway. When out on circuit they usually heard appeals at a local hotel[89] or at the offices of the surveyor.[90] Assessment Committees often sat at the local Poor Law Union offices, usually the board room of the local Board of Guardians. The Railway Commissioners of 1873 sat in a committee room of the House of Lords, but by the legislation of 1888 they were to sit in the Royal Courts of Justice,[91] a location which increased the

---

Income Tax in 1920: 'Report of the Royal Commission on the Income Tax', *HCPP* (1920) (615) xviii 97 at p. 185, para. 365 (d).

[83] Inclosure Act 1845, 8 & 9 Vict. c. 118 s. 55, 'some convenient place'.

[84] Triple Assessment Act 1798, 38 Geo. III c. 16 s. 63.

[85] The Valuation of Property (Metropolis) Act 1869, 32 & 33 Vict. c. 67 s. 63 provided that appeals were to be heard in 'any room maintained out of the proceeds of any rate levied wholly or partly in the metropolis'.

[86] For example, the proceedings for the tithe commutation for Brampford Speke in Devon in 1841 were held in the New London Inn and in the Seven Stars Inn, both in nearby Exeter (TNA:PRO IR 18/1116); those for the commutation in Newton St Cyres in Devon in 1841 were held at the Crown and Sceptre in the village, at the Ship Inn in Crediton and at the New London Inn in Exeter (TNA:PRO IR 18/1419); those for the commutation of the tithes of Isleham in Cambridgeshire from 1844 to 1849 were held at the Griffin Inn (TNA:PRO IR 18/13595).

[87] See for example the commutation of tithes for the parish of Hatley Saint George in Cambridgeshire (TNA:PRO TITH 2/12).

[88] For example the General Commissioners in Leek sat in the George Inn in 1860 (TNA:PRO IR 40/1052 (1860)).

[89] *Broughton and Plas Power Coal Co. Ltd* v. *Kirkpatrick* (1884) 2 TC 69.

[90] *Leeds Permanent Benefit Building Society* v. *Mallandaine* (1897) 3 TC 577.

[91] 51 & 52 Vict. c. 25 s. 5(2).

202 *Legal Foundations of Tribunals in 19th-Century England*

popular perception of the commission as closely resembling a court of law.

An issue which was of fundamental importance in achieving the aims of the legislators to create an efficient tribunal through accessible procedures was the ease with which a party aggrieved by any decision of the administrative process could make any objection, dissent or appeal to the tribunal to have it heard and determined. Knowledge as to how to initiate the proceedings was a prerequisite to any successful process, and accordingly the legislation invariably gave clear guidance as to the steps he should take. The initiation of litigation in the ordinary courts was not only primarily through the medium of a professional lawyer, but invariably a complex and formal process. Even after the recasting of the procedures of the superior courts by the Supreme Court of Judicature Acts 1873 and 1875,[92] the process of writ of summons, indorsements, pleadings, statements of claim, defences, demurrers and interrogatories, even before the trial was arrived at, were complex, lengthy and invariably expensive.

As with any new institution, the absence of a tradition and general knowledge of its procedures necessitated clear measures to ensure public information. Any procedures that were laid down in the statutes would be available for public scrutiny in that form. While the legislation was physically accessible to many individuals, since most private town libraries and reading rooms possessed copies of the *Statutes*, it was the intellectual preserve of the lawyers. The language was technical and arcane, the Acts were expressed in continuous sentences with no punctuation, they were rarely single Acts relevant to a particular topic and so several statutes had to be located and read together, and the result was an incoherent and apparently illogical statement of the law which was of little if any assistance to the vast majority of readers. The Acts did, however, usually make provision for public information. The traditional way of doing this was by the affixing of notices to the church door[93] and, as the number and availability of newspapers increased, the publication of relevant notices in the local journals. The parent Acts of the new tribunals were scrupulous in this

---

[92] 36 & 37 Vict. c. 66; 38 & 39 Vict. c. 77.

[93] Earlier tax Acts sometimes also provided for an announcement in church immediately after divine service: see for example Houses and Windows Duties Act 1747, 20 Geo. II c. 3 s. 12.

Procedure and Practice 203

respect. They almost invariably made express provision for the giving of public notice as to the holding of meetings to hear the complaints of any aggrieved parties. In the tax tribunals this followed a particular pattern. The date, time and place of the appeal meetings were generally included by the commissioners in their instructions to the collectors,[94] and were publicised by means of notices on the church door, in the market place or on the cross in the locality, 'that all Persons who shall think themselves over-rated may know when and where to make their Appeal to the said Commissioners'.[95] The official returns and notices of the income tax process sent to individual taxpayers also publicised, with varying degrees of clarity, the right to appeal against their tax assessments.[96] So too with the land rights tribunals, following the tradition of publicising proposed inclosures on the church door as required by the standing orders of the House of Commons in the days of private inclosure Acts. Tithe Commissioners often not only affixed notices to the church door, but also to the door of the meeting room, usually the inn.[97] Where they were determining parish boundaries the Inclosure Commissioners acting under the authority of private Acts of Parliament, were to give ten days' notice of their setting of the boundaries, by fixing a notice to the church door, by advertising in the newspapers and by depositing the notice at the homes of the lords of the manor.[98] The key documents themselves were made available for public inspection. The draft tithe commutation award and apportionment, for example, were to be available for inspection 'at some convenient Place within the said Parish' by everyone interested in the lands or tithes,[99] and in practice were deposited in a local inn[100] or at the

---

[94] *Ibid.*; Land Tax Act 1692, 4 Will. & M. c. 1 s. 20. The same provision was in force 100 years later: 38 Geo. III c. 5 s. 8.

[95] Land tax: 38 Geo. III c. 5 s. 8 (1797); Schedule D income tax: 43 Geo. III c. 122 s. 145 (1803).

[96] TNA:PRO IR 9/2, Form 64 (1868); TNA:PRO IR 9/4 Pt 2, Form 65 (1850s).

[97] See for example the commutation of the tithes of the parish of Isleham in Cambridgeshire, TNA:PRO IR 18/13595 (1844–9).

[98] Inclosure Clauses Consolidation Act 1801, 41 Geo. III c. 109 s. 3. See too the Common Fields Inclosure Act 1836, 6 & 7 Will. IV c. 115 ss. 1, 7, 8, which mentioned as an alternative 'some conspicuous public place'.

[99] 6 & 7 Will. IV c. 71 ss. 51, 61.

[100] For example, the draft award in the tithe commutation for Brampford Speke, in Devon in 1841 was deposited for inspection at the Agricultural Inn in the village of Brampford Speke, TNA:PRO IR 18/1116. In the commutation of the

204 *Legal Foundations of Tribunals in 19th-Century England*

house of a prominent resident.[101] The description of boundaries set by Inclosure Commissioners was to be deposited at the home of the churchwarden or overseer,[102] and the valuation list made by the parish overseers was by statute to be deposited for public inspection so that all persons assessed to the poor rate could inspect the list and take extracts from it.[103]

In order to ensure that the process was as expeditious as possible, and yet fair, time limits were set both for making the appeal and for the hearing of it,[104] though provision was often made for appellants who were prevented from adhering to the time limits through sickness or absence.[105] The usual pattern in the tax tribunals was that appeals were to be initiated within ten or fourteen days, and heard within a reasonable time.[106] The aim was to ensure that appeals were speedily dealt with, and that the collection of the revenue was not hindered.[107] In the case of inclosures, objectors were given at least twenty-one days to object to claims,[108] though notice of an appeal against a boundary determination had to be made within one month of the publication of the boundaries.[109] A similar pattern was adopted in the tithe commutation process, and meetings could be adjourned to consider the objections or make further inquiries.[110] The rating legislation laid down clear time limits to ensure that ratepayers were

---

tithes of Isleham in Cambridgeshire the draft apportionment was deposited for inspection in the Griffin Inn where the meeting for the hearing of objections was to be held, TNA:PRO IR 18/13595 (1844–9).

[101] For example, the draft award of the tithe commutation of the parish of Newton St Cyres in Devon was deposited for inspection at a private house, TNA:PRO IR 18/1419 (1841).

[102] 8 & 9 Vict. c. 118 s. 39.

[103] 25 & 26 Vict. c. 103 s. 17.

[104] With the land tax the appeal meetings were to be held at least thirty days after the duplicates had been delivered to the collectors: 38 Geo. III c. 5 s. 8 (1797). In the inclosure process, fourteen days' notice was given of meetings at which objections to claims would be heard and determined by the valuer: 8 & 9 Vict. c. 118 s. 48, and thirty days of the meeting at which the commissioners heard appeals from the valuer's determinations: 8 & 9 Vict. c. 118 s. 55.

[105] The Triple Assessment Act allowed a late appeal within reasonable time if there was proof of 'sufficient cause' for lateness: 38 Geo. III c. 16 s. 67 (1798). See 43 Geo. III c. 122 ss. 145, 146 (1803).

[106] Schedule D income tax: 43 Geo. III c. 122 s. 146 (1803).

[107] The Triple Assessment Act required ten days' notice: 38 Geo. III c. 16 s. 55 (1798) as did Schedule D income tax appeals: 43 Geo. III c. 122 s. 144 (1803).

[108] 8 & 9 Vict. c. 118 s. 48.   [109] *Ibid.*, s. 39.

[110] 6 & 7 Will. IV c. 71 ss. 51, 61.

Procedure and Practice 205

given sufficient time to examine the valuation lists and take any necessary extracts before they made a formal objection to the list. If any overseer or ratepayer wanted to object to the list, he had to do so within twenty-eight days from the notice of the deposit of the list[111] and the Assessment Committee had to give twenty-eight days' public notice of the holding of the meetings to hear and determine objections.[112] The whole process from the first deposit of the list to the final approved list could take some four months. The Railway Commission too imposed time limits by its general orders to ensure the expeditious resolution of complaints.[113]

Once the public were made aware of their right to object or appeal, the interests of speed and simplicity had to be served in relation to making the objection itself. The initiating of a tax appeal was direct and simple, consisting of a relatively informal written communication to the commissioners or some subordinate official[114] stating the desire to appeal or object. This was sometimes a pre-printed form, sometimes a letter. As with the institution of an appeal to the General Commissioners of Income Tax, that to the Special Commissioners was simple and straightforward, an aggrieved taxpayer merely having to give notice to the surveyor as instructed in his notice of first assessment. Objections to claims in inclosures were made in writing directly to the valuer and the claimant,[115] and appeals from the determination of the valuer were initiated by the aggrieved party writing to the commissioners.[116] In practice, however, objections were often made at the various meetings themselves with no prior communication with the officers. This was the general rule in the case of tithe commutations where the process was strikingly informal, with objections to the award or the apportionment being made at the meetings themselves.[117] Similarly in the case of objections

---

[111] 25 & 26 Vict. c. 103 s. 18.   [112] *Ibid.*, s. 19.

[113] General Orders made under the Railway and Canal Traffic Act 1873 (36 & 37 Vict. c. 48) Ords. 23, 25.

[114] With the land tax it was the assessor: 38 Geo III c. 5 s. 8 (1797); with the triple assessment it was the commissioners: 38 Geo. III c. 16 s. 65 (1798); and with the income tax it was either the assessor or the surveyor: 43 Geo. III c. 122 s. 144 (1803), for Schedule D.

[115] 8 & 9 Vict. c. 118 s. 48. Under the Inclosure Clauses Consolidation Act 1801, 41 Geo. III c. 109 s. 6, the objection had to be made directly to the commissioners, and could be made at the meeting itself.

[116] 8 & 9 Vict. c. 118 s. 55.   [117] 6 & 7 Will. IV c. 71 ss. 51, 51.

206 Legal Foundations of Tribunals in 19th-Century England

to valuation lists for the purposes of rating, the Union Assessment Committee Act 1862[118] and the Valuation of Property (Metropolis) Act 1869[119] – to be read with it and making special provision for London – provided that if a person felt aggrieved by the valuation, on the basis that it was incorrect or unfair, he could make his objection to the Assessment Committee. This stage of the appellate process was not expressed in the usual terms of appeals to be heard and determined, merely of objections being made prior to any revision of the valuation list, and as such was even more unambiguously part of the administrative process of raising rates. The objection had to be in writing and was usually on a printed form provided by the committee. It also had to state the grounds of the objection and the correction that the objector desired, though the other party could expressly waiver any insufficiency in the notice.[120]

In the more obviously judicial processes of the railway tribunals, even after the demise of the Court of Common Pleas as the implementing body, the procedure to be followed to make a formal complaint was laid down not in the parent legislation itself, but in the general orders the Railway Commission was permitted by statute to make. These laid out the steps in the process in considerable detail. Under the Railway and Canal Traffic Act 1873, an application to have a complaint resolved by the Railway Commissioners was relatively straightforward. It was to be made in writing or in print and signed by the applicant in a prescribed form. It had to contain a clear statement of the facts and the remedy asked for.[121] The application was for a writ of summons calling upon the railway or canal company complained of to show cause why a writ of injunction should not issue against it. Three copies and their accompanying documentation were to be left at the commissioners' office.[122] One or two commissioners would then hear the application and grant leave, or refuse, to issue a summons.[123] This procedure was judicial in tone and outline, but considerably simpler than the processes of the regular courts.

---

[118] 25 & 26 Vict. c. 103 s. 18.
[119] 32 & 33 Vict. c. 67 s. 11.   [120] *R.* v. *Justices of London* [1897] 1 QBD 433.
[121] General Orders made under the Railway and Canal Traffic Act 1873 (36 & 37 Vict. c. 48) Ord. 2 and Form 1 in the Schedule.
[122] *Ibid.*, Ord. 13.   [123] *Ibid.*, Ord. 18.

Procedure and Practice 207

An aggrieved party would, therefore, have little difficulty in setting his complaint in motion and finding out when and where his grievance would be heard. The parent legislation, however, was largely silent as to the conduct of the actual hearing, and most aggrieved parties had little idea as to what would happen when they appeared before the tribunal. This situation was exacerbated if the hearings were private, for there would be no opportunity for the development of any general knowledge of the process within the community. In the case of the regular courts including the justices of the peace, the general rule was that they constituted an open court of a judicial nature to which the public had free access and could not be denied.[124] It was, indeed, 'one of the essential qualities of a Court of Justice that its proceedings should be public'.[125] Only in exceptional cases were court hearings to be private. There were repeated arguments for the same degree of openness to be adopted in relation to non-judicial decision-making bodies. The procedures adopted by the early railway bodies in the 1840s were essentially closed with parties heard separately and in secret, and so the opposing parties did not know the arguments put against them, which laid the bodies open to suspicion. Viscount Howick said that to deny openness to the proceedings of the Railway Committee of the Board of Trade in its scrutiny of railway bills before they went before the private bill committees of Parliament, even though those recommendations were not binding, was to 'open a door to corruption and jobbing of the grossest and rankest nature'.[126] This secrecy contributed significantly to the downfall of the earliest regulatory bodies. When the constitution of a new controlling body was debated in 1852, publicity and a fair hearing of parties in the presence of each other were regarded as indispensable to the effectiveness of any system of dispute-resolution.[127]

The same publicity was adopted in relation to the hearings of the first tribunals as in the courts of law, though for different reasons. Lacking the status, legal expertise and established

---

[124] See *Collier* v. *Hicks* (1831) 2 B & Ad 663.

[125] *Daubney* v. *Cooper* (1829) 10 B & C 237 at 240 *per* Bayley J.

[126] *Parl. Deb.*, vol. LXXVII, ser. 3, col. 146, 5 February 1845 (HC) *per* Viscount Howick.

[127] 'Minutes of Evidence before the Select Committee on Railway and Canal Bills', *HCPP* (1852–3) (246) xxxviii 175 at qq. 1951–7 *per* Edmund Denison MP.

208 *Legal Foundations of Tribunals in 19th-Century England*

procedures of the regular courts, the need for obvious safeguards against incompetence, error, mismanagement and political bias was all the more pressing. One of the principal procedural safeguards was that of publicity of the proceedings themselves.[128] This was particularly desirable in the case of the land rights tribunals, for a general knowledge of changed property rights had always been valued in English law as a safeguard against fraud. Inherent in all the processes of the land rights tribunals, therefore, was not only a meticulous system of public notice, but also of holding public meetings at each stage in the process, with the resolutions of such meetings signifying an element of consent to the proceedings, and the airing and resolution of objections. These meetings were well attended by those with a peripheral interest as well as by the landowners and other interested parties, and, of course, the presiding Assistant Commissioner and the legal representatives of the parties if they had such representation. Objectors would be given full opportunity to voice their objections and to have them addressed by the Assistant Commissioner. The parent legislation usually assumed the public nature of the hearings, and expressly addressed only the attendance of certain key personnel, namely the officials. Undoubtedly, however, a large proportion of the administrative work of the tribunal, which included decision-making if not dispute-resolution, was undertaken in private, in the government offices of the commissioners. It was this secrecy, rather than that of the discrete adjudicatory elements of the tribunals' jurisdiction, which led Lord Hewart to observe in the following century that '[i]t is a queer sort of justice, that will not bear the light of publicity'.[129]

The sensitivity of the commercial community to revealing their dealings to the public gaze was well known and indeed was a factor in the popularity of the private process of arbitration as a method of dispute-resolution. The publicity of proceedings was one of the reasons for the failure of the specialised Court of Bankruptcy created in 1831. Creditors did not want their names published in the newspapers and debtors resented the criminal overtones of a public hearing. A Royal Commission on the Bankruptcy Laws concluded that publicity was 'an important and necessary incident

---

[128] The ultimate safeguard was the right of appeal to the regular courts.

[129] Lord Hewart, *The New Despotism* (London: Ernest Benn Ltd, 1929), p. 49.

Procedure and Practice

to every Court of Justice', and that 'the principle must be preserved without being unduly pressed'.[130] While the demand for secrecy was not fruitful in relation to bankruptcy proceedings, in one important instance there was a strong and ultimately successful resistance to open hearings.

When William Pitt introduced income tax in 1799, he made provision for a separate body of commissioners to assess commercial income in order to meet the concerns of the mercantile community. The merchants feared that if no special provision were made, their rivals in trade and creditors would learn of their financial affairs to the detriment of their livelihoods.[131] The principal precaution then introduced was the examination of witnesses 'apart'[132] and a slightly later provision ensured that Commercial Commissioners could examine persons in the presence of their clerk or anyone sworn to secrecy under the Act,[133] the implication being that this was limited to persons for whom the Act provided an oath. Though these provisions were introduced in the administrative context of assessment to the income tax, they constituted the authority for the hearing of income tax appeals in camera. It applied equally to the General and the Special Commissioners of Income Tax since they too had to take an oath of secrecy to the effect that they would not disclose any information received in the course of the performance of their duties with respect to commercial income.[134] Indeed, when the tax was reintroduced in 1842 the privacy of the process was part of the raison d'être of the extended powers given to the Special Commissioners. Since the provision for secrecy in income taxation was a procedural provision that was political in nature and peculiar to the income tax, it did not extend to the other taxes, whose appeal hearings were public.

Even in the sphere of income tax, however there was a strong current of opinion that secrecy was undesirable. It was condemned in the House by some commentators. Charles Buller observed that the secrecy of income tax proceedings would

---

[130] 'Report of the Royal Commission on Bankruptcy', *HCPP* (1854) (1770) xxiii 1 at p. 20.

[131] See C. Stebbings, 'The Budget of 1798: Legislative Provision for Secrecy in Income Taxation' (1998) *British Tax Review* 651.

[132] 39 Geo. III c. 13 s. 98.   [133] 39 Geo. III c. 22 s. 22.

[134] Income and Property Taxes Act 1842, 5 & 6 Vict. c. 35, Schedule F.

210 *Legal Foundations of Tribunals in 19th-Century England*

'violate the great rule of the publicity of all penal proceedings, and to subject to penalties upon evidence taken in secret, and not given to the public afterwards. A tax that could only be collected by such means must be very bad.'[135] Thomas Wakley too objected to the secrecy of the proceedings. 'Every man', he said, 'ought to have a public investigation if he wished it. If the commissioner should have a desire to act unjustly, the appearance of the public would serve as a check upon him.'[136] Peel was adamant, however, and the rule of secrecy was maintained. It was the political price he had to pay, as Pitt had had to, for the imposition of the tax.[137] Though public opinion became less concerned about private hearings in income tax as the nineteenth century progressed,[138] nevertheless the oath and its consequences were retained and the rule endured for over two hundred years.[139]

In one aspect of publicity the tribunals did not follow the practice of the courts of law. Even if the hearings were in public, tribunals usually gave no reasons for their decisions and simply announced their finding. This tended to undermine public confidence in the tribunals in question, since the parties did not know how decisions were arrived at, and such ignorance bred suspicions of bias and of arbitrary adjudication. Furthermore, it made it impossible for an aggrieved party to know or anticipate the view the tribunal would take on his particular situation, and so could not judge whether it was sensible for him to pursue his case or not. And it was important for him to know, for though the tribunals did not follow strict precedent, they inevitably developed certain principles of action and decision. Appellants to the General and Special[140] Commissioners felt this keenly, for while these

---

[135] *Parl. Deb.*, vol. LXII, ser. 3, col. 1000, 22 April 1842 (HC).
[136] *Ibid.*, col. 1024.
[137] *Ibid.*, col. 1000 *per* Charles Buller; *ibid.*, col. 1024 *per* Thomas Wakley, and *ibid.*, col. 1025 *per* Sir Robert Peel.
[138] See 'Minutes of Evidence before the Departmental Committee on Income Tax', *HCPP* (1905) (2576) xliv 245 qq. 1941–8 *per* Arthur Chamberlain JP, representing the Birmingham Chamber of Commerce, where he observed that 'There is nothing nowadays to hide. Why should not a man do it? All officials have their income known. Why should it be possible for every official to bear to see his income published in a red book, and business men alone feel that they cannot bear publicity.'
[139] It was ended in 2003 as a result of the implementation of European Human Rights legislation.
[140] See for example TNA:PRO IR 86/3.

Procedure and Practice

211

tribunals kept the briefest minutes of their meetings for their own private guidance, they were certainly not available to the public. One taxpayer represented the majority when he remarked in 1905:

Now, half the beauty of the law, is that when one is arguing before judges one can quote previous cases, and we know where we are. We say, " *This* has been decided *there*, and *that* has been decided *there*, " and so you can go from one to the other. But with the Commissioners we do not know what they have decided in the cases of the last thirty men they have had before them. We do not know how much they have allowed off Brown and refused off Smith, because Brown had a more pleasing manner or a more ready wit. That is where the income tax appealer is at a disadvantage, that he has no knowledge of their proceedings.[141]

This lack of publicity, and the consequent reliance on hearsay and gossip, left appellants with a sense of injustice; they suspected, though could not know, that they had not been treated fairly and equally with their fellow taxpayers. Such perceptions undermined the accessibility of the tribunal. Indeed, in the case of the Special Commissioners, so slight was publicity surrounding them that most taxpayers had never heard of the tribunal, let alone know of their right to appeal to it.[142] Having at least some idea as to how the tribunal might decide in their own particular case, they would have felt more able to approach it. In contrast, while the land rights commissioners did not publish their reasoned decisions as such, the processes were considerably more open throughout. The public meetings aired discussions, debates and objections, and the various stages of the processes were reduced to writing and made available for public inspection for further debate. The Assistant Commissioners hearing and determining disputes in the locality made their formal reports to the commissioners in London. Exceptionally, but with their close affinity to the regular courts of law, the Railway Commissioners always gave reasons for their judgments and were careful to state their grounds and why they arrived at particular conclusions on questions of fact. The Assessment Committees reported their proceedings

---

[141] 'Minutes of Evidence before the Departmental Committee on Income Tax', *HCPP* (1905) (2576) xliv 245 q. 1940 *per* Arthur Chamberlain. See too *ibid.*, q. 1953.

[142] See the confusion of Arthur Chamberlain, *ibid.*, qq. 1950–3. See generally C. Stebbings, 'Access to Justice before the Special Commissioners of Income Tax in the Nineteenth Century' (2005) *British Tax Review* 114.

212 *Legal Foundations of Tribunals in 19th-Century England*

through the Board of Guardians to the Poor Law Board, but in relation to the objectors they merely granted or refused relief. The disadvantages of the secrecy of income tax hearings were compounded by its natural consequence that the decision of the tribunal could not be reported.

While tribunals could not determine their procedures contrary to express or implied provisions in their governing legislation, the legislation was silent as to the detail of the appeals process and the practical application of the procedural rules. The rules gave little more than broad guidance and enabled an aggrieved person to see the place of his objection or appeal in the overall context of the administrative process. As to the conduct of the hearing itself, the legislation provided little if any direction, and it was left to the discretion of the commissioners. It was for them to decide how they were going to hear an appeal, for example whether they would give appointments for appeals or direct all appellants to arrive at the same time and wait; which party was to be the first to speak; the admissibility of some evidence; and degree of latitude allowed in conduct of the cross-examination. And, of course, there were matters that could not be legislated for and were material in the tribunal process. Such matters concerned the manner in which the tribunal personnel behaved in the human intercourse of the occasion, such as the degree of courtesy and respect shown to complainants and the commissioners' attitude to the government representative. The conduct of the tribunals' process was central to their public reception and, accordingly, to their efficacy. What was clear was that the procedure during the hearings of most tribunals was almost invariably significantly less formal than that of the regular courts. There was no inflexible adherence to rules about which party should first present his case nor to rules as to the admissibility of evidence. With no traditional etiquette of conduct, much depended on the force of personality and expertise of the chairman and the nature of the attendance.

With their wide attendance and common rights and interests, the land rights meetings were larger and generally more boisterous than the hearings of other tribunals. They often had the tone of a public meeting, with the Assistant Commissioner acting as chairman, mediator, conciliator and adjudicator. The evidence suggests that Assistant Commissioners were almost invariably patient, even-handed and knowledgeable in their conduct of the

Procedure and Practice 213

process.[143] Certainly the voluminous notes of individual tithe commutations show the painstaking and often frustrating work of the Assistant Commissioners, striving to bring the parties together. Occasionally even the patience of an Assistant Tithe Commissioner is seen to break. In the commutation of the tithes of the parish of Isleham in Cambridgeshire in 1844, the Assistant Commissioner was faced with repeated delays and non-attendance, and wrote to the board in London that he thought that 'the Commission has been trifled with in a very unwarrantable manner'.[144]

The hearings of the fiscal tribunals, in contrast, were generally restrained affairs, partly because their attendance was restricted to the parties, the commissioners and their clerk. The hearings of the Special Commissioners in many ways resembled an arbitration, with all the parties gathered together privately and seated not in a courtroom but at tables in an ordinary chamber. Conversely, the hearings of the General Commissioners were often perceived as an extension of the jurisdiction of the justices of the peace, primarily because General Commissioners were often justices as well and often sat in larger panels, but exacerbated if the premises used were the local courtrooms. The evidence reveals, however, that in all the tribunals, the government official usually concerned conducted himself in a non-confrontational and constructive way, seeking a fair and just conclusion to the proceedings.

The procedure for the hearing of objections to a rating valuation list by the Assessment Committee was intended to be informal and inexpensive, and not a full preliminary hearing prior to appeal to Quarter Sessions with a similar burden of formal legal procedures. To have done that would have been in effect to assimilate the objections before the committee with the appeal before the justices, and that would have constituted a considerable burden on both the ratepayers and the committee. Accordingly, the procedures were informal and the numerous objections were dealt with 'in a practical spirit',[145] with successive meetings and adjournments, correspondence and discussion. 'In most cases',

---

[143] See for example the tithe commutation for Swavesey in Cambridgeshire, TNA: PRO IR 18/13644 (1838).

[144] TNA:PRO IR 18/13595 (1844–9).

[145] *Gateshead Union Assessment Committee* v. *Redheugh Colliery Ltd* [1925] AC 309 at 329 *per* Lord Shaw.

214 *Legal Foundations of Tribunals in 19th-Century England*

observed Lord Shaw in the following century, 'the valuer and the ratepayer or his representative meet together and endeavour to get at an agreed figure or to understand each other as to what is the real difference to be determined by the committee.'[146] The matter was to be settled 'by such conferences and methods as may seem applicable'.[147] There were no rules of evidence and no oaths were to be taken.

The structure of the dispute-resolution process was often determined by statutory provision on two key matters: the summoning and examination of witnesses and the production of documentary evidence. The power to summon witnesses and examine them on oath was a valuable authority in achieving the objective of the tribunals. It was, of course, a defining power in the regular courts of law, but equally one that the legislators saw was necessary to the implementation of the new legislation. Most of the statutory tribunals of the nineteenth century were given this essentially judicial power to achieve their administrative ends. Even the Poor Law Commissioners of 1834 were given the power to summon and examine witnesses, though their adjudicatory functions were minimal.[148] One tribunal that did not have that authority, however, was the Assessment Committee, which could not summon witnesses to the meeting for the hearing of objections to the valuation list nor evidently examine them on oath. However, the Assessment Committee for Chesterfield Union in 1863 observed that it was their practice to 'call before them such persons as they think best able to give them information to arrive at the correct annual value'.[149] In the fiscal context the power to examine under oath had long been regarded as necessary for the effective raising of taxes and the power was invariably given for the assessing functions of the tribunals. There was some variation as to the extent to which the taxpayer himself could be summoned and examined on oath. The Land Tax Act 1797 did not directly address the issue but in the specific case of a complaint of charging in excess of the pound rate on lands, the taxpayer was to produce proof upon oath that he had been overcharged.[150] The Land Tax

---

[146] *Ibid.*   [147] *Ibid.*, at 335 *per* Lord Carson.   [148] 4 & 5 Will. IV c. 76 s. 2.

[149] 'Abstracts of Reports from Guardians of Unions as to Proceedings of Assessment Committees under the Union Assessment Committee Act 1862 s. 12', *HCPP* (1863) (540) lii 867 at p. 895.

[150] 38 Geo. III c. 5 s. 84 (1797).

Procedure and Practice 215

Redemption Appeal Commissioners were given the express power to examine all interested parties on oath, and indeed anyone else willing to be examined in connection with the dispute, and to examine any documentation produced under oath to them.[151] In hearing and determining the appeals of those who felt aggrieved by an assessment to the window tax, the commissioners could examine the appellant on oath concerning the number of windows in his house, and upon this examination or their own knowledge they could finally reduce or increase the assessment.[152] The examination of the appellant and witnesses under oath continued as an established feature of assessed taxes appeals jurisdiction.[153]

Under the recast income tax legislation of 1803,[154] whereby the General Commissioners became the supreme assessing and appellate body, the appellate procedures remained broadly the same as they had been in 1799.[155] The commissioners could summon the appellant to verify his schedule of income and property on oath, signing his name to the truth of the contents, but could not submit him to oral examination under oath. He was to answer the questions in writing or could, if he so chose, appear in person before the commissioners, though in that case he was entitled to refuse to answer any question.[156] While the appellant could not be examined under oath, he could be required to swear to the truth of the answers he had given under written or oral examination.[157] Other witnesses could be summoned and examined on oath,[158] though in practice oaths were rarely sworn. The effect of the legislation was to allow each party to appear and give evidence to support their own case; the person charged to show the assessment made upon him was too high, the Crown to show the assessment was correct. The commissioners were impliedly limited to a consideration of this evidence to ascertain whether in that light the assessment was correct. The commissioners' powers remained largely unchanged throughout the nineteenth century, and were only slightly extended thereafter.[159] The Special

---

[151] Land Tax Redemption Consolidation Act 1802, 42 Geo. III c. 116 s. 197.
[152] 20 Geo. II c. 3 s. 12 (1747).
[153] For example the Inhabited House Duty Act 1778, 18 Geo. III c. 26 s. 40; Horses and Carriages Duties and Taxes Management Act 1785, 25 Geo. III c. 47 ss. 30, 31.
[154] 43 Geo. III c. 122.   [155] 39 Geo. III c. 13 ss. 16, 64.
[156] 43 Geo. III c. 122 s. 151.   [157] Ibid., s. 152.   [158] Ibid., s. 153.
[159] 8 & 9 Geo. V c. 40 ss. 133–52.

216 Legal Foundations of Tribunals in 19th-Century England

Commissioners were similarly empowered to summon any person to appear before them, but only in the context of their exercise of their appellate powers.[160] Otherwise they had to proceed by affidavit, a provision originally enacted for the convenience of the taxpayer. In practice, many appeals before the fiscal tribunals did not require personal attendance. If all the information required by the commissioners had been forthcoming, and the parties were in agreement, the cases were normally settled by correspondence and in such cases the appellant would not have to attend personally.

The land rights tribunals of the 1830s were given similar powers for the collection of evidence, though their adjudicatory jurisdiction was more fully integrated into the administrative process. Where there were objections to the decisions of the Tithe, Copyhold or Inclosure Commissioners, or where there were boundary disputes, the commissioners all had the power to summon and examine witnesses under oath.[161] When the Tithe Commissioners' jurisdiction over boundary disputes was extended in 1837, they were given the power to examine witnesses on oath and any other legal method they saw fit to employ,[162] the same power given to Inclosure Commissioners under the Inclosure Clauses Consolidation Act 1801 which in turn reflected earlier practice.[163] A typical tithe commutation process involved a number of meetings, often attended by counsel, the examination and cross-examination of witnesses,[164] and the collection and analysis of evidence that was often complex and conflicting,

---

[160] Income Tax Act 1842, 5 & 6 Vict. c. 35 s. 23. See too *Minutes, Income Tax, 1919* q. 13,489 *per* G. F. Howe, presiding Special Commissioner.
[161] 6 & 7 Will. IV c. 71 s. 10; 4 & 5 Vict. c. 35 s. 39; 41 Geo. III c. 109 s. 33. The Inclosure Commissioners were able to make use of the statutory declaration, introduced in 1835 by 5 & 6 Will. IV c. 62 to address the growing abuse of the oath in business and public life and its degeneration into a mere formality. The fact that the statutory declaration was to be used in place of all oaths excepting those of allegiance and those used in courts of justice, is further evidence that the Inclosure Commission, and bodies like it, were not perceived as courts in the usual sense of the term: 8 & 9 Vict. c. 118 s. 9.
[162] 7 Will. IV & 1 Vict. c. 69 s. 2.   [163] 41 Geo. III c. 109 s. 3.
[164] See for example *Girdlestone* v. *Stanley* (1839) 3 Y & C Ex 421. See too the boundary disputes in Kirkby Stephen in Westmorland in 1843 (TNA:PRO TITH 1/44) and in Waldershare and Coldred in Kent in 1843 (TNA:PRO TITH 1/83).

Procedure and Practice 217

addressing questions of both law and fact.[165] In some instances this evidence was as challenging as any presented in a court of law. While the underlying procedures laid down for the restructuring of these various land rights were inquisitorial, the conduct of the adjudicatory aspects of the tribunals' jurisdiction tended more to the adversarial, the tribunal determining the disputes on the basis of the evidence adduced to them and not, at the dispute stage, initiating their own inquiries. When a dispute was referred to the Tithe Commissioners from the Assistant Commissioners, for example, the former would only examine the minutes of the evidence taken by the assistant to ensure he had come to a correct decision on it, or else they could direct the assistant to collect further evidence on a particular point.[166]

The land rights commissioners all delegated the task of examining witnesses and taking factual evidence to their various subordinate officers, and the taking of the evidence in the locality was an important aspect of the procedures. The ability to take evidence on oath locally was of considerable importance to the land rights tribunals and a very real advantage since it entailed little if any expense to the parties. In so doing the Assistant Tithe Commissioners were 'bringing justice to their doors'.[167] It saved considerably on the cost to individual witnesses, who were spared the journey to London and the expense of accommodation there for a lengthy trial. Indeed, the governing legislation often imposed limits on how far a witness could be required to travel to attend the tribunal.[168] This went far towards ensuring that local interests were fully represented and so furthered public acceptance of both the tribunal and the legislative regime it existed to implement.

The Railway Commissioners, the tribunal most resembling a court of law, had the power to summon and examine anyone they thought fit, require answers and returns to their inquiries, and administer oaths.[169] They also had the same power as the superior

---

[165] See for example *Re the Appledore Tithe Commutation* (1845) 8 QB 139. A legally qualified Assistant Commissioner generally conducted the proceedings, as in *Re Dent Tithe Commutation* (1845) 8 QB 43.

[166] See the evidence of Revd Richard Jones, Tithe Commissioner, in *Minutes, Commons' Inclosure, 1844* q. 23.

[167] *Ibid.*

[168] See for example the Inclosure Clauses Consolidation Act 1801, 41 Geo. III c. 109 s. 34 and the Inclosure Act 1845, 8 & 9 Vict. c. 118 s. 9.

[169] Railway and Canal Traffic Act 1873, 36 & 37 Vict. c. 48 s. 25.

218 *Legal Foundations of Tribunals in 19th-Century England*

courts to enforce the attendance of witnesses.[170] Most small traders, however, wanted the simplicity and informality of arbitration, with the calling of witnesses only by consent of the parties and the determination achieved as far as possible on the basis of written statements and without oral argument, but the railway companies were not in favour of that kind of adjudication, believing their interests to be too large. It was true that the exchange of written documents did not give the same opportunities to address the other party's arguments and evidence as oral evidence could. The outcome was a compromise of written preliminary process followed by an oral hearing. It was understood that the Court of Common Pleas' procedure, though modified, had been inappropriate and cumbrous. Application had been by affidavits on motion for a rule nisi, followed by the granting of the rule, then there was showing cause, and upon showing cause it was referred to a master for a further report, and upon that report a further agreement. The formality was a deterrent to potential users.

The procedures of the regular courts of law provided for the compulsory disclosure of relevant documents. Though the power to call for documentary evidence was a power that could greatly increase the expense and delay involved in a tribunal hearing, most of the new tribunals were given the power by statute. The Poor Law Commissioners had the power to call for certain documents in their administrative functions[171] and the Railway Commissioners could require the production of documents they deemed important.[172] The power to call for documentary evidence was of particular importance in the land rights tribunals, because of the complexity of the subject-matter and its traditional redaction to documentary form. All three were given this power in their founding legislation, though in the case of the Tithe Commissioners they found their initial powers in this respect to be inadequate. They were originally empowered to call for books, deeds, contracts, accounts, maps and other documents relating to the commutation of tithes, but could not compel the production of any document relating to the title of any lands or tithes because

---

[170] *Ibid.*, General Ord. 33. [171] 4 & 5 Will. IV c. 76 s. 2.
[172] Railway and Canal Traffic Act 1873, 36 & 37 Vict. c. 48 s. 25, and see General Ords. 30, 31.

Procedure and Practice 219

they did not possess the power to make determinations as to title.[173] This proved a hindrance to effective and inexpensive commutation in practice, since the only possibility was a bill of discovery in Equity, which entailed such a considerable expense that its threat could be used coercively in tithe litigation before the commissioners.[174] The full judicial power of compelling the production of documents, even documents of title if they related to the matter before the commissioners, was granted four years after the original commutation legislation and proved very effective.[175] This power was made explicit in relation to the Copyhold Commissioners in 1841.[176] When the Inclosure Commissioners were formed in 1845, Walter Coulson, who drafted the commons' inclosure bill, adopted the clause from the Copyhold Act, but omitted the proviso as to documents of title.[177] The commissioners were thereby given the widest power to demand the production of court records, plans, maps, surveys and other documents as they thought necessary.[178] In practice it was thought that since the Inclosure Commissioners had no jurisdiction in matters of title, they would very rarely need to call for documents of title, but they undoubtedly could do so if they felt it was necessary to their adjudication.[179] The regular courts regarded the production of documents as a matter of great importance, and were always circumspect in enforcing it.[180] They only allowed it if the documents related strictly to the matter in question. Documentary evidence was not invariably requested. A large number of inclosures were arrived at by the Inclosure Commissioners on the basis only of the oral evidence of the witnesses, the farmers and other inhabitants of the neighbourhood.[181]

The General Commissioners of Income Tax could issue a precept once an appeal had been initiated, requiring the appellant

---

[173] 6 & 7 Will. IV c. 71 s. 10.

[174] See the evidence of the Tithe Commissioners in *Minutes, Commons' Inclosure, 1844* qq. 83, 474.

[175] Tithe Commutation Amendment Act 1840, 3 & 4 Vict. c. 15 s. 24.

[176] 4 & 5 Vict. c. 35 s. 43. See too Enfranchisement of Copyholds Act 1852, 15 & 16 Vict. c. 51 s. 5.

[177] See the evidence of Walter Coulson in *Minutes, Commons' Inclosure, 1844* qq. 5569–70, 5575.

[178] 8 & 9 Vict. c. 118 s. 9.

[179] *Minutes, Commons' Inclosure, 1844* qq. 476–88.

[180] See *Pickering* v. *Noyes* (1823) 1 B & C 262.

[181] *Minutes, Commons' Inclosure, 1844* qq. 1966–9.

220 *Legal Foundations of Tribunals in 19th-Century England*

to provide a schedule containing information as to the appellant's property or occupation and his profits, detailed as to their source.[182] This evidence would form the basis of the appeal, as there was no power to call for the trader's books.[183] The Special Commissioners had the power to demand any further particulars as they could request under the authority of the primary legislation, but since the legislation of 1842 did not specify which documents they could call for, not only were the Special Commissioners themselves in some doubt as to the extent of their powers in this respect,[184] but some appellants were reluctant to co-operate on the basis of an absence of express authority in relation to specific documents. Clearly a wide and potentially intrusive discretion had been left in the hands of the commissioners, as a result of which appellants did not know precisely what an appeal would entail.[185] Appellants were often reluctant to provide balance sheets, trading accounts and profit and loss accounts.[186] The appellant had to go to the trouble and expense of providing his business accounts for the past three years, but that was not peculiar to the Special Commissioners; he was required to provide this information if he appealed to the General Commissioners. The perception of this by tradesmen was, predictably, that it was both onerous and intrusive.

At the heart of the notion that the procedures of dispute-resolution by the new tribunals should be inexpensive and expeditious was the limitation of the extent to which professional lawyers were permitted to become involved in the process. Although it was a matter for the discretion of the judges of the regular courts whom they would allow to participate in the proceedings before them, being one aspect of their right to determine their own procedures, long usage had established an undisputed right of certain advocates[187] to plead before the superior courts. It

---

[182] 43 Geo. III c. 122 s. 148 (1803); 5 & 6 Vict. c. 35 s. 120 (1842); *Minutes, Income and Property Tax, 1852* q. 1528.

[183] *Minutes, Income and Property Tax, 1852* q. 1533. Though often appellants did bring them along to the hearing.

[184] *Ibid.*, qq. 1195–1200 *per* James Dickens and Edward Cane, Special Commissioners.

[185] *Minutes, Income Tax, 1919* qq. 13,471–5 *per* G. F. Howe.

[186] *Ibid.*, q. 13,473 *per* G. F. Howe.

[187] Qualified barristers in the superior courts, with the added requirement of the rank of serjeant to appear in the Court of Common Pleas.

Procedure and Practice 221

was undoubtedly the case that the charges of solicitors and counsel, if briefed, constituted the most significant expense in any litigation. When lawyers participated in the proceedings, it introduced a 'nicety of discussion, and subtlety of argument'[188] that added to the length and complexity of the proceedings, which then reinforced the demand for professional legal representation, and which increased the costs. Indeed in 1861 in the context of an arbitration under the Friendly Societies Act[189] the court held that it was not necessarily in the interests of justice to allow legal representation, and thought it might even be contrary thereto by increasing the expense of the proceedings and by making the outcome of the case depend on 'the relative merits of the counsel rather than upon the intrinsic merits of the case'.[190] It was this self-perpetuating character of legal representation and its inherent and considerable expense that led the authors of the statutory tribunals to avoid the participation of lawyers. In general they did not prohibit it, but intended that the procedures would be so simple and straightforward that it proved unnecessary. Furthermore, arguably the expertise demanded of the adjudicators themselves rendered counsel unnecessary, at least insofar as counsel were not needed to explain to the judge the meaning or significance of the technical evidence.[191] The object with each new tribunal was that it 'would be judge, jury, and arbitrator all in one'.[192] If other expenses were kept low, and if legal representation was avoided, the issue of costs became largely irrelevant. Indeed there should be no costs other than the parties themselves going to appear at the tribunal. The land rights tribunals, however, had the power to ensure that expenses were equitably borne.[193]

The absence or limited use of legal representation – through a hoped-for lack of necessity or, more rarely, by express prohibition – was a deliberate and key feature distinguishing the statutory tribunals from the courts of law. The underlying policy decision to

[188] Collier v. Hicks (1831) 2 B & Ad 663 at 670 per Lord Tenterden CJ.
[189] Re Macqueen and the Nottingham Caledonian Society (1861) 9 CB NS 793.
[190] Ibid., at 796 per Erle CJ.
[191] See for example Parl. Deb., vol. LXXXIX, ser. 3, cols. 1180–1, 11 February 1847 (HC) per Edward Strutt, Chief Commissioner of Railways.
[192] Minutes, Railway Amalgamation, 1872 q. 3338 per Frederick Broughton, manager of the Mid-Wales Railway.
[193] See for example the Tithe Commutation Act 1836, 6 & 7 Will. IV c. 71 ss. 73 ff.

222 Legal Foundations of Tribunals in 19th-Century England

render professional legal assistance unnecessary coloured the entire procedures of the new tribunals. It created a tension too, in that legal representation in a hearing, particularly in a tribunal where the adjudicators were themselves untrained in legal principles of evidence, ensured that through expert oral examination and cross-examination, evidence was thoroughly tested and the material facts were correctly found. As such it constituted one of the most important safeguards to the parties, contributed materially to ensuring fair adjudication and was not a right to be denied lightly.

In certain relatively rare cases where there were clear reasons of policy on practical grounds, the representation of the parties by professional lawyers was expressly forbidden. This was the case with the General Commissioners of Income Tax. The prohibition on legal representation dated from the recasting of the income tax in 1803, since the Taxes Management Act of that year prohibited the representation of either party by any 'barrister, solicitor, attorney, or any person practising the law', and the prohibition extended to oral and written pleading.[194] Since that Act applied to all taxes under the management of the Commissioners for the Affairs of Taxes, prima facie the Land Tax Commissioners would have been affected in their administration of the land tax and the assessed taxes. However, it applied only to the General Commissioners of Income Tax since the Land Tax Commissioners acting under the Triple Assessment Act were expressly directed to hear a person by his 'attorney or agent' if he was unable to attend his appeal hearing in person,[195] and the Land Tax Commissioners were expressly excluded in relation to the land tax itself.[196] The reason was one of policy in the light of thousands of potential litigants and the need to keep the process swift so as to assess and collect the tax efficiently and regularly to finance government expenditure. Parties thus necessarily represented themselves, or, as in the case of commercial taxpayers appearing before the Special Commissioners, were represented by a partner,[197]

---

[194] 43 Geo. III c. 99 s. 26 (1803). The same provision is found in the Taxes Management Act 1880, 43 & 44 Vict. c. 19 s. 57(9).

[195] 38 Geo. III c. 16 s. 65 (1798).

[196] The Land Tax Commissioners were expressly excluded: see *ibid.*, s. 65.

[197] In *Watney & Co.* v. *Musgrave* (1880) 1 TC 272, when the Special Commissioners heard an appeal by a brewing partnership against an

Procedure and Practice 223

director[198] or officer.[199] There was a public demand for legal representation before the income tax commissioners, for the prohibition had been shown to cause hardship, particularly among female appellants,[200] and it was finally permitted in 1898.[201] Even then, however, it was relatively rarely used. Accountants were preferred where representation was desired before the General Commissioners, and tax barristers were employed only for the largest cases where the party had the means and the will to fight the Inland Revenue to the highest court.[202] Similarly legal representation was forbidden, though implicitly, in hearing municipal election petitions under the Corrupt and Illegal Practices Prevention Act 1883.[203] That Act provided that a person should be heard 'by himself', and those words were held to exclude legal representation.[204] Parliament had doubtless appreciated the inconvenience of allowing legal representation to possibly hundreds of persons, and since the tribunal in question had been recently created, no established practice had developed.

In most instances, legal representation was permitted by the statutes, either expressly or by implication. When the legislation regulating the railways was implemented by the Court of Common Pleas, legal representation before the court was both natural and expected. The Railway and Canal Traffic Act 1873 made no express reference to legal representation and it was allowed by implication, but when the Railway and Canal Commissioners were appointed in 1888, the parent legislation expressly provided that the parties could be represented by counsel, a solicitor, a parliamentary agent or could represent themselves.[205] The public

---

assessment, the younger partner, James Watney junr, represented the partnership. See too *Goslings and Sharpe* v. *Blake* (1889) 2 TC 450.

[198] In *Andrew Knowles & Sons Ltd* v. *McAdam* (1877) 1 TC 161 the company was represented by David Chadwick MP, who was also one of its directors. See too *Reid's Brewery Co. Ltd* v. *Male* (1891) 3 TC 279.

[199] In *San Paulo (Brazilian) Railway Co. Ltd* v. *Carter* (1895) 3 TC 344 the appellant company was represented by its secretary.

[200] See the introduction of the new clause by Lord Edmond Fitzmaurice in *Parl. Deb.*, vol. LIX, ser. 4, cols. 128–9, 13 June 1898 (HC). See too 'Minutes of Evidence before the Departmental Committee on Income Tax', *HCPP* (1905) (2576) xliv 245 at q. 55 *per* W. Gayler, a member of the committee.

[201] Finance Act 1898, 61 & 62 Vict. c. 10 s. 16.

[202] *Minutes, Income Tax, 1919* q. 15,927 *per* A. M. Bremner, barrister, on behalf of the General Council of the Bar of England.

[203] 46 & 47 Vict. c. 51 s. 38.   [204] *R.* v. *Mansel Jones* (1889) 23 QBD 29.

[205] 51 & 52 Vict. c. 25 ss. 50, 51.

224 *Legal Foundations of Tribunals in 19th-Century England*

were largely unaware of this, and it being the almost invariable practice for barristers to appear, it was widely assumed that representation by counsel was a requirement of the legislation. The widespread practice of appointing counsel was the result of the immense sums at stake in railway litigation, the complexity of the issues in question, and the considerable wealth and power of the railway companies. The issues brought before the commission were often complicated and despite the expertise of the commissioners were thought to require counsel conversant with the subject-matter. J. H. Balfour Browne, barrister, author and sometime secretary to the Railway Commission, said he would always recommend that parties employ counsel to appear before the commission because of the intricacy of the subject-matter.[206] The railway companies protected their interests fiercely, and since legal representation was not forbidden, they employed the best counsel they could. In order to fight the case on equal terms with the railway companies, private individuals then felt obliged to employ equally expensive legal representation, and the costs escalated accordingly.[207] The 'long purse' of the railway companies distorted the accessibility of the commissioners, for they were not inherently an expensive tribunal. The fees for appearing before them were small. The real expense lay in the appointment of counsel. In the natural way of things, therefore, the Railway Commission lost its character as a cheap and expeditious dispute-resolution body.

The Railway Commission became an expensive tribunal not only because the usual practice was to employ counsel, but also because of the cost of the particular barristers they appointed. The railway companies retained experienced railway counsel whose practices had been built up in the age of railway building when parliamentary counsel appeared to conduct railway cases before the parliamentary private bill committees, a branch of litigation in which fees were notoriously high.[208] 'Here', it was said, 'the funds were large, the fees enormous, and the costs

---

[206] *Minutes, Railways (Rates and Fares), 1882* q. 1207.

[207] *Minutes, Railways, 1881* q. 418 *per* Professor William Hunter; qq. 9377–9 *per* Robert Baxter, solicitor, parliamentary agent and coal owner. See *Minutes, Railways (Rates and Fares), 1882* qq. 1208–9 *per* J. H. Balfour Browne.

[208] 'Report from, and Minutes of Evidence before, the Select Committee on Private Bill Legislation', *HCPP* (1863) (385) viii 205.

Procedure and Practice 225

untaxed.'[209] The etiquette of the parliamentary bar demanded higher, minimum and daily fees as well as brief fees, and the practice of the bar required multiple counsel. When those same barristers were retained to conduct cases before the commissioners, they continued to charge comparable professional fees. The considerable fees charged by them, and the domination of the private bill committee process by experienced counsel,[210] contributed to a suspicion of, and disinclination to allow, legal representation before later statutory tribunals. The legislature remembered the expense, delays and unhealthy control caused by the counsel in this context.

The legislation permitted the parties to be represented by their solicitor, a right denied to suitors in the regular superior courts of law, where appearance had to be in person or by counsel. In practice, however, this concession was not taken advantage of even by the poorer party, primarily because of the great railway companies' determination to appoint the best railway counsel they could and the other party's acceptance that he had to attempt to match this expertise or fail in his action. There was also evidence that in practice the Railway Commissioners themselves did not allow it, though Balfour Browne saw no tension between the commission insisting on full legal representation and its nature as a 'popular tribunal'.[211] As a barrister himself he might be expected to take that view, but he was unusual in this respect and it was generally accepted that the refusal to hear solicitors sat uneasily with the notion of a publicly accessible tribunal. The Railway and Canal Traffic Act 1888 gave generous powers of representation before the commission. A party could appear by himself in person, or by counsel, by solicitor or parliamentary agent,[212] though again in practice solicitors and parliamentary agents were rarely used.[213] It was clear just a few years later that

---

[209] See Anon., 'The New Tribunals for Railway and Other Private Bills' (1846–7) 5 *Law Review and Quarterly Journal of British and Foreign Jurisprudence* 53 at 56.

[210] *Parl. Deb.*, vol. LXXVII, ser. 3, cols. 286–7, 11 February 1845 (HC) *per* Thomas Wakley.

[211] *Minutes, Railways (Rates and Fares), 1882* q. 1366.

[212] 51 & 52 Vict. c. 25 ss. 50, 51.

[213] 'Minutes of Evidence before the Select Committee on Railway Rates and Charges', *HCPP* (1893–4) (462) xiv 535 at q. 1412 *per* Walter Macnamara, registrar to the Railway and Canal Commission.

226 Legal Foundations of Tribunals in 19th-Century England

the parties continued to employ counsel, and that the relaxation of the rules regarding representation had done little to reduce the expense of appearing before the commission.[214] The magnitude of the interests concerned precluded any economy in legal representation, since it was necessary to ensure sufficient time for close consideration of the matter, and it was time that constituted the central expense, essentially the time of professional counsel. The alternative was a 'slap-dash decision', 'the benevolent despot under the palm tree who will go and give his decision straight away',[215] and no one with property at stake would be prepared to tolerate this. Even if a party could have his case adequately fought by a solicitor before the Railway Commissioners, that was impossible on appeal to the superior courts and there professional representation was an absolute necessity. It was the natural response of any litigant: where important issues arose, the best advocacy would be sought and where it could be paid for, it would be paid for. Even small traders felt that if it was worth engaging in litigation, it was worth doing it properly. To a large extent, therefore, cheap litigation was impossible.

The expense of litigation before the Railway Commissioners, comparable to that in the courts of law, caused considerable resentment. Court fees were low, but the expense of legal representation before the commission was so great that it was prohibitive for any but the large traders. One example given before the Select Committee on Railways in 1881 was a case before the Railway Commissioners lasting thirteen days and costing £6,000, of which £4,000 was spent before the commissioners themselves.[216] The cost of the Railway and Canal Commissioners of 1888 was equally high. One witness remarked in 1893 that a case fought by leading counsel and fully argued would cost in the region of £200 a day.[217] In condemning the expense of the Railway Commissioners in 1881 a Hull merchant observed that 'you

---

[214] *Ibid.*, at qq. 1423–8.

[215] 'Minutes of Evidence taken before the Departmental Committee appointed by the Board of Trade to consider the law relating to Railway Agreements and Amalgamations', *HCPP* (1911) (5927) xxix Pt 2, 51 at q. 18,918 *per* W. Guy Granet, general manager of the Midland Railway Company.

[216] *Minutes, Railways, 1881* q. 10,240 *per* Edward Lloyd, engineer and general manager of the Warwick and Birmingham Canal Company.

[217] 'Minutes of Evidence before the Select Committee on Railway Rates and Charges', *HCPP* (1893–4) (462) xiv 535 at q. 7298 *per* James Beale, solicitor.

Procedure and Practice

might as well say that the London Tavern is open to a man who is starving'.[218] There were other deterrents to engaging in litigation before the Railway Commissioners, which, when added to the expense, made most small traders prepared to put up with injustice and hardship. Not only was the time involved in litigation considerable, the odium of the railway companies towards a trader who challenged them[219] was not to be taken lightly. Many feared that they might 'make martyrs of themselves, and sacrifice their own private trades for the benefit of the community', who might then show little appreciation.[220] Another deterrent was the fear raised by the provision of powers of appeal and the potential enormous expense that might entail, with railway companies having the resources and motivation to fight cases to the highest court.[221] And since the Railway Commission had the power to award costs,[222] a trader could find himself liable to pay heavy costs if he failed in his contention. If costs were not allowed he would be free from the risk and his own costs would be a matter for his own discretion. The costs were in the discretion of the commissioners but they tended to follow the judicial pattern whereby costs followed the event. Just as in railway cases where the sums involved were potentially or actually substantial and so parties regarded it as a sound investment to pay for skilled legal representation, where the issues involved were perceived as essentially legal in nature and potentially financially significant – as in the commutation of tithes and the enfranchisement of copyholds – the practice was again for the parties to seek to be professionally represented. In the three land rights tribunals, parties were regularly professionally represented, even at the preliminary stages.[223] Both counsel and

---

[218] *Minutes, Railways, 1881* q. 9763 *per* Frederick Grotrian.

[219] *Ibid.*, q. 5765 *per* Benjamin Hingley, chairman of Ironmasters' Association of South Staffordshire.

[220] *Ibid.*, q. 7705 *per* Frederick Brittain, president of the Sheffield Chamber of Commerce and steel manufacturer.

[221] *Ibid.*, q. 5847 *per* C. F. Clark, president of the Wolverhampton Chamber of Commerce.

[222] 36 & 37 Vict. c. 48 s. 28.

[223] See *Church* v. *Inclosure Commissioners* (1862) 11 CB NS 664 where the plaintiff appeared at a meeting called by the Assistant Inclosure Commissioner to take assents and dissents to a proposed inclosure, and was represented even at that stage by counsel. Legal representation was equally usual in tithe commutation: see for example *Girdlestone* v. *Stanley* (1839) 3 Y & C Ex 421.

228 Legal Foundations of Tribunals in 19th-Century England

solicitors were used.[224] Assessment Committees would hear barristers or solicitors representing persons appealing against the valuation lists,[225] and often did, but commercial objectors were sometimes represented by an officer of their business.

The procedures conceived by the legislative draftsmen for the new tribunals on the whole enabled them to operate simply, cheaply, effectively and expeditiously to achieve their specific aims. This was achieved largely by ensuring that the procedures were sufficiently simple to enable an aggrieved party to represent himself. Though the procedural codes were largely self-contained, the tribunals were not permitted to operate entirely in isolation from the judicial world. The pervasive rules of natural justice whereby the regular courts ensured that all inferior bodies with adjudicatory powers conformed to a judicial norm of conduct, and the provisions for further appeal from the various tribunals to the regular courts of law, drew the tribunals inexorably into some relationship with the judicial system.

---

[224] In the commutation of tithes for the parish of Seabridge in Staffordshire, for example, the rector was represented by his solicitor, the landowners by counsel: TNA:PRO IR 18/9487 (1843).
[225] This is clear from the argument of the Assessment Committee in *R. v. Assessment Committee of St Mary Abbotts, Kensington* [1891] 1 QB 378.

6

JUDICIAL SUPERVISION

The statutory tribunals of the nineteenth century were conceived as self-contained semi-independent bodies to achieve an administrative objective. Though they had judicial functions to perform, their status as part of the executive meant that they were prima facie outside the regular court system and free from its control. Arguably, however, this control was necessary; the very qualities of tribunals that distinguished them and made them so well suited to their particular tasks rendered them vulnerable to error, ignorance, mismanagement and slackness. They lacked, furthermore, those safeguards inherent in courts of law, namely legal expertise, established procedures and independence. They had judicial functions to perform and yet they were diverse in nature, each procedurally self-contained and jurisdictionally specialised, with informal procedures, wide discretion and lay adjudicators untrained in law. There were two main forces pressing for and ultimately obtaining judicial supervision – the users of the tribunals, who pressed for the right to appeal from tribunals' decisions to the regular courts, and the judiciary, who pressed for the right to control the conduct of the tribunals. While between them these two methods of judicial supervision were comprehensive, they were theoretically and practically distinct, with appeal going to the merits of the decision itself, addressing potentially issues of both law and fact, and enabling the superior court to replace the tribunal's decision with its own. Review, on the other hand, related to the proceedings, embracing the extent and exercise of the tribunal's powers and procedures. In exercising that jurisdiction, a superior court could only quash the tribunal's decision. Both appeal and review, however much they constituted necessary and effective safeguards to the public, amounted to a degree of supervision and potential procrastination that fundamentally

230 Legal Foundations of Tribunals in 19th-Century England

undermined the nature and qualities of the statutory tribunals and put an end to any concept of judicial isolation.

Any popular demand for the right of appeal revealed a certain tension and inconsistency. On the one hand litigation in the regular courts of law was feared and avoided because of its expense and long duration, but on the other it was respected as the ultimate safeguard against abuses by the executive. There was a fundamental trust of the judicial system, and so the usual antipathy to the regular courts did not extend to their being ousted altogether. While members of the public, appreciating the boon of cheap and swift procedures, were in general content to have their disputes decided by the tribunals in the first instance, the denial of any recourse to the regular courts was, in most cases, a step too far. Indeed, the right to appeal to a higher court to prevent conclusive injustice in a lower one had long been regarded as inherent in natural justice, and in *Bentley*'s case in 1723 the right of appeal was described as 'the glory and happiness of our excellent constitution'.[1] The public demand for a right of appeal to another, implicitly higher, body, was determined. It was strongest where the tribunal's jurisdiction addressed complicated legal questions or issues of considerable financial importance to the parties. Not only was it widely believed that the existence of a right of appeal to the regular courts made tribunals more careful and considered in their determinations,[2] it was natural and reasonable where large interests were at stake to have recourse to a body of the highest legal calibre. The various bodies of commissioners inevitably adjudicated on questions of both fact and law. While their ability to decide questions of fact was rarely challenged, their ability to decide questions of law was often doubted and there were cogent reasons why appeals on questions of law should be allowed.[3] It has been seen that the legal component of tribunals differed widely in nature, with more or less qualified clerks, some legally trained assistants, access to external legal expertise and occasionally a legally qualified commissioner. Most tribunals were regarded as incapable of determining questions of law of any complexity.

---

[1] *R. v. Cambridge University, ex parte Bentley* (1723) 1 Str 557 at 564–5 *per* Pratt CJ.

[2] See for example *Minutes, Income and Property Tax, 1852* q. 1556.

[3] In the tax sphere, see *Parl. Deb.*, vol. CXXVII, ser. 3, col. 537, 23 May 1853 (HC); *Minutes, Income and Property Tax, 1852* qq. 1548, 1554.

Judicial Supervision

There was indeed a clear correlation between the status of the tribunal personnel, the nature and extent of their powers, and the demand for powers of appeal. The more highly qualified the members of the tribunal, in the sense of legal knowledge, the greater the confidence of the parties in the correctness of the decision and the less the demand for appeal powers. The lower the status and the greater the powers, the more the suspicion of error, and the higher the demand for appeal provisions. Where a tribunal had a distinct appellate function, as with the General and Special Commissioners of Income Tax, and as such was at the top of an internal multi-tiered structure, the reasons for allowing a further appeal to the regular courts were less powerful, for arguably the parties in such instances had had their cases fully heard and argued. It was not just the public who asked for the right of appeal; the judges favoured it because an appeal on a point of law ensured the law remained correct and consistently applied, an external discipline which would assist in introducing a measure of uniformity among adjudicating bodies which had little in common other than their statutory creation, specialist subject-matter and lay constitution. Though undoubtedly the judges also saw it as a way of ensuring their authority over the tribunals, it was arguably the best way not only of giving strength and stability to the tribunals, but also of protecting the liberties of the subject.[4]

The legislature, however, was reluctant to grant rights of appeal. The summary nature of the new tribunal procedures and the avoidance of professional legal involvement would count for nothing in the overall attainment of the legislative aims if the tribunals' decisions could be appealed against to the regular courts. Such an appeal would bring with it all the problems the tribunals had been designed to avoid, namely delay, expense and the absence of specialist expertise in a particular sphere of activity. Appeals to the regular courts would prolong litigation and so unacceptably delay the implementation of government policy,

---

[4] Though such considerations were mentioned in the nineteenth century, as in *Minutes, Income and Property Tax, 1852* qq. 1556, 1557, they became particularly important in the twentieth century. See for example and generally, 'Minutes of Evidence before the Committee on Administrative Tribunals and Enquiries' (London: HMSO, 1956) Cmnd 218, p. 194, para. 14, p. 678, para. 11(e). See Bowen LJ in *R.* v. *Justices of County of London and London County Council* [1893] 2 QB 476 at 492.

232 *Legal Foundations of Tribunals in 19th-Century England*

since it would entail not only the appeal to the lowest tier of the superior courts, but another two stages to the appropriate court of appeal and thence to the House of Lords. This would be exacerbated if there were a flood of appeals. It would add complexity to the entire process, because the system of appeals in the regular legal system throughout most of the nineteenth century was acknowledged as being complex, 'various and discordant',[5] and the inclusion of the tribunals in this system could only undermine the simplicity of process which characterised the tribunals. It would require the participation of professional lawyers, the payment of court fees and the danger of costs, all increasing the expense of litigation considerably and acting as a deterrent. Traders, for example, fearing the potential escalation of costs, objected to any right of appeal from the Railway Commission because they knew that the railway companies would fight a case through every court open to them, and would do so with the best counsel they could find. Expensive litigation invariably favoured the wealthier party, and this would undermine a fundamental if implied objective of the tribunals, namely to hold the balance between the individual and the state or, in the case of the railway tribunals, a similarly wealthy, powerful and unequal party. Another major disadvantage was the absence of relevant expertise in the regular courts, and this was a considerable hindrance to the granting of powers of appeal on matters of fact. 'You cannot appeal upon anything except law', it was said in relation to railway matters, as 'you have no cognate court to appeal to.'[6] It has been seen that the need for specialist expertise was one of the very reasons why certain legislation was entrusted to new tribunals. And finally, it was not in the broader interests of the state to allow appeals to the regular courts from the determinations of the tribunals, since such a power would enable wealthy and litigious parties considerably to hinder the implementation and progress of government policy. In every way, the right of appeal was seen, even by some lawyers, as contrary to the spirit of summary justice.

One possible approach would have been to prohibit appeals to the regular courts entirely. That would have been consonant with

---

[5] 'First Report of the Judicature Commissioners', *HCPP* (1868–9) (4130) xxv 1 at p. 23.
[6] *Minutes, Railways, 1881* q. 9382.

Judicial Supervision

233

traditional attitudes to judicial appeals. The right of appeal – in the sense of submitting a complaint to another and superior body, that the decision of the original body was wrong in fact or law – was not a right allowed by the Common Law and was unusual in the eighteenth and early nineteenth centuries. Indeed, at Common Law there was a presumption the other way. Appeals were not thought necessary within the formal legal system, because a jury was generally involved in both civil and criminal trials, and juries were regarded as the best, and so the final, arbiters of fact.[7] The regional knowledge of local adjudicators was often regarded as essential to the fair determination of facts.[8] Practically, too, the finding of facts involved assessing the credibility of witnesses, and that could not be determined from written notes, while rehearing or ensuring a complete record of the evidence would be prohibitively expensive, impracticable and would prolong litigation in the interests of no one. To allow appeals on questions of fact, therefore, was perceived as both unnecessary and undesirable as drawing out litigation,[9] and so it was a general principle of law that there should be no appeal from such questions. Questions of law, on the other hand, were felt to be the province of the judges. While the judges were on occasion accused of insensitivity to the conditions, needs and aspirations of the people on whom they sat in judgment,[10] the small size of the judiciary and its generally high standing resulted in legal issues being left to it with confidence.[11] And yet it was this distinction that was ultimately to guide the granting of powers of appeal. It was accepted that appeals could be permitted only by express provision and would be granted only restrictively. A possible compromise was to allow appeals to the courts on questions of law but not on questions of fact. This would not only overcome the problems of excessive and expensive

---

[7] See H. J. Stephen, *New Commentaries on the Laws of England*, 1844 edition printed for Henry Butterworth, London, 4 vols. (New York: Garland Publishing Inc., 1979), vol. III, pp. 622–3.

[8] A view that began to weaken by the 1870s.

[9] 'Minutes of Evidence to Second Report of the Judicature Commissioners', *HCPP* (1872) (631) xx 245, Answers to Questions 23–8. See too 'Report of the Royal Commission on the Income Tax', *HCPP* (1920) (615) xviii 97 at para. 590; Appendix to Third Report of the Judicature Commissioners, *HCPP* (1874) (957) xxiv 13, Answers to Questions 14–15.

[10] See generally A. H. Manchester, *A Modern Legal History of England and Wales 1750–1950* (London: Butterworths, 1980), pp. 79–83.

[11] See Stephen, *New Commentaries*, vol. III, pp. 622–3.

234 Legal Foundations of Tribunals in 19th-Century England

litigation before a court deemed unsuitable, but would ensure that the law itself remained consistent and would address any weakness in the concept of a lay bench.

The contribution of appeal provisions to the popular acceptance of the tribunal in question was appreciated, and the legislature generally took a pragmatic and politically expedient view. Despite the fear of litigation, there was some discomfort at expressly preventing parties from having recourse to the courts of law to sustain their rights if that is what they chose to do, and the view that a system of arbitrary determination should replace the regular courts of law was a minority one in the early Victorian period. Accordingly, while the primary safeguards which the legislature provided in response to popular anxieties as to adjudication by lay commissioners were those of personal integrity and ability, and the publicity of the process, it recognised that the ultimate precaution against incompetence, error and mismanagement, and the one which was of profound significance to the popular acceptance of the entire machinery, was the right of appeal to the regular courts of law. Though the traditional approach to appeal provision within the regular legal system was one of restraint, the reforms in legal process throughout the nineteenth century resulted in increased provision for appeal within the system of superior courts. The Judicature Commissioners reported that they wanted a system of appeals from all divisions of the Supreme Court exercising jurisdiction in the first instance to be made 'simple and uniform',[12] and by the latter part of the century the Judicature Act 1873 provided that an appeal was to lie from every judgment and order of the High Court, and established the appeal by motion as the one method to be used.[13] Appeals were generally provided to lie to the superior courts from inferior courts such as the County Courts and the Quarter Sessions, and when from the 1830s the growth of central government gave rise to numerous new tribunals in a variety of specialist fields, the statutes creating these bodies generally made provision for appeal from at least some of their determinations. Though the nature and extent of the powers of appeal were as diverse as the

---

[12] 'First Report of the Judicature Commissioners', *HCPP* (1868–9) (4130) xxv 1 at p. 20.
[13] 36 & 37 Vict. c. 66 s. 19.

Judicial Supervision 235

tribunals themselves, the underlying view was that inferior courts and lay tribunals were, like juries, the best bodies to decide questions of fact, but that their constitutions and the interests of the law itself made it desirable that there should be the possibility of appeal to the superior courts on questions of law It was felt that the need for the superior courts to supervise and control the decisions of inferior courts was 'so great and so obvious', in order 'that the law in its principles and practice may flow in an uniform and continuous channel from the fountain head'.[14]

The legislature had to strike a balance between ensuring public confidence on the one hand, and the risk of expense, delay and possible abuse on the other. It took the view that there was little danger of a flood of appeals to the superior courts if the quality of the tribunal and its procedures was carefully ensured. If the procedures were sufficiently open, with regular opportunities to be heard if a party disagreed with any decision taken in the process, and if the parties were confident that their disputes had been fully investigated and adjudicated by a competent tribunal, then the parties, even if they disagreed with the decision, would be unlikely to incur the undoubted expense and delay in making an appeal to the courts, since they would feel the decision would be unlikely to differ. Indeed, this was the case with the Tithe Commissioners. In their report for 1840, they observed that 'angry appeals are the very rare exception; contented acquiescence is the general rule', giving as the reason the ample time allotted to the valuers to arrive at a correct valuation.[15] Parties bringing disputes to the tribunal for determination were in general so satisfied with the decisions of the Assistant Commissioner and his handling of their case that the power of appeal to the regular courts was rarely used. In one instance an Assistant Commissioner heard 148 disputes. In 42 cases the parties did not proceed to determination because they were satisfied with the Assistant Commissioner's recommendation as to the dispute, and in 106 they proceeded to a decision. Of those 106, only 10 were appealed against to the superior courts. Of those 10, 3 were confirmed, 3

---

[14] 'Report of the Royal Commission on Bankruptcy', *HCPP* (1854) (1770) xxiii 1 at p. 38.
[15] 'Report of the Tithe Commissioners for England and Wales' *HCPP* (1840) (215) xxviii 139.

236 Legal Foundations of Tribunals in 19th-Century England

quashed and 4 were pending.[16] Providing a power of appeal to the regular courts was not, in practice, necessarily an invitation to excessive litigation. Its practical effect could ultimately be very small and so it could be granted without ill effect. This was seen in relation to appeals from the decisions of the County Courts.[17] In the fiscal sphere too, it was felt that a right of appeal would not be abused. In relation to the assessed taxes, a surveyor observed in 1852 that he did not take a case out once in five years.[18]

The orthodox view was that even if appeals were to be permitted, they were not to be encouraged. The legislature almost invariably provided that the decision of a body of commissioners was to be final, a provision that effectively excluded all rights of appeal other than any that might subsequently be expressly provided for. All adjudicatory decisions taken by the Land Tax Commissioners, as in boundaries, distress or exemptions, were expressed in the Act of 1797 to be final 'without any further Appeal, upon any Pretence whatsoever',[19] and the legislation also included a general provision to the effect that on all questions and disputes touching the rates, duties, assessments or collections their determinations were to be final and not to be questionable in any court.[20] The finality of their determinations ran through the whole land tax, since their decisions as to distress were expressly provided to be 'determined and ended' by them,[21] and their determinations on disputes as to the assessment of lands belonging to certain hospitals and almshouses were to be final.[22] When the Land Tax Commissioners were entrusted with the administration of the window and house duty in 1747, their decisions were final, with no further appeal whatsoever,[23] and their determinations of appeals against the triple assessment were also to be final.[24] The decisions of the Commissioners of Appeal for the

---

[16] Evidence of the Revd Richard Jones, Tithe Commissioner, in *Minutes, Commons' Inclosure, 1844* q. 23. See too the evidence of another Tithe Commissioner, William Blamire, *ibid.*, qq. 269, 271.

[17] See 'Minutes of Evidence to Second Report of the Judicature Commissioners', *HCPP* (1872) (631) xx 245, Answers to Questions at pp. 254 ff.

[18] *Minutes, Income and Property Tax, 1852* q. 1559, and see too q. 1555.

[19] 38 Geo. III c. 5 s. 8 (1797).

[20] *Ibid.*, s. 23.   [21] *Ibid.*, s. 17.   [22] *Ibid.*, s. 28.

[23] 20 Geo. II c. 3 s. 13, though see the provisions of the amending Act 21 Geo. II c. 10 s. 10 (1748).

[24] 38 Geo. III c. 16 s. 54 (1798).

Judicial Supervision 237

Redemption of the Land Tax were to be final and conclusive upon all the parties.[25] Though the Income and Property Taxes Act 1799 did not expressly provide that the decision of the then appellate body, the Commissioners of Appeal, was final, the administrative powers granted by an early taxes management Act in 1798[26] were to be read into the 1799 Act, and that Act provided that the determination of the commissioners on appeals by aggrieved taxpayers 'shall be final'.[27] Statute provided that the appeal determinations of the General Commissioners under the 1803 legislation were final and could not be altered, 'except always in such Cases where the Opinion of the Judges shall be required according to the Provisions of any Act or Acts concerning the same'.[28] Since no such provisions existed for income tax, the policy of the 1799 Act and the finality of the commissioners' decisions continued. It was re-enacted in the legislation of 1842 and so applied to both the General Commissioners and the Special Commissioners in their appellate capacity. Though there were early demands for the right of appeal from the decisions of private Inclosure Commissioners, the breadth of their powers giving rise to fears of their arbitrary exercise, their award had always been final as to the claim to common land and the allotment, and the later land rights tribunals adopted similar provisions. The dispute determinations of the Tithe Commissioners were expressed to be final,[29] as were those of the Copyhold Commissioners[30] and the commissioners under the general Inclosure Act.[31] The decisions of the Railway Commissioners in both 1873 and 1888 were not, however, expressed in the legislation to be final.

The parent legislation of the nineteenth-century tribunals, having provided the decisions of the commissioners were final, in most instances compromised and proceeded to provide that that was subject to the limited right to appeal to the regular courts on questions of law. Although when statutory tribunals proliferated in the first half of the following century the right of appeal was the exception rather than the rule, an issue which became one of real concern,[32] it was not so in the nineteenth century when nearly all tribunals had a right, albeit limited, of appeal to the superior

---

[25] 38 Geo. III c. 60 s. 121 (1798).   [26] 38 Geo. III c. 16.
[27] *Ibid.*, s. 54.   [28] 43 Geo. III c. 99 s. 29.   [29] 6 & 7 Will. IV c. 71, s. 45.
[30] 4 & 5 Vict. c. 35 s. 39.   [31] 8 & 9 Vict. c. 118 ss. 54, 57.
[32] Lord Hewart, *The New Despotism* (London: Ernest Benn Ltd, 1929), pp. 155–6; 'Minutes of Evidence before the Committee on Administrative Tribunals and

238 *Legal Foundations of Tribunals in 19th-Century England*

courts. The preferred method of appeal was the case stated, a method which built on the Common Law tradition of leaving questions of fact to be decided finally by the jury, while allowing in some limited instances a review on a question of law to a court of high standing, and a popular procedure for enabling this to be done. This Common Law procedure was known as the 'special case'[33] procedure, and was a well-established alternative to express statutory appeal. It allowed the decision of a judge and jury at nisi prius to be reviewed through argument before the full court at Westminster.[34] The procedure was, furthermore, well suited to a lay adjudicatory body which was not a court of record and which decided questions of both fact and law. The case stated was the statutory version of the special case, and it was phrased purely in terms of a question of law: whether the determination was contrary to the 'true Intent and Meaning of [the] Act' being put to the judges for their opinion at the request of one or other of the parties. The result was not that the commissioners' determination should be quashed, but that it should be amended or confirmed in the light of the judicial finding. The special case procedure was widely used in tax cases. When the establishment of a system of county courts was debated in Parliament in 1842, Lord Wynford believed that as to appeals 'the best which could be devised would be to follow out the practice of the tax acts, by drawing up special cases in small causes, and then there would be a uniformity of proceeding'.[35] So when the legislature decided to allow appeals on questions of law it was natural for it to do so by way of case stated. When the Judicature Commissioners examined its efficiency and popularity in 1872, they found that the consensus was in its favour as a form of appeal because 'it affords the opportunity of precisely and distinctly stating the point in dispute unincumbered by irrelevant matter'.[36] Its only disadvantage was

---

Enquiries' (London: HMSO, 1956) Cmnd 218, qq. 2137–8 *per* Sir Patrick Spens, giving evidence of the Inns of Court Conservative and Unionist Society.

[33] See generally The Law Society, *A Compendium of the Practice of the Common Law* (London: R. Hastings, 1847), pp. 383–4; M. J. Pritchard, 'Nonsuit: A Premature Obituary' (1960) *Cambridge Law Journal* 88 at 92–6.

[34] The predecessor of the modern Divisional Court.

[35] *Parl. Deb.*, vol. LXV, ser. 3, col. 238, 18 July 1842 (HL).

[36] 'Minutes of Evidence to the Second Report of the Judicature Commissioners', *HCPP* (1872) (631) xx 245, Answers to Questions, at p. 273 *per* William Raines, judge.

Judicial Supervision 239

that someone had to draft it. And when the same commissioners investigated proposals for the establishment of Tribunals of Commerce in 1874,[37] the consensus among lawyers and commercial men was that the decisions of such tribunals should be final on questions of fact, but that there should be appeal to the regular courts on questions of law.[38]

In the tax tribunals, where the various bodies of commissioners hearing the great majority of appeals were distinguished by a consistency in their lack of specialist knowledge, there is a remarkable paucity of appeal provisions. All the fiscal commissioners except for the Special Commissioners of Income Tax possessed little more than property qualifications, some commercial expertise and a somewhat haphazard local knowledge, and yet the parent legislation did not consistently provide for appeal to the superior courts. The finality provisions applicable to the determinations of the Land Tax Commissioners were not subject even to a limited right of appeal on a point of law. The regular courts had a role to play in the matter of the redemption of the land tax only where the sum in question exceeded £500 of stock, for then an aggrieved party had to bypass the Appeal Commissioners entirely, and appeal directly from the determination of the Land Tax Redemption Commissioners to the Court of Chancery or Exchequer.[39] This was consistent, however, with the context of the redemption of the land tax, for the Redemption Appeal Commissioners were justices of the peace hearing the smaller appeals at Petty Sessions. The entire appellate machinery was of the character of a regular court of law, though an inferior one, rather than of a specialist administrative tribunal. By contrast, and even though the same administrative and adjudicatory machinery as the land tax was used, appeals by way of case stated were permitted for the assessed taxes from the mid-eighteenth century. If either the surveyor or appellant were dissatisfied with a determination he could require the commissioners to state a case to be

---

[37] 'Third Report of the Judicature Commissioners', *HCPP* (1874) (957) xxiv 1.

[38] Within that broad consensus there were varying demands for financial minima for cases to be taken to appeal, generally £50 or £100, with lesser cases being final on both fact and law: 'Third Report of the Judicature Commissioners', Appendix, Answers to Questions and Minutes of Evidence, *HCPP* (1874) (957) xxiv 13, Answers to Questions 14–15. See too Arbitration Act 1889, 52 & 53 Vict. c. 49, for a provision for appeal by case stated from decisions of arbitrators.

[39] 38 Geo. III c. 60 s. 121 (1798).

240 *Legal Foundations of Tribunals in 19th-Century England*

transmitted to the King's Bench, Common Pleas or Exchequer.[40] This power was widely used, and the resulting case law was extensive.[41] When the income tax was introduced in 1799, the Act did not follow the precedent of the assessed taxes in relation to appeal provision, but preferred the model of the land tax with its absolute finality of decision.

The denial of rights of appeal on questions of law from the determinations of income tax tribunals was based on public policy. Even in those statutes that gave a right of appeal, as in the assessed taxes, it was clearly intended that it be strictly limited. In 1848 Parke B observed in relation to a tax on horse dealers that if the right of appeal were not limited, there would be a 'flood of litigation'. 'Actions would be innumerable,' he continued, 'juries would have to decide on facts without end, judges on law, and cases would be carried to the highest tribunal, when the exigencies of the state required a speedy determination.'[42] The object of any tax was to raise revenue, and to do so quickly and consistently, an objective that was threatened by extensive appeal powers. The reasons for denying the right of appeal in income tax cases were not expressed in contemporary debate. The new tax was immensely unpopular, and while a power of appeal might have helped to lessen the resentment, the depth of the antipathy might have resulted in so many appeals as to paralyse the tax in practice. The assessed taxes had been equally unpopular,[43] but they were in essence voluntary, and could be avoided by not purchasing the items subject to the tax; the income tax was mandatory, and an appeal offered the only legitimate means of escaping liability. The denial of rights of appeal, however, was always unpopular, particularly in relation to the General Commissioners. 'There is no power', complained a surveyor of taxes in 1851, 'of going beyond

---

[40] 21 Geo. II c. 10 s. 10 (1748); 17 Geo. III c. 39 ss. 21, 22 (1777); 18 Geo. III c. 26 ss. 41, 42 (1778); 25 Geo. III c. 43 ss. 38, 39 (1785); 25 Geo. III c. 47 ss. 33, 34 (1785).

[41] See generally W. R. Ward, *The Administration of the Window and Assessed Taxes 1696–1798* (Canterbury: Phillimores, 1963).

[42] *Allen* v. *Sharpe* (1848) 2 Ex 352 at 363. See too Platt B at 367. This was particularly important in tax matters, where the executive would pursue a case to the highest court where a matter of principle was involved: see 'Report of the Royal Commission on the Income Tax', *HCPP* (1920) (615) xviii 97 at p. 233, para. 594.

[43] Ward, *Window and Assessed Taxes*, pp. 15–16.

Judicial Supervision 241

the general commissioners, which I think is an unfortunate part of the Property Tax Act; because, if the same power were given as under the assessed taxes, of appeal to some superior tribunal, it would remove a great many difficulties which now present themselves.'[44] If the Crown officer, the surveyor, felt the decision was contrary to law, he could do nothing about it. The Special Commissioners were better suited to determining questions of law, being highly experienced full-time civil servants, and the demand for a right of appeal was correspondingly muted. Furthermore, in relation to the Special Commissioners certain internal review procedures existed, in the form of an early kind of special case to the Board of Inland Revenue, though it was rarely used.[45] By the latter years of the nineteenth century, once the Judicature Acts had given wide powers of appeal from inferior courts of law, where often the claims were trivial compared with the sums in question in income tax appeals, the demand could no longer reasonably be resisted. Accordingly an Act of 1874[46] gave the Crown and the taxpayer the right to require both the General Commissioners and the Special Commissioners to appeal by way of case stated to the High Court, on the grounds that their decision had been erroneous in point of law.[47] The procedure differed slightly from that in operation in the assessed taxes, in that legal argument was allowed, and reasons for the ultimate decision expected. Though the Board of Inland Revenue, in its annual report of 1874, described the change in the law as 'new and important' [48] there was very little public discussion of the development.

The three legislative regimes introduced in the 1830s and 1840s to restructure private property rights in tithes, copyholds and

---

[44] *Minutes, Income and Property Tax, 1852* q. 1548.
[45] Income and Property Taxes Act 1842, 5 & 6 Vict. c. 35 s. 131; *Minutes, Income and Property Tax, 1852* qq. 1061, 1124 *per* James Dickens, Special Commissioner. Its abolition was recommended in 1920: see 'Report of the Royal Commission on the Income Tax', *HCPP* (1920) (615) xviii 97 at para. 596.
[46] Customs and Inland Revenue Act 1874, 37 Vict. c. 16. The procedure was founded on the Queen's Remembrancer's Act 1859, 22 & 23 Vict. c. 21 s. 10.
[47] See generally C. Stebbings, 'The Appeal by Way of Case Stated from the Determinations of General Commissioners of Income Tax: An Historical Perspective' (1996) *British Tax Review* 611. Note that there was a precedent for the use of the case stated procedure within the internal income tax structure itself: *ibid.*, 617.
[48] 'Seventeenth Report of Her Majesty's Inland Revenue on the Inland Revenue for the Year Ended 31 March 1874', *HCPP* (1874) (1098) xv 673.

242 *Legal Foundations of Tribunals in 19th-Century England*

common land conferred on bodies of commissioners far-reaching powers in a complex field, and one where the private rights in question could be of considerable value. Where rights to minerals were concerned, for example, the setting of a boundary could cost one or other party several thousand pounds.[49] The underlying objective of the legislature in these regimes was to achieve the restructuring voluntarily if that were possible, and to do so the process had to be such that the parties had confidence that their respective rights would be fairly adjusted, and the provision of appellate powers contributed to this confidence. This was so despite the complexity, length and expense of tithe litigation before the regular courts. It was clear from contemporary debate that the determination of disputed questions of such moment by summary process in the hands of lay commissioners possessing considerable powers, with no intervention even at an appellate stage of a regular and authoritative court of law, was unacceptable.[50]

A material factor in the considerable success of the tithe commutation of the 1830s[51] was the provision of generous powers of appeal. Three types of appeal to the regular courts were laid down. The first was the appeal on questions of fact by way of feigned issue to the Assizes, and this was the method prescribed for appeals from any decision of the commissioners where the yearly value of the payment in question was more than £20.[52] This was to prevent a flood of small actions, and was a considerable limitation in practice, as many individuals did not come within this monetary restriction, and it was impracticable to join a number of such individuals together to appeal. The feigned issue was a judicial wager, which was the standard mode of appeal on matters of fact to the regular courts. It involved the appellant by a fiction saying that he wagered with the respondent that a certain event or state of affairs was a fact and stating positively that the fact was so. The respondent admitted the wager but denied the

---

[49] *Minutes, Commons' Inclosure, 1844* qq. 4679–87 concerning the Inclosure Commissioners' power to determine disputed boundaries.

[50] See for example the diversity of opinion in relation to inclosures: *ibid.*, qq. 400, 655, 1107–8, 1458, 2633, 2636, 4050–60, 4363, 4679–87.

[51] Essentially the process was admirable: it was inclusive, flexible, well informed, sensitive and yet independent.

[52] 6 & 7 Will. IV c. 71 s. 46.

Judicial Supervision

fact. The issue thus being joined, it was to be decided by a jury.[53] This method of appeal was used because it allowed a matter in dispute to be determined without the formality of pleading, and so saved both time and expense. In this, therefore, while the legislation allowed appeal to the regular courts, it selected a process that as far as possible did not undermine the rationale behind the creation of tribunals, and their process. It also conformed to the prevailing view of the Common Law that questions of fact were properly to be decided by a jury. The appeal by way of feigned issue was abolished in 1845, and replaced by the writ of summons, though maintained the same process.[54] If the appeal concerned a question of law only, and the parties were agreed as to the facts, the party could request a case to be stated for the opinion of a court of law.[55] And finally the commissioners' power to settle disputed parochial boundaries at the request of a parish was subject to an appeal by certiorari to the Court of Queen's Bench.[56]

These were generous and robust appeal provisions to high-level courts, and compared favourably to appeal provisions in other tribunals. The appeal provisions in the copyhold commutation and enfranchisement process of 1841 were identical.[57] When it was proposed to make copyhold enfranchisement compulsory at the request of either party, and that all questions of law and fact on any enfranchisement should be referred to the commissioners, it was argued that there should be an appeal from the decision of the commissioners to one of the superior courts, in the same way as the decisions of revising barristers were subject to appeal to the Court of Common Pleas. This was strenuously resisted by Henry Aglionby, who said 'he never would consent to have any appeal from the first decision. He would rather, for his part, submit to an unjust decision than be driven about from pillar to post in the manner in which people were treated in the Court of Chancery

---

[53] Sir William Blackstone, *Commentaries on the Laws of England*, 1783 edition printed for W. Strahan and T. Cadell, London and D. Prince, Oxford, 4 vols. (New York: Garland Publishing Inc., 1978), vol. III at p. 452. An example of its use, and one showing the precision necessary in framing the issue, was the case of *Earl of Stamford and Warrington* v. *Dunbar* (1844) 12 M & W 414.

[54] Gaming Act 1845, 8 & 9 Vict. c. 109 s. 19 and Schedule 2. See *Luard* v. *Butcher* (1846) 15 LJ NS CP 187 which decided that the feigned issue was not unlawful and could still be used.

[55] 6 & 7 Will. IV c. 71 s. 46.   [56] 7 Will. IV & 1 Vict. c. 69 s. 3.

[57] 4 & 5 Vict. c. 35 s. 40.

244 Legal Foundations of Tribunals in 19th-Century England

and the Courts of Common Law, in appealing from one tribunal to another.'[58] Such an appeal, he felt, would undermine the inexpensive expediency of the tribunal. Walpole retorted that the House had not yet dispensed with appeals to the superior courts on questions of law and that the commissioners' decisions should not be final. He suggested a power in the commissioners to certify there was cause for appeal in a case on a question of law, and then that the matter should be referred to a superior court which would be competent to decide on the matter.[59] The consensus was that an appeal to the superior courts on questions of law was highly desirable, and the Act retained the appeal provisions by way of case stated on the model of that of the Tithe Commissioners.[60] The appeal by way of feigned issue was no longer available. The finality of the Copyhold Commissioners' determinations was thus subject to appeal on a question of law.

The private Inclosure Acts from which the procedure of the new centralised processes of 1845 were taken, provided for appeals from the Inclosure Commissioners' decisions as to the setting out of roads, for example, to the commissioners and local justices of the peace, who were to 'hear and determine' such disputes 'to the best of their Judgment', an expression redolent of tax administration statutes. Any decision to stop a road entirely had to be made with the concurrence of two justices, but was subject to appeal to the Quarter Sessions,[61] as were the all-important boundary determinations.[62] The decisions of the justices as to parish boundaries were final and conclusive.[63] Appeals to the Quarter Sessions from the decisions of the commissioners were regarded as expensive and difficult, particularly as to the collection of evidence, and were relatively rare. The Common Fields Inclosure Act 1836,[64] which provided a process for an entirely voluntary inclosure, with or without commissioners, made extensive use of the justices in Quarter Sessions as an appellate body. If commissioners were employed, they were to hear and determine disputes as to the division of the land,[65] but if

---

[58] *Parl. Deb.*, vol. CXX, ser. 3, col. 965, 21 April 1852 (HC).
[59] *Ibid.*
[60] Enfranchisement of Copyholds Act 1852, 15 & 16 Vict. c. 51 s. 8; Copyhold Act 1894, 57 & 58 Vict. c. 46 s. 53.
[61] 41 Geo. III c. 109 s. 8.   [62] *Ibid.*, s. 3.   [63] *Ibid.*   [64] 6 & 7 Will. IV c. 115.
[65] *Ibid.*, s. 15, though they could not determine issues as to title.

Judicial Supervision 245

a party were dissatisfied with any determination of the commissioners with respect to any claim or objection, he was permitted to bring an action on a feigned issue to the Assizes. The decision in that court was to be 'binding, final and conclusive'.[66] If commissioners were not employed, the first tier of dispute-resolution was put in the hands of the justices in Quarter Sessions, and they were to hear and determine any objections.[67] But the Quarter Sessions was the court adopted in a general provision giving a party aggrieved by anything done by virtue of the Act the power to appeal to a court of law.[68] The determination of the justices was to be final and conclusive, and no further appeal was permitted.

Under the 1845 Act, where much of the day-to-day inclosure process was carried out by the valuer rather than the centrally appointed commissioner, the need for effective appeal procedures was especially necessary. In the specific instance of stopping up roads and exchanging lands, there was an appeal against the valuer's decisions to the justices of the peace at Quarter Sessions, the matter to be settled by a jury.[69] A party aggrieved by the determination of the commissioners as to a claim could choose to appeal to a superior court of law by feigned issue at the next Assizes,[70] as in the other land rights tribunals and whose decision would be final, or alternatively submit the issue to arbitration if the parties agreed,[71] the decision of the arbitral tribunal being equally binding on both parties. The appeal provisions in relation to boundary determinations were particularly robust, possibly to make the resolution of such potentially important property rights by a central board more acceptable. The appeal to Quarter Sessions was replaced with a choice between the determination of a jury on the matter presided over by an Assistant Commissioner, a device which had been questioned in Select Committee as possibly lacking in sufficient authority,[72] or an application to the Queen's Bench to remove the determination by certiorari.[73] The jury of twelve 'sufficient and indifferent men' would be

---

[66] *Ibid.*, s. 17.   [67] *Ibid.*, s. 44.   [68] *Ibid.*, s. 53.   [69] 8 & 9 Vict. c. 118 ss. 63, 64.
[70] *Ibid.*, s. 56.   [71] *Ibid.*, s. 60.
[72] See the evidence of Thomas Woolley, an Assistant Tithe Commissioner, in *Minutes, Commons' Inclosure, 1844* qq. 4051–60. He believed a further appeal to a regular court was desirable.
[73] 8 & 9 Vict. c. 118 s. 39.

246 *Legal Foundations of Tribunals in 19th-Century England*

empanelled by the sheriff, and would be empowered to inspect the boundaries and hear the examination of witnesses. The cost was to be borne by the appellant if he was unsuccessful, or as an expense of the inclosure if he succeeded.[74] There was thus, in 1845, an alternative appeal procedure, though both entailed considerable expense. If the appellant chose the certiorari route, the decision of the Queen's Bench was to be final and conclusive as to the boundary.[75] Such, therefore, was the importance of the determination of property claims in the context of inclosure, that a three-tier system of decision and appeal was provided by the Act, comprising all the known methods of dispute-resolution – lay tribunal, jury, the regular courts of law and arbitration.

In relation to railways where the interests concerned were of considerable financial importance, rights of appeal were a highly contentious issue. When the implementation of the railway legislation was given to the Court of Common Pleas in 1854, it necessarily brought with it full rights of appeal through the court structures, and this was consonant with the railway companies' wishes at least insofar as they felt that where issues of such magnitude were being decided, the tribunal should be strong in legal knowledge and ability. If this were not the case, then their view was that there should be the widest right of appeal.[76] So when the original bill for the creation of the Railway Commission in 1873 provided that the determinations of the commissioners were to be final,[77] opposition was so intense that the finality clause was deleted, and provision was made not only for the commissioners to rescind or vary their own orders, but also for them to state a case in writing for the opinion of any superior court on a point of law.[78] This question would be heard and determined by the superior court, which could reverse, affirm or amend the

---

[74] *Ibid.*, s. 42.   [75] *Ibid.*, s. 44.

[76] This was so in respect of the Railway Commissioners, who heard cases of great financial importance: *Parl. Deb.*, vol. CCCXII, ser. 3, col. 142, 14 March 1887 (HL).

[77] *HCPP* (1873) (34) iv 325, cl. 22.

[78] 36 & 37 Vict. c. 48 s. 26 and General Ord. 42. There was also provision for a party aggrieved by a decision made by one or two commissioners to have his case reheard by all the commissioners: see General Ord. 43. See speech of Christopher Denison in the debate on the Railway and Canal Traffic Bill, *Parl. Deb.*, vol. CCXV, ser. 3, cols. 367–8, 31 March 1873 (HC). See Geoffrey Alderman, *The Railway Interest* (Leicester: Leicester University Press, 1973), pp. 35–40.

Judicial Supervision 247

commissioners' determination or remit the question to the commissioners. The decision of the superior court was final. By the amendment in committee the commissioners' determinations on questions of law were thereby no longer final, but by implication their determinations of fact were.

Views were polarised. The railway companies opposed even the limited provision, since the right to appeal was in effect in the hands of the commissioners themselves, for it was for them to decide whether in their view there was a question of law at issue.[79] 'It was not to be reasonably supposed', it was argued, 'that the Railway Companies would submit their interests to any body of gentlemen, however distinguished, without appeal.'[80] Indeed, the Railway Commissioners were criticised for their approach to allowing appeals by case stated, and were accused of restrictively interpreting their powers, a 'uniform discouragement of appeals' and behaviour 'inconsistent with the spirit which should animate a court of justice'.[81] They defended themselves saying that it was not necessarily easy to distinguish questions of law from questions of fact, and that such issues had to be carefully considered.[82] Some years later it was put to Edward Pember QC, a barrister with extensive railway experience, that 'it is doubtful whether the railway companies would have been satisfied even if the Archangel Gabriel had been the president of the court without an appeal', and he replied that he thought 'they would have preferred the Archangel Gabriel with an appeal, to a subordinate official without an appeal'.[83] The railway companies thought the right of appeal was utterly inadequate and practically illusory. It was inconsistent both with the magnitude of the interests in question and with the contemporaneous provisions for appeal in the Judicature Acts even for cases before the High Court where often much smaller sums were at stake, questions of fact were simpler and questions of law were of equal complexity.[84] Ralph Littler

---

[79] Railway and Canal Traffic Act 1873, 36 & 37 Vict. c. 48 s. 26 and General Ord. 42.

[80] *Parl. Deb.*, vol. CCXV, ser. 3, cols. 367–8, 31 March 1873 (HC) *per* Christopher Denison, a railway director.

[81] *Minutes, Railways, 1881* q. 13,518 *per* James Grierson, general manager of the Great Western Railway Company, reading a paper previously prepared for the Board of Trade by the railway companies.

[82] *Minutes, Railways (Rates and Fares), 1882* q. 2998 *per* Sir Frederick Peel, Railway Commissioner.

[83] *Ibid.*, at q. 1494.   [84] *Minutes, Railways, 1881* q. 13,518 *per* James Grierson.

248   *Legal Foundations of Tribunals in 19th-Century England*

QC, another barrister with wide experience of railway law and practice, said in 1881 that he believed that the omission of the Railway Commission from those provisions had been an oversight,[85] but it seems the commissioners were definitely excluded. The railway interest demanded an appeal on fact and law as of right from the commissioners' decision at least to a regular court of first instance. On the other hand, most informed opinion and small traders, with some justification, felt the right of appeal was too generous, the potential expense thereof acting as a deterrent, and they wanted the commissioners' decision to be final.

A compromise proposed by a Select Committee in 1882[86] was that there should be a limited right of appeal as of right, to the Court of Appeal possibly, and that only at the instance of that court should a further appeal by the railway company to the House of Lords be allowed, possibly with a stipulation that the railway company pay the costs in any event.[87] The Railway and Canal Traffic Bill 1887 did not provide for any appeal on questions of fact, but allowed appeals on questions of law to the Court of Appeal and thence to the House of Lords. The president of the Board of Trade, at the second reading of the bill in the House of Lords, appreciated that the trading community had been opposed to frequent appeals because it favoured the wealthier railway companies, but believed there had been a change of perception and that the public at large would accept this appeal provision.[88] Ultimately the Railway and Canal Traffic Act 1888 repealed the provision in the 1873 Act which permitted appeal on a question of law only by way of case stated, and allowed an appeal on questions of law to the Court of Appeal and thence, with some limitations, to the House of Lords.[89] It did not permit an appeal on a question of fact.

The legislative provisions for the rating of property had traditionally preferred the justices of the peace as the usual appellate body, both within the initial administrative process, and as a second-tier body to hear appeals within the regular court system.

---

[85] *Minutes, Railways (Rates and Fares), 1882* q. 3363.
[86] 'Report from the Select Committee on Railways (Rates and Fares)', *HCPP* (1882) (317) xiii 1 at p. 16.
[87] *Minutes, Railways (Rates and Fares), 1882* q. 1243 *per* J. H. Balfour Browne, barrister.
[88] *Parl. Deb.*, vol. CCCXII, ser. 3, col. 132, 14 March 1887 (HL) *per* Lord Stanley of Preston, president of the Board of Trade.
[89] 51 & 52 Vict. c. 25 s. 17.

Judicial Supervision 249

When a uniform mode of rating for the relief of the poor was introduced in 1836, appeals against an unfair rate lay to the justices of the peace in Special Session initially, and then to the justices in Quarter Session.[90] When in 1862 the Union Assessment Committee Act[91] introduced Assessment Committees as the first-tier appellate tribunal, the second-tier appeal to the justices was retained. While the Assessment Committee new heard the objections to the valuation list,[92] if thereafter any overseer of any parish in the union believed any parish was aggrieved by any incorrect valuation of any hereditament in the valuation list, he could, with the consent of the vestry, appeal to the justices in Quarter Sessions.[93] The justices were empowered to adjourn any such appeal and to order an independent survey and valuation of the parishes, in order to hear and determine the appeal at the later date having received the results of the survey.[94] There had been some objection to the continued use of the Quarter Sessions in this way in Parliament. It was felt that it was 'a most inconvenient tribunal to decide matters of law',[95] though that objection was dismissed as groundless since the Quarter Sessions could always state a case for the opinion of the Court of Queen's Bench. The expense involved in an appeal to Quarter Sessions, however, was undeniable.

Nevertheless, under the Valuation of Property (Metropolis) Act 1869[96] – an Act which made special and more generous provision for the rating of London – ratepayers, overseers and surveyors of taxes were empowered to appeal against the decision of the Assessment Committee with respect to an objection to the list to the justices of the peace in Special Session.[97] The jurisdiction of the Special Sessions, however, was limited to the question of the valuation of a hereditament.[98] The justices of the peace in a General Assessment Session, however, had a wider jurisdiction,[99] and in their powers and procedures they resembled a court of Quarter Sessions. Any ratepayer, surveyor of taxes or overseer who felt aggrieved by any decision of the Assessment Committee as to his objection, or by any decision of the Special Sessions, could

---

[90] Parochial Assessments Act 1836, 6 & 7 Will. IV c. 96 ss. 6, 7.
[91] 25 & 26 Vict. c. 103.   [92] *Ibid.*, s. 19.   [93] *Ibid.*, s. 32.   [94] *Ibid.*, s. 33.
[95] *Parl. Deb.*, vol. CLXV, ser. 3, col. 415, 17 February 1862 (HC) *per* William Bovill, later Lord Chief Justice of the Court of Common Pleas.
[96] 32 & 33 Vict. c. 67.   [97] *Ibid.*, ss. 18, 19.   [98] *Ibid.*, s. 20.   [99] *Ibid.*, s. 23.

250 *Legal Foundations of Tribunals in 19th-Century England*

appeal to the Assessment Sessions, and any Assessment Committee, overseer or ratepayer could appeal if they were aggrieved by reason of a valuation of their parish.[100] The justices in Assessment Sessions were to hear and determine the appeals and alter the valuation list accordingly. In the context of metropolitan rating, however, there was a two-tier recourse to the regular courts, since if an appellant was dissatisfied with a decision of the justices in Assessment Sessions, he could appeal on a point of law 'by special case and certiorari or otherwise' in the same way as was laid down for questioning the decision of justices in General or Quarter Sessions.[101]

The supervision exercised by the courts through their appellate jurisdiction was an important safeguard, but, like the tribunals themselves, was statutory in its nature and so of inconsistent application. Some tribunals were subject to the safeguard, some not. Any supervision of the tribunals by the courts through their inherent power to supervise inferior jurisdictions was, however, based on the Common Law and was theoretically more consistent in its application. It was potentially a more effective method of judicial control of the new tribunals. By the time of the inception of the new regulatory statutory tribunals the power of the superior courts of law to control the exercise of jurisdiction in inferior courts and bodies was well established. The superior courts ensured that their inferior brethren kept within their jurisdiction, kept records and observed the rules of natural justice. The juridical basis of this control was the royal prerogative. 'All lawful authority', observed Willes J in 1867,[102] 'is derived from and must be traced to the royal authority. Any exercise, however fitting it may appear, of jurisdiction not so authorized, is an usurpation of the prerogative, and a resort to force unwarranted by law.'[103] The control was exercised through the writ of error, and the prerogative writs of prohibition, certiorari and mandamus. These methods of control were conceived, implemented and developed in the context of courts of inferior jurisdiction, a concept that was clearly delineated and understood.

---

[100] *Ibid.*, s. 32.   [101] *Ibid.*, s. 40.
[102] *Mayor and Aldermen of City of London* v. *Cox* (1867) LR 2 HL 239.
[103] *Ibid.*, at 254.

Judicial Supervision   251

The principal method whereby the decisions of the Common Law courts were reviewed in the nineteenth century was the writ of error.[104] Errors in the superior courts were reviewed by the Court of Exchequer Chamber, while those in inferior courts were reviewed by the King's Bench. The reviewing court required the record of proceedings in the court in question to be sent to it for review for an error 'in the foundation, proceeding, judgment or execution of a suit',[105] in other words, for an error of law.[106] The court would examine the record upon which the judgment in the lower court was made, and would affirm or reverse it as appropriate. The writ was extensively employed in a wide range of instances,[107] and had given rise to a considerable body of law. The principal condition for the application of the writ of error was that the court in question should be a court of record,[103] since by its very nature it required the existence of a record of the judgment of the lower court to be sent to the reviewing court. However defined, the new statutory tribunals, with the exception of the Railway Commissioners after 1888,[109] were not courts of record and so could not employ the writ of error. Neither could they use the analogous writ of false judgment,[110] a writ which overcame the

---

[104] See generally note to *Jaques* v. *Caesar* (1670) 2 Wms Saund 100.

[105] Sir Edward Coke, *The First Part of the Institutes of the Laws of England*, 1628 edition, 2 vols. (New York: Garland Publishing Inc., 1979), vol. II, p. 288b; *Jaques* v. *Caesar* (1670) 2 Wms Saund 100 n.

[106] Errors in the determination of fact could not be reversed by the writ. Error in fact referred to a situation where the party against whom the judgment was given had not been properly brought before the court, as for example where he was an infant and appeared by attorney, or where the party died before verdict or interlocutory judgment.

[107] See generally Matthew Bacon, *A New Abridgement of the Law*, 7th edition, 8 vols. (London: printed by A. Strahan for J. Clarke et al., 1832), vol. III, tit. Error; Joseph Dixon (ed.), *Lush's Practice of the Superior Courts of Law*, 3rd edition, 2 vols. (London: Butterworths, 1865), vol. II, pp. 657–86.

[108] Bacon, *Abridgement*, vol. III, tit. Error A3. See too Coke, *First Institutes*, vol. II, p. 288b; *Groenvelt* v. *Burwell* (1698) 1 Salk 144; *Scott* v. *Bye* (1824) 2 Bing 344; *Bruce* v. *Wait* (1840) 1 Man & G 1 at 2 n. (a).

[109] Railway and Canal Traffic Act 1888, 51 & 52 Vict. c. 25 s. 2. The old Commissioners of Sewers had been constituted a court of record: see Sir John Comyns, *A Digest of the Laws of England*, 4th edition, 6 vols. (Dublin: Luke, White, 1793), vol. VI, tit. Sewers D; Edith G. Henderson, *Foundations of English Administrative Law* (Cambridge, MA: Harvard University Press, 1963), Chapter 3.

[110] See Sir F. Pollock and F. W. Maitland, *The History of English Law*, 2nd edition, 2 vols. (Cambridge: Cambridge University Press, 1898 reissued 1968), vol. II, pp. 666–8; *Dyson* v. *Wood* (1824) 3 B & C 449.

252 Legal Foundations of Tribunals in 19th-Century England

absence of a record by commanding that one be drawn up and used by inferior regular courts in place of error,[111] because the tribunals did not satisfy the precondition that they be courts of the Common Law.[112] Their processes, personnel and jurisdiction were quite different. The distinctions were fatal to tribunals' use of both error and false judgment, for it had been settled since the late seventeenth century that those remedies were not available to 'a Court newly instituted, impowered to proceed by methods unknown to the Common Law'.[113] Furthermore, even if they had been available, their complexity and technicality would have been quite inappropriate to the notion of a specialised, informal and expeditious mode of proceeding in an administrative sphere that was embodied in the new statutory organs.

With error and false judgment being unavailable in principle, and appeal often strictly limited or non-existent, litigants before the new tribunals felt the need for some method of redress for their grievances. A possible alternative to review by error was review by the prerogative writs, in particular that of certiorari.[114] Indeed as early as 1700 Holt CJ had said that if a jurisdiction created by Act of Parliament acted either summarily or in a course different from the Common Law, then the writ of error did not lie, but he went on to say that the appropriate remedy was certiorari, 'and that as good as a writ of error'.[115] The suggestion was that certiorari would lie whenever the writ of error did not, to enable the superior court to do justice where the inferior court had not.[116] The writ of error resembled certiorari in that it required the removal of the record to another court.

The ancient writs of prohibition, certiorari and mandamus had developed to enable the superior courts, primarily the Court of King's Bench, to control the proceedings of inferior courts and to

---

[111] Notably by the old County Courts, Courts Baron and the Hundred Courts. When the writ of false judgment lay to the County Court it was known as *recordari facias loquelam*, and when it lay to remove proceedings from the Court Baron or the Hundred Court it was known as *accedas ad curiam*.

[112] See below, pp. 297–300.

[113] *Groenvelt* v. *Burwell* (1697) 1 Ld Raym 454 at 469; see too 3 Salk 265 (1696); Carth 421 (1697); Holt KB 184, 395, 536 (1697, 1700); 1 Ld Raym 213 (1697); 3 Ld Raym 278 (1697); 1 Salk 200, 263, 396 (1698, 1700); Carth 491 (1699); 12 Mod 386 (1700); 1 Comyns 76 (1700); see too *Scott* v. *Bye* (1824) 2 Bing 344.

[114] *Ibid.*, 12 Mod 386 at 389 (1700).   [115] *Ibid.*

[116] See counsel's argument in *R.* v. *Coles* (1845) 8 QB 75 at 79.

Judicial Supervision 253

ensure that they conducted themselves as bodies that formed part of the legal system should.[117] They ensured that inferior courts kept within their jurisdiction, that any error that appeared on the face of the record of the proceedings was addressed, and that they observed the rules of natural justice.[118] Specifically, prohibition addressed the boundaries of jurisdictions and the interpretation of the charters or statutes on which those jurisdictions were founded, and prohibited the inferior court in question from going beyond its proper jurisdiction.[119] Certiorari, an analogous writ addressing past decisions rather than future ones as prohibition did, ordered that the records of causes in the inferior courts be brought into the King's Bench which, thus armed with the information, reviewed their proceedings and decisions to ensure they were within the jurisdiction and showed no apparent error, and quashing them if they fell short. Finally mandamus, which was distinct from prohibition and certiorari in that it possessed a non-judicial character derived from its original purpose in controlling borough and city authorities, ordered them to perform some public duty or to show why they had failed to do so. It could issue to ensure that a statutory discretion was exercised, or properly exercised. The King's Bench did this 'by the Common Law'[120] by reason of its 'great superiority',[121] in other words by its inherent power. The reason for this jurisdiction was public policy: the courts could not allow these inferior bodies to remain uncontrolled by the superior courts.

From the seventeenth century certiorari was commonly used to supervise inferior courts, particularly justices of the peace, previously controlled largely through Star Chamber, and also specialist tribunals such as the Commissioners of Sewers.[122] In 1701

---

[117] See generally Louis L. Jaffe and Edith G. Henderson, 'Judicial Review and the Rule of Law: Historical Origins' (1956) 72 *Law Quarterly Review* 345; S. A. de Smith, 'The Prerogative Writs' (1951) 11 *Cambridge Law Journal* 40; Henderson, *English Administrative Law*; J. H. Baker, *An Introduction to English Legal History*, 4th edition (London: Butterworths LexisNexis, 2002), pp. 135–54.

[118] R. M. Jackson, *The Machinery of Justice in England*, 7th edition (Cambridge: Cambridge University Press, 1977), pp. 167–8.

[119] See *Re Tithes of Crosby-upon-Eden* (1849) 13 QB 761; *Worthington v. Jeffries* (1875) 10 LR CP 379; *Mayor and Aldermen of City of London v. Cox* (1867) LR 2 HL 239.

[120] 1 Ld Raym 454 at 469.   [121] 12 Mod 386 at 390.

[122] They had been subject to the control of the King's Bench since 1643: *Commins v. Massam* (1643) March NR 196. See generally Jaffe and Henderson, 'Judicial Review'.

254 *Legal Foundations of Tribunals in 19th-Century England*

the Court of King's Bench rejected the argument that it could not grant a certiorari to remove proceedings from a new jurisdiction created by Act of Parliament, in that case a jurisdiction given to justices to levy money to repair a bridge. It held that it would examine the proceedings of all new jurisdictions erected by Act of Parliament, '[a]nd if they, under pretence of such Act, proceed to incroach jurisdiction to themselves greater than the Act warrants, this Court will send a certiorari to them, to have their proceedings returned here; to the end that this Court may see, that they keep themselves within their jurisdiction: and if they exceed it, to restrain them'.[123]

Despite Holt CJ's confidence in certiorari as an alternative to the writ of error, and his broad statement of its application, its use by the new statutory tribunals of the nineteenth century was problematic. The early authorities made it clear that originally there were three fundamental and interrelated requirements to the application of certiorari. They were that the body should be a court proceeding according to the Common Law, that it should be a court of record and that it should be a court within the usual designation of that term. While these were satisfied by courts within the regular legal system, even inferior courts of specialised jurisdiction, they were potentially insuperable obstacles for the new statutory tribunals.

It has been seen in the context of the writ of false judgment that the new statutory tribunals did not proceed according to the Common Law, and indeed that was inherent in their creation. Neither were they, in general, formally courts of record, a feature which had denied them access to the writ of error. While it was early established that, in contrast to error, the court did not need to be a court of the Common Law for certiorari to lie,[124] the status

---

[123] *R.* v. *Inhabitants in Glamorganshire* (1701) 1 Ld Raym 580; see too S.C. *The Case of Cardiffe Bridge* (1700) 1 Salk 146.

[124] Holt CJ held that it applied to the censors of the College of Physicians: *Groenvelt* v. *Burwell* (1697) 1 Ld Raym 454. Though it was established that certiorari did not lie to an ecclesiastical court, inter alia because the Common Law courts felt unable to question the decision of a court administering canon law. See *R.* v. *Chancellor of St Edmundsbury and Ipswich Diocese* [1948] 1 KB 195. There was a difference in degree here; a tribunal was a court of limited jurisdiction, which while not a Common Law court in procedure, was a Common Law court in substance. An ecclesiastical court stood wholly outside the Common Law.

Judicial Supervision 255

of a court of record was more difficult. Had the courts insisted on the status as a court of record, while the tribunals might have been able to exploit judicial differences of opinion as to qualification for that status, it would have hindered their access to the writ. In practice, by the beginning of the tribunal movement in the early nineteenth century, the requirement had been overcome. The absence of formal status as a full court of record had become essentially a matter of procedure, conveniently transformed into a requirement for the existence of a record. Tribunals were able to acquire a record of their proceedings by employing the writs of false judgement,[125] the old requirement for status as a court of Common Law to permit the use of those writs having been overcome by a generous interpretation of the term.[126] The real problem lay with the requirement that the tribunal be a court, since it was clear that whatever features a tribunal might share with a court of law, any judicial function it had was subsumed by its dominant administrative purpose. The courts could have taken the view that this lack of status as a traditional court, illustrated predominantly by the administrative rather than the judicial function, was fatal to the application of certiorari to the statutory tribunals, because it had long been settled that certiorari would not lie in relation to acts which were purely ministerial in nature.[127]

The courts did not, however, wish to favour this strict approach, particularly in the face of the immense growth in adjudicating bodies in the nineteenth century. They wanted to keep such bodies firmly under their control. Since the authorities did not specifically or expressly address the issue of certiorari, the courts took the view that they were no bar to ultimately finding that full status as court of law was unnecessary for certiorari to apply.[128] They turned instead to the interpretation of the term 'judicial act'. In 1892 Lopes LJ stated that the term could refer to the discharge of the duties of a judge in court, or alternatively to

---

[125] *Edwards* v. *Bowen* (1826) 5 B & C 206; *Ex parte Phillips* (1835) 2 A & E 586.

[126] See C. Stebbings, 'The Origins of the Application of *Certiorari* to the General Commissioners of Income Tax' (1997) *British Tax Review* 119.

[127] See *Re Lediard* (1751) Sayer 6; *Miller* v. *Seare* (1777) 2 Black W 1141 at 1146; *R.* v. *Edward Pryse Lloyd* (1783) Cald 309; *Re Constables of Hipperholme* (1847) 5 Dowl & L 79.

[128] *R.* v. *Assessment Committee of St Mary Abbotts, Kensington* [1891] 1 QB 378.

256 *Legal Foundations of Tribunals in 19th-Century England*

administrative duties that had to be discharged with a 'judicial mind', namely 'a mind to determine what is fair and just in respect of the matters under consideration'.[129] The latter meaning was much wider in scope than the order of an inferior court, and it was adopted for the purposes of certiorari. 'In short', observed Fletcher Moulton LJ in 1906, 'there must be the exercise of some right or duty to decide in order to provide scope for a writ of certiorari at Common Law.'[130] If a tribunal had the duty to hear and determine issues which affected the rights of subjects,[131] and had to act judicially in the sense of conducting its proceedings with fairness, impartiality and in good faith, then there was sufficient analogy with a court to allow the application of the writs.[132] Even licensing justices of the peace were embraced by this interpretation,[133] though it was clearly easier for the courts to come to that conclusion in relation to them than other tribunals, for justices were legal officers with predominantly judicial duties, but with a natural predisposition to discharge their many administrative duties in a judicial manner. This cloaking of administrative functions in judicial form served the statutory tribunals well. It allowed the courts to follow their inclination and allow the more general application of certiorari. The statutory tribunals, with a judicial function inherent in the duty to hear and determine disputes and the duty on all commissioners to bind themselves by oath to act judicially, satisfied these conditions.

While this view had been adopted in relation to some tribunals many years earlier, by the end of the nineteenth century the principle of control of statutory tribunals by the superior courts

---

[129] *Per* Lopes LJ in *Royal Aquarium and Summer and Winter Garden Society Ltd v. Parkinson* [1892] 1 QB 431 at 452. See too *Sharp* v. *Wakefield* [1891] AC 173 at 179 *per* Lord Halsbury.

[130] *R.* v. *Woodhouse* [1906] 2 KB 501 at 535.

[131] See *R.* v. *Electricity Commissioners* [1924] 1 KB 171.

[132] *R.* v. *North Worcestershire Assessment Committee* [1929] 2 KB 397; see *R.* v. *London County Council* [1892] 1 QB 190; cf. *R.* v. *Legislative Committee of the Church Assembly* [1928] 1 KB 411.

[133] *R.* v. *Woodhouse* [1906] 2 KB 501; see too *R.* v. *Sunderland Justices* [1901] 2 KB 357 and *R.* v. *Johnson* [1905] 2 KB 59. Licensing justices had been held not to be a court of summary jurisdiction in *Boulter v. Kent Justices* [1897] AC 556 and in *R.* v. *Sharman* [1898] 1 QB 578 and *R.* v. *Bowman* [1898] 1 QB 663 the decisions of liquor licensing justices had been held not to be subject to certiorari as being administrative in nature.

Judicial Supervision 257

was firmly established, and it was applied to each new tribunal as it was created. In 1882 Brett LJ stated the principle thus:

> wherever the Legislature entrusts to any body of persons other than to the superior Courts the power of imposing an obligation upon individuals, the Courts ought to exercise as widely as they can the power of controlling those bodies of persons if those persons admittedly attempt to exercise powers beyond the powers given to them by Act of Parliament.[134]

Instances abound of the granting of certiorari in cases where there was clearly neither court nor lis inter partes,[135] but where there was a duty to act judicially. So in the case of *R. v. Aberdare Canal Company* in 1850,[136] the court held that an order made by commissioners appointed under the provisions of an Act incorporating a canal company approving the building of a bridge was a judicial act and that it could be brought up by certiorari. This body of commissioners quite clearly did not constitute a court in anything like the traditional sense of the term; any person owning freehold or copyhold property worth £100 a year was to be appointed a commissioner, and accordingly the tribunal was very large and its proceedings necessarily informal. However, the commissioners were appointed to determine differences that arose between the proprietors of land and the company, and in so doing could take evidence on oath and determine compensation. By their governing Act they were to take an oath to execute their powers truly and impartially. So they were bound to act judicially and accordingly certiorari could, and would, apply. Where there had been an excess of jurisdiction in holding an inquisition to ascertain the value of property taken under an Act of Parliament, it was said obiter that the usual course was to apply for a certiorari.[137] By the early years of the twentieth century, certiorari applied in principle to bodies of an unambiguously executive nature. It lay to the Board of Education on the basis that when a government department was entrusted by Act of Parliament with questions of public

---

[134] *R. v. Local Government Board* (1882) 10 QBD 309 at 321. In that case the court refused to decide whether or not prohibition applied to a Local Government Board as there was no need to do so. See too *R. v. Board of Education* [1910] 2 KB 165 at 179 *per* Farwell LJ.

[135] A dispute, with arguments heard on both sides supported by evidence, which was analogous to a suit in law.

[136] *R. v. Aberdare Canal Company* (1850) 14 QB 854.

[137] *Chabot v. Lord Morpeth* (1844) 15 QB 446 at 457.

258 Legal Foundations of Tribunals in 19th-Century England

importance, 'it becomes a tribunal charged with the performance of a public duty, and as such amenable to the jurisdiction of the High Court, within limits now well established by law'.[138] In that case the board had acted on a mistaken construction of the Education Act 1902 and arrived at a decision which the court regarded as 'so perverse as really to amount to a non-exercise of the jurisdiction' and accordingly it was quashed.[139] Again, it was held to lie to the Electricity Commissioners[140] where they had prepared a scheme for the better organisation of the electricity supply in London that was found to be ultra vires.[141] That case was primarily concerned with prohibition, but Atkin LJ said he saw no distinction in principle between prohibition and certiorari, except that prohibition could be invoked at an earlier stage.[142]

In some instances the availability of certiorari was expressly allowed by a tribunal's parent Act, in which case the Common Law requirements for its application with respect to the nature of the tribunal were superseded. In this way it applied to the Poor Law Commissioners under the Poor Law Amendment Act 1834,[143] and to certain acts of the Tithe Commissioners. In *Re Dent Tithe Commutation*[144] there was a motion for a certiorari to bring up the award of an Assistant Tithe Commissioner in which he had purported to settle disputed parish boundaries under the Tithe Commutation Amendment Act 1837.[145] Though denied in general by the principal Act,[146] certiorari was expressly allowed in relation to the commissioners' decisions as to boundaries under the Amendment Act.[147] The Act provided that the judgment or determination of the commissioners was to be removed by a person dissatisfied with it to the Court of Queen's Bench and that the decision of that court was final. When the objectors to the boundary determination argued that certiorari lay only on the

---

[138] *Per* Farwell LJ in *R. v. Board of Education* [1910] 2 KB 165 at 179.
[139] The decision of the Court of Appeal was affirmed by the House of Lords: *Board of Education v. Rice* [1911] AC 179.
[140] A statutory body set up under the Electricity (Supply) Act 1919, 9 & 10 Geo. V c. 100.
[141] *R. v. Electricity Commissioners* [1924] 1 KB 171. The case is useful for its full review of the authorities.
[142] *Ibid.*, at 206.
[143] 4 & 5 Will. IV c. 76 ss. 105, 106; *R. v. Poor Law Commissioners* (1837) 6 A & E 1.
[144] (1845) 8 QB 43.
[145] 7 Will. IV & 1 Vict. c. 69 (1837).   [146] 6 & 7 Will. IV c. 71 s. 95 (1836).
[147] 7 Will. IV & 1 Vict. c. 69 (1837) s. 3.

Judicial Supervision 259

basis of a want of form in the award, and the commissioners argued that it lay only to the merits of the decision, the court held it empowered them to examine both. By the provision the legislature had 'given a further effect to the writ of certiorari, and made [the court] a Court of appeal upon the merits', but had not removed the court's usual jurisdiction on certiorari, namely to examine the proceedings and to decide whether on their face they were good or bad.[148] The objectors were entitled to see the jurisdiction of the commissioners on the face of the award, and when the award showed defects in this respect, the court quashed it for insufficient jurisdiction.[149] The provision allowing certiorari in effect provided for an appeal from the determination of the commissioners. Whether this was deliberate or not is unclear, though Patteson J thought it was in all likelihood a mistake. 'Probably', he said, 'the framers of the Act did not know what a certiorari meant, and thought only of giving an appeal.'[150] This view was supported by the absence of any other appeal provision relating to parochial boundary disputes in the Tithe Commutation Amendment Act. The same provision was found in relation to boundary determinations under the Inclosure Act 1845, though as an alternative to the determination of the matter by a jury.[151] The decision of the Court of Queen's Bench would be final and conclusive.

Certiorari applied where a body had acted in excess of its proper jurisdiction, but it also operated in two other spheres. Where a body had acted within its proper jurisdiction, but had made an error, and that error was apparent on the face of the record, certiorari would apply to quash it, and indeed this was the original and primary use of certiorari in the seventeenth century.[152] At first this use of certiorari was very common, in keeping with an earlier emphasis on form. The records called up by the writ were examined by the court for any defects in form such as

---

[148] *Re Dent Tithe Commutation* (1845) 8 QB 43 at 59–60 *per* Lord Denman CJ.

[149] The award did not state that the district was one of which the tithes were to be commuted, and did not, as the statute required, state that the request was signed at 'a parochial meeting called for that purpose', but only at 'a meeting called for that purpose'. Both were essential to show jurisdiction.

[150] *Re Dent Tithe Commutation* (1845) 8 QB 43 at 48.

[151] 8 & 9 Vict. c. 118 ss. 39, 44.

[152] See H. W. R. Wade, *Administrative Law*, 2nd edition (Oxford: Clarendon Press, 1967), pp. 85–9.

260 *Legal Foundations of Tribunals in 19th-Century England*

error, and that error would usually be one of law, for example a mistake as to the construction of a statute or the application of a rule of law. Certiorari was used in this way to quash the decisions of justices of the peace, since a record with the evidence and the finding was necessary to its operation. In relation to magistrates' criminal convictions, this was brought to an end in practice in 1848 when a full record was no longer required and so errors no longer appeared on the face of the record.[153] Thereafter this use of certiorari largely fell into disuse.[154]

Where a body had acted within its jurisdiction but had breached the rules of natural justice in so doing, the decision could be quashed as an exceeding of jurisdiction by certiorari. It was clear by the nineteenth century that there existed certain precepts of judicial conduct and personal quality to which persons and bodies exercising judicial or quasi-judicial functions should adhere. These rules had been largely developed by the Court of King's Bench in its historic role of controlling inferior judicial bodies, and accordingly justices of the peace were obliged to abide by these rules. In the course of the nineteenth century a similar expectation emerged in relation to the new statutory tribunals. These precepts, which came to be known as the principles of natural justice but had long been known to the law, were essentially two – *nemo judex in re sua*, namely that a man could not be a judge in his own cause, and *audi alteram partem*, that the parties in litigation should be heard.

The principle that a man could not be a judge in his own cause, namely that he was to be independent and free from bias, that all his adjudication was to be impartial, was of ancient origin and had been repeatedly affirmed by leading jurists and judges.[155] In the leading case of *Dimes* v. *Grand Junction Canal*[156] in 1852 in the House of Lords, Lord Campbell said that 'it is of the last importance that the maxim that no man is to be a judge in his own cause should be held sacred', not only where a judge was a party to a cause, but equally where he had an interest in it.[157] In that case

---

[153] Summary Jurisdiction Act 1848, 11 & 12 Vict. c. 43.
[154] To be revived in the twentieth century: see *R.* v. *Northumberland Compensation Appeal Tribunal* [1951] 1 KB 711; [1952] 1 KB 338.
[155] See Coke CJ in *Dr Bonham's Case* (1610) 8 Co Rep 113b at 118a and Holt CJ in *City of London* v. *Wood* (1702) 12 Mod 669 at 687.
[156] (1852) 3 HLC 759.   [157] *Ibid.*, at 793.

Judicial Supervision 261

Lord Cottenham LC had affirmed a number of decrees made by the Vice Chancellor in a suit involving a canal company in which the Lord Chancellor was a shareholder to the extent of several thousands of pounds, and as such was a party to a suit in whose outcome he had a considerable interest. While the Vice Chancellor was held not to be affected by the Lord Chancellor's interest, the interest was held to render voidable the decree the latter had made. Lord Campbell observed that, as Chief Justice of the Court of Queen's Bench, he had again and again set aside proceedings in inferior tribunals because an adjudicator had an interest in the cause. For the House of Lords to set aside a decree because the Lord Chancellor of England had an interest in the cause would have, he said, 'a most salutary influence on these tribunals'. 'This will be a lesson', he continued, 'to all inferior tribunals to take care not only that in their decrees they are not influenced by their personal interest, but to avoid the appearance of labouring under such an influence.'[158]

The principle was not articulated as such in the statutory procedures of the new tribunals as it was assumed Parliament intended them to be read into the processes. So where an adjudicator, whether he was judge, justice or commissioner, decided a case in which he had a direct interest, he was in breach of the maxim that a man cannot be a judge in his own cause, and any determination would be set aside by certiorari.[159] It was not unusual for administrative decisions by justices of the peace to be quashed for bias,[160] and in their judicial activities justices would have their decisions quashed if any direct pecuniary interest, however small, were shown.[161] In relation to the statutory tribunals there were some specific expressions of the rule, notably in the oaths the various commissioners and officials had to take, swearing to their impartial conduct in the performance of their duties. The parent Acts made some provision to ensure that obvious abuses of procedure did not occur and that the process was demonstrably fair. Accordingly any Land Tax Commissioner

---

[158] *Ibid.*, at 793–4.   [159] *R. v. Rand* (1866) LR 1 QB 230 at 232–3.

[160] See for example, *Foxham Tithing Case* (1705) 2 Salk 607; *Great Charte v. Kennington* (1742) 2 Str 1173; *R. v. Cheltenham Commissioners* (1841) 1 QB 467.

[161] *R. v. Rand* (1866) LR 1 QB 230. Though a justice in Special Session could hear an appeal against a rate in a valuation list even if he was himself a ratepayer of the parish in question: *R. v. Bolingbroke* [1893] 2 QB 347.

262 Legal Foundations of Tribunals in 19th-Century England

was required to withdraw from the discussion and relinquish his vote when there was a difference as to the personal assessment to tax of one of them[162] to ensure he was not perceived to be judge in his own cause. The same provision applied to an Assistant Commissioner under the Triple Assessment Act.[163] The Inclosure Clauses Consolidation Act 1801 guarded against self-interest by providing that no commissioner could purchase any land involved in the award for five years following the award.[164] When the duty of implementing the Railway and Canal Traffic Act 1854 was consigned to the Court of Common Pleas, in the common situation where the judges were holders of shares in the companies appearing before them, the judges in question would decline to take part in the discussion of the case.[165] Similarly, the parent Act of the Railway Commissioners of 1873 not only provided that no commissioner should be permitted to exercise any jurisdiction under the Act in any case in which he is directly or indirectly interested, unless the parties consent, but also provided that commissioners were not to be interested in railway or canal stock and had to sell any stock within three months of appointment.[166]

Such obvious instances of potential bias were easily addressed. Far more intractable, and largely ignored, was the inherent possibility of bias introduced by the close and pervasive relationship of the new tribunals with their parent department of the executive. For example the status of the Special Commissioners of Income Tax as members of the Inland Revenue was to cause concern among some lawyers in the next century, particularly the very evident conflict of interest and danger of bias in the system of internal appeal to the Board of Inland Revenue.[167] More

---

[162] 1 Will. & M. c. 20 s. 18 (1688). Assessments favourable to individual commissioners had been common, and this was one attempt to prevent this. See too 4 Will. & M. c. 1 s. 22 (1692); 38 Geo. III c. 5 s. 23 (1797).
[163] 38 Geo. III c. 16 s. 61 (1798). [164] 41 Geo. III c. 109 s. 2.
[165] See for example *Jones* v. *the Eastern Counties Railway Company* (1858) 3 CB NS 718 where both Cockburn CJ and Crowder J owned shares in the Eastern Counties Railway Company and withdrew. The editor to the *English Reports* observed that the Lord Chief Justice, when there was a similar occurrence in a subsequent case, stated he would take care to remove the difficulty by disposing of his shares.
[166] Railway and Canal Traffic Act 1873, 36 & 37 Vict. c. 48 s. 5. This provision was a Lords' amendment.
[167] *Minutes, Income Tax, 1919* q. 23,898 *per* Randle F. W. Holme, solicitor, on behalf of The Law Society.

Judicial Supervision

263

problematic was the exacerbation of any perceived lack of independence by a certain carelessness in the conduct of the tribunal hearings, a slackness which was possible because the conduct of the hearing was entirely in the discretion of the commissioners. A recurrent and common complaint about appeals to the General Commissioners of Income Tax, for example, was that the surveyor – the Crown officer – remained in the room when the appellant had withdrawn to allow the commissioners to arrive at their determination. Where this happened it was a gross breach of the principles of natural justice, for even though justice may well have been done, it was certainly not seen to be done. Such carelessness as to the appearance of even-handed justice significantly contributed to a perceived lack of independence of the commissioners. As both procedurally and jurisdictionally tribunals were their own masters, supervision by the regular courts was of particular importance.

The requirement for a fair hearing where both sides were heard was an ancient and established precept of judicial process when the statutory tribunals were created in the early nineteenth century. It was stated in its classic form in 1911 by Lord Loreburn LC as comprising a duty on the adjudicators to 'act in good faith and fairly listen to both sides',[168] and it was 'a duty lying upon every one who decides anything'.[169] In 1874 Kelly CB observed that the rule was 'not confined to the conduct of strictly legal tribunals, but is applicable to every tribunal or body of persons invested with authority to adjudicate upon matters involving civil consequences to individuals'.[170] The procedures of the tribunals reflected the fundamental requirement for parties to be heard, and the provisions as to notice and attendance were directed to this end. The issue was more clearly addressed in the adjudicatory elements of their jurisdiction and processes, and much of the judicial debate was directed to the application of the maxims to purely administrative actions. The maxim was applied in its full vigour to the new statutory tribunals of the nineteenth century. The courts held that they could require a fair hearing where a tribunal was acting judicially, and, just as the courts did in relation to the application of the prerogative writs, they interpreted

---

[168] *Board of Education* v. *Rice* [1911] AC 179 at 182. [169] *Ibid.*
[170] *Wood* v. *Woad* (1874) LR 9 Ex 190 at 196.

264 *Legal Foundations of Tribunals in 19th-Century England*

that term so widely as to include administrative acts. So where a local Board of Works demolished a house because they had not, as statute required, been informed of its construction, Byles J said that because the board 'had to determine the offence, and ... had to apportion the punishment as well as the remedy' they were acting judicially and the rule applied.[171] '[A]lthough', he continued, 'there are no positive words in a statute, requiring that the party shall be heard, yet the justice of the Common Law will supply the omission of the Legislature.' In the same case Willes J said that he apprehended 'that a tribunal which is by law invested with power to affect the property of one of Her Majesty's subjects, is bound to give such subject an opportunity of being heard before it proceeds: and that the rule is of universal application, and founded on the plainest principles of justice'.[172] Some years later Wills J famously observed that '[i]n condemning a man to have his house pulled down, a judicial act is as much implied as in fining him £5', and went on to hold that the tribunal doing so was subject to the maxim.[173] In applying certiorari to the new statutory tribunals, the law was responding to changing conditions and new circumstances, though its motive in so doing was to retain the control over inferior courts that it had possessed for so long. It was pragmatic and flexible when it felt it had to be, and this could be portrayed as a fine quality of the law. As Bankes LJ observed when discussing the application of prohibition to the Electricity Commissioners, '[i]t has ... always been the boast of our Common Law that it will, whenever possible, and where necessary, apply existing principles to new sets of circumstances'.[174]

The prerogative writ of prohibition was analogous to certiorari. Like certiorari it was predominantly concerned with an absence of jurisdiction but could also lie for error on the face of the record or breach of the rules of natural justice. It was, however, broader in its scope than certiorari in that a wider range of bodies was subject to it. It controlled the jurisdiction of all inferior courts, including the Ecclesiastical Courts, Admiralty Courts, County Courts and justices of the peace, its preconditions being primarily that a body should have a jurisdiction that it purported to exceed, and that the

---

[171] *Cooper* v. *Wandsworth Board of Works* (1863) 14 CB NS 180 at 194.
[172] *Ibid.*, at 190.
[173] *Hopkins* v. *Smethwick Local Board of Health* (1890) 24 QBD 712 at 714–15.
[174] *Per* Bankes LJ in *R.* v. *Electricity Commissioners* [1924] 1 KB 171 at 192.

Judicial Supervision 265

body had not yet made its final determination so that there was something to prohibit.[175] The theoretical restriction to acts of a judicial nature also existed, but was not regarded as such a serious obstacle as it was with certiorari. Not having traditionally been confined to courts of record of the Common Law, it was applied with more ease to the new statutory tribunals. It was accepted that it would issue to the Tithe Commissioners if they proposed to act outside their jurisdiction. When in 1841 in the course of a commutation in Norfolk a dispute between the rector and a landowner as to the existence of a modus arose, it was heard and determined by an Assistant Commissioner, who found it had not been established.[176] The landowner appealed by feigned issue to the Assizes, and the action was still pending when he claimed a modus in a smaller amount over the same land, namely the same modus by another description. The commissioners argued that they could not make their final award without hearing and determining this second disputed modus, but the rector argued they had no jurisdiction to do so and that a prohibition should issue to ensure they did not. He argued on the basis of the provision in the governing statute to the effect that when a dispute over a modus or exemption hindered the commissioners in arriving at their award, they should hear and determine it and their determination was final and conclusive.[177] The court held that a prohibition would not issue as the commissioners had jurisdiction to determine the second claim, and indeed were bound to do so though they should wait until the appeal relating to the first modus had been disposed of by the court. On the true construction of the statute, their jurisdiction came to an end only when they made their final award. Until then their determinations were not final and binding for all purposes. Their determination as to the existence of the first modus was conclusive only as to the existence of that particular modus, and not as to whether any other modus existed over the land.[178]

While a prohibition would not issue where there was no excess of jurisdiction, the court entertained no doubt that in appropriate

---

[175] *Hall* v. *Norwood* (1663) 1 Sid 165 at 166. See too *Chabot* v. *Lord Morpeth* (1844) 15 QB 446.
[176] *Barker* v. *the Tithe Commissioners* (1841) 9 M & W 129.
[177] Tithe Commutation Act 1836, 6 & 7 Will. IV c. 71 s. 45.
[178] *Barker* v. *the Tithe Commissioners* (1841) 9 M & W 129 at 151 *per* Parke B.

266 Legal Foundations of Tribunals in 19th-Century England

circumstances the writ would issue. Though it was queried in 1844, the point was conceded as the commissioners themselves suggested it as an appropriate remedy and a prohibition issued to prevent them from determining a disputed boundary that divided counties as well as parishes.[179] In the following year, in the course of a tithe commutation in Kent, the rent charge calculated to be paid in lieu of tithes had been confirmed, but its sharing out among the lands of the parish was disputed when the valuer assessed some pasture on the basis of the possibility of future culture. Though the court held that a prohibition did not issue to prevent the commissioners from confirming the apportionment of the rent charge, it decided on the basis that they had acted within their statutory jurisdiction and according to law in allowing future culture to be taken into account when arriving at the apportionment.[180] Again in 1849, when the Tithe Commissioners were once more challenged under the provision in the Tithe Commutation Act 1836 that any suits pending in the courts had to be determined before the commissioners could make an award for commutation, a prohibition issued to prevent them making their award before these suits were decided, on the grounds that if they proceeded to do so they would be acting without jurisdiction. As such it provided clear grounds for the issue of the prerogative writ.[181] Just as prohibition issued to prevent the Tithe Commissioners from exceeding their jurisdiction, so it applied to the Inclosure Commissioners. In 1862 it issued to them to prevent them from proceeding with an inclosure without having sought the consent of an owner of brick earth, the Assistant Commissioner having mistakenly declined to take such minerals into account when ascertaining the value of the interests for the purpose of consents.[182] The writ was later seen to apply to the various fiscal tribunals where the commissioners had acted without jurisdiction.[183]

In theory prohibition faced the same restriction as certiorari to judicial acts. The argument was occasionally raised in court but seldom pursued. Occasionally it prevailed, as in 1844 when one of

---

[179] *Re Ystradgunlais Tithe Commutation* (1844) 8 QB 32 at 39.
[180] *Re the Appledore Tithe Commutation* (1845) 8 QB 139.
[181] *Re Crosby Tithes* (1849) 13 QB 761.
[182] *Church v. Inclosure Commissioners* (1862) 11 CB NS 664.
[183] *R. v. the Commissioners for the General Purposes of the Income Tax for Kensington* [1914] 3 KB 429.

Judicial Supervision 267

the reasons put forward for the non-application of prohibition was the ministerial nature of the act it was sought to prohibit, namely the formal recording of a jury's valuation of land which had been compulsory acquired by the Commissioners of Woods and Forests.[184] If the court had done so, said Lord Campbell CJ, it would be 'interfering with proceedings not judicial, but belonging to the executive Government of the country'.[185] When it was argued in 1924 that the writ of prohibition did not apply to the Electricity Commissioners because their proceedings were executive and not judicial, Bankes LJ accepted that originally the writ had doubtless applied only to inferior courts properly so called, but numerous authorities had since shown that it applied to 'a body exercising judicial functions, though that body cannot be described as being in any ordinary sense a Court'.[186] So wide and far-reaching were the powers given to the Electricity Commissioners, affecting individuals and property, that they were to be exercised judicially and not ministerially. The court thus rejected the traditional argument for a restrictive application of prohibition and held that it did apply to prevent the commissioners acting on a scheme that, creating two electricity authorities in one district, was ultra vires as they had jurisdiction to create only one. One tribunal in relation to which prohibition was extensively used was the Railway Commission of 1873. The railway companies regarded the statutory appeal provisions as totally inadequate to their needs, and avoided their full effect by using the writ of prohibition. It seems that where the Railway Commissioners refused leave to appeal on a point of law, the railway companies set about, successfully, in having the decision of the commissioners set aside by prohibition in the regular courts, alleging that they had exceeded their jurisdiction.[187] This practice was condemned, one barrister observing that 'the writ of prohibition as used in modern times is a most pernicious thing',[188] and in 1882 a Select

---

[184] *Chabot v. Lord Morpeth* (1844) 15 QB 446, cited with approval on this point by Avory J in *R. v. Kensington Income Tax Commissioners* [1913] 3 KB 870 at 895.

[185] *Chabot v. Lord Morpeth* (1844) 15 QB 446 at 459. See *R. v. Light Railway Commissioners* [1915] 3 KB 536 at 548; *Re Clifford and O'Sullivan* [1921] 2 AC 570 at 582.

[186] *R. v. Electricity Commissioners* [1924] 1 KB 171 at 194.

[187] For the use of prohibition as an appeal, see 'Sixth Annual Report of the Railway Commissioners', *HCPP* (1880) (2504) xix 287 at p. 289.

[188] *Minutes, Railways (Rates and Fares), 1882* q. 1533 *per* Edward Pember QC.

268 Legal Foundations of Tribunals in 19th-Century England

Committee recommended that prohibition and certiorari should be forbidden.[189] The Railway and Canal Traffic Act 1888 provided that no order of the Railway and Canal Commissioners could be reviewed by certiorari or prohibition.[190]

Finally, the writ of mandamus, compelling the performance of a public duty, was from its earliest days the broadest of the prerogative writs. It was also, according to Bowen LJ, the 'most cumbrous and most expensive'.[191] It applied to all public authorities, whether individual, body or court, with a public duty to perform, even if that was a ministerial duty of an administrative body.[192] Indeed in the eighteenth century Lord Mansfield stated the writ should be used 'upon all occasions where the law has established no specific remedy, and where in justice and good government there ought to be one'.[193] It was, he said, 'a very beneficial writ'.[194] Not being limited to a judicial act, there was no difficulty in applying it to the new tribunals created by statute. They could not refuse to exercise their proper jurisdiction and would, in appropriate cases, be instructed to hear and determine a dispute according to the law.[195] It would issue to the Tithe Commissioners to compel them to make their award,[196] to the Commissioners of the Land Tax to compel them to elect a clerk,[197] to the Board of Education to instruct them to address the correct question,[198] and to the Special Commissioners of Income Tax to compel them to issue orders for repayment of sums which the General Commissioners had certified had been overpaid by the taxpayers.[199] The three remedies of certiorari, mandamus and prohibition were not mutually exclusive and were often used together in some combination, to prevent a wrongful act from taking

---

[189] 'Report from the Select Committee on Railways (Rates and Fares)', *HCPP* (1882) (317) xiii 1 at p. 16.
[190] 51 & 52 Vict. c. 25 s. 17(6).   [191] *Re Nathan* (1884) 12 QBD 461 at 479.
[192] See generally Comyns, *Digest*, vol. V, tit. Mandamus.
[193] *R. v. Barker* (1762) 3 Burr 1265 at 1267.
[194] *R. v. Commissioners of the Land Tax for St Martin in the Fields, Westminster* (1786) 1 TR 146 at 148.
[195] *R. v. the Vestry of St Pancras* (1890) 24 QBD 371.
[196] *Earl of Stamford and Warrington v. Dunbar* (1844) 12 M & W 414 at 420 *per* Lord Abinger CB.
[197] *R. v. Commissioners of the Land Tax for St Martin in the Fields, Westminster* (1786) 1 TR 146.
[198] *R. v. Board of Education* [1910] 2 KB 165.
[199] *R. v. Commissioners for Special Purposes of the Income Tax* (1888) 21 QBD 313.

Judicial Supervision 269

place, to quash one which had already occurred and to order the performance of the correct one. While prohibition and certiorari were unaffected by the existence of methods of appeal, mandamus was traditionally not available where another remedy was available, true to its original purpose of supplying defects of justice.[200]

Certiorari, mandamus and prohibition were all used in relation to statutory tribunals from the early eighteenth century. By the time of the great expansion in statutory tribunals in the early nineteenth century, the foundations of the use of the writs outside the sphere of inferior but regular courts were laid. In principle, therefore, all the prerogative writs lay to the new statutory tribunals. It was clear, however, that the concerns that had led the legislature to limit rights of appeal, namely the excessive prolongation and expense of litigation in areas that all too often would result in public inconvenience and a hindrance to government policy, were equally present in legal provision for judicial review. This led to a certain prudence on the part of the judiciary as to when to allow the writs to lie, as where certiorari was cautiously granted to the Commissioners of Sewers otherwise 'great inconveniences may follow by inundations in the mean time',[201] and forbidden to lie to remove the poor rate itself,[202] for 'great inconveniences and delays would follow' and in the meantime the poor might starve.[203] Similar arguments were raised against the grant of certiorari to remove an assessment of the land tax,[204] and it was not until 1904 that it was expressly stated that in principle certiorari would apply to the General Commissioners of Income Tax.[205] It also led to the widespread inclusion of clauses in the parent legislation that purported to exclude or limit the scope of the prerogative writs in relation to the new tribunals,[206] itself an indication that, despite some theoretical obstacles, the consensus was that the prerogative writs applied. This long tradition of

---

[200] See Bowen LJ in *Re Nathan* (1884) 12 QBD 461 at 478–9.
[201] *Case of the Commissioners of Sewers for Yorkshire* (1724) 1 Str 609. See too *Dr Grenville* v. *College of Physicians* (1700) 12 Mod 386 at 390.
[202] *R.* v. *Inhabitants of Uttoxeter* (1732) 2 Str 932. See too *R.* v. *Justices of Shrewsbury* (1733) 2 Str 975.
[203] See *R.* v. *King* (1788) 2 TR 234.   [204] *Ibid.*
[205] *R.* v. *Commissioners of Income Tax for the City of London.* (1904) 91 LT 94.
[206] See generally S.A. de Smith, *Judicial Review of Administrative Action* (London: Stevens & Sons, 1959), pp. 226–30.

270 *Legal Foundations of Tribunals in 19th-Century England*

restrictive clauses[207] was adopted by the new tribunals of the nineteenth century, who nearly all included such provisions. Provisions broadly divided into two types – the designation of commissioners' decisions as 'final', and the more explicit clauses that expressly excluded certiorari.[208]

Finality clauses were repeatedly and early held to exclude only appeals to higher courts, and not to affect the right of the King's Bench to bring proceedings before it by certiorari.[209] Certiorari could be excluded only by the clearest words to that effect. The reason behind this strict construction of the statutory provisions was, paradoxically, a desire on the part of the King's Bench to retain its control over inferior jurisdictions. 'The King', it was observed in 1754, 'has ... an inherent Common Law right ... to have a *certiorari*.'[210] Even the addition of general words purporting to exclude certiorari but not expressly saying so were held not to be effective. A provision in the Conventicle Act 1670[211] to the effect that not only were decisions of the justices under that Act final, but also that 'no other court whatsoever [should] intermeddle', was held not to exclude certiorari. This was so despite a provision to the effect that the statute should be construed 'most largely and beneficially for the suppressing of conventicles ... and that no record, warrant or mittimus to be made by virtue of this Act, or any proceedings thereupon, shall be reversed, avoided or any way impeached, by reason of any default in form'.[212] Despite counsel querying 'to what purpose should a certiorari issue, when the Court can neither intermeddle with the fact or form',[213] the court held that certiorari was not taken away, and that only express words would suffice to do so.[214] Some tribunals, notably the three land rights tribunals, tended to be more expansive in their exclusion clauses, expressly providing that

---

[207] Bacon, *Abridgement*, vol. II, tit. Certiorari E.
[208] H. W. Arthurs, *'Without the Law': Administrative Justice and Legal Pluralism in Nineteenth-Century England* (Toronto and Buffalo: University of Toronto Press, 1985), pp. 147–9.
[209] *R. v. Moreley* (1760) 2 Burr 1040; Bacon, *Abridgement*, vol. II, tit Certiorari B. See *R. v. Nat Bell Liquors Ltd* [1922] 2 AC 128 at 160.
[210] *R. v. Berkley and Bragge* (1754) 1 Keny 80 at 102.
[211] 22 Car. II c. 1 s. 6. These Acts were aimed at suppressing religious meetings not conforming to the Church of England, 'conventicle' designating an irregular religious meeting.
[212] *Ibid.*, s. 13.   [213] *R. v. Moreley* (1760) 2 Burr 1040 at 1041.
[214] *Ibid.*, at 1042.

Judicial Supervision

decisions were not to be questioned in any court by certiorari or otherwise. The Inclosure Clauses Consolidation Act 1801, which frequently formed the model for the other legislation in this area, provided in relation to the determination of boundary disputes by the commissioners that an appeal lay by an aggrieved person to the justices of the peace in Quarter Sessions, but that the decision of the justices was to be 'final and conclusive and shall not be removable by Certiorari, or any other Writ or Process whatsoever, into any of his Majesty's Courts of Record at Westminster or elsewhere'.[215] Under the Common Fields Inclosure Act 1836, justices could hear appeals on a variety of issues from the determinations of the commissioners, and their decisions were to be 'final and conclusive', 'and no such Complaint, Appeal, or Proceeding shall be removed or removeable by Certiorari or any other Writ or Proceeding whatsoever into any of His Majesty's Courts of Record at Westminster or elsewhere'.[216] When the inclosure process was centralised in 1845, the same clause was adopted.[217] The Tithe Commutation Act had used a similar clause in 1836,[218] and the Copyhold Act employed it in 1841.[219] Similar restrictions on the review of justices' appellate decisions from tribunals were found in the Parochial Assessments Regulation Act 1836.[220] These comprehensive express provisions were effective to a limited degree in excluding certiorari, but were always narrowly construed. They did not fundamentally affect the regular courts' power to supervise the new tribunals, and certiorari would still issue in cases of exceeding jurisdiction, irregular composition and breaches of the rules of natural justice.[221] It left only errors on the face of the record that did not go to jurisdiction free to be subject to the clause.[222] Indeed, the limited effect of these exclusion clauses resulting from the determination of the judiciary to ensure control over all inferior dispute-resolution

---

[215] 41 Geo. III c. 109 s. 3. The clause was regarded as effective: see *Minutes, Commons' Inclosure, 1844* q. 4366.
[216] 6 & 7 Will. IV c. 115 s. 53. [217] 8 & 9 Vict. c. 118 s. 166.
[218] 6 & 7 Will. IV c. 71 s. 95. [219] 4 & 5 Vict. c. 35 s. 96.
[220] 6 & 7 Will. IV c. 96 s. 7.
[221] See *Colonial Bank of Australasia Ltd v. Willan* (1874) LR 5 PC 417.
[222] *R. v. Chantrell* (1875) LR 10 QB 587.

272 Legal Foundations of Tribunals in 19th-Century England

bodies coupled with the popular demand for the right of appeal, resulted in most errors of process or law being subjected to the supervision and correction of the regular courts of law. The extent to which this contributed towards establishing them in the legal system itself, however, was a matter of considerable uncertainty.

7

PRINCIPLES, PLACE AND PERCEPTION

On the eve of the Great War, an event in world history that was to change social and economic conditions in Britain as radically as the industrial revolution that had opened Victoria's reign, the legal and political system found that it had created a new institution. For over eighty years the statutory tribunal had effectively addressed the considerable problems to which the industrial revolution had given rise. Indeed it was a body that was to endure to meet radically changing conditions into the future and to become one of the major legal institutions in Britain, challenging the traditional courts of law in terms of numbers of disputes heard and determined. In 1914 there were a number of such bodies, extra-judicial administrative organs possessing limited judicial powers, bodies that are today known as statutory, or administrative, tribunals. To the modern legal eye they are instantly recognisable as examples of a hybrid species of dispute-resolution body hovering somewhat uncertainly between the judicature and the executive. From their inception, these bodies had clear common features in their personnel, procedures and broad function, because their requirements were in essence the same whatever the nature of the legislation they were created to implement. All required speed, efficiency, cheapness and a specialist composition. It has been seen that the regular courts could not be adopted wholesale for the implementation of the new legislation, not only because of the inherent shortcomings of personnel and process, but also because the new reforming legislative codes required more than an instrument of dispute-resolution. Nevertheless the evidence, not least the tribunals themselves, shows that it was the courts of law and other expressions of the regular legal system that provided the legal foundations of the essential components of the modern statutory tribunal.

273

274 *Legal Foundations of Tribunals in 19th-Century England*

One of the most striking characteristics of the statutory tribunal was its lay composition. The administration of justice by laymen with no formal legal qualification was, however, a familiar feature of English life and indeed the sole contact the majority of the population had with the regular courts was with a lay judge in the form of a justice of the peace. Similarly, the resolution of disputes of fact had always, within the principles and procedures of the Common Law, been left to a lay jury. Indeed, this was one of the fundamental tenets of the Common Law. Arbitration too, a widely used instrument of dispute-resolution for hundreds of years, was an example of lay adjudication. Whether the legislators deliberately and consciously drew on these influences in their creation of lay legal institutions is not always evident. In some instances, however, the foundations were clear and acknowledged. The qualification, selection and appointment of the Land Tax Commissioners and the General Commissioners of Income Tax were identical in principle with the justices of the peace, and indeed all justices of the peace could act as Land Tax Commissioners by an Act of 1827.[1] In this sense, therefore, the fiscal tribunals were not novel, indeed they were clearly based on established legal antecedents. The various commissioners composing the land rights tribunals resembled arbitrators in their specialist experience and mode of proceeding, and the influence was reflected in the terminology of the process. The term 'award' was the name given to the final determination of arbitrators in a traditional private arbitration, and not only had it long been used in relation to inclosures,[2] it was used to describe the final outcome and decision of a commissioner in the commutation of tithes. The personnel and processes of tithe commutation were frequently compared and contrasted with arbitration, and the taking of arbitration as a comparator is revealing. In inclosure, it has been suggested that the origins of the office of private commissioner, which in turn greatly influenced the composition of the centralised tribunal, lay in the appointment of an arbitrator for the mutual convenience of the parties striving to arrive at an agreement as to the inclosure of land.[3] While the concept of voluntary and private

[1] 7 & 8 Geo. IV c. 75 s. 1.
[2] Inclosure Clauses Consolidation Act 1801, 41 Geo. III c. 109 s. 35.
[3] E. C. K. Gonner, *Common Land and Inclosure*, 2nd edition (London: Frank Cass & Co. Ltd, 1966), p. 94.

Principles, Place and Perception

arbitration sat uneasily with a mandatory statutory restructuring of land rights, if it could be incorporated into the process it did serve to make any obligatory process more acceptable to the public, bringing with it the illusion, if not the reality, of personal control of the process.

The concept of specialist expertise in a particular field of activity to inform, among other things, the dispute-resolution duty of the tribunal was another feature familiar to the regular legal system. In one sense it had been a requirement of the justices of the peace, since local knowledge was regarded as an important qualification, and was implicit in the residency requirements of that office. But more prominently, it formed the essence of certain specialist courts of justice, and had done so from the earliest days of the formation of the English legal system, and was not unknown in regular courts of general jurisdiction. In his original Railway and Canal Traffic Regulation Bill in 1854, Edward Cardwell expressly looked to the judicial form in this respect. The Chancery Reform Act 1852[4] gave the Court of Chancery the power to consult experts such as engineers, actuaries, accountants or merchants in technical matters and to call for a report in order to enable the court to arrive at a judgment in any matter. Furthermore, there was a long tradition of appointing a specialist arbitrator where the subject-matter of arbitration was of particular technicality. While various approaches were adopted to ensure an appropriate composition, each being dictated by the subject-matter of the tribunal, all drew heavily, explicitly, implicitly or merely culturally, on established practices.

Not possessing the well-established right of judicial bodies to determine their own procedures, a right enjoyed by all the superior courts and justices of the peace,[5] and unable to call on ancient usage to supply guidance as to procedures, the new tribunals were entirely dependent on, and constrained by, the provisions of their parent legislation.[6] Though mindful of the need to ensure that the new regulatory legislation was implemented swiftly and cheaply, the parent legislation of the tribunals was rarely prescriptive as to procedures in the dispute-resolution

---

[4] 15 & 16 Vict. c. 80.
[5] *Collier* v. *Hicks* (1831) 2 B & Ad 663; *Ex parte Evans* (1846) 9 QB 279.
[6] *R.* v. *Assessment Committee of St Mary Abbotts, Kensington* [1891] 1 QB 378.

276 *Legal Foundations of Tribunals in 19th-Century England*

aspect of their jurisdiction, with most procedural rules dealing with the overall administrative function and doing so in considerable detail. Within that framework, and even when the dispute-resolution element of the process was discrete and prominent, the dispute-resolution aspects were largely unregulated. The most judicial of the tribunals, notably the Railway Commissioners, drew unambiguously on judicial procedures, for that was the pragmatic and obvious solution, but it is clear from the evidence that the majority of tribunals arrived at their own procedures for the hearing and determining of disputes. To do so, however, they drew on patterns of dispute-resolution that were familiar to them, and these were often orthodox legal processes. They were techniques and approaches employed by them in some instances through their own experiences as magistrates, or promoted by the experience of the legally qualified members of the tribunal such as the legal commissioner himself or the clerk, and which they regarded as either desirable or the only practical option. The procedures of formal legal dispute-resolution provided some appropriate guidance. That simplicity and informality of proceedings before the tribunals which was regarded as essential for the efficient implementation of legislation, though in stark contrast to the formal procedures of the courts of law, was not unknown to some sections of the regular legal system and was certainly a feature of arbitration. The concepts of notice, of statements of claim, of balanced arguments, of reasoned if not explicit judgments were all fundamental concepts taken from the regular legal system.

Alternatively the tribunals constructed procedures upon codes of conduct that they understood through an accepted general culture of fair decision-making that owed more to a moral sense of what was right and equitable than to any written procedural guidelines. Even this, however, reinforced the orthodox legal foundation of tribunal procedures, since the procedures of the regular courts of law – though surrounded by intricate formalities, developed at an early stage in the evolution of the legal system as a safeguard in the context of an undeveloped substantive law – were themselves based on fundamental tenets of natural justice. The concept of a fair hearing, and all that implied, formed the basis of all dispute-resolution, from the exercise of the judicial power of the state in the regular courts, to private adjudication in

Principles, Place and Perception 277

arbitration. All looked to the same fundamental natural requirements of fairness. In that sense, the tribunal procedures recognised the universal roots of fair adjudication common to the exercise of judicial powers in the widest sense of the term, a recognition which was unaffected by the overall administrative nature of the body's function. Since the essential aims of the dispute-resolution elements of the procedure were the same as in the regular courts, and recognised as being so, it was natural that the forms of court procedures should provide the underlying legal foundation of tribunal procedure. The similarity of essential procedure design particularly to the processes at Quarter Sessions, constitutes evidence of its legal foundation in the procedure of the regular courts, a foundation reinforced by the courts insisting on intervening if the rules of natural justice were broken. Again the justices of the peace are seen to be a formative influence on the modern statutory tribunal. The standards of judicial conduct reflected in the evolving rules of natural justice were developed and enforced in the context of justices of the peace in the eighteenth century. Their application to a body possessing both judicial and administrative functions predisposed the judicial mind to allow the application of the prerogative writs to the new tribunals.

It was the shedding of excessive formality and technicality, necessary to achieve the cheapness and speed required, which distinguished the tribunal procedures from those of the regular courts. Court rules of procedure were not adopted wholesale, and certain elements which were not deemed necessary to ensure a fair and disciplined hearing, and which served only to lengthen the process, were discarded. Such informality and flexibility were characteristic of arbitration, with the courts holding that an arbitrator had a general discretion as to the mode of directing the proceedings and could refuse to hear counsel. In 1847 Maule J observed that '[i]t is a very proper, and in some cases a very indispensable, thing that arbitrators should, within proper limits, be allowed to deviate from the ordinary rules which govern courts of justice: for instance an arbitrator may properly and conveniently take the examination of a sick or infirm person at his own house'.[7] Some tribunals were more legalistic with respect to

---

[7] *Tillam* v. *Copp* (1847) 5 CB 211 at 214.

278 *Legal Foundations of Tribunals in 19th-Century England*

procedures than others. The Railway Commissions of 1873 and 1888, for instance, were heavily influenced by their origins in the jurisdiction of the Court of Common Pleas. For example, the commission's refusal to hear solicitors was the direct result of the transfer of jurisdiction from the Court of Common Pleas and an adherence to its procedures.[8] Furthermore, the commission used the practice rules of the regular courts as their default law. Where the Act or the orders did not expressly provide for a particular case, the general principles of practice in the superior courts of law could be adopted and applied at the discretion of the commissioners.[9] This adherence to judicial procedures resulted in an external perception that was significantly more court-like than other tribunals, but was not unreasonable in view of the nature of the tribunal's cases.

The flexible procedures of arbitration undoubtedly influenced the development of those of tribunals. Not only was it included within the regulatory legislation as the preferred method of dispute-resolution in some instances, but its procedures bore a strong resemblance to the procedures of many tribunals. The Railway Clauses Consolidation Act 1845, for example, made wide use of arbitration as a method of dispute-resolution regarding railways.[10] It expressly specified that a number of disputes were to go to arbitration and laid down the processes to be followed in some detail, and in language strikingly similar to that used to express the dispute-resolution jurisdiction of tribunals such as the Tithe Commissioners, the Land Tax Commissioners and the General Commissioners of Income Tax.[11] The railway arbitrators had power to call for books and documents, they could examine the parties or witnesses on oath,[12] and each arbitrator had to make a declaration that he would faithfully and honestly, to the best of his skill and ability, hear and determine the matters given to him by the Act.[13] The greatest contribution of arbitration, however, was the consensual approach adopted by tribunals in the conduct of their proceedings. Even the Railway Commission saw itself as a

---

[8] *Minutes, Railways (Rates and Fares), 1882* q. 1365 *per* J. H. Balfour Browne, barrister.
[9] General Ord. 54, printed after the Railway and Canal Traffic Act 1873 in *The Practical Statutes* (London: Horace Cox, 1865–1900), 1873.
[10] 8 & 9 Vict. c. 20 s. 129.   [11] *Ibid.*, s. 126.   [12] *Ibid.*, s. 133.
[13] *Ibid.*, s. 134.

Principles, Place and Perception 279

court of arbitration,[14] and all other tribunals repeatedly expressed their aspiration to an arbitral character. With ideological resistance to compulsion, most tribunals to a greater or lesser degree relied on persuasion.[15]

Such an approach to the construction of procedural codes, however, inevitably resulted in a lack of uniformity and a haphazard growth through practice, as well as the establishment and continuation unchecked of insufficiently robust processes. The legislature having refused to address fundamental issues of natural justice through a prescriptive approach to procedure, it was left to the regular courts to ensure procedural correctness through their own supervisory jurisdiction, and as such they proved the only safeguard. Beyond this there was no recognised need for consistency and no common principles. The development of procedures was entirely pragmatic.

The nature of the jurisdiction of the statutory tribunals was notable in two ways: it was strictly circumscribed and was both administrative and judicial. Both characteristics were found in the regular legal system. A jurisdiction limited by subject-matter was the predominant feature of the specialist courts of justice whose number and very existence so exercised the Judicature Commissioners in the latter years of the nineteenth century. The concept of a body administering a specialist body of law was therefore familiar to legislators and was in that sense unremarkable. Similarly the possession by an organ of both administrative and judicial powers was not peculiar to the statutory tribunals, since this too was known to the regular legal system. Justices of the peace were the prime example, for since their inception in the fourteenth century they were endowed with a wide criminal jurisdiction and extensive administrative powers in the field of local government and licensing. Local government was almost exclusively in their largely uncontrolled hands from the seventeenth to the nineteenth century. Justices formed the connection between the administration

---

[14] *Minutes, Railways (Rates and Fares), 1882* q. 3113 *per* Sir Frederick Peel, first chairman of the Railway Commission. See too *Minutes, Railway Amalgamation, 1872* q. 413 *per* James Allport, general manager of the Midland Railway; q. 7457 *per* Thomas Farrer, permanent secretary of the Board of Trade.

[15] A number of types of arbitration existed, some of which closely resemble statutory tribunals. See H. W. Arthurs, *'Without the Law': Administrative Justice and Legal Pluralism in Nineteenth-Century England* (Toronto and Buffalo: University of Toronto Press, 1985), p. 63.

280 *Legal Foundations of Tribunals in 19th-Century England*

of the country and the inferior courts of justice, and, procedurally at least, gave the former the character of the latter. They used judicial processes in the exercise of all their duties.[16] There had been earlier examples in the legal system, notably the Star Chamber and indeed the Court of Chancery. This ancient, close and enduring connection between the administration of the country and its judicial process made the admixture of the functions acceptable in an implementing body, and also predisposed the statutory tribunals of the nineteenth century to cloaking administrative functions in judicial form. That statutory tribunals could draw on influences of established legal and governmental institutions in the creation of their particular jurisdictions is undeniable. Whether they did so in practice is less evident. The evidence suggests that, at most, the existence of precedents made the creation of a limited and dual jurisdiction unexceptionable. The highly specialised jurisdiction was never the subject of comment or question, and neither was the fact that there was a duality of function. This general acceptance of tribunals' jurisdictional features suggests clear legal foundations in established institutions.

The legal foundations of the principal characteristics of the new statutory bodies of the early nineteenth century lay, explicitly and implicitly,[17] in the two well-established institutions of the justices of the peace and arbitration, with considerable influences and traditions taken from the regular and specialist courts of justice and from the private bill committees of the Houses of Parliament. Though the latter were theoretically predominantly legislative, in conducting their inquiries they inevitably had to decide contentious issues which were judicial in nature, and it was felt that such matters should, as far as possible, be decided in a judicial manner and according to judicial principles.[18] In this they clearly informed and influenced the development of the statutory tribunals, particularly those concerning the restructuring of land rights and the regulation of railways since those had their roots in the private bill process. When it was seeking to improve the

---

[16] R. M. Jackson, *The Machinery of Justice in England*, 7th edition (Cambridge: Cambridge University Press, 1977), pp. 170, 176.

[17] See Arthurs, *Without the Law*, p. 86.

[18] See the evidence of Thomas Erskine May in 'Minutes of Evidence before the Select Committee on Private Bill Legislation', *HCPP* (1863) (385) viii 205 at q. 3004.

Principles, Place and Perception 281

procedures for the consideration of railway bills in the 1840s, under the pressure of huge numbers of bills coming before it, Parliament was feeling its way towards a tribunal procedure, albeit an inquisitorial one. All the principal challenges which tribunals were created to address were seen in relation to the private bill committees, notably expense and formality of procedure, legal representation, expert adjudicators, jurisdiction, openness and fairness, political independence and, indeed, the usurpation of the powers of another branch of the state. The extensive debates in Parliament and in Select Committee as to the constitution and functions of a specialised body to supervise the railways revealed normal expectations and demands of litigants and the public in quasi-judicial decision-making processes.[19]

Strong as these formative influences were, amounting in many instances to as much as a clear and pervasive legal foundation, no legal institution went so far as to constitute a model for the statutory tribunal. In the intensive debate of the nineteenth century, the established institutions were not called upon to act as a model for the new bodies. This was so despite the clear common features that in some instances they purported to share and of which the tribunals themselves are evidence – the facts of lay membership, informal procedures and jurisdictional specialisation. There was no explicit drawing on the experiences of, for example, the Courts of Requests. The use of a model to provide consistency within the regular legal system was itself not unusual, and again the Courts of Requests show that some attempt was made to attain a measure of uniformity.[20] The justices of the peace differed fundamentally from the statutory tribunals in that although they possessed administrative and judicial functions, those were kept distinct, and while they exhibited a duality of function, it was not an integration of function as found in the tribunals. Moreover, their procedures had the formality of those in the courts of justice, and they were unequivocally part of the regular legal system. Arbitration was equally no more than an influence, contributing

---

[19] See Anon., 'Railway Tribunals' (1846) 3 *Law Review and Quarterly Journal of British and Foreign Jurisprudence* 415; Anon., 'The New Railway Board' (1846–7) 5 *Law Review and Quarterly Journal of British and Foreign Jurisprudence* 354.

[20] See Arthurs, *Without the Law*, p. 26.

282 *Legal Foundations of Tribunals in 19th-Century England*

certain features but too informal and too personal an arrangement to be adopted in its entirety. The evidence also reveals that even though the requirements of the new bodies were in essence the same whatever the nature of the legislation they were to implement – namely speed, efficiency and cheapness – no model tribunal was adopted. There was no blueprint, no basic design of statutory tribunal that legislators looked to when they needed a body to implement a new legislative regime, and amend as they chose to suit their particular needs in that instance. The common denominators were there – a strictly circumscribed jurisdiction composed of administrative and judicial functions, simple procedures, lay and specialised personnel – and in that sense a rudimentary framework which was universally adopted was established in the minds of the legislators. But there existed no fully formed single model, with established and consistent procedures and provisions for appeal, no uniform powers or jurisdiction, no pattern of composition.

While no fully formed model transcended subject boundaries and each tribunal was to that extent independently and separately conceived, there is evidence that one model was generally employed within cognate subject areas. This is most striking in the group of land rights tribunals. When the choice of implementing organ was being determined in relation to tithes, copyholds and inclosure, there was a precedent for the form, for although the reform of the inclosure procedure was the last in time of the three, it was the earliest to have a tradition of employing commissioners. The model in that instance was the private Inclosure Commissioners of the eighteenth century, and it was adopted in most respects when centralised inclosure was introduced,[21] being amended in that essential feature, namely central control. The procedures, powers, duties and appeal provisions relating to the commissioners for tithes, copyholds and inclosures are consistent. Since the qualifications and machinery of the Tithe Commissioners were well suited to the enfranchisement of copyholds, the provisions could be, and were, adopted in their entirety.

---

[21] For example the procedures of the central Inclosure Commissioners were largely based on those of commissioners under the old private Acts: see W. E. Tate, *The English Village Community and the Enclosure Movements* (London: Gollancz, 1967), pp. 113–15.

Principles, Place and Perception 283

Similarly, the draftsman of the inclosure bill, Walter Coulson,[22] barrister and follower of Jeremy Bentham, adopted and sometimes modified many of the clauses in the Copyhold and Tithe Acts.[23] It was recognised that the principle of the Tithe Act could apply to inclosures.[24] Ultimately the enfranchisement of copyhold was given to the Tithe Commissioners themselves under, *mutatis mutandis*, identical legislation, and in the case of inclosures it was overtly proposed in Parliament to use the earlier model of tithe commutation.[25]

Not only was there a willingness to adopt a model within a subject area, there was also a marked sharing of experience and good practice. For example where the Tithe Commissioners had had favourable experience of legally qualified Assistant Commissioners, the Inclosure Act 1845 accepted the need for legal advice and provided for access to a barrister to act as an assessor. Where certain controls on the remuneration of valuers had been introduced in the Inclosure Act, it was proposed that it should be incorporated in the Act introducing the compulsory enfranchisement of copyholds.[26] Similar modelling can be seen in relation to the land rights commissioners' oaths, the judicial oath of the Inclosure Commissioners of 1845 being identical to that of the Tithe Commissioners of 1836, and both being attenuated versions of the old and lengthy Inclosure Commissioners' oath under the private Acts. Similarly in the sphere of taxation, the Land Tax Commissioners, themselves founded on the justices of the peace, formed the basis of the Assessed Taxes Commissioners, the Land Tax Redemption Commissioners and the General Commissioners of Income Tax.[27] This pattern gave strength and unity to the class of tribunals, though at the expense of a degree of insularity.

---

[22] Hugh Mooney, 'Walter Coulson (1795–1860)', in *Oxford Dictionary of National Biography* (Oxford: Oxford University Press, 2004), vol. XIII. Coulson was a newspaper editor, barrister and parliamentary counsel. He was tutored by Jeremy Bentham and acted as his amanuensis.

[23] *Report, Copyholds Enfranchisement, 1837–8* at p. 192.

[24] *Minutes, Commons' Inclosure, 1844* q. 3431 *per* Thomas Woolley, land agent and Assistant Tithe Commissioner.

[25] *Parl. Deb.*, vol. LXXXII, ser. 3, col. 18, 4 July 1845 (HC), in the debate on the inclosure of commons and waste lands bill.

[26] *Minutes, Copyholds Bill, 1851* q. 1418.

[27] Indeed in Ireland, where no assessed taxes machinery existed on which to model that of income tax when it was extended to that country in 1853, a new institution had to be found. The solution lay in the Special Commissioners.

284 *Legal Foundations of Tribunals in 19th-Century England*

Furthermore, in the fiscal field the same tribunal was often given subsequent new functions. The existing commissioners responsible for administering the assessed taxes, for example, were given the task of administering the triple assessment of 1798.[28] Established practices within the field were adhered to, with, for example, William Pitt adopting the same policy of separate appeal commissioners in both his original income tax in 1799 and in the redemption of the land tax in the same year.

Why the fiscal tribunals were not adopted as an acknowledged model of tribunal form and function is problematic. They had a long history, with an established practice reaching back into the sixteenth century and before, and settled principles of jurisdiction, personnel, procedures and appeals suited to the efficient and inexpensive administration of statutory law by the time the new reforming legislation required new implementing bodies in the 1830s. Their parent branch of the executive, the Treasury, was one of the earliest, most highly developed and most active. Indeed, along with justice and defence, it formed part of the small nucleus of central government that was, in the 1830s, approaching any degree of strength and efficiency.[29] Furthermore, the popular impact of the army, navy and law courts was minimal compared to that of the Treasury, for the payment of taxes was something which affected a significant proportion of the population. It would have been natural for the organs of the Treasury to be looked at as models for similar emerging institutions, but in this period of immense growth and development of new dispute-resolution bodies, the institution which could be regarded as the prototype, the Commissioners of the Land Tax, was rarely if ever mentioned as an appropriate or useful model. For example, even in the context of inclosure, where the chief Commissioner of Woods, Forests, Land Revenues, Public Works and Buildings was taken from his department in the Treasury to act as presiding Inclosure Commissioner, the connection was not made and the fiscal boards and commissions were not drawn upon. Tax law and institutions seemed to be ignored by lawyers, government and people; their

---

[28] 38 Geo. III c.16 s. 43.
[29] See David Roberts, *Victorian Origins of the British Welfare State*, reprint of Yale University Press edition 1960 (Hamden, CT: Archon Books, 1969), pp. 12–22.

Principles, Place and Perception   285

impact was limited, being essentially inward looking and self-contained.

The reason why one overall model, the obvious being the fiscal model, was not employed was the importance attached to subject-specificity, a conclusion supported by the clear use of models within cognate subject areas. While the fundamental features of tribunals were found in established legal institutions, in their more refined details the form was determined by the subject-matter of the tribunal's work. The subject-matter of the tribunal determined the detail of its composition, its procedures and, most importantly, its jurisdiction. In the thousands of pages of reported official investigation, parliamentary debate, newspaper reporting and judicial opinion, the occasions on which a tribunal in a different subject area is considered as a possible model are exceptional. It is striking, therefore, when in 1832 the Commissioners of Real Property asked the bishops whether they approved of the establishment of commissioners along the lines of the Commissioners for the Redemption of the Land Tax to enfranchise copyhold land;[30] when in 1845 Viscount Palmerston commented that Colonel Sibthorp had difficulty in accepting the temporary nature of Inclosure Commissioners in the light of the ostensibly temporary income tax with its associated commissioners;[31] when in debating the constitution of the government board to conduct a preliminary examination of railway bills in 1846 there was an allusion to the Tithe Commissioners and the Inclosure Commissioners and their practice of bringing the parties together to discuss their differences, in the nature of an arbitration;[32] and where one witness in 1882 wanted to take features from the new Divorce Court and model a Railway Court on it.[33] In the 1840s when a specialist lay railway tribunal was being extensively discussed by numerous Select Committees, questioners proposing

---

[30] 'Third Report of the Commissioners of Real Property', *HCPP* (1831–2) (484) xxiii 321 at p. 406. The bishops in general approved of the task being undertaken by a body of commissioners. The Bishop of Carlisle favoured the model of the private Inclosure Commissioners, as they resembled arbitrators, *ibid.*, at p. 417.

[31] *Parl. Deb.*, vol. LXXXII, ser. 3, col. 41, 4 July 1845 (HC), in the debate on the inclosure of commons and waste lands bill.

[32] 'Minutes of Evidence before the Select Committee of the House of Lords (on Railways)', *HCPP* (1846) (489) xiii 217 q. 45 *per* George Webster, parliamentary agent.

[33] *Minutes, Railways (Rates and Fares), 1882* q. 3919 *per* Ralph Littler QC.

286 *Legal Foundations of Tribunals in 19th-Century England*

the creation of such a body never suggested a comparable body to the witnesses to aid their understanding of the concept. Witnesses were expected to consider the idea de novo.

General subject-specificity was itself limited. Even in the closely related and analogous branches of the restructuring of land rights there was some hesitation expressed in adopting a model tribunal. Tithe and inclosure, for example, were in some ways regarded as very different, with common proceedings sometimes being inappropriate.[34] This would suggest there was very precise subject-specificity at work. Often subject-specificity was impossible, as with the railway tribunals. They could clearly be distinguished from the land rights and fiscal tribunals, which were long established in both form and subject-matter of operation. Railways were quite new and unknown, with no cognate institutions or systems to draw upon, since in scale and nature they were fundamentally different from canals. It is unsurprising that it was in this field that there was the most intense debate as to the most appropriate form of tribunal to undertake the implementation of the legislation. The various influences and foundations, the thought processes of creation and function of a new institution are most clearly seen in relation to the railway tribunals. Indeed, it is the Railway Commission of 1873, with its composition of experts in practical railway management and lawyers, and its inexpensive, swift, though relatively formalised procedures, which a retrospective analysis shows was in essence the model for the modern statutory tribunal in its composition, procedures, appeal provisions and inherent flexibility.[35] It, rather than its successor of only fifteen years later, can claim this honour, for the latter had already diverged from the model. Although the Railway Commissioners of 1873 exhibited clear legal foundations and were among the more judicial type of tribunal, their successors in 1888, by a change in personnel and in legal status, became a full court of law. Its foundations in established institutions of the regular legal system were so numerous and were adopted in such a pure form that the tribunal closely resembled a regular court of law. Its unambiguous modelling on judicial lines was reflected in its legal

---

[34] *Minutes, Commons' Inclosure, 1844* q. 28 *per* Revd Richard Jones, Tithe Commissioner.
[35] See R. E. Wraith and P. G. Hutchesson, *Administrative Tribunals* (London: George Allen and Unwin, 1973), p. 27.

Principles, Place and Perception 287

standing, and it was granted the status of a court of record by its parent Act.

The railway tribunal reveals a paradox. It began as unequivocally a department of the executive, an extension of the old Railway Committee of the Board of Trade, sifting railway projects and reporting on them to save time and expense at the private bill committee stage, though largely modelled on the practices of arbitration and often referred to in the 1840s as a Court of Arbitration. Ultimately, however, it was one of the most judicial of statutory tribunals. As such it is the prime example of the judicialisation of a tribunal. Its tendency to model itself on the regular courts, notably in relation to legal representation, procedures and appeal provisions, was clear even before it was made a court of record. Sir Frederick Peel, the first chairman of the commission, contemplated allowing the same right of appeal from his decisions as parties would have under the Judicature Acts from the decisions of a division of the High Court.[36] Furthermore, under the 1888 Act the registrar to the Railway and Canal Commission dealt with interlocutory matters, and the rules provided that if a person was affected by the decision of the registrar in a matter of law, he could appeal to the ex officio commissioner.[37] This right of appeal was that which existed from the decisions of all masters of the Supreme Court to the judge, the functions of the registrar to the Railway and Canal Commission being analogous to those of a master of the High Court. This strong judicial flavour of the railway tribunals was a cause of complaint by many potential litigants.

With legal influences falling short of a legal model, and only a degree of modelling within subject areas, what emerges is that tribunals were individually conceived, self-contained and were, to a large extent, ad hoc. While common aims gave rise to a similarity in their fundamental features, one formula for personnel and composition, one common code of procedure and one system of appeals were all impossible. This was because the requirements of individual tribunals were very different, and the details of the tribunals were dictated by the subject-matter each tribunal was formed to address. It was this need for subject-specificity that led

---

[36] *Minutes, Railways (Rates and Fares), 1882* q. 3073.
[37] Rule 53 of the Railway and Canal Commission Rules.

288 *Legal Foundations of Tribunals in 19th-Century England*

inevitably to each tribunal being essentially sui generis and lacking underlying principles, and it explains the considerable challenge faced when attempts were made in the following century both to classify the growing numbers of tribunals and ultimately to reform them. Other factors nurtured this approach. Ideologically, politically and administratively the culture was one of pragmatism and reaction. Views on centralisation and state intervention were inconsistent. Utilitarians such as Edwin Chadwick demanded the reform of unacceptable evils through state intervention, but shared the profound contemporary distrust of central government and so limited the powers of the new bodies strictly to the objective of the legislation. The Benthamites in general favoured a policy of reacting to events and legislating as it became necessary in view of a new factual situation, eschewing prescription and principle to ensure flexibility.[38] Furthermore, though historians may disagree as to the origins and nature of the social policy developments of the mid-nineteenth century, it is undeniable that the state's response to the problems posed by industrialisation were pragmatic and ad hoc in nature. The resulting growth of the English administrative state was complex, piecemeal and full of contradictions and ambiguities. It was not a tidy, systematic, coherent process.[39] As a result the structures of government were predisposed to the creation of ad hoc bodies, being themselves characterised by a lack of co-ordination and a pragmatic, individualistic, piecemeal and reactive development.[40] The various agencies even of central government were already somewhat chaotic and unsystematic. The statutory tribunals, with their integral dispute-resolution function, which were to develop into the modern organ, were integral to this system, and suffered from the same defects. So close was the connection between the new tribunals and the executive government that their nature was determined from their inception and they shared an unsystematic and reactive basis with the agencies of the government themselves.

---

[38] M. W. Thomas, 'The Origins of Administrative Centralisation' (1950) 3 *Current Legal Problems* 214 at 222.

[39] Roberts, *Victorian Origins*, p. 326.

[40] See generally Emmeline W. Cohen, *The Growth of the British Civil Service 1780–1939* (London: Frank Cass & Co. Ltd, 1965); Roberts, *Victorian Origins*, pp. 320 ff.; Derek Fraser, *The Evolution of the British Welfare State* (London: Macmillan, 1973), p. 108.

Principles, Place and Perception 289

Inconsistent government structures and political ideologies resulted in an inconsistent growth of implementing administrative and dispute-resolution organs, from which the modern statutory tribunal developed. Economic and social forces gave rise to the growth of the administrative state, and their ideological context and the available infrastructure determined its form and that, ultimately, of the modern statutory tribunals. The political context from which they sprang and the fundamental English dislike of a centralised administrative state, undermined an approach to social reform based on principle and permitted a piecemeal solution. It was this subject-specific, pragmatic, circumscribed and strictly focused constitution of the commissions achieving a compromise between the necessity for state intervention and an almost universal distrust of it that gave the tribunals their particular character. The public antipathy towards permanent commissions and the government capitulation even when temporary commissions were harmful,[41] contributed to this legislative policy of ad hoc creation of tribunals and the proliferation of individual and highly subject-specific bodies. The concept of a subject-specific body exercising administrative functions with strictly circumscribed and subordinate adjudicatory powers, created by central government though maintaining some distance from it through semi-independent personnel and local input, clearly reflected and encompassed contemporary attitudes and priorities.

An examination of the jurisdiction, procedures and composition of the statutory tribunals of the nineteenth century shows that they were individually conceived to suit the subject-matter of the legislation they sought to implement, but drew for their fundamental characteristics on the features and processes of established institutions of the English legal system in its widest sense. With influences and no model, guided by pragmatism rather than theory, the Victorians produced the concept of the bespoke tribunal. It drew on the features of the regular courts, of arbitration, of boards, of government departments, of juries and of parliamentary private bill committees. It selected those features and techniques of established legal or quasi-legal institutions that

---

[41] In the case of the Railway and Canal Commission of 1873 its temporary nature made some companies desist from using it, hoping that a paucity of work would make it amenable to abolition.

290 *Legal Foundations of Tribunals in 19th-Century England*

suited its purpose and invented new processes if none existed. The legislature had no hesitation in separating and re-amalgamating these features to form a new body. The outcome was a tribunal exhibiting a number of various features and influences, each determined by the tribunal's own administrative task and its practical requirements of speed, cheapness, impartiality, expertise and safeguards, and together forming a new body. There was no single model, a fact that was both a strength and a weakness.

It was a pragmatic strength. It was not hindered in any way by an archaic form, and in that sense reflected the Victorian desire to be rid of legal anachronisms and to reform the law by giving it the freedom to adapt to new conditions in the light of new values, and it was designed for its purpose. The archetypal bespoke tribunal was the Railway Commission. It sprang from the very particular and novel circumstance of railway expansion and could not, as such, call on any model. It was constructed de novo. Indeed, when the Lord Chancellor imposed essentially non-judicial duties on the regular courts by the Railway and Canal Traffic Act 1854, he felt justified in so doing by the novel state of affairs which the railways had created.[42] His approach was one of pragmatism. As he observed, '[t]he railway companies were perfectly satisfied with that provision; and if there was a prospect of its affording to both persons concerned a practical relief in an inexpensive and effectual mode, why should it not be attempted?'[43] It is undeniable that tribunals did not develop systematically, but the modern orthodox view that they showed no underlying principle can be challenged. While later certain features of tribunals were condemned as anomalous, their reason invariably lay in the subject-matter of the legislation they were originally created to implement. The secrecy of tax hearings provides just one example.

A short-term pragmatic strength, however, was a long-term weakness. Because the adjudicatory function of the tribunals was integral to administrative functions, and because administrative functions were strictly subject-specific, the growth in adjudicative powers by organs of central government grew virtually unnoticed. It is not that a clear understanding of the duties of the regular

---

[42] *Parl. Deb.*, vol. CXXXIII, ser. 3, col. 1138, 30 May 1854 (HL) *per* Lord Cranworth LC.
[43] *Ibid.*

Principles, Place and Perception 291

courts was lacking, nor that adjudication by non-judicial bodies was creeping in unseen, for when adjudicatory functions were proposed for a non-judicial body, it was done so openly and unambiguously. But in each case the development occurred in isolation, and as a result not only did extra-judicial dispute-resolution as a whole grow, but the problems that arose in one tribunal were rarely addressed in another. The complete segregation of each tribunal, its self-contained existence, stifled the benefits of experience and experiment. And finally, the ad hoc approach was to create significant problems of classification in the future.

Though the actual institutions of the regular or specialist courts, justices of the peace, arbitration and the private bill committees were rejected for wholesale adoption to implement the new legislation, it becomes clear that the new tribunals were not original in the sense of entirely newly conceived methods of dispute-resolution, but rather a conglomeration of elements drawn from existing legal traditions, practices and institutions set in an administrative context. Though features that were identified as being so characteristic of the new tribunals of the nineteenth century were in fact commonplace in English legal and public life, they were nevertheless novel institutions. It is apparent from the views expressed in Parliament, in the newspapers and through other media that the statutory tribunals were regarded as singular and unfamiliar institutions, to be welcomed, feared or distrusted, depending primarily on the vested interests or the ideologies of those in question. The legislators were aware even in the most judicial of the tribunals that they were being experimental. The Railway Commission of 1873 was clearly regarded as novel in its composition, procedures and jurisdiction, since the Joint Select Committee that recommended it acknowledged that there was no existing institution that met the requirements.[44] It 'started as an experiment in the direction of a lay tribunal'.[45]

The originality of the new tribunals lay in the very recasting of established judicial notions. The challenges facing the legal process demanded innovation and creation. Each field of activity raised its own particular problems, and the best solution was an ad

---

[44] *Report, Railway Amalgamation, 1872* p. 49.
[45] *Minutes, Railways (Rates and Fares), 1882* q. 1490 *per* Edward Pember QC.

292 Legal Foundations of Tribunals in 19th-Century England

hoc tribunal, especially created in each sphere of activity to meet the particular requirements the subject-matter demanded. In the search for a solution to the machinery of implementing legislation, the Victorians showed a remarkable open-mindedness and a readiness to be innovative, to improvise and to compromise. They were not afraid of looking outside the regular courts to create the appropriate body, but equally they were not constrained by established forms and techniques if they found they were potentially useful. The Victorian legislators were prepared to deconstruct established legal institutions, to extract the features of each that they regarded as serving their purpose, namely the administration of a regime of law, and to reconstruct them in the form of a statutory tribunal, and this deconstruction and reconstruction is revealed by the identification of their several legal foundations. Their originality, creativity and indeed their genius, lay in their willingness to split the bundles of powers and duties which constituted the various legal institutions and which had traditionally been regarded as capable of existence only in an indivisible entity and their selectivity once this had been achieved. They tried a number of different combinations: lay expert adjudicators, lay expert assessors, professional judges, part-time judges, legal experts who were not judges, costs, no costs, appeals, no appeals, limited appeals, legal representation by barristers, solicitors, parliamentary agents, or none at all, combinations of formal adjudication with arbitration or conciliation. They were prepared to experiment and to keep trying new combinations of features as many times as was necessary. They had a clear end in view, and used all the dispute-resolution tools at their disposal.

Ultimately the legislators selected the consensual approach from arbitration, while rejecting the private appointment of arbitrators; they chose certain modes of appeal to the regular courts and rejected others; they followed the fundamental features of legal processes while discarding its attendant formality; they were selective, though not always successfully, with the use of the prerogative writs; they adopted certain inquisitorial processes from private bill committees, and they chose specialists to adjudicate while ensuring access to expert legal advice. They were also prepared to enhance some features and depress others. So, for example, arbitration was often given prominence and adopted in its entirety though for a limited purpose within the new

Principles, Place and Perception

framework. Differences as to tithes that hindered the making of the parochial agreement could be referred to arbitration,[46] and when discussing the valuation of copyhold rights Sir Robert Peel suggested that it could be undertaken by a combination of private arbitrators and central commissioners.[47] Indeed under the Copyhold Act 1841 arbitration was used to resolve boundary disputes,[48] while leaving other dispute-resolution to the commissioners,[49] and yet others to valuers.[50] This imaginative and confident use of diverse established institutions or elements of them was characteristic of the age. The outcome was a hybrid organ, a combination of these features afresh in a new body fit for its very specialised purpose.

Such creativity in deconstruction and reconstruction was not unknown, and is one of the great achievements of the Victorian legislators. For example it occurred strikingly in the development of company law, when in 1837 the bundle of characteristics incident to incorporation was broken up and the ability to sue and be sued in a quasi-corporate name was extracted and given to unincorporated bodies.[51] Equally the corporate incident of limited liability was removed from the bundle of corporate incidents and the remainder granted to companies incorporated by registration under statute in 1844.[52] The trust, another major legal institution, was following a similar process of pragmatic adaptation to suit the changing needs of the Victorian age.[53] The radical rethinking of the whole of the legal system culminating in the Judicature Acts was another perspective on this confident innovation in legal and quasi-legal thinking. While not original in its component parts, the tribunal was as a whole both innovative and creative. In this, as in its pragmatism, it was entirely Victorian. It was an expression of the robust confidence the Victorians had in their ability to address the considerable challenges their age presented. Their tools were sufficient for the purpose, and they had the confidence and creativity to exploit them and recast them to achieve their aims.

---

[46] 6 & 7 Will. IV c. 71 s. 24.   [47] *Report, Copyholds Enfranchisement, 1837–8.*
[48] 4 & 5 Vict. c. 35 s. 22.   [49] *Ibid.*, s. 39.   [50] *Ibid.*, s. 29.
[51] Chartered Companies Act 1837, 7 Will. IV & 1 Vict. c. 73
[52] Joint Stock Companies Act 1844, 7 & 8 Vict. c. 110.
[53] See generally C. Stebbings, *The Private Trustee in Victorian England*, Studies in English Legal History (Cambridge: Cambridge University Press, 2002).

294 *Legal Foundations of Tribunals in 19th-Century England*

The statutory tribunal was innovative in another way. While the giving of dual administrative and judicial functions was known to the legal system, notably in the form of the justices of the peace, their integration as seen in the statutory tribunals was quite new. There, the judicial function was part of the overall administrative function, and for most of the nineteenth century was subsumed by it. Indeed, the challenge of the twentieth century would be to distinguish the judicial functions from the administrative, and not only at the extremes, a task which would not be without difficulty precisely because the tribunal had been conceived to achieve a contrary integration of function. The integration of function would cause considerable tensions in the next century: the overall administrative function of the tribunals inevitably brought with it an intimacy with the executive, which sat uncomfortably with the notion of independent adjudication, a feature which was essential to any judicial body.

This individualistic pragmatic approach was characteristic of Victorian thinking. It is seen even in the rationalisation of the legal system culminating in the Judicature Acts 1873 and 1875,[54] where the legal system as a whole was perceived as individualistic and empirical. For while it was recognised that the old system of local, communal and special courts was unsystematic and unsatisfactory, the dominant view was that the country should provide courts adapted to try all classes of cases in the way most suitable to the nature of the questions presented to it. This was maintained as an ideal, though a strictly circumscribed one, within the formal legal system itself, but it does go some way towards explaining why the subject-led, ad hoc, development of tribunals occurred. Furthermore, there was no real attempt to curb the proliferation of tribunals with dispute-resolution powers because their nature as individualistic administrative bodies with judicial foundations resulted in them having difficulty in establishing a place within the legal system so as to be subject to its rationalisation. So while there is no doubt that the judicial system had a powerful influence on the foundations on which the new tribunals' composition, process and personnel were laid, it did not, and could not, go to the extent of counteracting their ad hoc nature. The inability of the tribunals as a genre to secure a formal place in the machinery

---

[54] 36 & 37 Vict. c. 66; 38 & 39 Vict. c. 77.

Principles, Place and Perception 295

of justice in the nineteenth century became an almost insurmountable difficulty in legal classification in the twentieth. They could not form themselves into a recognisable class or group. This is possible only in retrospect, now that modern rationalisation has achieved if not a sound classification, at least some collective identity through the creation of the Council on Tribunals and the beginning of a policy of uniformity. Contemporary perception, even of the tribunals by themselves, was not of a legal genre, as evidenced by the circumscribed discussion of tribunals when arriving at an implementing body. At most it was a genre of administration, the derided 'government by commission'. Despite common underlying principles, there was no system of tribunals, and each tribunal, or subject-specific group of tribunals, developed in theoretical and practical isolation.

This evolutionary isolation suggested that the statutory tribunals would have no place or status in the regular legal system. The outcome of nearly a thousand years of development was a broadly hierarchical legal system composed of superior courts dominated by the Courts of the Common Law and the Court of Chancery, supported by a pragmatic and amorphous mass of inferior dispute-resolution bodies of limited jurisdiction. The latter included the justices of the peace, local courts, specialised courts and arbitration, and within the class the boundaries of central justice, administration and private settlement were often unclear. They shared the common features of lay adjudicators who possessed administrative functions as well as judicial ones, and whose jurisdictions were restricted by the size or subject-matter of the claim or the geographical locality. These common features were too generalised to permit any meaningful classification, but the inclusive nature of their personnel and the limitation of their powers resulted in a clear perception of inferiority to the central courts in Westminster, staffed by expert judges and possessing wide jurisdiction. Yet the breadth of the inferior dispute-resolution culture was such that the statutory tribunals could theoretically claim a place within it.

The jurisdiction of the statutory tribunals of the nineteenth century was, without exception, primarily administrative, in the sense that these bodies were created in order to carry out executive functions: it has been seen that in the case of the fiscal tribunals it was to manage, assess and collect the tax, and in the case of the

296 *Legal Foundations of Tribunals in 19th-Century England*

land rights tribunals it was to effect the restructuring of land rights and ascertain the appropriate monetary compensation. The railway tribunals were created to regulate the new system of transport, and the Assessment Committees' function was to arrive at a correct valuation list for the purposes of the poor rate. Their declared purpose was to implement specific legislation in a limited and specialist field of executive action, usually for an inherently limited time. There was no suggestion of a jurisdiction beyond the terms of a tribunal's parent Act, and any discretion was strictly circumscribed by the legislation that laid down precisely what the tribunal was to do. The primarily administrative nature of the jurisdiction of the new tribunals had a far-reaching effect. It coloured every aspect of their nature: their constitution, composition, procedures. The highly specialised jurisdiction necessitated specialist commissioners rather than lawyers; the integration of the adjudicatory with the administrative demanded informal or unusual procedures;[55] the administrative nature of the work meant there was no clear lis inter partes in the adjudication process, and, finally, the nature of the work inevitably gave rise to some connection between the tribunal and a government department. Other than these fundamental characteristics, each tribunal exhibited other, specific, features that were not found in any court of law. For example, the authority of the Railway Commissioners of 1873 to allow companies to explain an alleged violation of the law before formal proceedings began[56] was, in the view of informed commentators, a clear indication that the commission was not originally intended to be a court, for such a power would be an improper one for a court to exercise.[57] Furthermore the practice of advertising in the *Railway Times* calling for alleged contraventions of the Act for the commission to inquire into was not appropriate to a court of law, and their power to hold an inquiry and to enter buildings for the purposes of inspection if they thought fit were not powers generally given to a court of law. The income tax tribunals' practice of hearing cases in camera was unusual in a court of law, and the inquisitorial nature of the land

---

[55] One of the most notable is the hearing of tax appeals by the General Commissioners in camera.

[56] 36 & 37 Vict. c. 48 s. 7.

[57] In practice the commission did not use this power.

Principles, Place and Perception

rights tribunals sat uneasily with a predominantly adversarial legal system.

Nevertheless, it has been seen that each tribunal undeniably possessed to a greater or lesser extent an adjudicatory jurisdiction supported by procedures and powers that were judicial in character. Their power to 'hear and determine' disputes between parties so as to affect the rights of individuals was the fundamental characteristic of a court of law. It was the ancient command of the commission of oyer and terminer, giving to judges and certain others authority to inquire, hear and determine treasons, felonies and misdemeanours, and as such it carried unambiguously judicial connotations. Yet it was the foundation of the adjudicatory jurisdiction of all statutory tribunals in the nineteenth century. Neither were those features exhibited by the statutory tribunals and characteristic of them, notably a limited jurisdiction and a lay membership, peculiar to them, since the legal system was familiar with regular courts whose jurisdiction was subject to monetary, geographical or subject restrictions, and lay justices of the peace and commercial assessors were well known in the regular legal system. Through the possession of judicial qualities, and undaunted by the possession of special features, some individual tribunals, denied a place as a genre, sought the status of a court of law and, as such, a place in the regular legal system.

In any demand for judicial status, the statutory tribunals had a clear point of reference. If the juridical nature of tribunals was still poorly understood, the nature of courts of law in the regular legal system and the judicial process itself were clearly defined and known. The traditional formal status of a court of record had been defined by Sir Edward Coke as a court of justice having the power to hold pleas according to the course of the Common Law and whose proceedings were recorded on parchment,[58] and Sir William Blackstone had stressed the recording of the proceedings on parchment 'for a perpetual memorial and testimony',[59] and the

---

[58] Sir Edward Coke, *The First Part of the Institutes of the Laws of England*, 1628 edition, 2 vols. (New York: Garland Publishing Inc., 1979), vol. II, p. 260a; see generally Sir William Holdsworth, *A History of English Law*, 17 vols. (London: Methuen & Co. Ltd, 1924), vol. V, pp. 157–61.

[59] Sir William Blackstone, *Commentaries on the Laws of England*, 1783 edition printed for W. Strahan and T. Cadell, London and D. Prince, Oxford, 4 vols. (New York: Garland Publishing Inc., 1978), vol. III, p. 24.

298 *Legal Foundations of Tribunals in 19th-Century England*

indisputable nature of these records. Holt CJ regarded the power to fine and imprison as the distinguishing character of a court of record.[60] Similarly, judicial definitions of courts proceeding according to the Common Law emphasised the employment of writs, pleadings and jury trial, the conducting of proceedings in Latin, the formality of the judgments and the legal learning of the judges. More generally, by the time the new bodies were appearing to implement new regimes of statute law, it was accepted that a court of law possessed certain indicia. Over and above the fundamental right in an independent judge to adjudicate and to do so in a judicial manner, they included a number of characteristics generally concerning the conduct of the proceedings. The right of a court of law to summon witnesses and administer oaths to the persons it called to appear before it for examination had long been regarded as one of its essential characteristics.[61] Evidence was given upon oath in the regular courts because the law 'presumeth that no man will forswear himself for any worldly thing'.[62] Similarly the rights to demand the production of documents and to award penalties were characteristics of a court of law, and indeed the latter was one of the defining characteristics of a court of record. The right to appeal to a higher body, and the application of the prerogative writs of certiorari, mandamus and prohibition were equally regarded as characteristics of courts of law.

What was clear was that with very few exceptions, those being the Commissioners of Sewers[63] and the Railway and Canal Commission of 1888, statutory tribunals were not courts of record. It had been held that that lack of status precluded their use of the writ of error. Neither were they courts proceeding according to the Common Law, for it had been established that that lack of status precluded their use of the writ of false judgment.[64] The statutory tribunals constituted new jurisdictions established by Act of

---

[60] *Groenvelt v. Burwell* (1700) 1 Comyns 76 at 79; see too 1 Ld Raym 454 at 467; Carth 491 at 494; 1 Salk 396, and *Griesley's Case* (1588) 8 Co Rep 38a.

[61] *R. v. Assessment Committee of St Mary Abbotts Kensington* [1891] 1 QB 378 at 382.

[62] Coke, *First Institutes*, vol. II, p. 295a.

[63] See Sir John Comyns, *A Digest of the Laws of England*, 4th edition, 6 vols. (Dublin: Lake, White, 1793), vol. VI, tit. Sewers D; Edith G. Henderson, *Foundations of English Administrative Law* (Cambridge, MA: Harvard University Press, 1963), Chapter 3.

[64] *Groenvelt v. Burwell* (1697) 1 Ld Raym 454 at 469.

Principles, Place and Perception 299

Parliament to administer specialist rules in a limited sphere laid down in the parent Act, and to do so by methods very different from those of the Common Law courts. It has been seen that they enjoyed a large degree of informality, proceeded in English, eschewed written pleadings and jury trial, and were staffed by men ignorant of the rules of law.

The question still remained whether the new tribunals could be regarded as courts at all. It has been seen that in some ways they did not fit the usual profile of a court, not being presided over by a legally qualified person and having flexible procedures. On the other hand in exercising their powers of hearing and determining disputes, and undoubtedly affecting the rights of individuals by their determinations, the tribunals all possessed at least one of these accepted indicia of courts embodied in the original legislation of their creation. In their adjudicatory capacity the fiscal, land rights and railway tribunals had the power to summon witnesses and to hear evidence on oath, and indeed this was regarded as particularly valuable in the fiscal field. Some tribunals had the power to award penalties. The fiscal commissioners, for example, had wide powers of imposing penalties and could levy large fines and multiply the duty payable in case of various defaults. The Railway Commissioners of 1873 even had the power to punish for contempt just as an inferior court of record could.[65] All the tribunals had some aspect of their determinations which could be appealed against to the regular courts, though the extent of that right varied in degree and chronology,[66] and all commissioners were under a duty to act in a judicial manner as exemplified by their oath which bound them to act judicially, in the sense of fairly, impartially, honestly and to the best of their ability, when carrying out their duties. Indeed, it was this duty to conduct their proceedings with this judicial standard of conduct that ultimately constituted a sufficient analogy with the regular courts so as to allow the application of the prerogative writs. Judged by the possession of these various indicia, the fiscal, land rights and railway tribunals, and indeed many others, were judicial in character. The Assessment Committees were the least judicial in

---

[65] 36 & 37 Vict. c. 48 s. 25.
[66] See *National Telephone Company* v. *HM Postmaster General* [1913] AC 546 at 562.

300 *Legal Foundations of Tribunals in 19th-Century England*

that they did not possess the power to summon witnesses, administer oaths or compel the production of documents, but did have the power to hear and determine objections to the valuation list.[67]

The debate as to the judicial nature – or lack of it – of the administrative tribunals possessing adjudicatory jurisdiction was coterminous with their creation, but only gathered pace in the latter years of the nineteenth century when it came to be judicially considered. There were a number of reasons why this was so. When tribunals were first created they were invariably regarded as administrative bodies. Any ambiguity caused by their judicial powers rarely had time to make itself felt in any practical way, since most of the tribunals were temporary in nature: the income tax tribunals administered a temporary tax, albeit one renewed annually, but even then there was a period from 1816 to 1842 when the income tax was suspended. The Tithe Commissioners were in existence only for as long as was necessary to commute all tithes in the country, Copyhold Commissioners were there to enfranchise all copyholds, and the duties of the Inclosure Commissioners were similarly inherently limited. Even the Railway Commissioners of 1873 were to endure only five years and be renewable annually thereafter. By the mid-Victorian period tribunals had become both more numerous and more established. Many became permanent; some, like the fiscal tribunals, in practice, and others, like the land tribunals and ultimately the Railway and Canal Commissioners, in law. Their growing establishment caused them to become increasingly confident, and this was compounded as they grew in experience. In this sense the tribunals became established independently of their creating statutes. Feeling secure in their constitution, many tribunals sought a place in the regular legal system by asserting their status as courts of law, their aim being to claim one or more of the various privileges incident to traditional courts of law. The courts thereby addressed their juridical nature. The juxtaposition of the tribunals' judicial characteristics with their administrative function created an ambiguous jurisdictional relationship that was discerned by the courts with difficulty and dissent.

---

[67] *R. v. Assessment Committee of St Mary Abbotts, Kensington* [1891] 1 QB 378.

Principles, Place and Perception 301

An early exploration of the juridical nature of a tribunal in this way concerned a local marine board established under the Merchant Shipping Act 1854 and in this instance investigating a master's drunkenness. The court had to decide whether false swearing before such a tribunal constituted perjury,[68] a feature characteristic of judicial proceedings. The tribunal possessed the usual essential qualities of such bodies – a primarily, though not exclusively, specialist lay membership; an informal procedure; the power to examine witnesses on oath and to inflict penalties on the parties. One of its statutory duties was to investigate charges such as the one in this case,[69] to do so with express power to administer an oath or a declaration and with the power to impose a penalty in the form of a cancellation or suspension of the certificate of a master or mate.[70] 'The effect', concluded counsel for the Crown, was that 'the investigation is a judicial proceeding in every sense of the term'.[71] Cockburn CJ agreed and held that an indictment for perjury would lie. 'The inquiry was before a tribunal invested with judicial powers, and enabled to inquire on oath, and pass a sentence affecting the status of the person accused.'[72] To find otherwise, he said, would be 'highly inconvenient'. It would 'be fatal to the person accused, if he were not to have protection against witnesses who came to swear falsely'.[73] The decision to accord this tribunal an incident of judicial status was, therefore, based on public policy considerations: the jurisdiction of the tribunal, the taking of evidence under oath and the penalty it could inflict combined to introduce such a measure of compulsion and a potential severity of outcome that some protection of the accused was in the public interest. For this purpose, the proceedings were judicial in character.

The juridical nature of certain tribunals was repeatedly tested through claims of immunity from action for defamatory statements made in the course of proceedings before them. Judge, counsel and witness were all immune from actions for defamation in respect of the statements they made during judicial

---

[68] *R. v. Tomlinson* (1866) LR 1 CCR 49.   [69] 17 & 18 Vict. c. 104 s. 241.
[70] The power conferred on the Board of Trade to do so under *ibid.*, s. 242 was vested in the tribunal by the Merchant Shipping Act Amendment Act 1862, 25 & 26 Vict. c. 63 s. 23.
[71] *R. v. Tomlinson* (1866) LR 1 CCR 49 at 53.   [72] *Ibid.*, at 53–4.
[73] *Ibid.*, at 54.

302　*Legal Foundations of Tribunals in 19th-Century England*

proceedings[74] for reasons of public policy. The privilege was first extended beyond the traditional courts of justice to a military court of inquiry, set up to investigate and report on certain disciplinary offences in the army.[75] This body had no power to administer oaths, nor to compel attendance of non-military witnesses, nor could an action for perjury lie against a witness, and one of the Queen's regulations for the army expressly said that it was not to be considered as a judicial body. Its constitution thus seemed clearly to deny judicial status. Despite the absence of the usual judicial incidents, the proceedings were held to be privileged, obviously not because of the possession of judicial characteristics, but the fact that 'though not a court of record, nor a court of law, nor coming within the ordinary definition of a court of justice, [it was] nevertheless a court duly and legally constituted and recognized in the articles of war and many Acts of Parliament'.[76] This decision led other bodies to claim the privilege, and in 1881 it was again extended, this time to proceedings before a Select Committee of the House of Commons.[77] The committee, inquiring into the suspension of the plaintiff's schoolmaster's certificate, was of a more evidently judicial character than a military court of inquiry, because it had the power to summon persons and examine them on oath. When the defendant was sued for slander in respect of his evidence, he maintained his statements were privileged, and the court found in his favour. The rules of privilege would apply if the tribunal were a court of justice. The court agreed that it might be a hardship to allow defamatory statements to be made by affording them the protection of privilege, but that it was an instance where the interest of the individual was 'subordinated by the higher interest [of] public justice'.[78] As a matter of public policy, witnesses who were compelled to give evidence and to do so on oath, whether before a court of justice or no, should be free to give their evidence without fear of the consequences.

There was a limit, however, beyond which the courts would not go. While military courts of inquiry and Select Committees of the House of Commons were clearly not courts of justice in the strict

[74]　*Seaman* v. *Netherclift* (1876) 2 CPD 53.
[75]　*Dawkins* v. *Lord Rokeby* (1873) 8 LR QB 255.
[76]　*Ibid.*, at 266 *per* Kelly CB.　　[77]　*Goffin* v. *Donnelly* (1881) 6 QBD 307.
[78]　*Ibid.*, at 308 *per* Field J.

Principles, Place and Perception 303

and traditional sense of the term, they were judicial inquiries and as such analogous to them. In 1892 the courts refused to extend the privilege to a defamatory statement made in the course of the London County Council's proceedings to grant music and dancing licences,[79] in a case that explored the nature of courts of law in more depth. The granting of licences had been a function originally carried out by justices of the peace, and transferred to the council by the Local Government Act 1888,[80] the Act of its constitution. It had been held the previous year that the exercise even by justices of a licensing power was an administrative and not a judicial act,[81] and it would shortly be confirmed that in exercising such powers they did not constitute a court of summary jurisdiction and that a grant or refusal of a licence by them was not an 'order' within the Summary Jurisdiction Act 1879.[82] Licensing justices were not a court giving judgment in litigation in the traditional sense and there was no lis between the parties. The granting of a licence involved no controversy inter partes unless the applicant was regarded as one part and the entire public the other.[83] It was an administrative, not a judicial act. When the Local Government Act 1888 transferred those functions to the council, it expressly distinguished between judicial and administrative business, and provided that licensing was a purely administrative matter. Indeed, there was nothing in the Act to suggest the council was a court, and the Act provided that the council was not to be concerned with any judicial matter. In terms of function, therefore, the granting of licences was not a judicial act. In terms of process, the only judicial element was the requirement for the exercise of reason and judgment.

The court held that the privilege was not to be extended to the council in the granting of licences. In Lord Esher's view no analogy could be drawn with a court because of the administrative nature of the business the council was addressing. For him the determinant was the nature of the work, and the granting of licences was an administrative act.[84] Under Fry LJ's closer

---

[79] *Royal Aquarium and Summer and Winter Garden Society Ltd* v. *Parkinson* [1892] 1 QB 431.
[80] 51 & 52 Vict. c. 41. [81] *Sharp* v. *Wakefield* [1891] AC 173.
[82] *Boulter* v. *Kent Justices* [1897] AC 556. [83] *Ibid.*, at 569 *per* Lord Herschell.
[84] *Royal Aquarium and Summer and Winter Garden Society Ltd* v. *Parkinson* [1892] 1 QB 431 at 443.

304 *Legal Foundations of Tribunals in 19th-Century England*

analysis, the essential point was that to attract the privilege of immunity the body should be a court in law, a definition which included, but was wider than, a court of justice. The duties did not, therefore, need to be judicial; they could be consultative, legislative or investigative. On the other hand, courts had certain characteristics, notably a specially qualified president and a fixed and dignified procedure, which were generally absent from bodies that were not courts and were absent in the case before him.[85] In granting licences the council was not constituted a court in law. It was under no duty to hear and determine, nor was it bound by any fixed procedures, and the granting of licences was not judicial business. He based his reasoning on an integrated constitutional and functional test. It was clear that acting judicially – in the sense of acting fairly and impartially as a judge should do in conducting judicial business, and as tribunals were obliged to do by their oath – did not of itself mean that the body in question was a court of justice.[86] As Lopes LJ observed,

The word 'judicial' has two meanings. It may refer to the discharge of duties exercisable by a judge or by justices in court, or to administrative duties which need not be performed in court, but in respect of which it is necessary to bring a judicial mind – that is, a mind to determine what is fair and just in respect of the matters under consideration.[87]

Exercising a judicial function did not make the body in question a court in law. It was the overall purpose that the judicial function served that was critical. If that function was an administrative one, the body was not a court in law.

In 1891 an Assessment Committee – one of the bodies mentioned by Fry LJ in the *Royal Aquarium* case as being under a duty to act in a judicial manner and yet not having the status of a court – had claimed the right to determine its own procedure, a privilege inherent in judicial bodies. In the leading case of *R. v. Assessment Committee of St Mary Abbotts, Kensington* in 1891,[88] a householder objected to the valuation list, as he was entitled to do under the governing legislation. He did not appear before the committee himself, but appointed an agent to conduct the case on his behalf. The committee refused to hear him on the grounds that he was not a barrister or solicitor, nor a member of the household of the householder. The juridical nature of the committee was

[85] *Ibid.*, at 448. [86] *Ibid.*, at 447. [87] *Ibid.*, at 452. [88] [1891] 1 QB 378.

Principles, Place and Perception

central to the resolution of the correctness of its decision not to hear the ratepayer's agent, because it was argued that in hearing and determining objections to the valuation list the committee was acting judicially, and that this gave them the power to regulate their own proceedings and to impose reasonable limits on the appearance of objectors through agents if it so wished. The committee compared itself to magistrates acting in summary proceedings and in Quarter Sessions,[89] both settled as courts of justice with all the privileges that brought with it. Counsel argued against this saying that the committee was not a judicial tribunal, and supported this contention by stating that it possessed none of the principal characteristics of judicial bodies: it had no power to summon witnesses, nor to compel the production of documents, nor to administer an oath.

At first instance Pollock B said that it was true that the committee had the statutory duty to hear and determine objections, 'but in other respects there is no fair analogy to the position of a court'.[90] Accordingly, it did not have any inherent right to determine its own procedures. Having so decided, he could only look to the governing statute to determine the rights of audience. The statutory provision that gave the committee its power to hear and determine objections to the valuation lists made it clear that their power was to hear the objection, not necessarily the objector.[91] The section contained no limitation on how the committee was to do this. He felt that if the objector was unable through absence, illness or incompetence to conduct his appeal, and he found someone to represent him, the committee could not decline to hear him. Charles J too could find nothing in the statute to show that the objector had to appear in person, and so his Common Law right to appoint an agent was unaffected.[92]

When the Assessment Committee appealed, the Court of Appeal upheld the decision and observed that the committee was merely

a certain number of persons, in this case selected vestrymen, to whom power has been given by statute to hear objections, which have been made

---

[89] *Collier v. Hicks* (1831) 2 B & Ad 663; *Ex parte Evans* (1846) 9 QB 279.
[90] *R. v. Assessment Committee of St Mary Abbotts, Kensington* [1891] 1 QB 378 at 380.
[91] Union Assessment Committee Act 1862, 25 & 26 V ct. c. 103 s. 19.
[92] On the authority of *Re Schmidt's Trade-Mark* (1887) 35 Ch D 162 at 172–3.

306 Legal Foundations of Tribunals in 19th-Century England

to the valuation list, and to decide whether such objections are well founded. I do not think that they are a court or a tribunal exercising judicial functions in the legal acceptation of the terms.[93]

Though tribunals resembled justices of the peace in many ways, and certainly in a lack of expertise, those created under the Union Assessment Committee Act 1862 were not judicial bodies, at least for the purposes of regulating their own procedures.[94] It was again clear that a duty to act judicially did not suffice to endow a body with the formal status of a court. Both the *St Mary Abbotts* and the *Royal Aquarium* cases confirmed that possessing a judicial function did not alone constitute that body a court in law. The overall purpose was the decisive factor, and if that was administrative in nature, then the body itself was administrative and not judicial. Any judicial function merely served the principal function and left its overall nature unaffected.

By the close of the nineteenth century, the courts had confirmed the statutory tribunals as juridically administrative and not judicial bodies, thus placing them outside the regular judicial system and denying them the privileges of courts of law. Where the primary function of a tribunal was administrative, its jurisdiction was administrative and its nature was administrative. They placed them, rather, as institutions of government. They did so on the basis of the nature of the jurisdiction of the tribunals, on their purpose. Their judicial function taken in isolation was indistinguishable from that of regular courts of law: it was to hear and determine disputes in a judicial manner. In exercising their adjudicatory functions, it has been seen that the tribunals were

---

[93] *R. v. Assessment Committee of St Mary Abbotts, Kensington* [1891] 1 QB 378 at 382 *per* Lord Esher MR.

[94] Nor according to Fry LJ's obiter dictum in *Royal Aquarium and Summer and Winter Garden Society Ltd* v. *Parkinson* [1892] 1 QB 431 at 447. The successors of the Assessment Committees were the local valuation courts which, despite their name, were held in *Society of Medical Officers of Health* v. *Hope* [1960] AC 551 not to be courts of law. See too *Shell Company of Australia Ltd* v. *Federal Commissioner of Taxation* [1931] AC 275 at 296–7; *AG* v. *BBC* [1980] 3 All ER 161 where a valuation court was held not a court of law so as to allow the jurisdiction of the Divisional Court to apply to it in relation to contempt. See generally N. A. D. Willshire, 'Valuation for Rates: The Existing and the Proposed New Local Tribunals', in R. S. W. Pollard (ed.), *Administrative Tribunals at Work: A Symposium* (London: Stevens & Sons, 1950), pp. 79–101; W. A. Robson, *Justice and Administrative Law*, 2nd edition (London: Stevens & Sons, 1947), pp. 1–13.

Principles, Place and Perception   307

behaving as courts of law did. They were deciding questions of fact and law; they were finding facts and arriving at their determinations by applying objectively legal rules and principles. Furthermore, they possessed many of the procedures adopted by the courts of law. And yet despite this, they were denied the status of courts. The judges in the nineteenth century were challenged by the classification of tribunals, a challenge compounded by the lack of any satisfactory definition of a court. They adopted different approaches to the problem, broadly either the functional or the indicia tests, but neither proved definitive. The presence or absence of key indicia was a popular approach, but it depended too greatly on externals and, relying on process rather than principle, avoided the fundamental issue of jurisdiction. It was also of limited value in that the possession of judicial functions, even if those functions were not exclusive, more often than not demanded possession of certain, generally procedural, features of courts of law such as the power to summon witnesses and to hear evidence on oath. As those flowed from the possession of the judicial function, which tribunals undeniably had, this analysis did not reveal the nature of the tribunal itself. The functional analysis was more valuable, looking to the functions the tribunal performed, but it was too limited in that if the tribunals' power of adjudication were taken in isolation, they were identical with those of the courts: both had the jurisdiction to hear and determine disputes. Superficially, in both functions and features, tribunals and courts were very similar. To discern the distinction between them, a more profound analysis was required.

The distinction lay in the context of the adjudictory powers. It has been seen that the doctrine of the separation of the constitutional functions of government, refined and developed after 1688, put legislation in the hands of Parliament, administration in the hands of the executive, and adjudication – being the state's power to decide controversies between its subjects, or itself and its subjects – into the hands of the courts. The administration of justice was the purpose of the courts, their principal and proper function in which they were to be supreme. Exercising the judicial power of the state, they constituted the judicial system. Their adjudicatory power was, therefore, an end in itself. They were created to exercise it, and in so doing were exercising the judicial power of the state. This was so even where the court in question

308 *Legal Foundations of Tribunals in 19th-Century England*

was one of limited jurisdiction, whether the limitation was geographical, monetary or of subject-matter. Those limitations left the purpose of the court unchanged: resolution of the dispute before it was its sole object.

Tribunals, on the other hand, were created not to adjudicate, but, as was clear from their parent Acts, to implement certain defined and limited statutory regimes. The legislation invariably stated in unambiguous terms that the function of the new tribunals was exclusively to execute and implement the legislative regime of the parent Act. In this they were so highly specialised that they were not a tribunal enforcing the judicial power of the state to protect the rights of the subjects, but instruments of the executive to implement the law. That was the function of government, not of the judiciary. The tribunals, therefore, existed to exercise the executive power of the state, and so their purpose was administrative, not judicial. As undoubtedly there would be disputes arising within the implementation of the law, as part of the administrative process[95] they were given the power to adjudicate. The adjudicatory power of tribunals was limited to resolving every dispute arising within the context and as a result of the administrative process of raising income tax, commuting tithes or whatever the object of the legislation was. The adjudicatory powers they possessed were given to them by Parliament in that context, and not in their own right. They were not given to such organs as stand-alone powers, but as a necessary and inevitable part of their administrative function.[96] As an administrative body with merely incidental judicial powers they were not exercising the judicial power of the state, so could not be courts and so could not be constituents of the judicial system. The administrative nature of the dominant object of the tribunal was fatal to the designation of the tribunal as a court in law, as a court of judicature. Its judicial functions were subsumed by the overall administrative purpose of the tribunal. Tribunals did not administer justice, they administered a specific regime of statutory

---

[95] Confirmed by the commissioners' duty to 'allow' the central administrative decision after the adjudication, as in allowing the assessment, the tithe commutation or the inclosure.

[96] See Henry Parris, *Government and the Railways in Nineteenth Century Britain* (London: Routledge and Kegan Paul, 1965), p. 210.

Principles, Place and Perception 309

law, and their purpose was decisive in determining their juridical nature.

The limitation of the jurisdiction of the tribunals to the implementation of a specific statutory regime was, therefore, the defining characteristic of the new tribunals. Their special features of specialised personnel, informal procedures, a close relationship with a government department and the absence of a discernible lis even when exercising adjudicatory jurisdiction all flowed from their primary function as organs to implement a statutory regime in an administrative field. It was ultimately this, their purpose, which determined their juridical nature and denied them the status of courts. It did not, however, determine their juridical nature in a positive sense. The problem was that neither outcome – court or organ of the executive – was satisfactory, because the new tribunals embodied a genuine mixture of functions. There was a clear, and necessary, duality of function. That duality was as evident in the context of the statutory tribunals as it was in the exercise of the varying functions of the justices of the peace. The latter, however, were not interdependent; they had judicial and administrative functions, but in entirely distinct fields and the distinction was thus easier to maintain. They had an extensive criminal jurisdiction, for example, and responsibility for licensing. Tribunals, on the other hand, were given judicial functions solely to achieve their administrative ones. It was this integration of the functions that made them more susceptible to confusion, and the overall juridical nature more difficult to discern. A more subtle classification was necessary, which did not exist. The ad hoc nature of the tribunals, created as and when each new legislative regime was introduced and with a resulting lack of uniformity in procedures and composition, militated against the establishment of tribunals as a genre of dispute-resolution. Their strong individuality, their lack of cohesion as a class, and their overriding executive function negated the influence of their judicial foundations and denied them a place in their own right in the regular legal system, especially the highly structured organisation created by the Judicature Acts. At most, they were regarded as bodies existing on the periphery of that class of inferior dispute-resolution bodies, while the justices of the peace, juries and the various local or specialised courts were unequivocally perceived by the law and the public as elements of the formal legal

310 *Legal Foundations of Tribunals in 19th-Century England*

system. Indeed while those bodies received the considered attention of the Judicature Commissioners in the debates prior to the recasting of the formal legal system by the Judicature Acts, the statutory tribunals played no part in the debate, even on an individual basis.

Furthermore, on those relatively rare occasions when the legislature intended a tribunal to be a court in the full sense of the term, it said so in the legislation in clear terms. The Railway Commission, for example, was stated to be a court of record in the legislation of 1888. A greater formality and exactitude was required of organs of the formal legal system,[97] and the lack of procedural and substantial uniformity that was characteristic of the tribunals was unacceptable within the Victorian formal legal system. When examining the powers of the County Courts in 1872, the Judicature Commissioners observed that 'it cannot be doubted that these inconsistencies call for alteration and correction'.[98] Their toleration among tribunals, the absence of any call for uniformity during the nineteenth century, confirms the exclusion of the tribunals from the legal system. They stood alongside that system, part of a wider, unstructured and less coherent judicial environment which, in order to ensure the individual was protected against bad justice, was subject to the supervision of the courts of law. Any judicial power or function was subsumed by the dominant administrative purpose. The supremacy of the functional test was confirmed some 100 years later, when Lord Scarman defined a court of law as 'a body established by law to exercise, either generally or subject to defined limits, the judicial power of the state' as opposed to a body created for a legislative or administrative purpose. '[T]he judicial power of the state', he continued, 'exercised through judges appointed by the state remains an independent, and recognisably separate, function of government. Unless a body exercising judicial functions can be demonstrated to be part of this judicial system, it is not, in my judgment, a court in law.'[99] On balance, in terms not only of their functions, but also of their procedures and

---

[97] See for example *Re Dent Tithe Commutation* (1845) 8 QB 43.
[98] 'Second Report of the Judicature Commissioners', *HCPP* (1872) (631) xx 217 at p. 228.
[99] *AG* v. *BBC* [1980] 3 All ER 161 at 181–2.

Principles, Place and Perception 311

constitutions, most of the new statutory tribunals could not be classified as courts.

Nevertheless, the judiciary was not prepared to disown the tribunals entirely. It has been seen that the great variety of procedures and personnel within bodies which undoubtedly had a judicial function, albeit a subordinate one, gave rise to a need for the formal supervision of the courts to ensure an acceptable quality of judicial activity. The judges saw it as their duty to supervise the tribunals' decision-making to keep them within the proper jurisdictional bounds Parliament had set, and were vigilant in doing so,[100] despite tribunals' efforts to exclude them, and did so through the prerogative writs. Since such jurisdictional control was regarded as 'a necessary and inseparable incident to all tribunals of limited jurisdiction',[101] it constituted an affirmation of the essential qualities required of an adjudicatory body which claimed a place in the legal system of the country and thereby accorded the tribunals a position, albeit a subordinate and tenuous one, within the legal system and judicial hierarchy. It was, however, more an affirmation of the dominance of the superior courts over all decision-making than a revealing feature of the nature of the tribunals. And the fact that the application of certiorari could be achieved only through extensive adaptation of the rules of the Common Law suggests that statutory tribunals were not by their essential nature a part of the regular legal system. Furthermore, it was clear by the nineteenth century that there existed certain precepts of judicial conduct and personal quality to which persons and bodies exercising judicial or quasi-judicial functions should adhere. Justices of the peace were obliged to abide by these rules and the regular courts similarly demanded them of the new tribunals in the nineteenth century. This required adherence to the norms of judicial behaviour was more revealing. It affirmed their place as dispute-resolution bodies effecting the rights of individuals, in other words as bodies, at least in part, of a judicial character. In the following century, the application of judicial review to the statutory tribunals would be seen as a clear

[100] See for example *Mayor and Aldermen of City of London* v. *Cox* (1867) LR 2 HL 239 at 295 *per* Lord Westbury.
[101] *R.* v. *Shoreditch Assessment Committee* [1910] 2 KB 859 at 880 *per* Farwell LJ.

312 Legal Foundations of Tribunals in 19th-Century England

judicialisation of such bodies, a strengthening of their place in the legal system.[102]

The statutory provisions for appeal to the courts of the established legal hierarchy, which were equally the result of the highly individualistic nature of the tribunals, like judicial review gave the tribunals a place in the formal legal system at their very inception. The judges were concerned to ensure the integrity of the law and to prevent erroneous decisions of law remaining uncorrected. The public wanted to ensure that if they were dissatisfied with a decision of the lay tribunal, the ultimate safeguard of recourse to a higher body would lie. The right of appeal created a recognised bond between the unstructured and somewhat random statutory tribunals and the stability of the formal legal system. This relationship in turn created a place for the institutions possessing such powers. The place was, again however, an inferior one. They confirmed the tribunals as subordinate adjudicatory bodies whose decisions were subject to an overriding power of amendment and, therefore, restraint. Its further significance, however, was somewhat limited. The power was essentially technical, to redress mistakes of law and thereby to ensure consistency and correctness of the administration of the law in the interests of both the law itself and the protection of the subject. It accorded a formal or conventional place in the judicial hierarchy, rather than a substantial one. The statutory powers of appeal from tribunals to the superior courts are accordingly revealing as to the legislative perception of the place of the former in the legal system. Where rights of appeal were non-existent, as with the Land Tax Commissioners and the General Commissioners of Income Tax for example, the tribunals were a self-contained organism lying almost entirely outside the formal legal system.[103] The place that resulted from formal and legitimate judicial supervision, however, fell short of a real status within the legal system. It was not a place in the sense of a true integration in the regular legal system, though the subjection of tribunals to judicial review involved some degree of such integration as it recognised tribunals as

---

[102] Jackson, *Machinery of Justice*, pp. 174–7; Carol Harlow and Richard Rawlings, *Law and Administration*, 2nd edition (London: Butterworths, 1997), pp. 391–422, 456–94.

[103] There was, of course, the possibility of a special case at Common Law, and of judicial review.

Principles, Place and Perception   313

bodies sufficiently judicial in nature to require control by the regular courts. It was a relationship with the courts based on power that set tribunals in their wider juridical context. Structurally, functionally and procedurally the tribunals were set apart from the regular courts and different standards pertained.

The individualistic nature of tribunal development and the judicial ambivalence towards them was accurately reflected by popular perceptions as to their nature. This was most evidently illustrated by the absence of any consistency in contemporary nomenclature. The fiscal tribunals were often called courts and courts of appeal, and the Railway Commission of 1873 was variously called a Board of Control, a Board of Appeal, a Court of Conciliation, a tribunal, a court, a Court of Equity and a Court of Arbitration. It was in 1882 referred to in a Select Committee as 'a popular tribunal', one of the first times there was any attempt to give a generic term to a dispute-resolution body which was neither court nor government department.[104] Some tribunal members saw themselves as courts, and one of the Tithe Commissioners referred to the land rights tribunals as 'judicial' tribunals.[105] In practice the distinction between an administrative body and a judicial one was not always apparent, and indeed not relevant, to the parties involved.[106]

However, in line with the intention of the legislators and the findings of the judges, the general consensus was that the tribunals were not organs of the administration of justice in any other than in a peripheral sense. Informed commentators adhered to this view. The tribunals in the nineteenth century were more firmly regarded as a branch of government, and the mixture of functions was more easily accepted than it was to be later. Both legally and popularly, the new statutory tribunals were part of the administration. Ralph Littler QC saw the Railway Commission of 1873 as a non-legal tribunal, at best a hybrid, whose decisions were not precedents in courts of law.[107] Sir Frederick Peel, its first chairman, said he preferred to refer to it as a mixed tribunal with a strong legal element in it rather than a lay tribunal.[108] William Price MP saw

---

[104] *Minutes, Railways (Rates and Fares), 1882* q. 1366 *per* J. H. Balfour Browne.
[105] *Minutes, Commons' Inclosure, 1844* q. 23 *per* Revd Richard Jones.
[106] Roberts, *Victorian Origins*, pp. 113–14.
[107] *Minutes, Railways (Rates and Fares), 1882* q. 3994.
[108] *Ibid.*, at q. 2969.

314 *Legal Foundations of Tribunals in 19th-Century England*

it as a purely administrative body. He drew a clear distinction, based on jurisdiction, between its functions and those of a judicial body:

The functions of the judges, of course, are purely judicial; they are simply interpreters of the law, and their function is a very simple one; they have not to concern themselves about what is right or what is expedient, but what the law provides. I take it that the body, such as we are talking of, must have rather wider discretionary powers; they would have to deal with matters that are not strictly matters of law in all cases, but questions of expediency, and I do not think that judges can deal with questions of expediency. I think that there is a great distinction between the two.[109]

Similarly the orthodox legal theorists of the late nineteenth century, notably A. V. Dicey, considered tribunals and the law they administered to be outside the regular legal system.

The general appreciation that the new statutory bodies were quite different in purpose and nature from courts of law was apparent from the lack of agreement as to the form and procedures of Tribunals of Commerce in the 1870s, even after forty years of experience of statutory bodies administering reforming legislation. Superficially the problems which that institution sought to address were similar to those which gave rise to the new statutory bodies, namely the need for summary procedures and a specialist bench in a subject-specific field of dispute-resolution, but there was a clear distinction between the two concepts. The Tribunal of Commerce was to be a court while statutory bodies were organs of the executive – the two were fundamentally different, and experience in one sphere counted for nothing in the other. Despite the Victorian aptitude for critical deconstruction of established institutions, and long experience of the mixing of administrative and judicial functions, the boundaries between judicial and administrative bodies once classified as such were not breached.

The individualistic nature of the tribunals meant that their effectiveness in implementing the regulatory legislation and resolving the disputes which inevitably arose in that process, was determined according to each specific tribunal and not as a genre of dispute-resolution. The annual reports of the various bodies of commissioners chart the progress and success or otherwise of their

[109] *Minutes, Railway Amalgamation, 1872* q. 3871.

Principles, Place and Perception 315

activities. The government assessed success on the basis of the objective of the legislation – the number of tithe commutations, copyhold enfranchisements or inclosures achieved; the amount of revenue raised; the number of complaints of breaches of the railway regulations for example. The tribunals themselves tended to assess their success not only on the extent to which they were able to achieve their objectives in implementing the legislation, but also on the number of appeals from their determinations. The public assessed the success of the tribunals on the basis of the treatment each individual received when he appeared before them. In practice the various perceptions were linked. It had always been evident that the tribunals would achieve the intentions of the legislature only if they proved accessible to the public and provided a satisfactory service. If the composition of a tribunal was in fact and in perception made up of high-quality men, independent, knowledgeable in their field, with access to expert legal advice, then, if in conjunction with expeditious, inexpensive and sensitive procedures, there was a tribunal considerably superior to a court of law and universally welcomed.[110] Such tribunals constituted a real service to the public and were not, as has been said of the regular courts, 'an adjunct of the honours system'.[111] Assessment Committees were generally regarded as satisfactory, and certainly considered themselves as good providers of an efficient public service. They congratulated themselves on their 'unwearied exertions in investigating every objection brought before them', and 'their earnest desire to carry into operation [a] just and necessary Act of Parliament'.[112] They devoted considerable time to their duties, meeting on average once a week for six months of the year, each meeting lasting six or seven hours.[113] But it was the Tithe Commission that lived up to this ideal. It was regarded as an outstanding success by all parties and accordingly achieved its objective of almost universal tithe commutation. Appeals from the commissioners' administrative and

---

[110] This view was expressed by Walter Coulson: *Minutes, Commons' Inclosure, 1844* q. 5759.

[111] Brian Abel-Smith and Robert Stevens, *Lawyers and the Courts* (London: Heinemann, 1967), p. 98.

[112] 'Abstracts of Reports from Guardians of Unions as to Proceedings of Assessment Committees under the Union Assessment Committee Act 1862 s. 12', *HCPP* (1863) (540) lii 867 at p. 881, referring to the Bellingham Union.

[113] *Ibid.*, pp. 867 ff.

316 *Legal Foundations of Tribunals in 19th-Century England*

judicial decisions were very few,[114] and parties appearing before them almost invariably felt they had been treated with courteous and expert efficiency. The popular acceptance of this centralising legislation was due in a large part to their conduct and calibre. In 1852 they reported that they had 'the satisfaction of feeling that the business of commutation has been conducted with general tranquillity and harmony'.[115] The parties almost invariably felt the same. One Assistant Commissioner having completed the commutation of tithes in the parish of Swavesey in Cambridgeshire observed in his formal report that the parties 'seem to be very well satisfied', and that they had all achieved a 'good bargain'.[116] A Newbury attorney ascribed their success to their nature as 'an independent authority, and ... a kind of arbitration'.[117] They conducted their work in that spirit, with delicacy and expertise, following a policy of minimal interference and promoting voluntary commutation wherever possible.[118] The flexibility of their procedures, their expert knowledge of the subject-matter, their sensitivity to local interests and a process which strove for agreement all contributed to the effective implementation of the legislation. While not receiving the same degree of praise, the Copyhold and Inclosure Commissioners were ultimately effective in the implementation of their own parent legislation and resolving the contentious issues that arose in its course.

This approach resembled the highest quality of arbitration, and was a process that was not popularly perceived as litigation at all. To settle a dispute in this way was, according to one witness before the Joint Select Committee on Railway Companies Amalgamations in 1872, to do so 'without any law whatever

---

[114] 'Report of the Tithe Commissioners for England and Wales for 1840', *HCPP* (1840) (215) xxviii 139 at p. 141.

[115] 'Report of the Tithe Commissioners for England and Wales for 1852', *HCPP* (1852) (1447) xviii 597.

[116] TNA:PRO IR 18/13644 (1838).

[117] *Minutes, Commons' Inclosure, 1844* q. 4282 *per* Robert Graham, attorney and solicitor. See too 'Minutes of Evidence taken before the Select Committee of the House of Lords (on Railways)', *HCPP* (1846) (489) xiii 217 at q. 45 which shows how both the Inclosure and the Tithe Commissioners were perceived as being arbitral in character.

[118] 'Report of the Tithe Commissioners for England and Wales for 1837', *HCPP* (1837–8) (127) xxviii 33 at p. 34.

Principles, Place and Perception   317

between the companies and the public'.[119] The popular perception of arbitration reflected the reality, namely that it was a process that was entirely private. When Lord Fawn suggested to Lizzie Eustace that the matter of the Eustace diamonds be settled by arbitration, she exclaimed: 'Arbitration? That means going to law?' to which Lord Fawn replied, 'No, dearest, – that means not going to law.'[120] Even when the Railway and Canal Commission had become a full court of record in 1888, it maintained that it acted in a less technical and more pragmatic spirit than the regular courts of law, though this was a perception not readily shared by the parties who used it. The common view was that the original ideal of the commission as an organ combining judicial skills with railway expertise to resolve disputes between traders and railway companies in a discursive and informal way had been lost.

Those tribunals which were perceived as conducting their hearings in a heavy-handed way were invariably condemned as 'star chambers', an appellation given to almost every tribunal in the nineteenth century at some point in its existence. General Commissioners of Income Tax were particularly susceptible. To many appellants it seems they amounted, in composition and spirit, to a Police Court, 'a perfect Star Chamber'. The inadvertent introduction of criminal connotations through the common appointment of justices of the peace and commissioners, a feeling that the commissioners did not listen to the appellants, and a strong resentment to being interrogated by men who were their fellows and equals, and in some instances commercial rivals, did not make for effective adjudication. Despite his acknowledgment that the Railway Commissioners were not a legal tribunal, Ralph Littler QC, a barrister with an extensive railway practice, said that when he appeared before them he felt he was 'in the presence of the correctional police'.[121] This perception of arbitrariness was exacerbated by the tribunals' power to exercise their discretion and make policy decisions based on expediency,[122] even though they had to adhere closely to the legislation. When the Railway

---

[119] *Minutes, Railway Amalgamation, 1872* q. 1744 *per* John Hutchinson, mayor of Halifax.

[120] Anthony Trollope, *The Eustace Diamonds* (1873), Chapter 10.

[121] *Minutes, Railways (Rates and Fares), 1882* q. 3672.

[122] *Minutes, Railway Amalgamation, 1872* q. 3871 *per* William Price, Member of Parliament for Gloucester and chairman of the Midland Railway Company.

318 *Legal Foundations of Tribunals in 19th-Century England*

Commission of 1873 was first proposed it was called despotic, 'a sort of Railway Star Chamber, capable of interpreting its own jurisdiction on the most elastic principles'.[123] Those members of the public voicing such opinions, however, were the users of the tribunals. Most, though not all, were people of some degree of wealth and influence whose own interests were affected, perhaps adversely, by the existence of the regulatory legislation and its machinery of implementation. Their opinions should, therefore, be noted in that context.

The effectiveness of the tribunals was also undermined by a common perception that the tribunals did not always – through choice, ignorance or bias – resolve disputes according to the strict letter of the law, a perception strengthened by the lay composition of the tribunals and their informal procedures. Swift and informal procedures were felt to lead to a 'slap-dash decision', 'the benevolent despot under the palm tree who will go and give his decision straight away'.[124] The railway companies accused the Railway Commissioners of not always preserving 'a strictly judicial attitude', and having 'a mission to protect traders against railway companies',[125] though again such views were coloured by a perceived threat of regulation to their own interests. There was a consensus among barristers practising before the Railway Commissioners that litigants often felt the commissioners would do something for them, even if they did not have a strict legal right to a remedy, that they might be prepared, in other words, to bend the rules.[126] The railway companies certainly thought the statutory tribunals were providing an inferior kind of justice to the courts of law, and vociferously demanded nothing less than the highest legal tribunals to address railway disputes.[127] They regarded the provision of a specialist tribunal rather than the

---

[123] *Parl. Deb.*, vol. CCXV, ser. 3, col. 368, 31 March 1873 (HC) *per* Christopher Denison, a railway director. See too *Minutes, Railway Amalgamation, 1872* qq. 7768–82 *per* Thomas Farrer.

[124] 'Minutes of Evidence taken before the Departmental Committee appointed by the Board of Trade to consider the Law relating to Railway Agreements and Amalgamations', *HCPP* (1911) (5927) xxix Pt 2, 51 at q. 18,918 *per* W. Guy Granet, general manager of the Midland Railway Company.

[125] *Ibid.*, at q. 13,785 *per* Claude Andrews, solicitor to the London and North Western Railway Company.

[126] *Minutes, Railways (Rates and Fares), 1882* q. 1661 *per* Richard Webster QC.

[127] *Parl. Deb.*, vol. CCCXII, ser. 3, col. 141, 14 March 1887 (HL) *per* Lord Brabourne.

Principles, Place and Perception 319

better-qualified and more prestigious judges of the courts of law as undermining their status and dignity and, possibly, their own commercial interests. It was suggested that this combination of judicial functions with a perceived policy of the protection of traders was one reason why the commission was reconstituted in 1888 with a judge at its head.[128] Though paradoxically this led to popular criticisms of the 'rough justice' meted out by the tribunals, there was a commonplace expectation of a kind of justice which was acknowledged to work for or against a party, and often led a party to embark on litigation even when he felt he might not have a strong case. The General Commissioners of Income Tax were criticised as an appellate body, primarily because of their lack of technical knowledge and of legal procedures. They were regarded, with some justification, as providing 'rough justice'.[129] One businessman condemned the commissioners as 'no good at all'. 'They do little,' he continued, 'they know little. Hardly one of them could open a set of books in double entry.'[130] These perceptions as to the quality of adjudication by the tribunals illustrate the real tensions which existed when the desire was for informality and specialist expertise without undermining the quality of the justice dispensed.

A potent obstacle to the effectiveness of the tribunals was their perception as inaccessible. While in the nineteenth century the concept of access to justice was not articulated as a discrete concept as it is today, that did not mean it was perceived as either unimportant or undesirable. The general consensus among legislators and reformers, with a few notable exceptions,[131] was that the main elements of accessibility – namely simplicity, cheapness, speed and proximity – were the right of any litigant in the English courts of law. The truth underlying the common saying that

---

[128] 'Minutes of Evidence taken before the Departmental Committee appointed by the Board of Trade to consider the Law relating to Railway Agreements and Amalgamations', *HCPP* (1911) (5927) xxix Pt 2, 51 at q. 13,785 *per* Claude Andrews.

[129] *Minutes, Income Tax, 1919* qq. 4903, 4905, 4912.

[130] See 'Appendix to the Report of the Departmental Committee on Income Tax, with Minutes of Evidence', *HCPP* (1905) (2576) xliv 245 q. 1978 *per* Arthur Chamberlain JP, putting forward the views of the Birmingham Chamber of Commerce on income tax.

[131] Not by all, however. See the speeches of Solicitor General Tindal in 1828 and Lord Lyndhurst in 1833: *Parl. Deb.*, vol. VIII, new series, col. 852, 29 February 1828 (HC); *ibid.*, vol. XVIII, ser. 3, col. 869, 17 June 1833 (HL).

320   *Legal Foundations of Tribunals in 19th-Century England*

justice through the courts was open to all, rich and poor, like the Ritz Hotel, was increasingly uncomfortable. Rather less altruistic was the undeniable need to streamline the procedures of the courts in order to keep pace with the growth in legal business engendered by immense commercial and technological development.

The regular courts of law were almost invariably perceived as inaccessible, and by the beginning of the nineteenth century the widespread public fear of litigation in the regular courts was accepted by most legislators and reformers to be unacceptable. Contemporary notions of access to justice were revealed in the debates on the establishment of local courts for the hearing of small civil cases that ultimately produced the system of County Courts. They were essentially that adjudication should be swift, cheap and effective. Throughout the nineteenth century there was a continuous programme of legislation simplifying the procedures in the superior Common Law courts by introducing uniform methods of starting actions, reducing or removing technicalities and fictions,[132] and in the creation of the County Courts in 1846.[133] These early reforms were not radical and were limited in their effectiveness, but constituted a considerable step towards the facilitation of the administration of justice in the regular courts.[134] Ultimately the demand for an accessible system of regular courts resulted in the complete recasting of the system of superior courts and a uniform code of procedure outlined in the schedule to the Supreme Court of Judicature Act 1873, the latter going far towards achieving the desired 'cheapness, simplicity, and uniformity of procedure'.[135] The context of the new tribunals was thus one of an increased awareness and appreciation of the desirability of access to justice. Though not the prime reason for

---

[132] Uniformity of Process Act 1832, 2 & 3 Will. IV c. 39, provided for a uniform writ of summons; Real Property Limitation Act 1833, 3 & 4 Will. IV c. 27. See too the Common Law Procedure Acts 1852 (15 & 16 Vict. c. 76) and 1854 (17 & 18 Vict. c. 125). For the simplification of pleading, see Sir William Holdsworth, 'The New Rules of Pleading of the Hilary Term, 1834' (1923) 1 *Cambridge Law Journal* 261.

[133] Recovery of Small Debts Act 1846, 9 & 10 Vict. c. 95.

[134] See generally Baron Bowen, 'Progress in the Administration of Justice during the Victorian Period', in *Select Essays in Anglo-American Legal History*, 3 vols. (Boston: Little, Brown & Co., 1907), vol. I, pp. 516–57.

[135] *Parl. Deb.*, vol. CCXIV, ser. 3, col. 337, 13 February 1873 (HL) *per* the Lord Chancellor.

Principles, Place and Perception 321

their creation, the desirability of accessible dispute-resolution bodies was the unstated premise in the creation of the new statutory tribunals. The tribunals were created in order to implement new, and often controversial, government policy. Pragmatic politicians and legislators recognised that policy could be implemented only if those members of the public with a perceived or real grievance were afforded an accessible and effective process for its resolution. Thus the constitution and procedures of the new tribunals reflected an acknowledged need for accessibility.

The fiscal tribunals were generally easily accessible, particularly the General Commissioners of Income Tax. Whatever the criticisms as to their quality, they were undoubtedly cheap, local and entirely informal. The Commissioners of the Inland Revenue fulsomely praised the appellate adjudication of local commissioners in relation to the assessed taxes. 'These Courts of Appeal', they wrote in 1862,

in truth fulfil every condition which has been considered desirable for the administration of justice, both in theory and in practice They afford to every person charged the means, without any expense, of having his objections, whether of law or of fact, inquired into by Judges whose high character and position, and whose entire independence of the Executive Government, place them beyond all suspicion of partiality. With the assistance of their Clerk and of the Surveyor, who are both necessarily conversant with the statutes and judicial decisions bearing upon the subject, they are not likely to fail in correctly interpreting the law; but in order that no security may be wanting on that point, whether for the subject or the Crown, the party dissatisfied with the decision of the Commissioners has the power of stating a case to be laid before two Barons of the Exchequer by our Board, and by this means the decision of the highest legal authorities of the kingdom is obtained with so little trouble or expense as to be scarcely worth mentioning . . . The attendance of the Surveyor at Appeals is a very important part of his duty. He is, in fact, the advocate for the Revenue, but a fair and candid advocate, and one whose assistance is very acceptable to the Commissioners.[136]

The Special Commissioners were not perceived as accessible in the sense that their existence and function were not widely publicised, a problem compounded by the almost total intellectual inaccessibility of tax legislation. Most taxpayers had little idea of their role in hearing appeals against assessments to tax, and as a

---

[136] 'Sixth Report of the Commissioners of Her Majesty's Inland Revenue on the Inland Revenue 1862', *HCPP* (1862) (3047) xxvii 327 at pp. 346–7.

322 Legal Foundations of Tribunals in 19th-Century England

tribunal the Special Commissioners were little used.[137] Once taxpayers were able to avail themselves of them, however, they were generally regarded as a very successful tribunal. The Royal Commission on Income Tax reported in 1920 that they had 'received no adverse criticism of any kind' as to the performance by the Special Commissioners of their duties, and that the tribunal 'evidently possess in a marked degree the confidence of the public'. One member of the Association of British Chambers of Commerce remarked that after many years of experience his opinion of the Special Commissioners was 'that they are absolutely excellent and fair in every particular'.[138]

Though the procedures of the new tribunals were designed so as to ensure swift and cheap justice, this policy of deliberate accessibility was not always successful. The unequal financial resources available to the parties distorted the accessibility of the various railway tribunals. The wealthy and powerful railway companies dominated both the commission and any subsequent appeals to the regular courts. Their considerable resources allowed them not only to approach any appeal with impunity, but permitted a determination to push the legal process as far as it would go, and to do so with the best legal advice money could buy. Individual traders with limited resources and fearing further litigation as much as the expense of appearing before the commission itself, could not compete. To them the commission was essentially inaccessible, or at least accessible only on the terms set by the railway companies. It was not just the expense that was prohibitive for the private trader. The ensuing intimidation of individuals by the railway companies was perceived as a real deterrent to making a complaint.[139] Furthermore, the railway companies had their own officials fully versed in the facts and figures of railway management, and could call upon solicitors well versed in the law. An individual trader might have none of these, if only because he would not have time aside from the single-handed conduct of his own business. In practice, therefore, the

---

[137] *Minutes, Income and Property Tax, 1852* qq. 1119, 1553 *per* Edward Cane, Special Commissioner. See too *ibid.*, qq. 1564–5 *per* Edward Hyde, surveyor, and q. 806 *per* Edward Welsh, surveyor.

[138] *Minutes, Income Tax, 1919* q. 8185 *per* H. Lakin-Smith.

[139] *Minutes, Railways*, 1881 qq. 933–5 *per* Professor William Hunter; qq. 4479–81 *per* Alfred Hickman, ironmaster.

Principles, Place and Perception 323

poorer trader tended to endure the hardship of violations of the legislation by the railway companies. Though the Railway Commission of 1873 was judged a success with regard to large cases involving issues of principle, and was felt to have addressed the evils of the railway monopoly by acting as a deterrent to the railway companies who disliked the threat of being taken before the commission, this was a somewhat negative success. The tribunal was widely perceived as 'very difficult of access' for ordinary litigants, a perception that was reinforced by the small number of cases that came before them.[140] The object of the commissioners to give an effective remedy to small traders had, accordingly, failed. Nevertheless the consensus of witnesses before the Select Committee on Railways in 1881, companies, traders and experts, was that the commission should continue, with attempts to make it more accessible in terms of both locus standi[141] and expense.

However, the recast commission of 1888 was regarded as equally inaccessible, and the complaints of the traders at the end of the 1890s were the same as those expressed in the 1850s. It was inaccessible to a large number of potential litigants, having become little different from a regular court of law in technicality and expense. Individual traders could not meet an expense of some £200 a day to appear before the commission. Even a chamber of commerce could not always do so. The Birmingham Chamber of Commerce, for example, had a yearly income of some £1,200 or £1,300, an income which could be exhausted, and even exceeded, by the expense of paying of counsel to take a case before the commission.[142] In many cases the expense, even if it could be borne, was simply not worth it. The representative of the Sheffield Chamber of Commerce recounted how his association had fought a case against a railway company for £3 and although they won, it cost them £120. Another case where £40 was at stake cost the association between £600 and £700.[143] This led the traders to

---

[140] *Ibid.*, q. 6825 *per* Thomas Dickson, member of Belfast Chamber of Commerce.
[141] Trade associations and chambers of commerce were not permitted to bring a case before the commissioners.
[142] 'Minutes of Evidence taken before the Departmental Committee appointed by the Board of Trade to consider the Law relating to Railway Agreements and Amalgamations', *HCPP* (1911) (5927) xxix Pt 2, 51 at q. 5780 *per* Henry Edmunds.
[143] *Ibid.*, at q. 7801 *per* Joseph Ward.

324 *Legal Foundations of Tribunals in 19th-Century England*

demand some other and cheaper form of dispute-resolution body, in the nature of a conciliation process or voluntary arbitration, even one within the Board of Trade.[144] Samuel Boulton, senior partner in a firm of timber merchants in London, criticised the Railway and Canal Commission in 1893: 'The expense and the complexity of the proceedings, the time that is taken; the difficulty in getting to them, and so on. We want something short, sharp, and decisive.'[145]

The most significant barrier to the effectiveness of the tribunals as dispute-resolution bodies, primarily because it undermined the confidence of the public in their operation, was their real or perceived lack of independence from the executive. It was the result of an accurate popular perception of the statutory tribunals as organs of the administration, or at most hybrid bodies, possessing administrative and judicial functions. That status led to a suspicion of their subordination to the will of the executive. When the tribunal was exercising its judicial function, and even in those tribunals which had progressed to a stage where the functions were more clearly separated, there was still a popular perception – and a correct one – that it was doing so as part of a process of the executive. That was unfortunate because it led to a popular and understandable view that in so doing the members of the tribunal could not be impartial and independent in their adjudication. This perception was, of course, considerably affected by the composition of the tribunal, but it began with the underlying duality of jurisdiction and accordingly theoretically applied to all tribunals to some degree. In some instances it was only a peripheral concern, as in the case of the railway tribunals where the disputes to be settled were between railway companies rather than between the state and the subject and indeed the common view inclined to some connection with government being beneficial. This was in clear contrast to the fiscal tribunals. The evident and material interest of the government in raising taxation, its wide applicability, an ever-present public fear of government rapacity and the clear identification of some tribunal personnel with a discrete department of government combined to make the fiscal tribunals

---

[144] 'Minutes of Evidence before the Select Committee on Railway Rates and Charges', *HCPP* (1893–4) (462) xiv 535 at qq. 2206, 2236–7, 2275–87 *per* William Barrett, colliery owner.
[145] *Ibid.*, q. 4649.

Principles, Place and Perception 325

the most open to the criticism of partiality. The General Commissioners, though themselves independent of government and more akin to the justices of the peace, were perceived – correctly in most cases – as being unduly influenced by the government surveyor who was considered as being primarily motivated to secure as high a revenue as possible.[146] And yet the Special Commissioners, of all the tribunals probably the one with the closest connection with central government – and unambiguously constituting an arm of the executive, and so most open to accusations of partiality – was, paradoxically, one which received the considerable approbation of the public.[147] The Special Commissioners took pains to emphasise their independence.[148] A Special Commissioner in 1906 said his tribunal was 'actually independent in every way of the Inland Revenue in the consideration of appeals, and we do our utmost to convey that fact to the public',[149] and the tribunal itself thought that the mixture of functions did not give rise to any inconsistency in practice.[150] Some lawyers, however, expressed their discomfort. A solicitor giving evidence in the early years of the twentieth century urged that these conflicting duties should not be imposed on the same tribunal. He warned that '[t]hose who exercise judicial should not also be called upon to exercise administrative functions – a distinction which, so far as I know, is carefully preserved in all other judicial bodies in the country'.[151]

A clear perception of independence was important because there was a sense in which the tribunals at their inception were regarded as buffers between the individual and more powerful interests. There was a growing realisation that if statutory tribunals were truly independent and expert, they could be a powerful expression of resistance to government interference or at least of control. In this sense the railway tribunals were affected. It was said that though the railway system was widely accepted as a boon

---

[146] *Ibid.*

[147] For the converse view see *Minutes, Income Tax, 1919* q. 1853 *per* G.O. Parsons, secretary to the Income Tax Reform League.

[148] *Ibid.*, at q. 13,812 *per* G. F. Howe, presiding Special Commissioner.

[149] 'Minutes of Evidence before the Select Committee on Income Tax', *HCPP* (1906) (365) ix 659 at q. 2709 *per* Walter Gyles, Special Commissioner.

[150] *Minutes, Income Tax, 1919* qq. 13,780–1 *per* G. F. Howe.

[151] *Ibid.*, at q. 23,891 *per* Randle F.W. Holme. At q. 24,017 he urged the separation of the administrative and judicial functions of the Special Commissioners.

326 Legal Foundations of Tribunals in 19th-Century England

to the people and the country, once it had reached the stage of a 'leviathan monopoly' it was in the public interest that there should be some arbitrator between the public and the railway companies, and that should be an accessible tribunal.[152] Accordingly the Railway Commissioners were conceived as an intermediary between the individual railway user and the immense power of the railway interest, and were described as 'a sort of watch dog upon the part of the public'.[153] The fiscal tribunals were intended to be particularly significant in this respect, to act as the 'natural safeguard'[154] of the individual taxpayer against the state, to ensure the state took no more, and indeed no less, than its fiscal due. To some extent they achieved this. The various commissioners based on the Land Tax Commissioners were at least independent, being unpaid and formally unconnected to the executive. The chairman of the Inland Revenue, perhaps unsurprisingly, said that he knew of 'no machinery that could be established to give such satisfaction'.[155]

With the exception of the Railway Commission, an exception largely explained by its highly judicial nature, the statutory tribunals were generally accessible to the public. Unfortunately, since they were not regarded as organs exercising the judicial power of the state, the special qualities of litigation before them were not regarded as the exemplar of judicial process. The speed, efficiency and expertise of dispute-resolution before the tribunals were as confined in their success as in their substance. Although the process before each tribunal had grown out of dissatisfaction with the procedures of the regular courts, there was little influence on the process of the regular courts even when the tribunal process had proved its worth. In the context of access to justice, therefore, the impact of the tribunals was limited. The reason lay in the fact that they were not integrated into a system of dispute-resolution, a situation that was not a failure of the legislature, merely a reflection of the true raison d'être of statutory tribunals.

---

[152] *Minutes, Railways*, 1881 q. 7543 *per* Henry Gilbey, chairman of the Council of the National Chamber of Commerce.
[153] *Minutes, Railways (Rates and Fares), 1882* q. 3675.
[154] 'Report of the Royal Commission on the Income Tax', *HCPP* (1920) (615) xviii 97 at p. 181, para. 344.
[155] 'Minutes of Evidence before the Select Committee on Inland Revenue and Customs Establishments', *HCPP* (1862) (370) xii 131 at q. 541 *per* Charles Pressly.

Principles, Place and Perception   327

Simplicity, efficiency and cost-effectiveness of process was achieved on a micro, but not a macro, level.

As the tribunals developed throughout the nineteenth century, the outlines of their future role and form were discernible. What is clear is that the statutory tribunals were originally conceived as an arm of the executive, though with varying degrees of independence, and that they were given primarily administrative functions with subsidiary judicial powers existing entirely to serve the former. That was their provenance. Just as had happened with the justices of the peace at an earlier stage, their function as primarily administrative bodies decreased in importance throughout the late nineteenth century. The reason was twofold. First an increase in the size and organisation of central government and the development of a bureaucracy permitted government itself to take on the administration of the various legislative regimes. Secondly, as the various spheres in which tribunals operated became more complex with the increasing sophistication of society, government and the economy, so they required and gathered increasingly specialised expertise. It was realised that the work was moving beyond the ability of temporary commissions or part-time lay personnel in permanent commissions, and that specialist, remunerated and permanent officials were needed. Similarly the making of policy decisions became more firmly placed in the government department. However, the tribunals' convenience as tools for dispute-resolution within those areas of activity was recognised and as they were divested of many of their administrative functions, that judicial power was left in their hands, for much the same reasons as had prompted their original creation. So the tribunals were gradually left with their judicial functions, often appellate, and increasingly arising from decisions made not by them but by the appropriate government department. This functional evolution was seen not only in the established tribunals of the nineteenth century, but also in the new creations of the opening years of the twentieth. First the Special and then the General Commissioners of Income Tax began to be stripped of their administrative assessing functions.[156] The Railway

---

[156] See J. Avery Jones, 'The Special Commissioners after 1842: From Administrative to Judicial Tribunal' (2005) *British Tax Review* 80; C. Stebbings, 'The General Commissioners of Income Tax: Assessors or Adjudicators?' (1993) *British Tax Review* 52.

328 *Legal Foundations of Tribunals in 19th-Century England*

Commissioners became a full court of record, and while retaining administrative functions their later development confirmed them as more akin to a court of law than an administrative body.[157] After a period of experimentation with a multiplicity of dispute-resolution techniques, the Liberal social welfare legislation of the early 1900s made use of specialist lay tribunals. In particular the legislative regime introducing old age pensions in 1908 placed the administration of the regulations in the hands of a Pensions Committee, but gave a right of appeal to the Local Government Board. The national insurance legislation of 1911 was to be administered by insurance officers appointed by the Board of Trade, with any disputes as to their decisions going to a Court of Referees and thence on final appeal to an Insurance Commissioner. These appellate tribunals were of such importance in the number of claims they addressed that the orthodox view is that the national insurance tribunals of 1911 constituted the first of the modern administrative tribunals, and indeed in composition, jurisdiction and process they are clearly recognisable to the modern lawyer.[158] In their conception and foundations, however, they were the product of over seventy years of administrative practice and legal refinement. They were primarily judicial bodies, concerned with adjudication and with less scope for making discretionary policy decisions.

The immediate effect of this shift in emphasis in the duties of tribunals and a growth in extra-judicial dispute-resolution generally, was to give rise to concern among judges and legal commentators as to the threat to the rule of law posed by such bodies undertaking judicial functions. The statutory tribunals had been relatively untroubled by theoretical considerations as to their standing, if any, in the judicial hierarchy for most of the nineteenth century, and they were received in much the same way as they were conceived. Their nature and function as organs of the executive were accepted and the close integration and subservient role of their judicial function prevented them from being

---

[157] See Robson, *Administrative Law*, pp. 92–101 and, generally, pp. 38–218.

[158] Wraith and Hutchesson, *Administrative Tribunals*, p. 33. See Sir Robert Micklethwait, *The National Insurance Commissioners*, Hamlyn Lectures, 33rd series (London: Stevens & Sons, 1976). Note, however, that Sir Robert observes that even the new tribunal was 'in part a novel experiment' at *ibid.*, p. 3.

Principles, Place and Perception 329

perceived as posing any challenge to either the regular courts or the rule of law, and not even to the uniform administration of the law as some inferior courts were, because they were not perceived as administering the judicial power of the state or indeed as creating a new type of dispute-resolution. They were rather regarded as a legitimate and effective administrative response to the challenges of over a hundred years of intensive industrialisation, and any anxiety was on the grounds of increasing state intervention into new spheres of human activity and its accompanying bureaucracy. While administration and adjudication were thus integrated in one process and one organ, the system was both logical and generally effective. When the functions became separated and the judicial function isolated in the tribunals and consequently more prominent, the original processes and constitutions of the tribunals became increasingly anomalous. This development was reflected in the nomenclature. It is during this period that the terms 'commission' and 'board', which were synonymous with public administration, began to fall into popular if not official disuse, to be replaced by the more modern appellation of 'tribunal', a term which, significantly, had stronger judicial connotations and would become synonymous with extra-judicial adjudication. Tensions developed, partly as a result of the ambiguous theoretical basis of the dual functions, but primarily because of an increased appreciation of the importance of independence in dispute-resolution. That, allied to a more rigid interpretation of the rule of law and the separation of powers, rendered their place in the public organism more equivocal than at their inception. The judiciary, as defenders of the rule of law, expressed their misgivings and the separation of powers was recognised as being inevitably undermined.

The unease Professor A. V. Dicey had expressed in the closing years of the nineteenth century was shared and engaged in by the leading jurists of the early twentieth century, and was expounded yet more strongly by Lord Hewart CJ in *The New Despotism*[159] in 1929, where he attacked the new tribunals and the increasing use the government was making of them as dispute-resolution bodies. Though mainly concerned with dispute-resolution by ministers

---

[159] Lord Hewart, *The New Despotism* (London: Ernest Bern Ltd, 1929). See too Robert Jackson, *The Chief* (London: Harrap & Co. Ltd, 1959), pp. 213–15.

330 *Legal Foundations of Tribunals in 19th-Century England*

and officials in a department, rather than independent or semi-independent tribunals, he took the view, like Dicey, that the creation of administrative bodies with dispute-resolution functions undermined the doctrine of the separation of powers. Their effect, and indeed their object, was 'to evade the Courts, and to render the will, or the caprice, of the Executive unfettered and supreme'.[160] His arguments served to highlight the weaknesses of tribunal adjudication as never before. The provision of safeguards in the form of judicial review, adherence to the rules of natural justice and appeals to the law courts did not diminish the scale of the breach of the rule of law nor the danger to the public. Features that had once been welcomed for achieving swift and specialised justice[161] were now condemned as abuses of citizens' rights, and standards of justice were found wanting compared to those in the regular legal system.[162] For not only were their constitutions, procedures and personnel diverse and entirely lacking any coherence or uniformity, they were considered to afford insufficient protection to individual rights.

Such was the force of Lord Hewart's criticism, and his position as a senior judge in office, that the government felt obliged to respond. It established a Select Committee in 1929[163] to examine delegated legislation and ministerial judicial decision-making. That committee, the Donoughmore Committee, like the Franks Committee[164] some twenty years later, was dominated by the traditional constitutional view of Dicey, with its fundamental belief in the rule of law and the separation of powers which guided the allocation of duties to courts or administrative tribunals according to the judicial or executive nature of the tasks to be undertaken. The committee accepted Dicey's statement of the rule of law as 'the best exposition of the modern doctrine',[165] and

---

[160] Hewart, *The New Despotism*, p. 17.
[161] Lack of publicity, not giving reasons for decisions, adjudication by non-lawyers, no legal representation.
[162] See Inns of Court Conservative and Unionist Society, *Rule of Law* (London: Conservative Political Centre, 1955), pp. 21–3.
[163] See 'Report of the Committee on Ministers' Powers', *HCPP* (1931–2) (4060) xii 341.
[164] 'Report of the Committee on Administrative Tribunals and Enquiries', Cmnd 218 (1957). See too Inns of Court, *Rule of Law*.
[165] 'Report of the Committee on Ministers' Powers', *HCPP* (1931–2) (4060) xii 341 at p. 418.

Principles, Place and Perception 331

Professor W. A. Robson later observed that the committee 'started life with the dead hand of Dicey lying frozen on its neck'.[166] The committee presupposed the possibility of both definition and extraction of 'judicial' and 'administrative' tasks, an approach which the nineteenth-century legislators had neither attempted nor debated, nor, indeed, thought particularly relevant, other than in the context of the overall function of the organ and not in relation to individual actions viewed in isolation. The Franks Committee concluded in 1957 that disputes should be allocated to a court of law unless special considerations made a tribunal more suitable,[167] but this is precisely what the early legislators of the nineteenth century accepted in the creation of each tribunal – that such special considerations existed, namely the nature of the legislation, and the need for expeditious, informal, inexpensive and specialist adjudication and administration.

Since function continued to determine the legal status of the organ, another effect of the new prominence of judicial activity was to render less tenable the hitherto relatively clear legal status of tribunals as primarily administrative bodies. The less of the highly subject-specific administrative duties of the tribunal and the isolation of the judicial function in one sense rendered the tribunals more uniform: the resolution of a dispute in land rights was not markedly different from the resolution of a dispute over assessment to tax. It had been the administrative functions that had differed through their subject-specificity, and so when these were shed the outcome was a more obvious consistency between the tribunals. This led to the natural formation of a discrete class of dispute-resolution bodies of broadly similar character possessing the same fundamental features of cheapness, speed, simplicity, informality, specialism and accessibility. Tribunals were implicitly given an identity when the Franks Committee was appointed to consider 'the constitution and working of tribunals'.[168] Not only did this demonstrate that tribunals were accepted and understood as a genre of dispute-resolution, the qualification of the term 'tribunals'

---

[166] Robson, *Administrative Law*, p. 318. For Professor Robson's account of the committee's proceedings, see *ibid.*, pp. 314–76.

[167] 'Report of the Committee on Administrative Tribunals and Enquiries', Cmnd 218 (1957), para. 406.

[168] Minute of Appointment of the Franks Committee, 'Report of the Committee on Administrative Tribunals and Enquiries', Cmnd 218 (1957), iii.

332 *Legal Foundations of Tribunals in 19th-Century England*

with the phrase 'other than the ordinary courts of law'[169] in the minute of appointment revealed the changed perception of such bodies over the hundred years since their inception. The emergence of the tribunal as a distinct class, however, and one whose primary activity was dispute-resolution, made it stand out as starkly anomalous in a political context, and flawed in a legal one. It was, as Wraith and Hutchesson were to observe, 'the orphaned child of both'.[170] The tribunals possessed certain features and functions that challenged accepted structures and institutions within the legal system. The fact that there was no attempt to classify them nor to integrate them into the contemporary legal system did not mean that any difficulties in so placing them were unimportant. Their ad hoc genesis masked the absence of underlying principle, and in its pragmatism denied the need for rigorous analysis of the juridical nature of these new adjudicatory organs. Tensions arose between the residual administrative functions and context, and the judicial functions. The inconsistencies that had been acceptable when tribunals were individually conceived organs of government could no longer be tolerated when they were increasingly performing similar functions to organs of the judiciary. The absence of all but the most basic common standards and the varying compositions, procedures and principles of accessibility that characterised the tribunals were incompatible with the increasing coherence and higher standards demanded of the regular judicial system. The independence of the tribunals became an even more significant issue. The reality by the middle years of the twentieth century was that the statutory tribunals were an integral part of the machinery of justice and were valuable to the preservation of the regular legal system by taking on a large proportion of small-scale specialised litigation.[171] The Franks Committee concluded that 'tribunals should properly be regarded as machinery by Parliament for adjudication rather than as part of the machinery of administration'[172] on the basis that Parliament had made deliberate

---

[169] *Ibid.*   [170] Wraith and Hutchesson, *Administrative Tribunals*, p. 17.

[171] 'Minutes of Evidence before the Committee on Administrative Tribunals and Enquiries', Cmnd 218 (1957), evidence of the Lord Chancellor's Department, p. 191, para. 10.

[172] 'Report of the Committee on Administrative Tribunals and Enquiries', Cmnd 218 (1957), para. 40.

Principles, Place and Perception 333

provision for an organ to resolve disputes independently of the executive department. Most scholars and lawyers were in agreement.

The political masters of the legislature had determined the nature of the new tribunals. Driven by a uniquely Victorian blend of ideology and pragmatism, the executive desired the effective implementation of their controversial centralising reforms with as little popular resistance as possible and, where necessary, the retention of some degree of executive control. Political demands were reflected in legislative provision, and Parliament, as conservative or creative as it wished to be, designed the tribunals to achieve that policy in each instance. An accessible dispute-resolution form was necessary to ensure government policy was implemented swiftly and effectively, but the creation of the tribunals was not part of any coherent policy of extra-judicial dispute-resolution with an idealistic objective of increased public accessibility. It was, rather, the outcome of a reaction to the demands of the new regulatory legislation and the demands of the executive, the result of a policy of government growth. It was legally and politically convenient to exclude disputes arising between citizens and public bodies from the ordinary court system: they were too trivial, too numerous and too specialised for the courts to undertake the task of determining them. There was a danger of clogging an already congested legal system with the burden of such litigation. Furthermore, court procedures were costly and slow, and inappropriately formal for disputes of this nature, particularly in the light of political pressures to implement swiftly often controversial legislation. Statutory tribunals were the expression of centralised government, state intervention and an accompanying professional bureaucracy and those conditions were, as Sir Cecil Carr astutely observed, all extant in the 1830s.[173] The statutory tribunal of the nineteenth century had developed piecemeal, driven by practical considerations to improvise and compromise, and with no intention of creating a new element in the machinery of justice. The evidence shows that it was originally and primarily a government body, and yet one whose essential features of lay specialist personnel, informal

---

[173] Sir C. T. Carr, *Concerning English Administrative Law* (London: Oxford University Press, 1941), p. 8.

334 *Legal Foundations of Tribunals in 19th-Century England*

procedures and a limited jurisdiction were consciously and deliberately drawn from recognisable institutions of the regular legal system. The legal character of the tribunals was the result of social, political and economic forces, with legal devices being employed in order to carry out controversial political policies. It was, however, an enduring success. It displayed such flexibility and utility, and so many advantages over the regular courts, that it became an indispensable and major public institution of the modern world, which in a hundred years since its inception, would overtake the regular courts of law in the quantum of litigation it undertook, and which was poised to remain a major instrument of dispute-resolution for the foreseeable future. During the nineteenth century, a period dominated by the pragmatism and imagination of creation, the tribunals' place was broadly as an appendage of government; during the twentieth, where the principal challenge would be the theoretical one of classification and place, it was broadly as an appendage of the regular courts; in the twenty-first, with its idealistic aspiration to coherence, effectiveness and direct participation, it would be as a genre of dispute-resolution in its own and formidable right.

INDEX

access to justice 70, 319–20, 326
Addington, Henry 26, 36, 115, 154–5
adjudicatory functions of tribunals 8,
    107, 182, 186, 282, 290, 297, 307–8
administrative functions of tribunals
    62, 147, 295–7, 306, 308
  and judicial functions 7, 182, 186,
    282, 290, 294, 300
Aglionby, Henry 98, 243
Alderson 133–4, 166
Anti-Centralisation Union 89
appeal by case stated 238, 239, 241,
    244, 247
  Railway Commission 248
appeal by certiorari 243–5
appeal by feigned issue 242–4
appeal by special case 238
arbitration 59–62, 104, 274, 277–9, 316
  consensual approach 292
  local knowledge 120
  as a model for the tribunals 50–1,
    280–1, 291
  private process of 208, 274
  procedures of 185, 278
  speed and expense of 51, 61
assessed taxes 20, 35, 149, 151, 156, 239
Assessed Taxes Commissioners 35, 66
Assessment Committees 101, 172, 304
  adjudicatory functions 173, 186, 299
  administrative functions 7, 173, 296
  composition of 69
  jurisdiction of 171–4
  legal representation 228
  places of meeting 201
  procedures of 194, 213–14
  reasons for decisions 211
  right of appeal to regular courts
    173, 249
  speed and expense of 69

success of 315
summoning and examination of
    witnesses 214
  time limits for appeals 205
Association of British Chambers of
    Commerce 322
Atherton, William 54
Atkin LJ 258
audi alteram partem, parties in litigation
    should be heard 260, 263–4

Balfour Browne, J.H. 224–5
Bankes LJ 264, 267
bankruptcy 57–8
Bankruptcy Act 1869 47
*Barrett v. the Great Northern Railway
    Company and the Midland Railway
    Company* 178–9
*Baxendale v. the Great Western Railway
    Company* 179
Baxter, Robert 127
Bentham, Jeremy 84–8, 105, 188, 283
Benthamism 84, 86, 95, 105, 288
Bentley's case 230
Birmingham Chamber of Commerce
    323
Blackstone, Sir William 90, 297
Blamire, William 111, 122
Board of Education 257, 268
Board of Inland Revenue 262
Board of Trade 60, 176
  Railway Committee 207, 287
  Railway Department 33
  and railway regulation 53–4, 56, 68,
    175, 182
Boulton, Samuel 324
Bowen LJ 268
Bramwell, Lord 44
Brett LJ 257

335

336   Index

Brougham, Henry, Lord 43, 55
Bruce, Vice Chancellor Knight 133
Buller, Charles 87, 209
bureaucracy 99, 100, 327, 333
Byles J 264

Campbell, Lord 267
  nemo judex in re sua 260
  railway regulation 44, 54–6, 177
Cardwell, Edward 37
  government centralisation 77
  railway regulation 25, 45, 52–4, 60,
    94, 194, 275
Carr, Sir Cecil 333
Caterham Railway Company v. the
  London, Brighton, and South Coast
  Railway Company and South
  Eastern Railway Company 178
certiorari, writ of 252–64
  appeal by 243, 245
  application of 256, 258–9, 264, 311
  requirements for the application of
    254, 270
Chadwick, Edwin 85, 111, 288
  public health 12, 23, 30
Chancery Reform Act 1852 275
Charles J 305
children, employment of 11, 23
church interests 93
Civil Superannuation Acts 144
Cockburn CJ 177–8, 301
Coke, Sir Edward 297
collectivism 84, 103, 109
Commercial Commissioners 124, 209
commercial income, taxation of 21, 26,
    64, 119, 123–4, 154, 190, 208
Commissioner of Woods and Forests
    86, 267
commissioners, lay 67, 110, 116, 128,
    133, 274–5, 281, 297, 328, 333
  appointment of 29, 112, 143–6
  impartiality of 114–20
  oaths sworn by 112–14, 257, 299
  residency and property qualifications
    of 114–18
Commissioners for the Redemption of
  the Land Tax
  administrative function 151
  appeals against 152
  finality of decisions 236
Commissioners for the Reduction of
  the National Debt 152

Commissioners of Appeal (income tax)
    115, 153
Commissioners of Sewers 254, 269, 298
Commissioners of the Inland Revenue
    321
Common Fields Inclosure Act 1836 92,
    163, 244, 271
Common Law 90–1,
  appeal methods 238
  questions of fact 274
  right of appeal 233
  role of juries 243
Common Law courts 188, 196, 251–72,
    297, 298
company law, development of 293
competiton 18, 25, 80, 81, 88
constitutional theory 63, 105
Conventicle Act 1670 270
Copyhold Act 1841 32, 96–7, 162, 271
  boundary disputes 293
  documentary evidence 219
Copyhold Commission 160
  adjudicatory functions 169
  appeal provisions 243–4
  arbitration 162
  dispute-resolution powers 66
  documentary evidence 219
  duties and powers 162
  finality of decisions 237
  inquisitorial function 7
  procedures of 191, 193
  success of 316
  summoning and examination of
    witnesses 216
Copyhold Commissioners 32, 101, 300
copyhold tenure 14–17
  compulsory enfranchisement 96–7
  enfranchisement 24, 69, 88, 92, 123,
    162–3, 283
  heriot 15
  prevention of improvement of the
    land 15
  reform of 23, 31, 48
  voluntary enfranchisement 95–7, 162
Corrupt and Illegal Practices
  Prevention Act 1883 223
Cottenham, Lord LC 260
Coulson, Walter 219, 283
Council on Tribunals 2, 295
County Courts 46–7, 196, 313, 320
Court of Bankruptcy 57, 196, 208
Court of Chancery 31, 43, 63, 239, 275,
    280

Index

337

Court of Common Pleas 55, 68, 178, 218
  jurisdiction of 57, 126, 177
  procedures of 218
  and railway regulation 127, 177, 194,
    223–8, 278
Court of Exchequer 239
courts of law 264, 291, 310
  accessibility of 320, 323
  creation of new courts 48
  and dispute-resolution 108
  documentary evidence 218–20
  expense of litigation 42, 185
  initiation of litigation 202
  ordinary 108–9
  oyer and terminer 297
  procedures of 42, 185, 188, 218–20,
    276
  public nature of proceedings 207
  purpose of 106, 297, 307
  regular courts 41, 64
  and regulatory legislation 56–7
  specialist courts 47–8, 275
  specialist knowledge 121
  superior courts 41–5, 250, 295, 311
  supervision of tribunals 279
  use of expert assessors 126–8
  writ of prohibition 264
Cowen, Joseph 76
Cresswell J 179
Cubitt, Sir William 50
customs and excise duties 20
Customs and Inland Revenue Act 1874
  241

Darwin, Charles 88
Denman, Lord CJ 169
Dicey, A.V. 84, 103, 108–9, 143,
  329–30
Dickens, Charles 43
Dimes v. *Grand Junction Canal* 260
discretion 72, 129, 212, 229, 277–9, 296
  Assessment Committees 172
  debates concerning 105, 108
  Railway Commission 136, 195
  Tax Commissions 220, 317
dispute-resolution 38–9, 63, 72,
  327, 332
  cheap and effective processes of
    39–40, 67, 70, 220, 326
  and the courts 73, 99, 104
dispute-resolution powers 3, 6, 41, 65,
  70, 104, 106, 186, 292
  and the rule of law 108

Dissenters 79
Donoughmore Committee 330

economics, classical 83, 85
Education Act 1902 258
education, and state intervention 82
efficiency 85, 187, 273, 282
Elder Brethren of Trinity House 126
Electricity Commissioners 258, 267
Erle J 123
error, writ of 251–72, 298
Esher, Lord 303
Evangelicals 76, 85
executive control 75, 288

factories 10, 23
  reform of
  regulation of 29, 37, 65, 74, 83,
    86, 91
fairness 40, 70, 187, 211, 276–7
  and public confidence 38, 184
false judgment, writ of 251, 254–5,
  298
Farrer, Thomas 44, 127
Fielden, Joshua 94
fiscal tribunals 7, 25, 157, 284–7,
  300
  access to legal advice 137
  accessibility of 321
  accounting knowledge 124
  adjudicatory functions 148–52,
    299
  administrative function 148–52,
    189–90, 295
  appeals 157, 236
  appointment of clerks 138–9
  independence of 324, 326
  jurisdiction of 156–8
  procedures of 213–14
  property qualification 137
  residence qualification 137
  specialist knowledge of
    commissioners 123
  subordinate officers 140–1
  summoning and examination of
    witnesses 214
Fortescue, Chichester 45
Franks Committee 330–2
free market economy 80
free trade policy 22
freedoms, individual 78, 84, 94–7, 184
  protection of 144

338 *Index*

Friendly Societies Act 221
Fry LJ 303

General Board of Health 30, 65–6, 93
General Commissioners of Income Tax
35–6, 111, 118, 278
accessibility of 198, 321
adjudicatory functions 157
administrative functions 154, 327
appellate jurisdiction 154
appointment of 115–16, 274
discretion 220
dispute-resolution powers 66
documentary evidence 219–20
finality of decisions 237
independence of 98, 145, 324
inquisitorial function 153
legal representation 222
nemo judex in re sua 263
places of meeting 201
procedures 201, 213
public perception of 119, 317, 319
reasons for decisions 210
right of appeal to regular courts 312
social status of 116
writ of certiorari 269
writ of mandamus 268
Girdlestone v. *Stanley* 165–6
Grimthorpe, Lord 135

Halsbury, Lord 136
Health and Morals of Apprentices Act
1802 83
Henley, Joseph 172
heriot 15
Hewart, Lord 208, 329–30
Hill, Rowland 199
Holt CJ 252, 254, 298
Howick, Viscount 207
Hume, Joseph 86–7
Hutchesson, P.G. 332

ideology 5, 73–109, 288, 333
Inclosure Act 1845 32, 86, 160, 163,
170, 282
boundary disputes 260
legal advice, access to 283
Inclosure Clauses Consolidation Act
1801 163, 170, 192, 216, 271
Inclosure Commission 131–3, 163–4, 192
appeal provisions 204–5, 244–6
Assistant Commissioners 131–3

boundary disputes 170, 245
centralised control 75
dispute-resolution powers 66, 169–70
documentary evidence 219
finality of decisions 237
inquisitorial function 7
procedures of 192–3
public information about 204
remuneration of clerks 142
role of valuers 123, 164, 170, 245
success of 316
summoning and examination of
witnesses 216
writ of prohibition 266
Inclosure Commissioners 32, 75, 300
local knowledge 120
oaths 112, 283
remuneration 141
specialist knowledge 120, 122
inclosure of common land 16, 92
arbitral commissioners 67
private Acts 122, 132, 163, 237, 282
reform of 23–4, 31–2, 48
Income and Property Taxes Act 1799
152, 237
Income and Property Taxes Act 1842
198, 241
income tax tribunals 20–1, 26, 35–6,
102, 152–6
abolition movement 119
appeals 153, 215–16, 240
bureaucratic dominance in 99
Commissioners of Appeal 153
complexity of law and practice 98
compulsory nature of 94
independence of commissioners 98
lay commissioners 119
oath of non-disclosure of information
113–14
property qualification for
commissioners 114–16
public information about 203
secrecy 212
individualism 75, 78, 84, 103
industrial revolution 3, 10, 12, 17, 26,
76, 83, 273
information, public 202–4, 211, 234
Ireland 156

Jervis, Lord 56
Joint Select Committee on Railways 68,
127, 180, 316

Index

339

Jones, Richard 167
judges 41, 44, 314
 and railway regulation 54–6
 and technical knowledge 41, 44, 46
Judicature Act 1873 65, 126, 135, 234, 247, 293, 294, 309
Judicature Act 1875 65, 247, 293, 294, 309
Judicature Commissioners 48, 64, 238, 279, 313
judicial acts 299
 and certiorari 257, 265
 definition of 154, 304
 and prohibition 266, 268
judicial functions of tribunals 7, 8, 10, 72, 147, 294, 301, 329
judiciary, independence from executive 107
justice 40, 43, 264
 access to 70, 319, 320, 326
 natural 260, 263, 277, 330
justices of the peace 48–9, 110, 256
 appointment of 274
 and arbitration 59–62
 and dispute-resolution processes 58–9, 248
 functions of 59, 142, 249, 309
 jurisdiction of 48, 51, 59, 279, 281
 and land tenure restructuring 31
 local knowledge 49
 as a model for the tribunals 277, 279, 280, 291
 procedures of 311
 and railway regulation 59
 supervision of 253
 and the tax tribunals 197

Kelly CB 263
King's Council 63

laissez-faire 75, 80–4, 85, 88, 95, 103
Land Clauses Consolidation Act 1845 61, 245
land rights tribunals 31, 159–71, 280
 accessibility of 197
 adjudicatory functions 186, 299
 administrative functions 189–90, 295
 appointment of clerks 138
 appointment of commissioners 144
 Assistant Commissioners 139
 balance of administrative and judicial functions 170

boundary disputes 131, 293
dispute-resolution powers 66, 164–71
documentary evidence 218
 hearings of 212–13
 inquisitorial function 7, 296
 legal dimensions of the work 130–3
 legally qualified Assistant Commissioners 132
 legislation 74, 86
 model for 282–4, 286
 procedures of 190–3, 212–13
 public information about 203
 reasons for decisions 211
 right of appeal to regular courts 241–6
 sharing of experience and practice 283
 specialist knowledge of commissioners 122, 123
 subordinate officers 139, 217
 summoning and examination of witnesses 216–17
 valuers 139
 writ of certiorari 270
land tax 20, 26, 35, 151
Land Tax Act 1688 35, 114
Land Tax Act 1797 148, 150, 214, 236
Land Tax Commissioners 20, 35
 adjudicatory functions 150
 appointment of 274
 dispute-resolution powers 66, 150, 151
 finality of decisions 236, 239
 house and window duty 236
 independence of 326
 jurisdiction of 278
 legal representation 222
 nemo judex in re sua 261
 property qualification 115
 remuneration of clerks 142
 residency requirements 116
 right of appeal to regular courts 312
 social status of 116
 writ of mandamus 268
Land Tax Redemption Acts
 consolidation 152
Land Tax Redemption Appeal Commissioners 59, 112, 198, 214, 239
Land Tax Redemption Commissioners 112, 115

340   *Index*

land tenure 10, 12, 16, 23–4, 39
  reform of 37, 48–9
law 1–71
  ordinary 108–9
  reform of 4, 22, 57
  uniformity of 29, 79, 91, 196, 281
Law Society 93, 103
legal representation before tribunals 61,
  129–33, 137, 220–8, 222, 223, 228,
  283
legislation, interventionist 73, 75, 83, 97
legislative reform 22, 28, 73, 74, 89,
  187, 275
  appeals processes 212–14
  conduct of hearings 207
  procedures specified in 188–9
  provision for public information
  202
Liberal party 77
Littler, Ralph QC 17, 128, 247, 313,
  317
local control 9, 30, 32, 89, 96
local government 27–8, 103, 279
Local Government Act 1888 303
Local Government Board 66
local knowledge 49, 118, 120,
  233, 275
localism 9, 75, 89, 90, 103
Locke, John 78, 105
Lopes LJ 255, 304
Loreburn, Lord LC 263
Lyndhurst, Lord 55

mandamus, writ of 252, 253, 268–9
Mansfield, Lord 268
Maule J 277
Merchant Marine Board 68
Merchant Shipping Act 1854 37, 68,
  301
Mill, John Stuart 82, 85, 88
ministerial responsibility 29, 87
Montesquieu, C.L. de 105
Morpeth, Viscount 90
Moulton, Fletcher LJ 256

National Insurance Act 1911 9
national insurance tribunals 328
nemo judex in re sua, a man cannot be a
  judge in his own cause 260–3

oaths sworn by commissioners 112–14,
  257, 299

inclosure 112, 283
income tax 113–14
poor law 113
tithes 112

Palmer v. *the London and Brighton
  Railway Company* 179–80
Palmerston, Viscount 102, 111, 285
Parke B 240
Parochial Assessments Act 1836 171, 271
Pasley, Major-General 62
Patteson J 259
Peel, Sir Frederick 134, 181,
  287, 313
Peel, Sir Robert 2003, 95
  arbitration 50, 293
  income tax 20, 26, 36, 155, 210
  land tenure 15, 122
  railway regulation 81
Pember, Edward QC 128, 134, 247
Pensions Committee 328
Pitt, William 20, 35–6, 38
  income tax 111, 123, 155
  redemption of the land tax 151
  tax commissioners 115, 152–6, 209,
  284
Pollock B 305
Poor Law Amendment Act 1834 23, 77,
  90, 113, 158, 159, 258
Poor Law Commission 90, 158–9
Poor Law Commissioners 30, 158–9
  dispute-resolution powers 65, 159
  documentary evidence 218
  remuneration 141
  summoning and examination of
  witnesses 214
poor laws 11, 58–9, 65, 86, 90, 158–9
  administration of 12
  rating for 26, 38, 69–70, 171, 248–50,
  249
  reform of 23, 30, 74, 79, 82–3, 86
population growth 10, 12, 76
postal system 199–200
poverty 11; *see also* poor laws
pragmatism 289–90, 294, 332–4
Price, William 313
privacy 78, 119, 207–12
private bill committees of Parliament
  45, 280, 291
  inquisitorial processes 292
privilege 302–3

Index

procedures of tribunals 184–228, 231, 263, 275–6, 279, 289, 332
procedural safeguards 112, 187, 208, 229–30, 234, 250, 330
simplicity of 72, 186–7, 232, 276–7, 281, 333
professions 93
prohibition, writ of 252–3, 264–8
property qualification for commissioners 114–18
tax commissioners 114–16, 124, 137
property rights 13, 17, 91–3, 159–71
and centralised government 78, 84, 99, 120
public health 12, 23, 74
dispute-resolution and 37, 59
reform of 30–1, 65, 86, 90–1
and state intervention 82
Public Health Act 1848 23, 62
Public Health Act 1875 66
public policy 301–2, 327
public revenue 10, 21, 25, 145; *see also* taxation

R. v. *Aberdare Canal Company* 257
R. v. *Assessment Committee of St Mary Abbotts, Kensington* 304–6
R. v. *Justices of London* 173–4
Radicalism 84
Railway and Canal Commission 34, 181–2, 298, 300, 324
composition of 134–7
cost of 226
legal representation 223
procedures of 61
Railway and Canal Traffic Act 1854 25, 177, 290
and Court of Common Pleas 57, 178, 180
implementation of 45, 180, 194
nemo judex in re sua 262
Railway and Canal Traffic Act 1873 25, 127, 195, 206, 223, 278
Railway and Canal Traffic Act 1888 225, 248, 268, 287
Railway Clauses Consolidation Act 1845 92, 278
Railway Clearing House 59
Railway Commission 174–5, 287, 290–1, 300, 313

accessibility of 200, 323
adjudicatory function 299
administrative function 180, 296
appeals 206, 237 247
appointment of commissioners 144
arbitration 52, 59, 158, 181
Assistant Commissioners 141–2
composition of 134–7, 286, 291
cost of litigation 101, 185, 226–7, 232
as a court of record 310, 317, 327
and the Court of Common Pleas 262, 277
creation of 3, 68, 81, 246
dispute-resolution powers 37, 39, 52–6, 175–6, 181
documentary evidence 218
independence of 326
inquisitorial function 176
judicial function 7, 175, 278, 287
powers of 195, 227, 299
procedures of 194–6, 201, 207, 276, 291
public perception of 317
purpose of 136
reasons for decisions 211
remuneration of commissioners 142
representation by solicitors 225–6
right of appeal to regular courts 232, 246–8
specialist knowledge of commissioners 125–6, 128–9
speed and expense of 224
success of 323
summoning and examination of witnesses 217–18
time limits for appeals 205
writ of prohibition 267
railway companies 19, 32, 175
and the courts 54–6, 178–9
duties of 52, 177–8
and the Railway Commission 318, 322
railway regulation 32–4, 44, 52–6, 74, 174–82, 223–8, 280, 286
and dispute-resolution 37, 52–6, 68, 275
railways 17–20, 24–5, 80
Joint Select Committee 19
monopoly 18–19, 33, 80, 323, 326
and public safety 25, 33, 39, 80, 174
Ransome v. the Eastern Counties Railway Company 179

342 Index

rates, local 26, 38, 69–70, 171, 248–50
rating tribunals 189–90, 204, 248–50
Re the Appledore Tithe Commutation 167
Re Dent Tithe Commutation 168–9, 258
Regulation of Railways Act 1840 174
rights, individual 78, 88
rights, legal 105
Robson, W.A. 330
Royal Aquarium case 306–7
Royal Commission on the Bankruptcy Laws 208
Royal Commission on the employment of children 11
Royal Commission on the Income Tax 125, 322
royal prerogative 250, 252, 292
rule of law 105–8, 328–30
Russell, Lord John 74, 95

St Leonards, Lord 55
Scarman, Lord 310
Select Committee on Commons' Inclosure 44, 87, 102
Select Committee on Railways, 1881 226, 323
self-help 88
self-interest 121
Senior, Nassau 77, 82
separation of powers 105–7, 307, 330
Shaftesbury, Lord 76
Shaw, Lord 214–18
Sheffield Chamber of Commerce 323
Sibthorp, Colonel Charles 101–2, 285
Smiles, Samuel 88
Smith, Adam 81–2
Smith, Joshua Toulmin 89
social conditions 5, 10, 26
social policy 82, 288–9
social welfare 9, 82, 328
Special Commissioners of Income Tax 35, 198
  accessibility of 198–200, 321
  adjudicatory functions 137, 156, 158
  administrative functions 155, 327
  appellate jurisdiction 124–5, 156, 198, 205
  commercial income 190
  dispute-resolution powers 66
  finality of decisions 237
  independence of 146, 325
  inquisitorial function 157

nemo judex in re sua 262
  procedures 201, 213
  public information about 211
  reasons for decisions 210
  remuneration 142
  use of the postal system 199–200
  writ of mandamus 268
Stanley, Lord 54
Star Chamber 63, 253, 280, 317
state 9, 78, 82, 100–1
  centralised 5, 22, 28, 79, 103, 107, 288
  growth of administration 8–9, 29, 71, 288–9, 327
state intervention 5, 37, 59, 73, 76–7, 79, 288
  compulsory 94–7
  deficiencies of 99
  laissez-faire and 83
  legislation for 73, 75
  opposition to 28, 40, 82
Stephenson, Robert 59, 125
subject-specific expertise of tribunals 39–40, 72, 275, 285–8, 292, 316, 327, 331
Summary Jurisdiction Act 1879 303
Supreme Court of Judicature Act 1873 188, 202, 320
Supreme Court of Judicature Act 1875 202

tax tribunals 34–6
  access to legal advice 137
  accessibility of 197–200
  adjudicatory functions 145–6
  appeals 59, 205, 209, 239–41, 296
  dispute-resolution powers 66
  independence of 145–6
  legal representation 223
  procedures 241
  sharing of experience and practice 283–4
  specialist knowledge of commissioners 239
  status of commissioners 144
  subordinate officers 141
  time limits for appeals 204
taxation 10, 20–2, 35, 49, 74, 79
  centralised control 75
  and laissez-faire 81
Taxes Management Act 1798 189, 237
Taxes Management Act 1803 156, 189, 222

Index

343

Tithe Commission 160–2, 166, 168, 278
  adjudicatory function 164, 167
  appeals 204–5, 235
  Assistant Commissioners 132,
    139–40, 165, 201, 217
  boundary disputes 167–9, 216, 258
  dispute-resolution powers 66, 278
  documentary evidence 218–19
  finality of decisions 237
  inquisitorial function 7
  local knowledge 316
  procedures of 193
  public information about 203–4
  right of appeal to regular courts 242
  subject-specific expertise 316
  success of 111, 242–3, 315–16
  summoning and examination of
    witnesses 216
  valuers 161
  writs 265, 268
Tithe Commissioners 32, 87, 101, 300,
  313
  appointment of 144
  oaths 112
  remuneration 141
  skill of 111
  specialist knowledge of 122, 316
tithe commutation 12–14, 79, 92
  compulsory 95–6, 161–2, 191
  reform of 13, 23, 48
  voluntary 160–1, 164, 191–2
Tithe Commutation Act 1836 24, 32,
  67–8, 131, 160, 191, 266, 271
  dispute settlement 165, 168
Tithe Commutation Amendment Act
  1837 168, 258–9
Tories 76, 86
Treasury 284–5
tribunals 2–3, 70, 102–3, 273, 289, 291,
  295, 329
  accessibility of 40, 70, 184, 315, 322,
    326, 332–3
  ad hoc nature of 64, 294, 309, 332
  appellate jurisdiction 6, 212–14, 231
  appointment of commissioners 29,
    112, 143–6
  balance of administrative and judicial
    functions 6, 71, 147, 186, 282, 294,
    309, 329
  and certiorari 254
  composition of 110–46, 230, 289,
    324, 332

costs of 101, 196
  as courts of record 251, 254–5, 297–9
  creativity of 292–4, 334
  documentary evidence 214–20, 298
  effectiveness of 187, 212, 318–19, 324
  efficiency 202–28
  and the executive government 288,
    296, 327
  finality of decisions 236, 270
  functional powers of 147–82
  functions of 62, 307, 309, 313, 327
  geographical location 185
  immunity from action for defamation
    301
  independence of 28, 40, 98–9, 143,
    324–9, 332
  individualistic nature of 314–16
  inquisitorial functions 186, 292
  judicial functions 10, 72, 147, 287,
    294, 301, 329
  judicial supervision 229–71, 279, 311,
    330
  jurisdiction of 147–82, 256, 279, 289,
    295–7, 307, 309
  legal character of 334
  legal foundations of 3, 273, 277, 280
  legal representation 61, 129–33, 137,
    185, 220–8, 231–2, 292
  location of 196–202
  model for 285
  nemo judex in re sua 261
  objectives of 1, 65, 221, 306, 308, 314
  perceptions of 313–34
  personnel 110–46
  political dimension of 36–7
  popular acceptance of 185, 212, 234
  practices of 184–228, 273–333
  public confidence in 110–11, 119,
    187, 210, 231, 235
  public information about 202–4, 234
  questions of law 230, 233, 235, 237,
    240–1
  reasons for decisions 210
  relationship with government
    departments 262, 324
  remuneration of personnel 29,
    141–3
  residency requirements of
    commissioners 116–18
  right of appeal to regular courts
    229–31, 312
  roles of 1, 29

344 *Index*

tribunals (*Cont.*)
  simplicity and informality of
  procedures 187, 232, 276–7, 281,
  333
  speed and expense of 72, 184, 205–7,
  228, 235, 273, 277, 282, 319, 326
  status in the legal system 182, 328
  subordinate officers 139
  summoning and examination of
  witnesses 214–18, 298
  theoretical context of 73–109
  weaknesses of 3, 330
Tribunals of Commerce 51, 129, 139,
  239, 314
Triple Assessment Act 1798 113, 142,
  150–1, 198, 222, 262

Union Assessment Committee Act
  1862 121, 171–4, 206, 249, 306
urbanisation 10, 12, 76
Utilitarianism 84–6, 88, 105, 188, 288

Valuation of Property (Metropolis) Act
  1869 206, 249
values 6, 75–6
vested interests 75, 91–4, 103
  church interests 93

  private property interests 91–3
  professions 93
  railway companies 94

Wakley, Thomas 87, 210
Webster, Richard QC 134
Whigs 76, 77, 86
Wilberforce, William 76
Willes J 250, 264
Wills J 19, 182, 264
  railway companies
  work practices 10–11
Workmen's Compensation Act 1897 62
Wraith, R.E. 332
writ of certiorari 252–64
  appeal by 243, 245
  application of 256, 258–9,
  264, 311
  requirements for the application of
  254, 270
writ of error 251–72, 252, 298
writ of false judgment 251, 254–5,
  298
writ of mandamus 252–3, 268–9
writ of prohibition 252–3, 264–8
Wynford, Lord 238

For EU product safety concerns, contact us at Calle de José Abascal, 56–1°,
28003 Madrid, Spain or eugpsr@cambridge.org.

www.ingramcontent.com/pod-product-compliance
Ingram Content Group UK Ltd.
Pitfield, Milton Keynes, MK11 3LW, UK
UKHW011312060825
461487UK00005B/29